VMware®
Certified Professional
Virtualization on vSphere 6.7
Exam 2V0-21.19
Study Guide

VMware®
Certified Professional Data Center Virtualization on vSphere 6.7 Exam 2V0-21.19
Study Guide

Jon Hall

Joshua Andrews

SYBEX®
A Wiley Brand

Copyright © 2021 by John Wiley & Sons, Inc., Indianapolis, Indiana

Published simultaneously in Canada

ISBN: 978-1-119-21469-4
ISBN: 978-1-119-21471-7 (ebk.)
ISBN: 978-1-119-21472-4 (ebk.)

No part of this publication may be reproduced, stored in a retrieval system or transmitted in any form or by any means, electronic, mechanical, photocopying, recording, scanning or otherwise, except as permitted under Sections 107 or 108 of the 1976 United States Copyright Act, without either the prior written permission of the Publisher, or authorization through payment of the appropriate per-copy fee to the Copyright Clearance Center, 222 Rosewood Drive, Danvers, MA 01923, (978) 750-8400, fax (978) 646-8600. Requests to the Publisher for permission should be addressed to the Permissions Department, John Wiley & Sons, Inc., 111 River Street, Hoboken, NJ 07030, (201) 748-6011, fax (201) 748-6008, or online at www.wiley.com/go/permissions.

Limit of Liability/Disclaimer of Warranty: The publisher and the author make no representations or warranties with respect to the accuracy or completeness of the contents of this work and specifically disclaim all warranties, including without limitation warranties of fitness for a particular purpose. No warranty may be created or extended by sales or promotional materials. The advice and strategies contained herein may not be suitable for every situation. This work is sold with the understanding that the publisher is not engaged in rendering legal, accounting, or other professional services. If professional assistance is required, the services of a competent professional person should be sought. Neither the publisher nor the author shall be liable for damages arising herefrom. The fact that an organization or Web site is referred to in this work as a citation and/or a potential source of further information does not mean that the author or the publisher endorses the information the organization or Web site may provide or recommendations it may make. Further, readers should be aware that Internet Web sites listed in this work may have changed or disappeared between when this work was written and when it is read.

For general information on our other products and services or to obtain technical support, please contact our Customer Care Department within the U.S. at (877) 762-2974, outside the U.S. at (317) 572-3993 or fax (317) 572-4002.

Wiley publishes in a variety of print and electronic formats and by print-on-demand. Some material included with standard print versions of this book may not be included in e-books or in print-on-demand. If this book refers to media such as a CD or DVD that is not included in the version you purchased, you may download this material at booksupport.wiley.com. For more information about Wiley products, visit www.wiley.com.

Library of Congress Control Number: 2020940831

TRADEMARKS: Wiley, the Wiley logo, and the Sybex logo are trademarks or registered trademarks of John Wiley & Sons, Inc. and/or its affiliates, in the United States and other countries, and may not be used without written permission. VMware and vSphere are registered trademarks of VMware, Inc. All other trademarks are the property of their respective owners. John Wiley & Sons, Inc. is not associated with any product or vendor mentioned in this book.

SKY10020379_081120

The authors would like to dedicate this book to their patient and understanding families.

Acknowledgments

This book would not exist today if it weren't for the help of several individuals. First and foremost, my co-author, Joshua Andrews, stepped in to make this book a reality when I realized just how overwhelming a project like this is. The bulk of the material you will be exposed to here is his creation, and I am proud to call Josh a good friend of mine and humbled that he was willing to help. I would also like to thank our excellent technical editors, Dave Davis and Ken Nalbone. Dave and Ken did amazing work double-checking our technical accuracy and pointing out any omissions, so hopefully you should find few, if any, errors. Any mistakes you may find that they didn't catch are mine and mine alone. Finally, I would like to thank Jim Minatel, Pete Gaughan, Candace Cunningham, and all the folks at Wiley who were extremely helpful and even more patient throughout this process.

—Jon Hall

About the Authors

Jon Hall began his career in IT as a technical educator for companies like SMC Networks, Compaq, and Hewlett-Packard, where he focused on networking, storage area networking, server administration, and datacenter virtualization technologies. Eventually, he became involved in technical certification and has continued to focus on certification for the past 15 years. Jon considers certification to be a critical part of the IT industry, and indeed it has become his passion. As a certification manager at VMware, Jon built an industry-leading program from a single certification to more than a dozen certifications across various technologies and levels of expertise. On the way, he helped over 100,000 IT professionals become virtualization evangelists. During that time he also worked as a technical editor on several VMware Press books and spoke at numerous VMware events across the globe. Today, Jon works as the certification manager for Nutanix, where he continues to create new evangelists in the hybrid and multicloud spaces. This is his first book. He can be reached at www.linkedin.com/in/halljon.

Joshua Andrews is a VMware expert, blogger, and certification enthusiast. His first certifications were Certified Novell Engineer and Microsoft Certified Systems Engineer. Over the years he has also received certifications from NetApp, IBM, and Dell. He currently holds numerous VMware certifications, including VCP6-DCV, VCAP6-DCV, VCIX-DCV, and VCIX-NV. He has also received the VMware vExpert designation every year since 2012.

In his IT career Josh has been a programmer, network engineer, system administrator, storage administrator, technical writer, and consultant, and a freelance instructor for VMware. He worked for VMware for several years as a member of the certification team, focusing on developing and administering the VMware Certified Advanced Professional exams. During that time he acted as technical editor for several books from VMware Press.

Josh has been working with VMware products since late 2001 when he put ESX 1.0 into production at Cass Information Systems in St Louis. He blogs at sostechblog.com and can be reached at josh@sostechblog.com.

Contents at a Glance

Contents

Table of Exercises

Introduction

Why should you learn about VMware vSphere? Although the concept of virtualization has been around since the days of mainframe computing, VMware was and is the company that made virtualization a mainstay in the x86/x64 space. Originally, VMware introduced a desktop virtualization product called Workstation followed by the server virtualization products GSX and ESX and a datacenter management product called VirtualCenter. Today, the ESX and VirtualCenter products have converged into the vSphere platform. This platform allows IT administrators to get greater utilization out of existing physical servers and reduce the overall datacenter footprint, sometimes by 50 percent or more. It also provides features to allow for high availability and scaling up with a predictable level of performance. Today, vSphere is used by 100 percent of Fortune 500 companies and distributed by over 75,000 partners.[1] This means that if you intend to get a job in the IT space, whether you are working for a large organization or a big partner, you are likely to be working with vSphere. Because of this, companies look for individuals who are certified. Holding the VMware certification lets companies know that you are qualified to work with vSphere at a guaranteed level of competency.

The purpose of this book is to help you pass the Professional VMware vSphere 6.7 (2V0-21.19) exam, exam number 2V0-21.19. The exam is closely tied to a version of vSphere. This book focuses on vSphere 6.x (6.5, 6.7). The current version of the certification, VMware Certified Professional - Data Center Virtualization 2020 (VCP-DCV 2020), is based on the 6.7 release of vSphere and covers installation, configuration, and administration. VMware's information about the exam is posted at
www.vmware.com/education-services/certification/
vcp6-7-dcv-exam.html

This book covers all of the objectives tested for in the exam and includes topical information, lab work, and review questions. Because this book covers many of the tasks an administrator would perform on a day-to-day basis, this book should remain a useful reference even after you have passed the exam and earned your certification.

What Is vSphere?

The datacenter virtualization platform known as vSphere consists of multiple components. At its core is ESXi, a bare metal hypervisor that allows an x86 server to be virtualized. This virtualization allows the server's compute resources, as well as attached networking and storage resources, to be utilized by virtual servers (known as virtual machines, or VMs). These VMs can each run individual workloads with defined resource settings, allowing all of the server's resources to be efficiently utilized. vSphere includes VMFS, a filesystem optimized for virtualization, and vCenter Server, a management tool used to

---

1. www.vmware.com/company/why-choose-vmware.html

collectively manage all of the virtualized servers in the datacenter as well as providing advanced features like vMotion (live migration), High Availability (designed to manage unplanned downtime and maximize VM uptime), and a Distributed Resource Scheduler (designed to optimize performance), just to name a few.

Why Become VCP-DCV Certified?

There are several good reasons to become VMware certified, particularly with the VCP-DCV certification:

Provides proof of professional achievement   There are basically two types of organizations that work with vSphere. First, there are companies that have a vSphere implementation. Second, there are partners of VMware that distribute and implement vSphere for their customers. In both cases, it is vital that the individuals working with the implementation know what they are doing. It is typical for these organizations to actively look for candidates who are certified so that they can feel confident that the person they are hiring is capable. Gaining the VCP-DCV certification shows organizations that you are one of these people.

Increases your marketability   Having the VCP-DCV certification establishes your capability to employers and indicates that you can potentially step right into the position with little or no training. This benefit to the employer can often translate into a better salary for you. Furthermore, out of all of VMware's certifications, this is the one that covers the core datacenter virtualization components. As a result, this certification is the one most often looked for by organizations.

Provides an opportunity for advancement   Most raises and advancements are based on performance. Individuals who become certified have a tendency to work with more of the features of a product and are able to get a more stable, better-performing implementation. Having an implementation that performs well and utilizes all of its desired features is certain to reflect positively on an employee and provide opportunities in their organization.

How to Become VCP-DCV Certified

The first step in becoming VMware VCP-DCV certified is to attend a VMware authorized training course. VMware requires all of its certification candidates to first complete a training course. There are over a dozen courses or course combinations to choose from, which provides options if you already have a certain level of expertise working with vSphere.

Next, you must take and pass the VMware vSphere 6.7 Foundations exam. This exam, as well as the VCP-DCV exam, is version specific, so you should take the exam that matches up to the version of vSphere you are working with if at all possible (since VMware periodically retires older-version exams).

Finally, you must take and pass the VCP-DCV exam. All of these steps must be completed before you earn the certification, and although the path above is the most logical (and recommended) order in which to complete all of the requirements, you can take the course and exams in whatever order you prefer.

The exam is administered by Pearson VUE and can be taken at any Pearson VUE testing center. To register for the exam, you must go to VMware's website. You will need a myLearn account if you do not already have one. Your results for the exam are presented to you immediately upon completion. If you pass, keep in mind that you will still need to fulfill the other requirements before you can obtain your certification. Shortly after you have completed all requirements, VMware will grant your certification. This is an automatic process, although it may take a few days following the completion of all requirements.

Who Should Buy This Book

Anybody who wants to become VCP-DCV certified will benefit from this book in multiple ways. The book covers all of the objectives on the exam and includes a large number of practice questions that can help you prepare. In addition, the book contains a collection of hands-on labs that can be performed in a vSphere environment. The labs can be done in your own environment or by using VMware's Hands-On Lab environment.

This book can also help a fledgling vSphere user increase their proficiency, both by learning about new or previously unused features and by practicing with the included labs.

Since this book focuses on the VCP-DCV certification, there is an expectation that you have enough of a background with vSphere to successfully pass the underlying vSphere Foundations exam and therefore have sufficient knowledge of the topics covered by that exam. That being said, we have done as much as possible to make this book usable to candidates who might have minimal exposure to vSphere.

In order to take advantage of all of the hands-on labs and exercises presented in this book, you will need to have a vSphere implementation. If you have an implementation already, we recommend that you perform these labs outside the production environment. If you do not have your own implementation, you can utilize one of VMware's Hands-On Lab environments. In particular, we recommend that you use the VMware Virtualization 101 hands-on lab, since this lab provides both vSphere and vCenter.

How This Book Is Organized

This book consists of 11 chapters plus supplementary information: a glossary, this introduction, and the assessment test after the introduction. The chapters are organized as follows:

Chapter 1, "What's New in vSphere 6.7," describes features that are new to vCenter Server, vSphere Operations, security, availability, storage, networking, developer and automation interfaces, and Host Lifecycle Management enhancements.

Chapter 2, "Configuring and Administering Security in a vSphere Datacenter," focuses on access to a vSphere environment and hardening of that environment, including how to configure and administer role-based access control, securing ESXi and vCenter Server, configuring and enabling SSO and identity sources, and securing vSphere virtual machines.

Chapter 3, "Networking in vSphere," focuses on configuring policies and networking features and verifying vSphere networking proper operations. This chapter also shows you how to configure Network I/O Control (NIOC).

Chapter 4, "Storage in vSphere," shows you how to set up storage for a vSphere implementation, including managing vSphere integration with physical storage, configuring software-defined storage, configuring vSphere Storage Multipathing and Failover, performing VMFS and NFS configurations and upgrades, and setting up and configuring Storage I/O Control (SIOC).

Chapter 5, "Upgrading a vSphere Deployment," is all about performing ESXi host and virtual machine upgrades, performing vCenter Server upgrades (Windows), and migrating vCenter Server to the VCSA.

Chapter 6, "Allocating Resources in a vSphere Datacenter," focuses on configuring multilevel resource pools and configuring vSphere DRS and Storage DRS clusters.

Chapter 7, "Backing Up and Recovering a vSphere Deployment," describes the process of backing up vSphere components, including configuring and administering the vCenter Server Appliance backup and restore operations, configuring and administering vCenter Data Protection, and configuring vSphere Replication.

Chapter 8, "Troubleshooting a vSphere Deployment," will show you how to troubleshoot major vSphere components, including vCenter Server and ESXi hosts, vSphere storage and networking, vSphere upgrades and migrations, virtual machines, HA and DRS configurations, and fault tolerance.

Chapter 9, "Deploying and Customizing ESXi Hosts," focuses on configuring Auto Deploy for ESXi hosts and creating and deploying host profiles.

Chapter 10, "Ensuring High Availability for vSphere Clusters and the VCSA," is all about configuring vSphere HA Cluster features and configuring vCenter Server Appliance (VCSA) HA.

Chapter 11, "Administering and Managing vSphere Virtual Machines," will show you how to create and manage vSphere virtual machines and templates, create and manage a Content Library, and consolidate physical workloads using VMware vCenter Converter.

Each chapter begins with a list of the VCP-DCV objectives that are covered in that chapter. The book doesn't cover the objectives in the order in which they are present in the exam, since the order is subject to change and exam items are randomly placed during the exam itself. At the end of each chapter, you'll find a couple of elements you can use to prepare for the exam:

Exam Essentials   This section summarizes important information that was covered in the chapter. You should be able to perform each of the tasks or convey the information requested.

Review Questions   Each chapter concludes with approximately 20 review questions. You should answer these questions and check your answers against the ones provided after the questions. If you can't answer at least 80 percent of these questions correctly, go back and review the chapter, or at least those sections that seem to be giving you difficulty.

The review questions, assessment test, and other testing elements included in this book are *not* derived from the official VMware exam questions, so don't memorize the answers to these questions and assume that doing so will enable you to pass the exam. You should learn the underlying topic, as described in the text of the book. This will let you answer the questions provided with this book *and* pass the exam. Learning the underlying topic is also the approach that will serve you best in the workplace—the ultimate goal of a certification like VMware's.

To get the most out of this book, you should read each chapter from start to finish and then check your memory and understanding with the chapter-end elements. Even if you're already familiar with a topic, you should skim the chapter; vSphere is complex enough that there are often multiple ways to accomplish a task, so you may learn something even if you're already competent in an area.

Bonus Contents

This book is accompanied by an online learning environment that provides several additional elements. The following items are available among these companion files:

Sample Tests   All of the questions in this book appear in our proprietary digital test engine—including the 30-question assessment test at the end of this introduction and the over 200 questions that make up the review question sections at the end of the chapters. In addition, there are two 55-question practice tests.

Electronic "Flashcards"   The digital companion files include 68 questions in flashcard format (a question followed by a single correct answer). You can use these to review your knowledge of the VCP-DCV exam objectives.

Glossary   The key terms from this book, and their definitions, are available as a fully searchable PDF.

 To register and gain access to this interactive online learning environment, please visit this URL: www.wiley.com/go/Sybextestprep.

Conventions Used in This Book

This book uses certain typographic styles in order to help you quickly identify important information and to avoid confusion over the meaning of words such as on-screen prompts. In particular, look for the following styles:

- *Italicized text* indicates key terms that are described at length for the first time in a chapter. (Italics are also used for emphasis.)

- A `monospaced` font indicates the contents of configuration files, messages displayed at a text-mode Linux shell prompt, filenames, text-mode command names, and Internet URLs.

- *`Italicized monospaced text`* indicates a variable—information that differs from one system or command run to another, such as the name of a client computer or a process ID number.

- **`Bold monospaced text`** is information that you're to type into the computer, usually at a Linux shell prompt. This text can also be italicized to indicate that you should substitute an appropriate value for your system. (When isolated on their own lines, commands are preceded by nonbold monospaced $ or # command prompts, denoting regular user or system administrator use, respectively.)

In addition to these text conventions, which can apply to individual words or entire paragraphs, a few conventions highlight segments of text:

 A note indicates information that's useful or interesting but that's somewhat peripheral to the main text. A note might be relevant to a small number of networks, for instance, or it may refer to an outdated feature.

 A tip provides information that can save you time or frustration and that may not be entirely obvious. A tip might describe how to get around a limitation or how to use a feature to perform an unusual task.

 Warnings describe potential pitfalls or dangers. If you fail to heed a warning, you may end up spending a lot of time recovering from a bug, or you may even end up restoring your entire system from scratch.

Sidebars

A sidebar is like a note but longer. The information in a sidebar is useful, but it doesn't fit into the main flow of the text.

 ### Real World Scenario

Real World Scenario

A real world scenario is a type of sidebar that describes a task or example that's particularly grounded in the real world. This may be a situation I or somebody I know has encountered, or it may be advice on how to work around problems that are common in real, working Linux environments.

Exercises

An exercise is a procedure you should try out on your own computer to help you learn about the material in the chapter. Don't limit yourself to the procedures described in the exercises, though! Try other commands and procedures to really learn about Linux.

Objective Mapping

Table I.1 contains an objective map to show you at a glance where you can find each VCP-DCV exam objective covered.

TABLE I.1 2V0-21.19 Objective Map

Exam Objective	Chapter
Section 1 – VMware vSphere Architectures and Technologies	
Objective 1.1 – Identify the prerequisites and components for vSphere implementation	3, 5. 9
Objective 1.2 – Identify vCenter high availability (HA) requirements	10
Objective 1.3 – Describe storage types for vSphere	4
Objective 1.4 – Differentiate between NIOC and SIOC	4
Objective 1.5 – Manage vCenter inventory efficiently	6
Objective 1.6 – Describe and differentiate among vSphere, HA, DRS, and SDRS functionality	4, 6, 10
Objective 1.7 – Describe and identify resource pools and use cases	6
Objective 1.8 – Differentiate between VDS and VSS	3
Objective 1.9 – Describe the purpose of cluster and the features it provides	2, 6, 10
Objective 1.10 – Describe virtual machine (VM) file structure	4, 11
Objective 1.11 – Describe vMotion and Storage vMotion technology	4, 11
Section 2 – VMware Products and Solutions	
Objective 2.1 – Describe vSphere integration with other VMware products	3
Objective 2.2 – Describe HA solutions for vSphere	10
Objective 2.3 – Describe the options for securing a vSphere environment	1
Section 3 – Planning and Designing	

(There are no testable objectives for this section.)

Exam Objective	Chapter
Section 4 – Installing, Configuring, and Setting Up a VMware vSphere Solution	
Objective 4.1 – Understand basic log output from vSphere products	8
Objective 4.2 – Create and configure vSphere objects	1, 2, 3, 4, 6, 10, 11
Objective 4.3 – Set up a content library	1, 11
Objective 4.4 – Set up ESXi hosts	1, 9
Objective 4.5 – Configure virtual networking	3
Objective 4.6 – Deploy and configure VMware vCenter Server Appliance (VCSA)	1, 5, 7
Objective 4.7 – Set up identity sources	1, 2
Objective 4.8 – Configure an SSO domain	1, 2
Section 5 – Performance-tuning and Optimizing a VMware vSphere Solution	
Objective 5.1 – Determine effective snapshot use cases	1, 7, 11
Objective 5.2 – Monitor resources of VCSA in a vSphere environment	5, 6, 8
Objective 5.3 – Identify impacts of VM configurations	8, 11
Section 6 – Troubleshooting and Repairing (There are no testable objectives for this section.)	
Section 7 – Administrative and Operational Tasks in a VMware vSphere Solution	
Objective 7.1 – Manage virtual networking	3
Objective 7.2 – Manage datastores	1, 4
Objective 7.3 – Configure a storage policy	4
Objective 7.4 – Configure host security	1, 2

TABLE 1.1   2V0-21.19 Objective Map *(continued)*

Exam Objective	Chapter
Objective 7.5 – Configure role-based user management	2
Objective 7.6 – Configure and use vSphere Compute and Storage cluster options	4, 6
Objective 7.7 – Perform different types of migrations	1, 6, 7, 11
Objective 7.8 – Manage resources of a vSphere environment	1, 3, 4. 6, 9
Objective 7.9 – Create and manage VMs using different methods	1, 7, 11
Objective 7.10 – Create and manage templates	1, 11
Objective 7.11 – Manage different VMware vCenter Server objects	1, 2, 3, 4, 6
Objective 7.12 – Set up permissions on datastores, clusters, vCenter, and hosts	2
Objective 7.13 – Identify and interpret affinity/anti-affinity rules	4, 6, 10
Objective 7.14 – Understand use cases for alarms	8
Objective 7.15 – Utilize VMware vSphere Update Manager (VUM)	1, 5
Objective 7.16 - Configure and manage host profiles	9

Assessment Test

1. Which component is a requirement for deploying vCenter Enhanced Linked Mode when using a combination of vCenter Server for Windows and vCenter Server Appliances?
   - **A.** External PSC
   - **B.** Embedded PSC
   - **C.** Load Balancers
   - **D.** vCenter High Availability

2. Which method should a virtual machine running a current version of Windows use to take advantage of PMem?
   - **A.** vPMemDisk
   - **B.** vPMem
   - **C.** NVDIMM
   - **D.** RDMA

3. What vSAN queue is responsible for managing witness traffic?
   - **A.** VM I/O Queue
   - **B.** Namespace Queue
   - **C.** Resync I/O Queue
   - **D.** Metadata Queue

4. An organization has an encrypted virtual machine whose Encrypted vSphere vMotion setting is set to Required. If encryption is later disabled for the VM, what happens to the Encrypted vSphere vMotion setting?
   - **A.** It is set to Disabled.
   - **B.** It reverts to the default (Opportunistic).
   - **C.** It remains set to Required.
   - **D.** Encryption cannot be disabled until the setting is changed to Disabled.

5. Which objects can be added to a Content Library prior to vSphere 6.7 Update 1? (Choose three.)
   - **A.** VMX files
   - **B.** OVA files
   - **C.** ISO images
   - **D.** VMTX files
   - **E.** Certificates

6. Where would an administrator configure EVC to support migration of a VM across a hybrid cloud environment?

   A. On the cluster

   B. On the datastore

   C. On the individual VM

   D. On the PSC

7. An administrator wants to configure RDMA over Converged Ethernet (RoCE). Which of these are requirements to support RoCE v1? (Choose two.)

   A. Lossless layer 2 network

   B. Lossless layer 3 network

   C. PFC priority enabled VLAN

   D. Teamed RoCE NICs

8. Which options would enable an administrator to create a distributed virtual switch? (Choose two.)

   A. 10gbE NICs

   B. vCenter Server/VCSA

   C. vSphere Enterprise Plus license

   D. Network I/O Control

9. What protocol can be enabled on vCenter Server to provide information about a vDS to management software?

   A. MPP

   B. LLDP

   C. SNMP

   D. NMP

10. Which two types of traffic, if selected for use by a VMkernel adapter, will cause the default TCP/IP stack to no longer be used for that traffic? (Choose two.)

   A. Fault-tolerant traffic

   B. Provisioning traffic

   C. vSphere Replication traffic

   D. vMotion traffic

11. Which technology cannot be used to prioritize specific types of traffic?

   A. SIOC

   B. Traffic shaping

   C. NIOC

   D. LACP

12. Which technology can be configured on an ESXi iSCSI adapter to ensure security and data integrity?

   A. Kerberos

   B. CHAP

   C. KVM

   D. AES-256

13. What provisioning technology should be used on a VM to allow for space reclamation in an all-flash array without needing to use the UNMAP command?

   A. ZeroedThick

   B. EagerZeroedThick

   C. Thin

   D. 2gbsparse

14. What feature can vSphere use to present a SAN LUN to a virtual machine?

   A. RDM

   B. FCoE

   C. CIFS

   D. SIOC

15. When using `esxtop`, which value will show you the average total response time for VMkernel operations?

   A. KAVG

   B. GAVG

   C. DAVG

   D. QAVG

16. Which DRS option is best for architects to establish usage based on predefined SLAs?

   A. VM Distribution

   B. Memory Metric for Load Balancing

   C. CPU Overallocation

   D. Proactive HA

17. What value is used by network-aware DRS to determine when a host has excessive network utilization?

   A. 70% utilization

   B. 75% utilization

   C. 80% utilization

   D. 85% utilization

18. What can be done to ensure that virtual machines with anti-affinity rules are restarted during an HA restart event?

   A. Nothing, anti-affinity rules are ignored for a HA restart

   B. Set the HA Advanced Option **das.respectvmvmantiaffinityrules** to *false*

   C. Configure admission control with sufficient resources

   D. Configure the Anti-Affinity Rule to **Must**

19. Which types of I/O filters are offered by VMware? (Choose two.)

   A. Replication

   B. Encryption

   C. Caching

   D. Storage I/O Control

20. Which patterns are valid for use with vSphere Auto Deploy? (Choose two.)

   A. Serial

   B. CPU type

   C. Domain

   D. Image profile

21. Where is the data plane located for vSphere Distributed Switches?

   A. On the vCenter server

   B. On the Platform Services Controller

   C. On the ESXi host

   D. On the Service Composer VM

22. What virtual machine hardware component was newly supported beginning with vSphere 6.5 (VM Hardware v13)?

   A. 3D video support

   B. NVDIMM controllers

   C. Virtual RDMA

   D. PCI Passthrough

23. Storage policies are assigned to a VM during which procedures? (Choose two.)

   A. Initial deployment

   B. Powering on

   C. Migration

   D. Placing in Standby mode

24. An administrator has upgraded the vCenter server to version 6.7. The cluster uses an external Platform Services Controller. What is the next component to be upgraded in the vSphere upgrade process?

    A. ESXi hosts

    B. Platform Services Controller

    C. Virtual appliances

    D. Virtual machines

25. How many additional vSphere Replication servers can be deployed to scale the solution to handle a large number of virtual machines?

    A. 1

    B. 2

    C. 5

    D. 9

26. What are two advantages to enabling compression for vSphere Replication? (Choose two.)

    A. It reduces network bandwidth requirements.

    B. It reduces CPU utilization.

    C. It reduces the amount of buffer memory.

    D. It reduces the RPO time.

27. Which three are valid failure events that Proactive HA can respond to? (Choose three.)

    A. Memory

    B. Network

    C. CPU

    D. Power Supply

    E. Shared Storage

28. A High Availability cluster has eight powered-on virtual machines whose total resource requirements add up to 12 GHz and 28 GB. These virtual machines are running on a cluster containing four hosts, whose total resources for running virtual machines equal 38 GHz and 112 GB. Based on this scenario, what is the current memory failover capacity for the cluster?

    A. 85%

    B. 75%

    C. 68%

    D. 58%

29. What is the advantage of creating a snapshot of a virtual machine that includes the VM's memory?

    A. The snapshot can restore the VM even if the VMDK file is corrupted.

    B. The size of the snapshot is significantly smaller.

    C.   The restored snapshot will include any open files.

    D.   Quiescing is automatically performed during the snapshot.

30. Which two options would not be considered if an administrator's use case is to share a GPU across multiple VMs? (Choose two.)

    A.   vSphere DirectPath I/O

    B.   NVIDIA vGPU/Grid

    C.   BitFusion FlexDirect

    D.   PCI Passthrough

Answers to Assessment Test

1. A. While VCSA includes an Embedded PSC that can be used with vCenter Enhanced Linked Mode, it can only be used with VCSA nodes and is not supported for Windows vCenter Server installations.

2. B. A virtual machine with VM hardware 14 or later and a current guest OS is PMem-aware and can use vPMem to take advantage of PMem.

3. D. The Metadata Queue manages objects that comprise a VM, such as witness traffic, cluster monitoring, and membership activities.

4. C. If encryption is disabled on a VM, the setting for Encrypted vSphere vMotion must be explicitly changed to Disabled. Until then, it remains set to Required.

5. B, C, E. A Content Library allows for OVA and OVF files to be used as templates and also allows for the management of support files like ISO images and certificates. vSphere 6.7 Update 1 introduced support for VM template files (.vmtx) in content libraries.

6. C. Configuring EVC at the individual VM level allows for migration support out of an on-premise cluster into an entirely different datacenter.

7. A, C. RoCE v1 requires a Lossless Layer 2 Network and a PFC-enabled VLAN, whereas RoCE v2 requires both Layer 2 and Layer 3 to be Lossless.

8. B, C. To create a vDS, you must have a license that allows it, such as Enterprise Plus. vDS creation and management is performed on the vCenter Server/VCSA.

9. C. SNMP allows for information, alerts, and errors to be sent to a receiver running management software. This includes information related to a vDS.

10. B, D. Once a VMkernel adapter has been linked to the vMotion or the provisioning TCP/IP stack, those traffic types will no longer be carried on the default stack.

11. D. SIOC, NIOC, and traffic shaping are all technologies specifically designed to optimize traffic. LACP (Link Aggregation Control Protocol) is used to combine the bandwidth of multiple network adapter interfaces into a larger, logical bandwidth.

12. B. The Challenge Handshake Authentication Protocol (CHAP) uses a three-way handshake algorithm on ESXi iSCSI adapters to verify the identity of the ESXi host and, if applicable, of the iSCSI target device.

13. B. The use of EagerZeroedThick provisioning zeroes out all storage in advance, saving an administrator from using the VMFS UNMAP procedure manually.

14. A. Raw Device Mapping (RDM) is used to map a SAN LUN on a physical storage device to a virtual machine.

15. A. The total time it takes for a VMkernel command to process is expressed by the ESXi Kernel Average Latency time metric (KAVG).

16. C. CPU Overallocation is a useful feature when establishing multiple SLAs or service tiers.

17. C. DRS observes the Transmit (Tx) and Receive (Rx) rates of a host's connected physical uplinks and avoids placing VMs on hosts whose physical NICs are greater than 80% utilized.

18. B. HA by default will enforce anti-affinity rules unless you set the advanced option **das. respectvmvmantiaffinityrules** to *false*.

19. B, D. I/O filters not offered by VMware are available from third-party partners.

20. A, C. Patterns include host-specific information like vendor or serial number and network information like IP address and domain.

21. C. The data plane for a vSphere Distributed Switch resides on each ESXi host.

22. C. Virtual RDMA support was new for VM Hardware v13. NVDIMM Controllers were not supported until VM Hardware v14, and PCI Passthrough and 3D video were supported prior to the vSphere 6.5 release.

23. A, C. Storage policies are applied when you create, clone, or migrate a virtual machine.

24. A. vSphere 6.7 is a complex set of products and features that include several upgradeable components. Understanding the correct upgrade sequence is vital for ensuring that all needed services are running and available.

The order of actions during a vSphere upgrade is as follows:
1. Back up the configuration.

2. Upgrade Platform Services Controller.

3. Upgrade vCenter Server.

4. Upgrade ESXi hosts.

5. Upgrade virtual machines and virtual appliances.

25. D. vSphere 6.x supports a maximum of 9 additional vSphere Replication servers (for a total of 10).

26. A, C. Using compression can reduce the amount of replication data that is transferred through the network, which helps save network bandwidth and reduces the amount of buffer memory used on the vSphere Replication server. However, compressing and decompressing data requires more CPU resources on both the source site and the server that manages the target datastore.

27. A, B, D. Proactive HA monitors the network, power, memory, local storage, and fan of each host.

28. B. The memory failover capacity for this cluster is 112 GB minus 28 GB divided by 112 GB, which is 75%.

29. C. Creating a snapshot that includes the VM's memory captures the live state of the VM. This includes any files that might be in memory that have not yet been committed to disk.

30. A, D. vSphere DirectPath I/O and the PCI Passthrough option are both used to link a host graphics card directly to a single VM.

Chapter

1

What's New in vSphere 6.7

2V0-21.19 EXAM OBJECTIVES COVERED IN THIS CHAPTER:

✓ **VMware Products and Solutions**

- Describe the options for securing a vSphere environment

✓ **Installing, Configuring, and Setting Up a VMware vSphere Solution**

- Create and configure vSphere objects

- Set up a content library

- Set up ESXi hosts

- Deploy and configure VMware vCenter Server Appliance (VCSA)

- Set up identity sources

- Configure an SSO domain

✓ **Performance-Tuning and Optimizing a VMware vSphere Solution**

- Determine effective snapshot use cases

✓ **Administrative and Operational Tasks in a VMware vSphere Solution**

- Manage datastores

- Configure host security

- Perform different types of migrations

- Manage resources of a vSphere environment

- Create and manage VMs using different methods

- Create and manage templates

- Manage different VMware vCenter Server objects

- Utilize VMware vSphere Update Manager (VUM)

VMware is continually updating all of the different components that make up vSphere. The ESXi hypervisors to vCenter management and all of the various subsystems continually receive bug fixes, enhancements, and new features. Major updates to the ecosystem are released as new versions (the last being 6.0, released in 2015), with "sub" or "point" releases containing important updates and enhancements released more often.

In addition to the version and point releases, VMware also releases "Updates," which tend to be mostly bug fixes but do often contain an extra or enhanced feature or two.

While keeping your environment up-to-date is important from a security standpoint, more critically for the purpose of this book is to ensure that you are studying the correct version of vSphere. The 2V0-21.19 exam at the time of this writing covers vSphere 6.7 U1. If you are going to download the binaries to install a practice environment, or are researching exam topics in the official documentation, make sure you are referencing the correct version and update number.

In this chapter, we will go over the latest updates and changes in vSphere 6.7 U1.

Accessing vSphere

Environments are primarily managed day to day by graphical tools. While command-line tools and APIs are in widespread use, they are typically for one-off or automated solutions. For VMware vSphere environments, there are several graphical utilities you might use, from the host console (DCUI, or Direct Console User Interface) to the ESXi host's HTML5 web client.

Prior to vSphere 6.5, primary management of the vSphere environment was managed by a Flash-based Flex client called the VMware vSphere Web Client. However, with the decline and fall of Flash as a development platform, VMware started working on an HTML5 client, using the new Clarity framework. Initially released as a fling (one of VMware's unsupported free tools) in March 2016, by vSphere 6.7 U1 this new client has almost achieved feature parity with the Flex client—and in fact some of the new features can only be accessed in the HTML5 client.

VMware vSphere Client

As shown in Figure 1.1 and Figure 1.2, the clients can be easily differentiated, yet the new client doesn't radically change the user interface. Note that while both clients are included with vSphere 6.7, this will be the last release that includes the Flex client.

FIGURE 1.1 The home page of the Flex vSphere web client

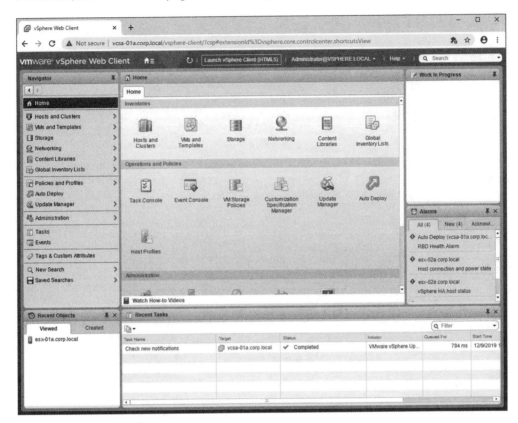

   While traditionally the VMware certification exams have tried to avoid "where is this setting in the GUI?" -type questions, with a new client being transitioned, it is possible some will show up. For starters, the new client is accessed by a different URL. Where the Flex client is still at `https://<vcenter FQDN or IP address>/vsphere-clientui/`, the new HTML5 client can be found at `https://<vcenter FQDN or IP address>/ui/`.

   You might have noticed in Figure 1.1 and Figure 1.2 that the home screen for the HTML5 client has performance information instead of icons for possible tasks (such as VM Storage Policies). Most of the tasks can be found under the same Navigator section. For instance, VM Customization Manager can be found under Policies and Profiles, although it has been renamed VM Customization Specifications as shown in Figure 1.3.

   However, System Configuration has changed. While it is still under the Administration section and shows all available vCenter servers (as shown in Figure 1.4), it no longer displays the full list of vCenter services as shown in Figure 1.5.

FIGURE 1.2   The home page of the HTML5 vSphere client

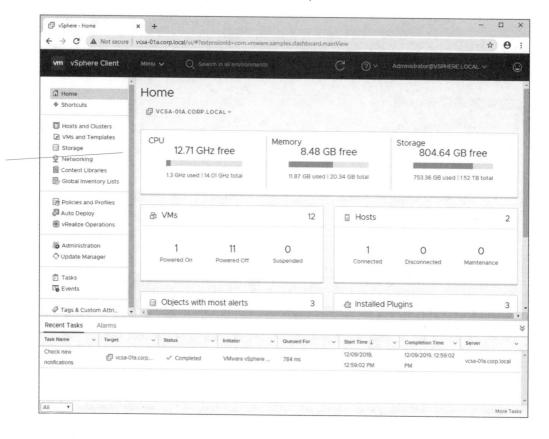

FIGURE 1.3   Policies and Profiles contains the renamed customizations tool.

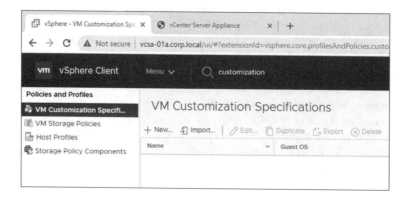

FIGURE 1.4   The Nodes section of the Flex client shows all the connected vCenter appliances.

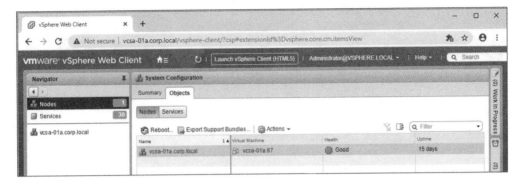

FIGURE 1.5   The Flex client System Configuration section shows vCenter services.

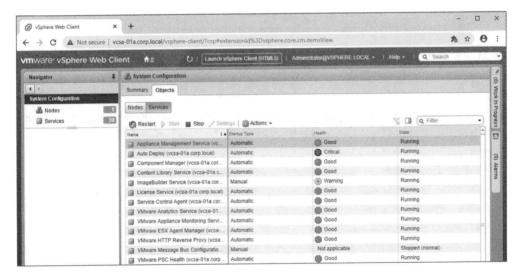

The list of services has been moved to the VAMI console, which can be accessed by clicking the hyperlinked name of the vCenter server as shown in Figure 1.6.

By clicking on the vCenter server, you can log into the updated VCSA management console, which has the list of services as shown in Figure 1.7.

FIGURE 1.6   The node list of the HTML5 client

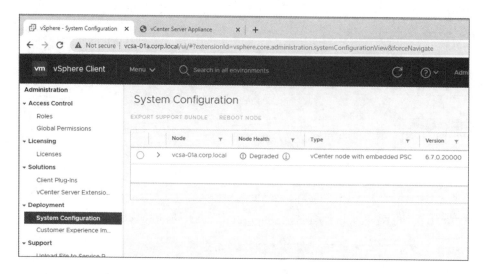

FIGURE 1.7   The VCSA console shows the available services that can be started.

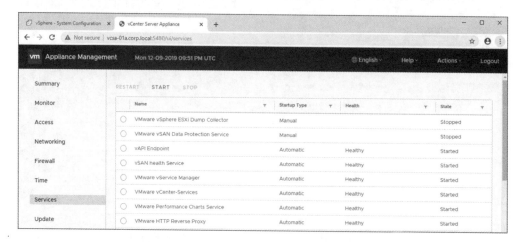

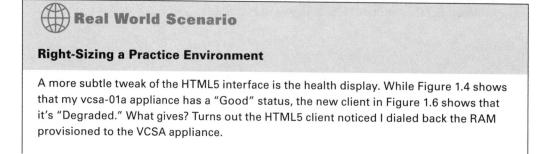

Real World Scenario

Right-Sizing a Practice Environment

A more subtle tweak of the HTML5 interface is the health display. While Figure 1.4 shows that my vcsa-01a appliance has a "Good" status, the new client in Figure 1.6 shows that it's "Degraded." What gives? Turns out the HTML5 client noticed I dialed back the RAM provisioned to the VCSA appliance.

If you are creating a nested environment for practice, you might want to manipulate the available RAM or CPUs to minimize the impact to your host system. This sometimes results in issues like upgrades failing when their checks show reduced RAM or random flags like this one. While perfectly fine in a demo environment, you will want to stick to the documented settings for a production environment, which for VCSA means only use the GUI to make changes to CPU/RAM.

One of the features not yet moved into the HTML5 client is the Virtual Flash configuration, as seen in Figure 1.8. If you wish to configure or manage Virtual Flash you'll need to use the Flex client.

FIGURE 1.8   The Virtual Flash settings are not yet ported to the HTML5 client (note the lack of a Virtual Flash section in the HTML5 client on the right).

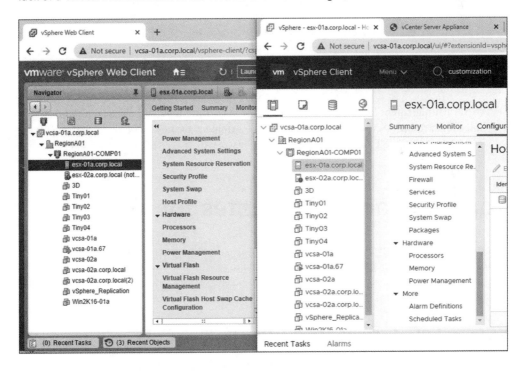

In the Update Manager section of this chapter, we'll talk about the limited Update Manager features available in the HTML5 client.

Application Programming Interface

For automation or access through other tools, VMware provides software development kits (SDKs), command-line tools (such as PowerCLI), and application programming interfaces (APIs). While there are some changes to the PowerCLI for 6.7, they are beyond the requirements of the VCP-level exams. However, VMware has referred to the new SDKs and APIs in blog posts and release notes and those could be considered fair game for the exam.

For in-depth documentation, visit www.vmware.com/support/pubs/sdk_pubs.html. To download the SDKs and explore the APIs, head over to code.vmware.com/sdks.

These updated SDKs were listed in the vSphere 6.7 release blog:

vSphere Management SDK   Bundle containing several vSphere SDKs: vSphere Web Services SDK, vSphere Storage Management SDK, vSphere ESX Agent Manager SDK, SSO Client SDK, and vSphere Storage Policy SDK.

vSphere Automation SDK   This is a family of SDKs for programmatic access from different programming languages—Java, Python, .NET, Perl—plus a REST SDK. Note that vSphere 6.5 included an Automation SDK for Ruby, but that has not been updated for 6.7 at the time of writing.

vSphere Client SDK   The Client SDK is intended to help the creation of extensions for the vSphere client.

vSAN Management SDK   This is a family of SDKs intended to help developers create solutions around vSAN. Languages available are Java, Python, .NET, Perl, and Ruby. There is also a REST SDK.

Topology and UI Updates for VCSA

The management platform for vSphere—VMware's vCenter server—has received some important changes for 6.7 and received further changes for U1. The topologies allowed for vCenter have undergone several changes with each release, along with different methods for changing topologies, and this is a prime topic for exam questions.

External Platform Services Controller

The Platform Services Controller (PSC) component of vSphere manages the Single Sign-On (SSO) domain for the environment. It can be installed embedded on the same Windows server or VCSA appliance as vCenter, or externally on a separate appliance or Windows sever.

In previous versions, the external deployment version was required for Enhanced Linked Mode, where multiple vCenter servers can be managed from the same client UI.

However, the embedded version now works with Enhanced Linked Mode and the external deployment is no longer recommended. VMware has stated that in a future release, the external PSC will no longer be supported, and new tools have been released to modify existing vCenter topologies to the recommended, embedded deployment.

First, VMware offers a vSphere Topology and Upgrade Planning Tool, which can be found at vspherecentral.vmeware.com; it will ask a series of questions before recommending a deployment topology with documentation links.

For existing deployments, you can migrate (VMware calls it "converge") from an external to an embedded PSC by using the new convergence tool, *vcsa-util*, available on the VCSA 6.7 U1 ISO as shown in Figure 1.9. There are Windows, Linux, and MacOS versions of the tool, and note that it is not available on the Windows-based vCenter Server ISO.

FIGURE 1.9   The convergence tool allows for migrating a PSC from external to embedded.

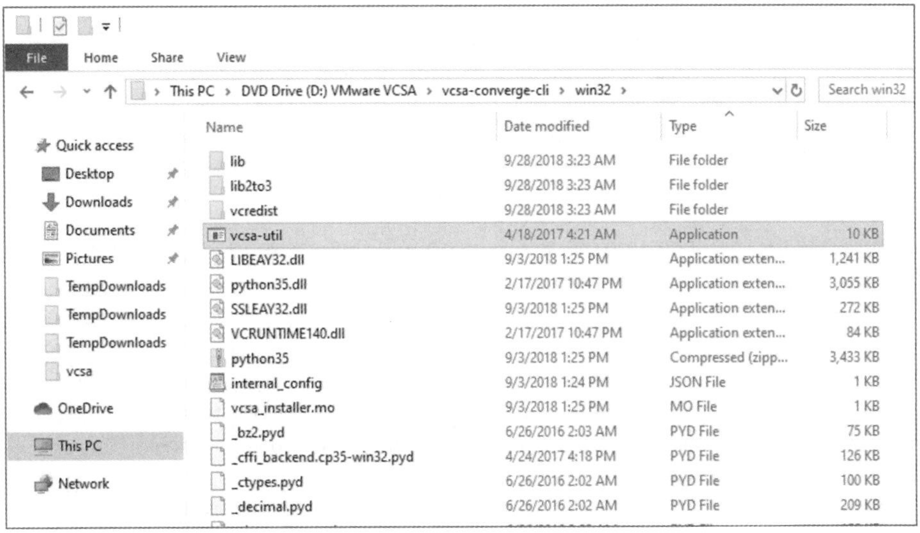

In addition to migrating a PSC from external to embedded, the tool can also decommission an external PSC. Either method requires a JSON template as shown in Figure 1.10. You should modify the sample JSON template for your environment, then submit that template when you run the *vcsa-util* tool.

Another tool included on the ISO is *cmsso-util*, which allows you to manipulate vCenter/PSC relationships, including consolidating or splitting vSphere domains. Using the tool you can complete the following tasks:

- Move a vCenter server to a different vSphere domain.

- Move all vCenter servers in a domain to a different domain.

- Point a vCenter server with an embedded PSC to an external PSC, including in a different domain.

FIGURE 1.10 A JSON file is required to pass the environment information to the conversion tool.

The *cmsso-util* tool can be run from VCSA or from C:\Program Files\VMware\ vCenter Server\bin\ on a Windows-based vCenter server.

Update Manager

With vSphere 6.7 U1, Update Manager gets a new look in the vSphere Client; however, the VM update functionality has not been ported, so updating VM hardware and VMware Tools still requires the Flex client.

As shown in Figure 1.11, Update Manager ships with two baselines (*Non-Critical Host Patches* and *Critical Host Patches*) and one group that combines those two baselines (*All Updates*).

While the HTML5 client doesn't yet include the functionality to manage baselines for VMs, you can still view and edit the VM remediation settings as seen in Figure 1.12.

FIGURE 1.11   Listing the baselines and baseline groups in Update Manager

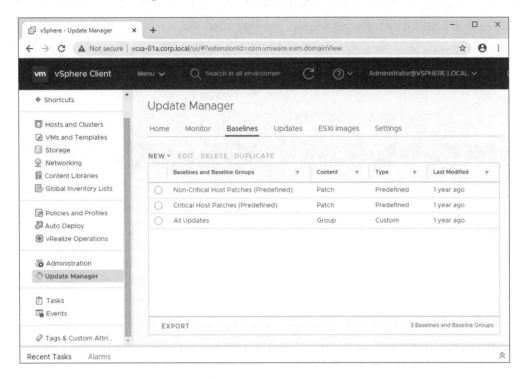

FIGURE 1.12   Changing the settings for VM remediation

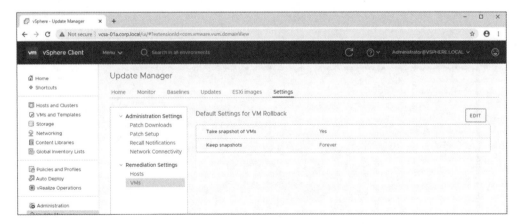

EXERCISE 1.1

Create a baseline and scan a host for compliance.

Requires a vCenter server with a datacenter created, one ESXi host, and the ISO for ESXi 6.7 U1.

1.   In Update Manager, Click Import to launch the import dialog.

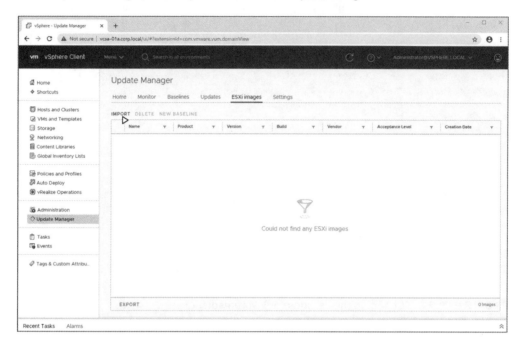

2.   Locate the ISO to begin uploading.

3. Click New Baseline to launch the wizard.

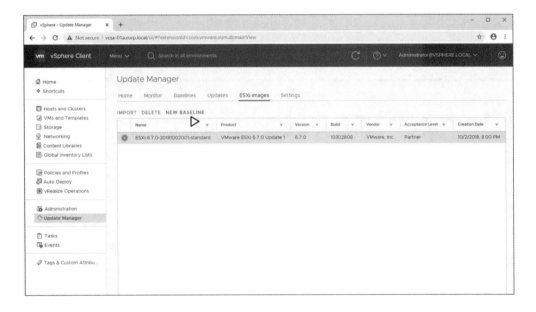

4. Enter a name for the baseline.

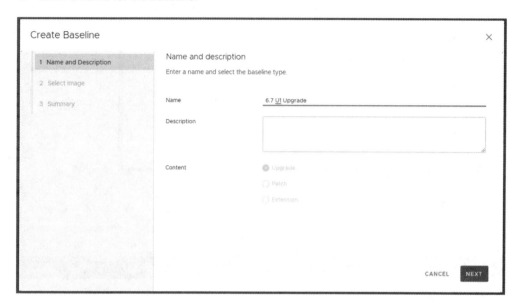

5. Select the ISO you uploaded.

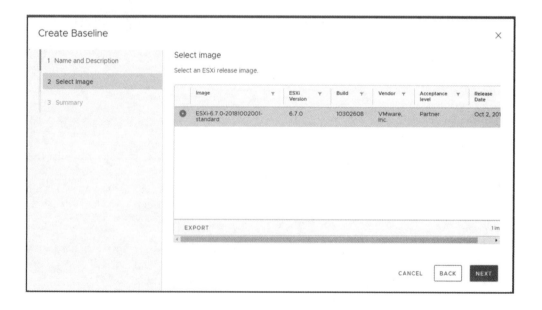

6.   Verify the settings and click Finish.

7.   Open the Updates tab for your host and click Attach.

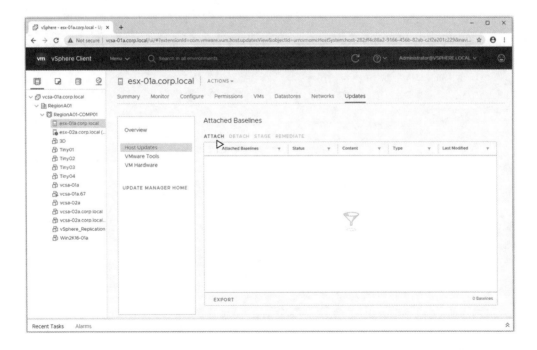

EXERCISE 1.1 *(continued)*

8. Select the new baseline you created and click Attach.

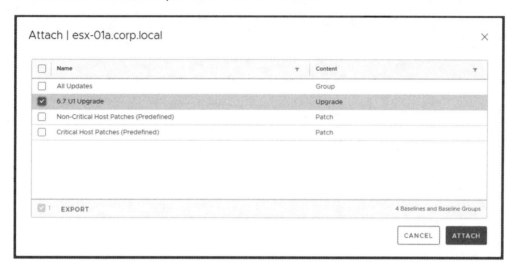

9. From the Overview section, click Check Compliance.

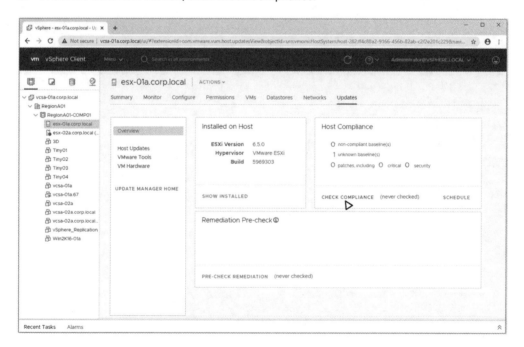

10. Note that it might take a few minutes for the Host Compliance to update. Assuming your host is not 6.7 U1, the host should report a noncompliant baseline.

The new-to-6.7 Quick Boot feature of ESXi ties into Update Manager. With Quick Boot, only the ESXi kernel is restarted when patches and updates are installed. Since the hardware, BIOS, and subsequent hardware checks are bypassed, rebooting ESXi is much faster.

You can see if your 6.7 hosts are compatible with Quick Boot in the Overview section of the Update Manager tab for the host, as shown in Figure 1.13.

You can disable Quick Boot, but only in the Update Manager UI of the Flex client, as shown in Figure 1.14.

There is also a command-line script available on 6.7 hosts to check Quick Boot compatibility. The script will also list any incompatibilities if Quick Boot cannot be enabled.

```
[root@esx-02a:~] /usr/lib/vmware/loadesx/bin/loadESXCheckCompat.py
Congratulation - your system is compatible with loadESX
```

Per VMware KB article 52477, the following issues are among those that could prevent Quick Boot from being enabled:

- The host platform is not supported.
- The host is configured to use a TPM.
- A pass-through device is configured for VMs on your host.

FIGURE 1.13   Viewing Quick Boot status of a 6.7 host

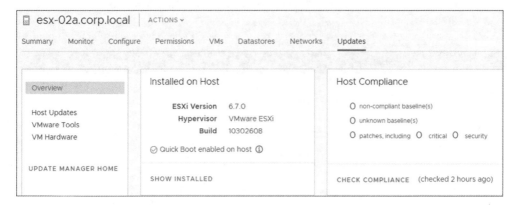

FIGURE 1.14   Disabling Quick Boot requires the Flex client.

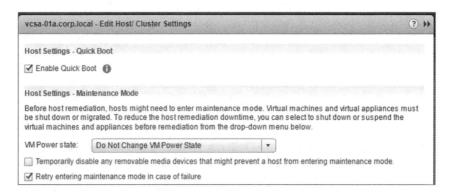

- There are vmklinux drivers loaded on your host.
- There are other noncertified drivers loaded on your host.

    Quick Boot is disabled in the Update Manager UI.

Storage Updates

Several different storage components are either updated or brand-new for vSphere 6.7 and 6.7 U1. There is support for new hardware, a new way to see extremely high I/O, and several vSAN updates. While studying vSAN outside this book, make sure you are reading only up to U1 as VMware is continually adding new features and enhancements for vSAN.

Persistent Memory

As costs come down and performance improves, the line between long-term storage, what used to be a spinning hard drive, and short-term storage (RAM) becomes closer. For the highest computing speeds, the closer you are to the CPU, the faster the storage should be; however, the faster the storage, the more expensive it is. The sticks of RAM in your server might cost 10 times more per GB than the solid-state drives that are holding the virtual machines.

While solid-state drives (SDDs) and the NVM Express (NVMe) interface have made long-term storage blazing fast, there is a new hardware family known as Persistent Memory (PMem) that takes the dynamic random access memory (DRAM) technology used for the system memory and adds battery backup and capacitors to ensure data is not lost during power cycles.

 PMem is also called Non-Volatile Memory (NVM), or NVDIMM, and is the same technology as Intel's Optane, if you have seen references to that on desktop and laptop computers.

A 6.7 ESXi host will automatically create a PMem datastore if it detects compatible PMem hardware. VMs can use PMem either as Virtual Persistent Memory (vPEM) or as a Virtual Persistent Memory Disk (vPMemDisk).

Newer operating systems that are PMem-aware and built on VMs with hardware version 14 and above can be configured with vPMem. With vPMem, applications can reference the storage in byte addressable random mode, which allows more granular use of the PMem storage.

Any operating systems can leverage vPMemDisk, which will show up in the guest as a virtual SCSI device.

PMem does have some drawbacks. For starters, a VM leveraging vPMem can only be migrated to a host with PMem (you can migrate a VM with vPMemDisk to a host without PMem, but you'll lose the performance benefits). If you want to shut down a host with PMem, you'll need to migrate off all VMs utilizing PMem, even if they are powered off. You also lose snapshot and HA support for VMs with PMem configured.

Remote Direct Memory Access

Another technology released with 6.5 and updated with 6.7 is Remote Direct Memory Access, or RDMA. RDMA improves network performance between hosts (for SMP-FT, NFS, and iSCSI traffic) or between virtual machines for use cases such as high-performance computing or big data applications.

RDMA improves I/O for virtual machines through the use of paravirtualized network adapters (PVRDMAs). With a PVRDMA configured, the ESXi kernel's network stack is bypassed and the VM can talk directly to another VM configured with PVRDMA on the same host or directly to the hardware of the host if the remote VM is on a different host. See Figure 1.15.

While RDMA supports network technologies such as iWARP, Infiniband, and RoCE, VMware only supports RoCE (RDMA over Converged Ethernet). There are three transport nodes: memcpy (when two VMs are on the same host), TCP (between hosts without host channel adapters), and RDMA for hosts with host channel adapters.

FIGURE 1.15   This graphic from VMware's white paper on RDMA shows the kernel bypass data path.

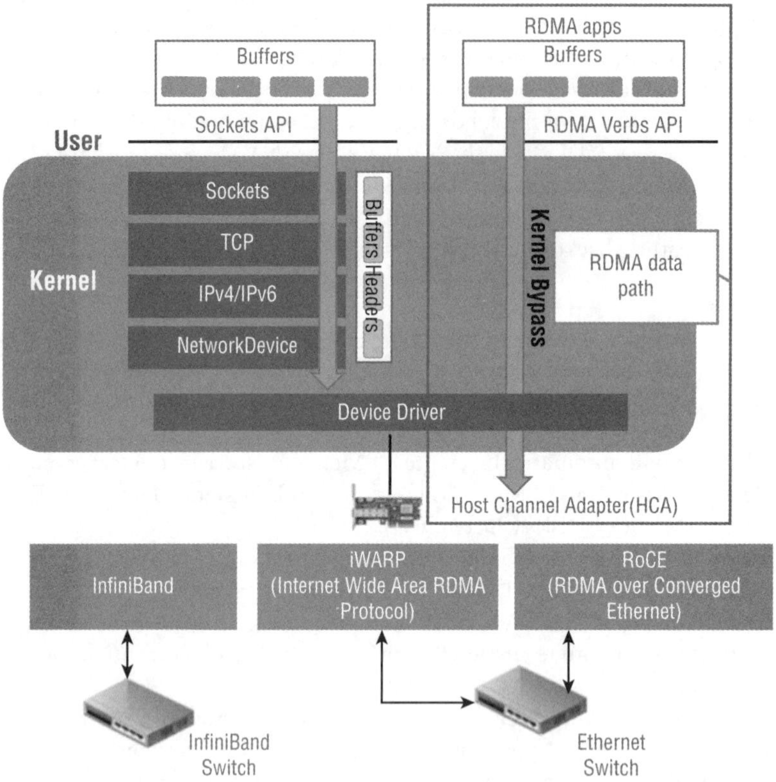

To take advantage of RDMA for your host's iSCSI connectivity, you will need to configure an iSCSI Extensions for RDMA (iSER) adapter. With an iSER adapter and RDMA-compatible NICs, you can see a significant performance boost for host storage traffic. You can enable iSER from the host's command line with the esxcli command:

```
esxcli rdma iser add
```

Once the adapter has been enabled, you configure and manage it just like a normal iSCSI adapter.

vSAN

While many of the vSAN updates for 6.7 and 6.7 U1 are more "optimizations" and enhancements, there are a couple of features that could show up on the VCP exam, including new Microsoft cluster support, new device and security features, plus some new network features.

Setting up vSAN is easier now as there is a quickstart wizard for cluster creation, as seen in Figure 1.16.

FIGURE 1.16   The quickstart guide will walk you through setting up a cluster.

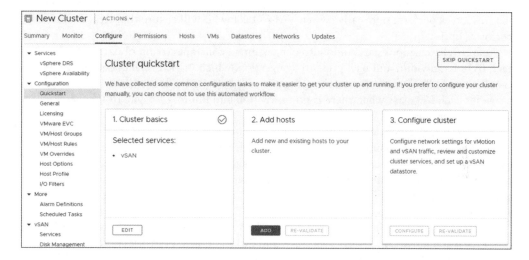

Once you add hosts to a cluster, the quickstart guide will validate them for the services you have chosen for the cluster (HA, DRS, vSAN), as shown in Figure 1.17.

FIGURE 1.17   This cluster shows a couple of warnings about its environment but is otherwise is ready to go.

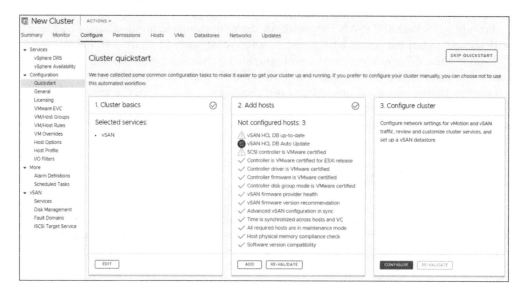

You can also use quickstart to add hosts to an existing cluster.

Another optimization with 6.7 is Adaptive Resync. This mechanism will balance the I/O requests between the four vSAN I/O queues (VM, Namespace, Resync, and Metadata). As the name implies, it's primarily to balance Resync I/O. During times of heavy VM I/O, when the hosts experience congestion, Adaptive Resync will prioritize VM traffic to ensure that resources perform optimally. When VM I/O is low, it will ensure that Resync traffic performs optimally.

Adaptive Resync looks at bandwidth congestion (a constant stream of data regarding each I/O's bandwidth) and backpressure congestion, which involves the queue length of each I/O class. With these inputs, the scheduler will balance the load, allowing maximum usage for each I/O class when there is no contention and limiting Resync I/O requests when there is contention.

To help storage efficiency, vSAN now fully supports TRIM/UNMAP commands sent by a guest OS. These commands (TRIM for ATA drives and UNMAP for SCSI) are used by the guest OS to indicate blocks of storage no longer in use. When vSAN receives the command, it can free up the underlying storage referenced by the guest. This can greatly improve the available storage in your vSAN cluster, especially for guests that have considerable disk usage.

With 6.7, vSAN now supports Microsoft's Windows Server Failover Clustering (WSFC). WSFC is available in Windows Server 2016 and 2019 and uses network connectivity to cluster multiple Windows servers together to improve availability and scalability. This is supported under vSAN by creating iSCSI targets and pointing the Windows guest software iSCSI adapter to those targets.

The final updates to mention for vSAN is the support for 4K Native Devices and FIPS 140-2 Level 1 Validation. 4K (or 4Kn) drives have a sector size of 4096 bytes, much larger than the 512-byte sector size of traditional drives (called 512n drives). Between sectors on a drive is a sector gap, and each sector needs room for an error correction code (ECC). With a larger sector size, the number of gaps is reduced, saving space for data.

Previously vSphere and vSAN supported 4K drives in emulated mode (512e), which helps with the space issue but comes with a performance hit compared to native 4K devices.

With vSphere 6.7, the VM Kernel Cryptographic Module used by vSAN's encryption setting has passed FIPS 140-2 validation. This is mostly important in the government datacenters that require solutions to carry this certification level. With the new validation, partners can build vSAN-based solutions that are FIPS certified to ensure that the highest standards of encryption are met.

Security Updates

The FIPS validation mentioned in the last section makes a good segue into VM encryption, as the same VM Kernel Cryptographic Module that is used by vSAN is also leveraged by the virtual machine encryption feature. In addition to the new FIPS certification for VMs at rest, there is an enhancement of a feature introduced in vSphere 6.5—Encrypted vMotion. Intended to protect VMs as they transition between hosts, with 6.7 it also protects VMs as they transition between datacenters, including to and from VMware on AWS.

Encrypted vMotion can be enabled on a per-VM basis from the VM Options menu as shown in Figure 1.18.

FIGURE 1.18   Enabling VMotion Encryption on a virtual machine

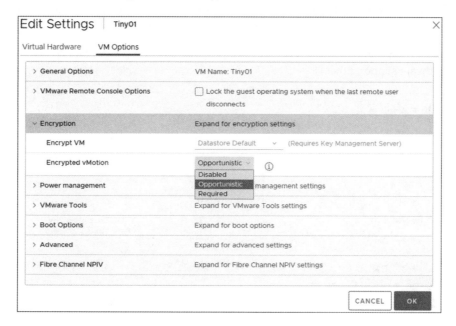

The choices for Encrypted vMotion are Disabled, Opportunistic (where encryption will be used if the destination host offers it), and Required (where the vMotion will fail if the host cannot support encrypted vMotion). While this was available with vSphere 6.5, with 6.7 you can use Encrypted vMotion between vCenter instances. However, this Cross-vCenter Encrypted vMotion currently is only available if your VM is not itself encrypted.

Another key security update is the support for Trusted Platform Module (TPM) version 2.0 hardware devices. These devices improve ESXi host integrity by leveraging Secure Boot to ensure that the running kernel and processes have not been tampered with. Additionally, the TPM 2.0 hardware can be provided as vTPM devices to guests that are compatible to ensure the integrity of their processes.

See VMware's vSphere 6.7 Security Guide for in-depth information on TPM 2.0 and how it is used.

One final security note looks back to the earlier section on topology and UI updates for VCSA. If you are repointing vCenter servers and migrating SSO domains, note that local users and groups will not be migrated to the destination. Using local users and groups is not a recommended practice, but some deployments utilize them.

Virtual Machines

There is a new VM hardware version for 6.7 (version 14) along with changes to the Content Library and a new EVC setting. These are not backward compatible, so keep that in mind if you run a mixed-version environment.

Hardware version 14 is required to enable some of the features we have discussed, such as vTPM and vPMem/NVDIMM, as well as the new EVC setting we'll discuss later on. See Figure 1.19 for the new device options for hardware version 14.

FIGURE 1.19   With hardware version 14, NVDIMM and TPM are available if your hardware supports them.

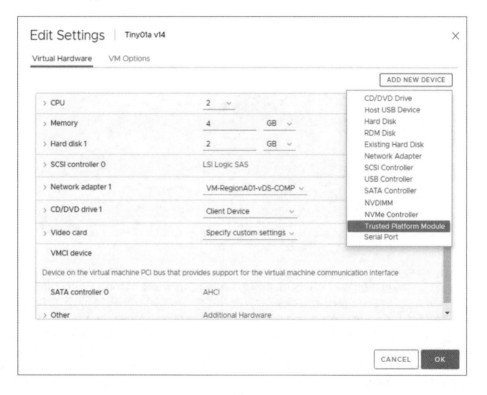

Content Library

The Content Library can now be accessed from within the HTML5 client, and virtual machines can now be stored as either Open Virtualization Format (OVF) or VM templates, as shown in Figure 1.20. Note that VM templates can only be stored in local libraries that are not shared externally.

FIGURE 1.20 Content Library showing a virtual machine uploaded as a VM template and OVF

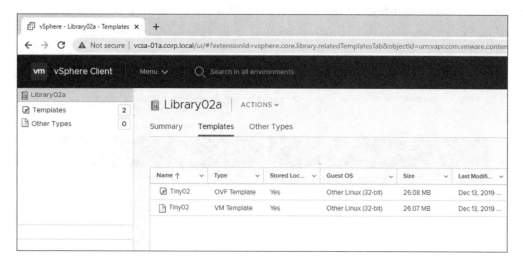

When vApps are uploaded to a Content Library, they will be stored as OVFs. New to vSphere 6.7, OVA files uploaded to a Content Library will be stored as an OVF, as shown in Figure 1.21. ISOs and other files will still show up in the Other Types tab in the Content Library UI.

FIGURE 1.21 An uploaded OVA stored as an OVF.

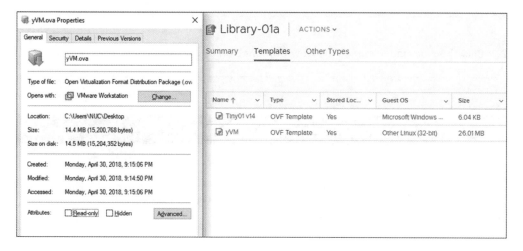

EXERCISE 1.2

Create a local Content Library in the HTML5 client and upload an OVA.

Requires a vCenter server with a datacenter created, an ESXi host with storage, and an OVA file.

1. Select Content Libraries in the HTML5 client.

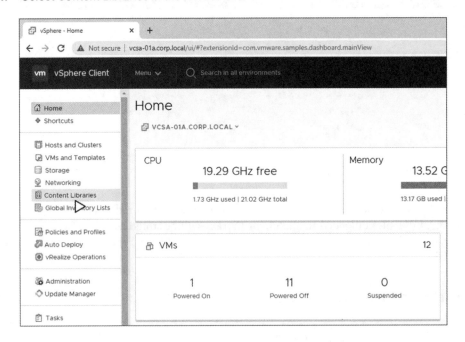

2. Click the plus sign to launch the New Content Library wizard.

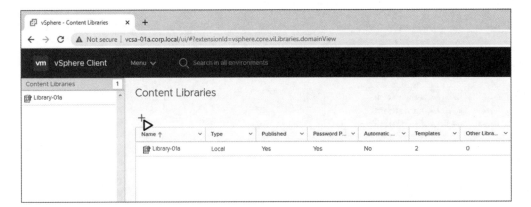

3. Enter a name for the library and click Next.

4. Leave the default Local Content Library selected and click Next. Do *not* check Publish Externally.

5. Select a storage location and click Next.

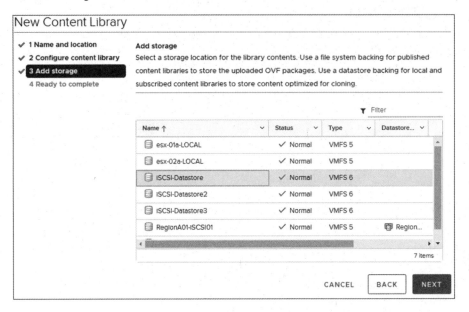

6. Verify the settings and click Finish.

7. Click the new library to open it.

8. From the Actions menu, select Import Item to launch the Import Wizard.

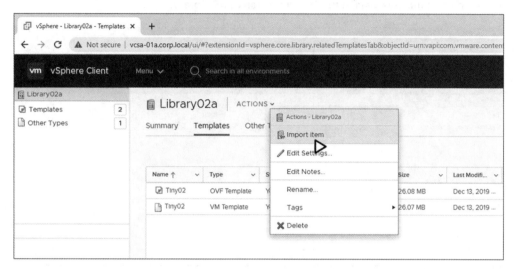

9. Select Local File, browse for the OVA file, and click Import.

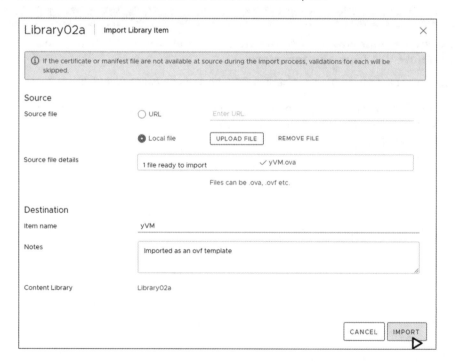

EXERCISE 1.2 *(continued)*

10. Verify that the file exists in the Templates tab of the library.

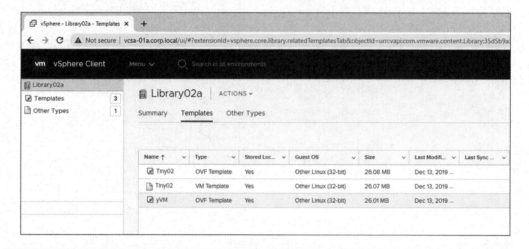

EXERCISE 1.3

Clone a virtual machine to a template in a local Content Library and deploy a new VM from the template.

Requires a vCenter server with a datacenter, ESXi host, and local Content Library.

1. Select the virtual machine to upload to the Content Library. Right-click the virtual machine and select Clone as Template to Library.

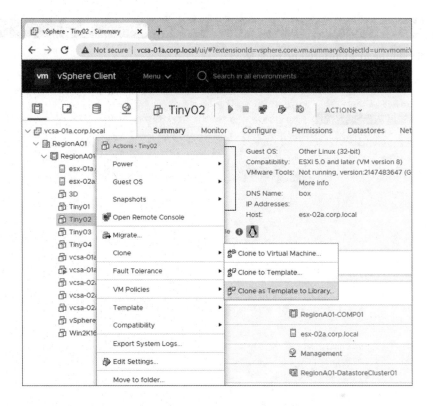

2. In the Clone Wizard, make sure VM Template is selected and click Next.

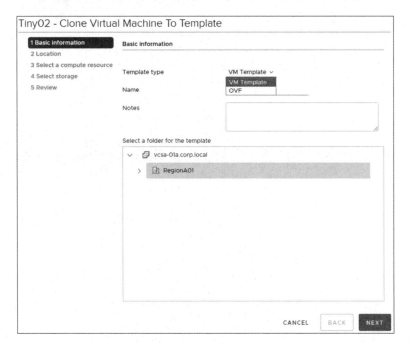

3. Select the local library and click Next.

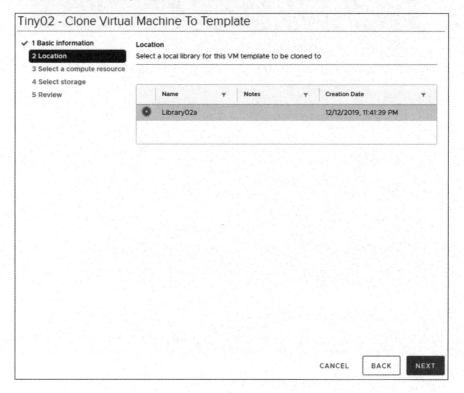

4. Select a compute resource and click Next.

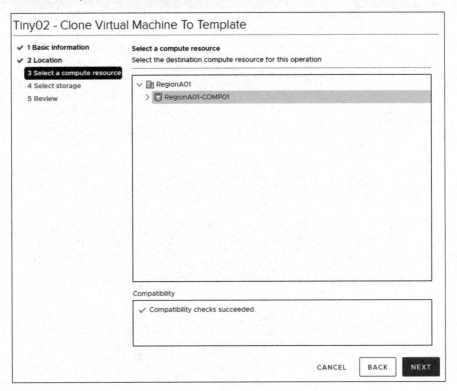

Tiny02 - Clone Virtual Machine To Template

✔ 1 Basic information
✔ 2 Location
3 Select a compute resource
4 Select storage
5 Review

Select a compute resource
Select the destination compute resource for this operation

∨ 🗄 RegionA01
  ⟩ 🗐 RegionA01-COMP01

Compatibility

✔ Compatibility checks succeeded.

CANCEL   BACK   NEXT

5. Select a storage location and click Next.

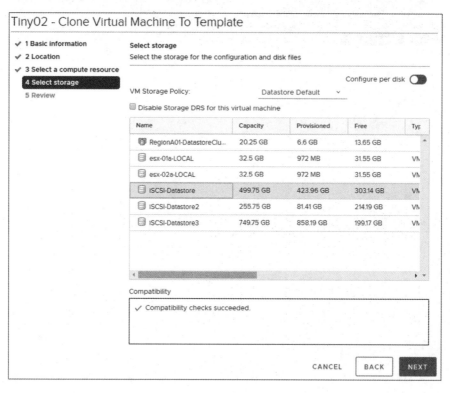

6. Verify the settings and click Finish.

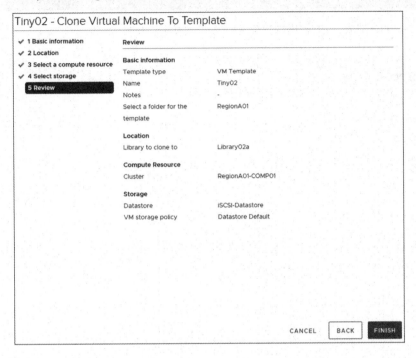

7. From the Templates tab of the Content Library, right-click the new template and select New VM from This Template.

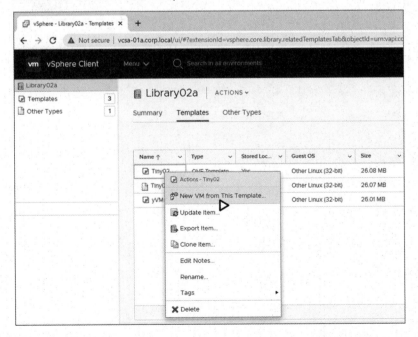

8. Enter a name for the virtual machine and a folder and then click Next.

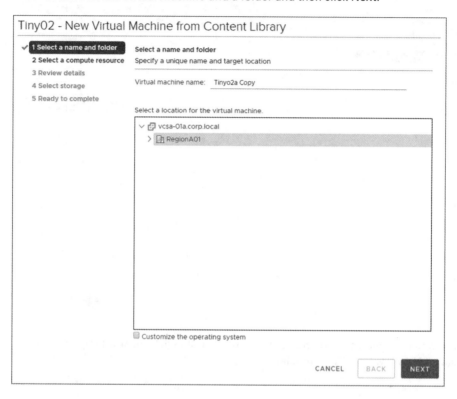

9. Select a compute resource and click Next.

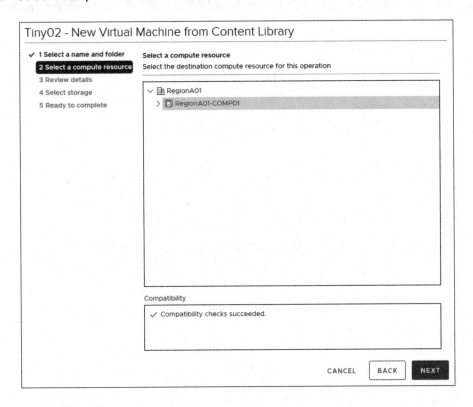

Tiny02 - New Virtual Machine from Content Library

✓ 1 Select a name and folder
2 Select a compute resource
3 Review details
4 Select storage
5 Ready to complete

Select a compute resource
Select the destination compute resource for this operation

∨ 🗄 RegionA01
   > 🖥 RegionA01-COMP01

Compatibility

✓ Compatibility checks succeeded.

CANCEL   BACK   NEXT

EXERCISE 1.3 *(continued)*

10. Review the template details and click Next.

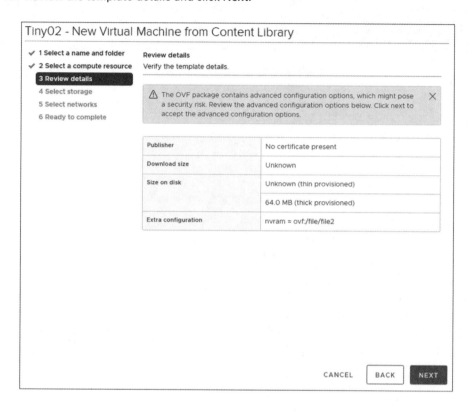

11. Select the storage and click Next.

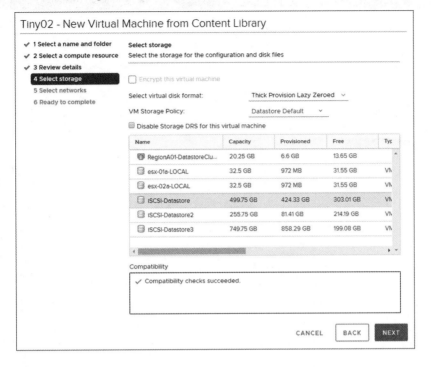

12. Select the network and click Next.

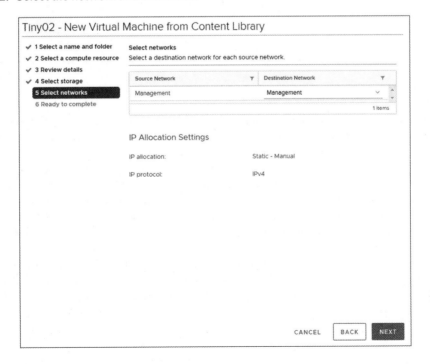

13. Reviews the settings and click Finish to deploy the VM.

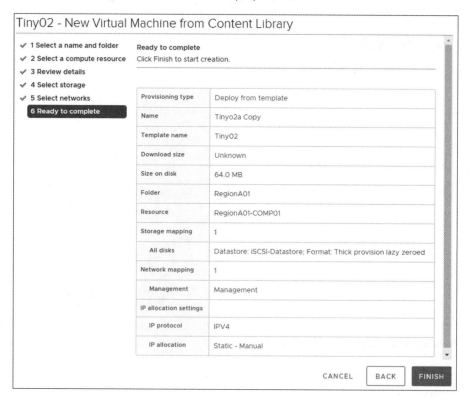

Per-VM EVC

VMware's vMotion technology allows a running virtual machine to be migrated between hosts. vMotion has had its improvements over the years, and now you can migrate running virtual machines up to your datacenter on VMware Cloud on AWS.

This ability isn't completely carefree, however. A guest OS tends to assume that the CPU instruction set available to it at boot time will continue to be available to it. A running VM that suddenly loses the ability to run some CPU instructions will not be a running VM for long. While one solution is to ensure that all of your hosts have the exact same CPU (or at least the same family), as datacenters grow and change that requirement becomes impossible to achieve.

Thus the debut of Enhanced vMotion Compatibility, or EVC, which can specify the CPU instruction set available to a host. By setting the EVC level to the oldest/least possible CPU that your ESXi hosts are running on, you can ensure that the VMs can migrate freely around your datacenter.

However, with stretched clusters, hybrid clouds like IBM offers, and of course VMware Cloud on AWS, a more granular approach is needed, one that allows the EVC setting on a per-VM basis.

Per-VM ECV is a setting available with VM hardware version 14 and is enabled in the Configure tab of the virtual machine, as shown in Figure 1.22.

FIGURE 1.22   Editing the EVC setting on a virtual machine

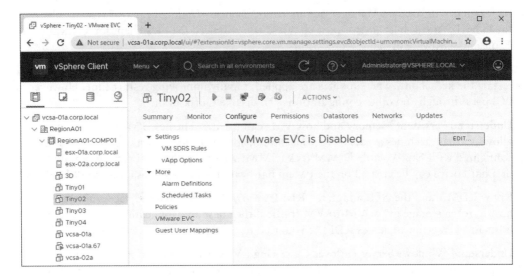

Summary

VMware is constantly improving its software. New releases provide stability and security and bring new features and enhancements to existing features—which turn into great material for exam questions.

The improvements to vSphere with 6.7 and 6.7 U1 include more functionality in the HTML5 client, changes to vCenter and the vCenter Appliance, feature enhancements, and new hardware support for the vSphere storage. There are also new security features as well as updates to virtual machines and the Content Library.

You should work with each of these new features and functions to build familiarity before taking the exam.

Exam Essentials

Understand vCenter topology changes.   The external PSC is being deprecated. It's still supported but not for much longer. The push is to migrate to embedded PSCs using the new command-line tools to modify the topology. Embedded PSCs now support hybrid linked mode.

Be familiar with Update Manager and its requirements.   Update Manager is available in the HTML5 client, but only for host updates. You still need the Flex client for VMware Tools and hardware updates.

Understand Quick Boot.   The new Quick Boot feature works with Update Manager to restart the kernel only when updates are applied, rapidly improving restart time. However, PCI pass-through and other configurations can disable Quick Boot.

Understand Persistent Memory and how VMs can use it.   The new PMem hardware allows virtual machines access to very fast storage that persists on restarts. VMs can be configured with Non-Volatile DIMM (NVDIMM) virtual hardware if the guest allows it, or a hard drive can be created on the PMem hardware for the VM's usage as a vPMemDisk.

Know RDMA and the iSER adapter.   RDMA provides for high-speed access either for a host to reach storage or for VM-to-VM traffic if the guest and application support it. For hosts to leverage iSCSI across RDMA, you need to configure the iSER adapter.

Understand Windows Server Failover Clustering (WSFC) support.   With vSphere 6.7 U1, support is provided for vSAN iSCSI targets to support Microsoft's Windows Server Failover Clustering (WSFC) configuration. The Windows guests will connect to the iSCSI targets using a software iSCSI initiator.

Understand the Content Library updates.   The Content Library can now import OVAs as OVFs and hold VM templates along with OVF templates.

Review Questions

The answers to the chapter review questions can be found in the Appendix.

1. Where can VCSA service management be found?
   A. VAMI UI
   B. Flex client
   C. HTML5 client
   D. Clarity client

2. What task still requires the Flex client?
   A. Backing up the VCSA appliance
   B. Managing a content library
   C. Configuring Virtual Flash
   D. Enabling Quick Boot

3. Which software development kit includes the vSphere Storage Management SDK?
   A. vSphere Automation SDK for Python
   B. vSphere Management SDK
   C. vSphere Client SDK
   D. vSAN Management SDK for Java

4. What vSphere topology supports Enhanced Linked Mode and is recommended by VMware for new deployments?
   A. Windows-deployed vCenter with an external VCSA PSC
   B. VCSA vCenter with an external VCSA PSC
   C. VCSA vCenter with an embedded VCSA PSC
   D. Windows-deployed vCenter with an external Windows PSC

5. What can help plan your vCenter topology?
   A. vSphere Management SDK
   B. VCSA Deployment Utility
   C. vSphere 6.7 Clarity client
   D. vSphere Topology and Upgrade Planning Tool

6. What tool is available to convert or migrate external PSCs to embedded PSCs?
   A. vSphere 6.7 Clarity client
   B. *vcsa-util*
   C. *cmsso-util*
   D. *loadESXCheckCompat.py*

7.   Which tool will help you consolidate SSO domains?

A.   vSphere 6.7 Clarity Client

B.   *vcsa-util*

C.   *cmsso-util*

D.   *loadESXCheckCompat.py*

8.   If your host does not show Quick Boot compatibility, what tool can report on Quick Boot incompatibilities?

A.   vSphere 6.7 Clarity Client

B.   *vcsa-util*

C.   *cmsso-util*

D.   *loadESXCheckCompat.py*

9.   What feature of ESXi can dramatically improve the time it takes to update a server?

A.   Quick Boot

B.   RDAM

C.   PMem

D.   iSER

10.   What new feature can be enabled on legacy operating systems to improve storage speed?

A.   NVDIMM

B.   iSER

C.   vPMemDisk

D.   Quick Boot

11.   What must you enable on each ESXi host to make use of iSCSI across RDMA?

A.   A new software adapter

B.   PMem

C.   WFCS

D.   Quick Boot

12.   What new feature of vSAN can help VM I/O traffic be prioritized during times of contention?

A.   PMem

B.   Adaptive Resync

C.   RDMA

D.   TRIM

13.   What feature allows guests to help drive storage efficiency?

A.   TRIM/UNMAP

B.   vPMemDisk

C.   NVDIMM

D.   iSER

14. What is required for vSAN to support Microsoft's Windows Server Failover Clustering (WSFC)?

   A. iSCSI target

   B. Virtual Volumes

   C. EVC

   D. RDM

15. What storage technology provides the best performance and efficiency?

   A. 512n

   B. 4K

   C. 512e

   D. ECC

16. What security hardware will ensure guest boot integrity?

   A. TPM 2.0

   B. OVF

   C. FIPS 140-2

   D. vPMem

17. What VM hardware version is required for NVDIMM?

   A. 140-2

   B. 2.0

   C. 6.7

   D. 14

18. What format are OVA files stored in for a vSphere 6.7 Content Library?

   A. OVA

   B. OVF

   C. VMX

   D. VMTX

19. What formats are available for virtual machines stored in a vSphere 6.7 Content Library? (Choose two.)

   A. OVA

   B. B. OVF

   C. VM template

   D. vApp

20. What virtual machine option can improve portability in a large diverse environment?

   A. Per-VM EVC

   B. GPU

   C. CPU affinity

   D. RDM

Chapter 2

Configuring and Administering Security in a vSphere Datacenter

---

2V0-21.19 EXAM OBJECTIVES COVERED IN THIS CHAPTER:

✓ **Section 1 – VMware vSphere Architectures and Technologies**

- Objective 1.9 – Describe the purpose of cluster and the features it provides

✓ **Section 2 – VMware Products and Solutions**

- Objective 2.3 – Describe the options for securing a vSphere environment

✓ **Section 4 – Installing, Configuring, and Setting Up a VMware vSphere Solution**

- Objective 4.2 – Create and configure vSphere objects

- Objective 4.7 – Set up identity sources

- Objective 4.8 – Configure an SSO domain

✓ **Section 7 – Administrative and Operational Tasks in a VMware vSphere Solution**

- Objective 7.4 – Configure host security

- Objective 7.5 – Configure role-based user management

- Objective 7.11 – Manage different VMware vCenter Server objects

- Objective 7.12 – Setup permissions on datastores, clusters, vCenter, and hosts

This chapter focuses on how to secure ESXi hosts, virtual machines, and other infrastructure components in a vSphere 6.x datacenter.

Securing all access points into a vSphere implementation should be considered even more important than securing a traditional datacenter. In a traditional datacenter, bypassing security on a single server would allow access to data on only that server. But a single ESXi host could be running dozens of virtual machines, each containing potentially valuable data. Also, in addition to taking security precautions within each virtual machine, you must also take precautions with the ESXi host itself, as well as other virtualized components within the vSphere environment.

The vSphere Web Client provides a centralized access point into the virtual machines running within the datacenter. One of the first steps that should be taken in securing the environment should be ensuring that each user and group has the smallest degree of access to each virtual machine as is appropriate for their role within the company. Normally, this could be cumbersome to administer, but vSphere provides the ability to customize roles as needed to provide the exact grouping of privileges required. It also allows that permission set to be propagated to child objects, simplifying the need to assign permissions on multiple objects within the hierarchy.

Next, steps should be taken to harden both the ESXi hosts running virtual machines and the vCenter Server system. The term *harden* comes into play because both the ESXi hosts and vCenter Server come with a degree of security out of the box. The idea behind hardening is to make adjustments to the inherent security of these vectors in order to reduce the attack surface as much as possible without overly impacting usability of the environment.

Identity management, certificate management, and licensing management for ESXi hosts and vCenter Server are provided by the Platform Services Controller (PSC). There are multiple methods of deploying the PSC depending on design requirements, including a high-availability solution available starting with vSphere 6.7. Once deployed, the PSC provides a SAML-token-secured, encrypted pathway for communications-critical components within the environment. Two-factor authentication is supported using smart card or RSA SecurID methods. Certificates are managed by the VMware Certificate Authority (VMCA), which can act on its own or as a subordinate of an enterprise or third-party CA.

The final point of security to be considered is the virtual machine itself. The guest OS in a virtual machine is subject to the same risks it would be subject to on a physical system, so the same security precautions should be taken. In addition, starting with vSphere 6.5, virtual machine encryption is supported, which can be used to protect virtual machine files, virtual disk files, and core dumps. Finally, some additional steps can be taken to harden this vector and further reduce the attack surface of the vSphere implementation.

Configuring and Administering Role-Based Access Controls

Security in a vSphere environment is a delicate balancing act. Users that perform day-to-day activities within the environment typically have a set of duties that require access to specific objects, along with the ability to perform actions on those objects. At the same time, a user should be restricted from accessing objects that are outside the scope of their duties. In the case where the user does have access to an object, they still should be limited to performing the actions on those objects that are necessary for their job.

In vSphere, these actions are referred to as privileges. When a user is granted one or more privileges on an object, the collection of privileges forms their permissions governing the use of that object. Finally, the collective group of permissions and objects a user can access makes up that user's permission set.

The determination of objects and privileges is closely tied to the user's duties, or job role. Because the defining of permissions is tied to a job role, this is referred to as role-based access control (RBAC). The following sections focus on RBAC.

What Is a Privilege?

A *privilege* is an action that can be taken in a vSphere environment. An example of a privilege is *Network.Assign network*, which assigns a network to a virtual machine. There are over 275 privileges that can be assigned in vSphere 6.7, which would be extremely cumbersome if an administrator were required to assign every privilege individually. Thankfully, this is not necessary, since privileges can be grouped together for easier assignment. This grouping is done based on tasks and roles.

What Is a Task?

A *task* is a duty a user has to perform as part of their job role. In many cases, multiple privileges are required to perform a task. An example of a task might be to create a virtual machine, which requires the following privileges:

- Virtual machine.Inventory.Create new
- Virtual machine.Configuration.Add new disk
- Resource.Assign virtual machine to resource pool
- Datastore.Allocate space
- Network.Assign network

Other common tasks and related privileges can be found in the vSphere Security Guide.

In some cases, it might be appropriate for a single user to have all of these privileges. For example, an administrator would typically have all of the above privileges. However, it may not always be advisable for a user to have all of these privileges even if it is part of their job role to perform the related task. In this case, if it is an application owner's duty to create virtual machines for related applications, the owner may be limited to a specific resource pool or network. So in some cases, it may be necessary for the owner to request some portion of the tasks to be performed by another user, such as a Resource Pool Administrator.

What Is a Role?

A *role* is a grouping of privileges based on a specific set of tasks that must be performed within a vSphere environment. If a user is in the job role of managing the content library for virtual machine administrators, they might be assigned the *content library administrator* role, which contains the following privileges:

- Content library.Add library item
- Content library.Create local library
- Content library.Create subscribed library
- Content library.Delete library item
- Content library.Delete local library
- Content library.Delete subscribed library
- Content library.Download files
- Content library.Evict library item
- Content library.Evict subscribed library
- Content library.Probe subscription information
- Content library.Read storage
- Content library.Sync library item
- Content library.Sync subscribed library
- Content library.Type introspection
- Content library.Update configuration settings
- Content library.Update files
- Content library.Update library
- Content library.Update library item
- Content library.Update local library
- Content library.Update subscribed library
- Content library.View configuration settings

There are two types of roles in vSphere: *system roles* and *sample roles*. There are five system roles, as follows:

Administrator Role   The Administrator role contains all possible privileges. Assigning a user or group this role against an object ensures that they can perform all possible actions on the object. This is also the *only* role that can be used to assign privileges to other users and groups. This role is assigned to the local administrator account by default.

No Cryptography Administrator Role   The No Cryptography Administrator role contains the same privileges as the Administrator role, except for cryptographic operations privileges. This role allows an administrator to assign administrator privileges to other users or groups while restricting them from encrypting or decrypting virtual machines or accessing encrypted data.

No Access Role   The No Access role restricts a user or group from viewing or changing an object in any way. This role is assigned to new users and groups by default to prevent access until appropriate privileges can be assigned. This role can be used in addition to normal privileges to mask specific areas of the hierarchy from a user or group.

Read Only Role   The Read Only role allows a user or group to view the state and details of the object it is applied to. A user or group with this role on a virtual machine would be able to view its attributes but would not be able to open a remote console to the VM.

Tagging Admin Role   The Tagging Admin role allows a user or group to manage tags that are applied to objects in the vSphere inventory. A user or group with this role can create, edit, delete, or modify tags as well as assign and unassign them.

System roles are permanent fixtures in vSphere, so it is not possible to make any changes to them. However, these are not the only roles available in vSphere. A number of sample roles are also included, and these can be modified as needed. The included sample roles are as follows:

Content Library Administrator Role   The Content Library Administrator role allows a user or group the ability to monitor and manage a library and its contents. Users and groups with this role can create, edit, and delete libraries, synchronize a library, configure library settings, and import/export items to/from a library.

Resource Pool Administrator Role   The Resource Pool Administrator role allows a user or group to create child resource pools or modify the configuration of existing child pools. This permission is usually assigned on a parent pool (or a cluster), which cannot be modified by users or groups assigned this role. Additionally, the role also allows the granting of permissions on child pools and the assignment of VMs to child or parent pools.

Virtual Machine Power User Role   The Virtual Machine Power User role allows a user or group to interact with and make changes to a virtual machine. Examples would be modifying vCPU or memory settings or adding a vDisk. This role also includes the ability to manage snapshots and schedule tasks on a VM.

Virtual Machine User Role   The Virtual Machine User role allows a user or group to perform power actions on a virtual machine. It is typically combined with additional permissions or roles and is very effective when used with VM folders to grant power users control over a group of virtual machines. Additional actions include the ability to insert media as well as open a remote console to the VM.

Datastore Consumer Role   The Datastore Consumer role allows a user or group to consume space on a datastore and restricts a user or group from viewing or changing an object in any way. It is typically combined with additional permissions or roles when a user or group needs to create snapshots or virtual machines.

Network Consumer Role   The Network Consumer role allows a user or group to assign virtual machines or hosts to a network, assuming the user or group also has the appropriate permissions on the related VMs or hosts.

VMware Consolidated Backup Role   The VMware Consolidated Backup role is for the most part a legacy role, but it still can be used to allow a user or group the appropriate permissions to perform snapshot and backup actions in conjunction with VMware Data Protection or a third-party backup platform.

To change one of these roles, select the role in the vSphere Web Client and click the Pencil icon. The Edit Role window is displayed, allowing privileges to be added or removed as necessary. For example, let's say you wanted to take the Datastore Consumer role, which is limited to allocate space, and expand it into a Datastore Administrator role, with all datastore privileges, including the ability to browse, configure, and move a datastore. An example is shown in Figure 2.1.

FIGURE 2.1   The Datastore Consumer role edited to include all datastore privileges

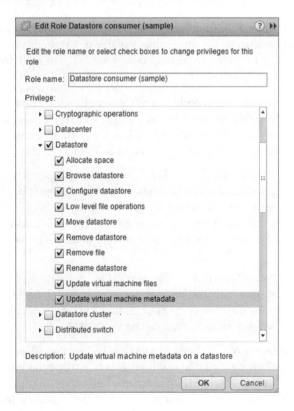

Although it is possible to edit these sample roles, they serve even better as templates in the creation of new roles. If used in this way, it would be preferable not to make changes to the sample roles. This is easily accomplished by cloning the sample role, then making changes and saving the result as a new role. For example, if you wanted to create a role similar to the Virtual Machine Power User role but wanted to add the ability to configure virtual machine fault tolerance, you would select the Virtual Machine Power User role in the vSphere Web Client, click the Clone icon, supply a name for the new role, and add the privileges as shown in Figure 2.2.

FIGURE 2.2   The Virtual Machine Power User role cloned to a new role that will include FT privileges

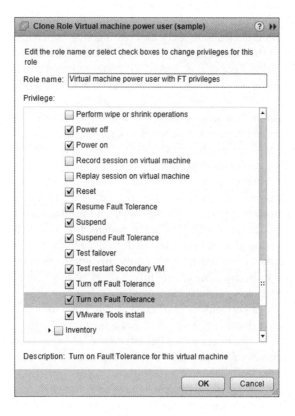

While cloning sample roles is a convenient way to create custom roles, you may sometimes need to create a new role from scratch, particularly if there are no sample roles that closely match your permission requirements. If you do need to create a role, it is a VMware best practice to grant permissions only to the objects needed in performing the tasks the role comprises and to use the minimum number of permissions required for each task.

Assigning Permissions

Now that you have an understanding of privileges, tasks, and roles, let's look at how to assign a user or group to an object with a specific set of privileges. To perform this action, begin by selecting an object. It is a VMware best practice to group both objects and users together to minimize management overhead. For objects, such groupings would include the entire datacenter, specific clusters, resource pools, or folders containing specific groups of virtual machines. Users should be grouped by job role whenever possible.

For the example shown in Figure 2.3, we are selecting the entire datacenter. This is because the group that we will assign to the datacenter is responsible for creating virtual machines within the both the Sales cluster and the Finance cluster. This assignment will also allow the group to create VMs regardless of future cluster, resource pool, or folder locations. The next step is to assign a user or group to the object. In this case, I have grouped together users who will share the same responsibility for creating virtual machines, and this is the group I am assigning to the object. Finally, I select a role for the group on this object. Since there is no system or sample role that is limited to creating virtual machines, I have created a custom role limited to the privileges necessary to perform this task. The workflow would look like Figure 2.3.

When assigning permissions on an object, think about both user and group require-ments as well as the collective objects that need to be utilized. This will help determine whether you make an explicit assignment to an object or propagate permissions to a group of objects. Take Figure 2.4, for example.

In this use case, the Finance group works with a number of virtual machines (VMs) on a regular basis. As a result, all of those VMs have been grouped into a folder labeled Finance. By assigning the Finance group to the Finance folder and propagating their permissions, not only does the group get access to each VM in the folder with the exact same permissions, but they will gain the same level of access to any future VMs that are placed into the folder. Not only does this follow best practice, it also minimizes management overhead as this assignment only needs to be done once. Any future users added to the group or VMs added to the folder will automatically acquire the same configuration.

However, in some cases you may need to explicitly assign a user to an object. In the use case, there is a Receivables user. This user does a very specific job and should not be granted access to other Finance-related VMs, only to the VM that runs the Receivables app. The explicit assignment provides the exact level of access needed, albeit at a higher level of management overhead.

The way permissions on inventory objects behave can change dramatically when a user has multiple possible permissions assignments to the object. There are two primary instances when this occurs. The first is when a user is assigned to multiple groups and those groups are assigned to the same object, as shown in Figure 2.5.

FIGURE 2.3 Assigning an object to a group, then assigning privileges for the group on that object

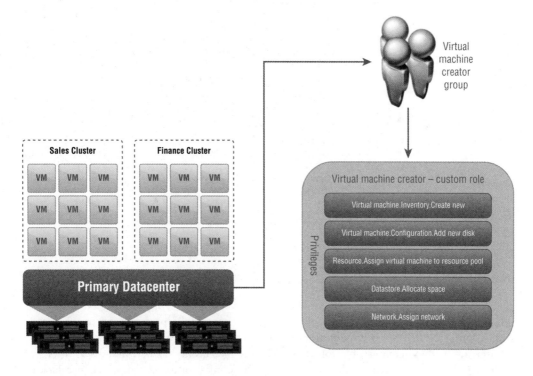

FIGURE 2.4 Example of propagated permission assignments

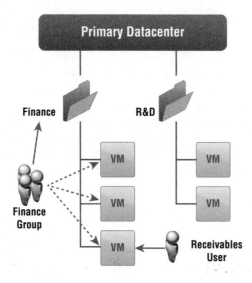

FIGURE 2.5 Example of combined propagated and explicit permission assignments

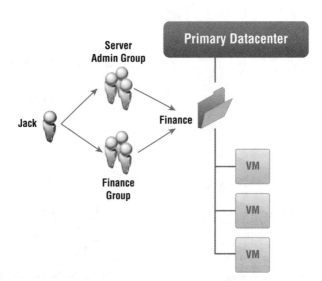

In this example, Jack is a member of both the Server Admin group and the Finance group. The Server Admin group has all permissions necessary to perform power options and to configure VM resources but no permissions to interact with the VM or guest (such as inserting media, opening a console, etc.). The Finance group has permissions to interact with the VM and guest but no ability to change VM configuration settings. Because Jack is a member of both groups, and both groups have been assigned to the Finance folder, Jack is given the aggregate of permissions for both groups. This means that Jack can change the configuration of the VM and interact with it as well.

The second instance occurs when a user is part of one or more propagated assignments but has an explicit assignment to a child object. Figure 2.6 provides an example of this.

When this situation occurs, the explicit assignment overrides any propagated permissions. A good example of this would be if Jack was a member of the Server Admin group, which can configure VMs in this folder, but Jack needs to have total access to the VM. Assigning Jack the Administrator role on this VM would override the propagated assignment and allow for complete access to the VM.

However, care should be taken when applying this type of assignment. If, for example, Jack was given a Read Only role on this VM, he would be restricted to those permissions, which would override the greater degree of control that was granted to him by the propagated role.

FIGURE 2.6   Example of explicit permission assignment overriding propagated permissions

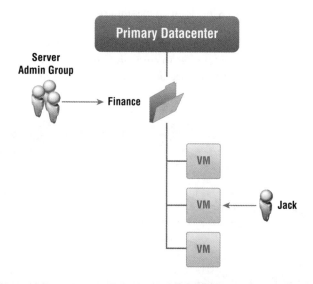

EXERCISE 2.1

Creating a custom role

1. Connect to a vCenter Server using the vSphere Web Client.

2. Click the Home button, then click Administration in the drop-down menu.

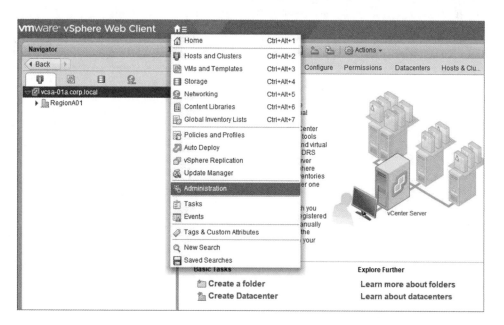

3. To create the custom role, we will clone an existing role. The user that will be assigned to this role will be responsible for all activities on the datastores assigned to the vSphere implementation. Therefore, a good starting place would be to clone the Datastore consumer (sample) role. To clone this role, begin by selecting Roles in the Navigator pane, then click on the Datastore Consumer (Sample) role. Finally, click the Clone Role Action icon.

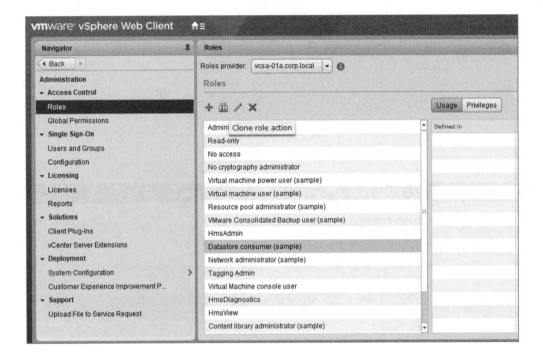

4. The Clone Role window is displayed, showing the privileges that make up the existing role.

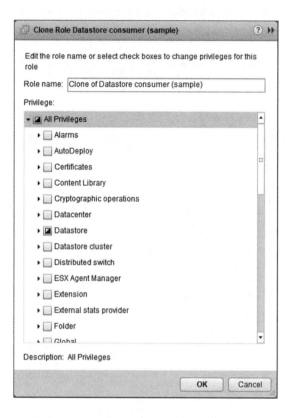

5. To create the new role, begin by changing the name of the role to Datastore Administrator.

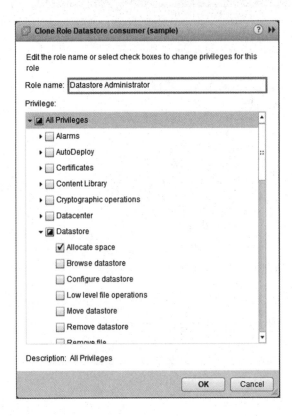

6. Next, select all of the Datastore privileges by clicking the Datastore box twice. The first click will deselect the current privileges, while the second click will select all privileges. Click OK to create the new role.

7. Once the role is created, you should see it displayed in the list of available roles.

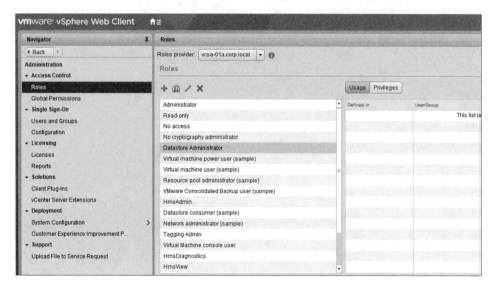

EXERCISE 2.2

Applying a role to a user on an object

1. Connect to a vCenter Server using the vSphere Web Client.

2. Click the Home button, then click Administration from the drop-down menu.

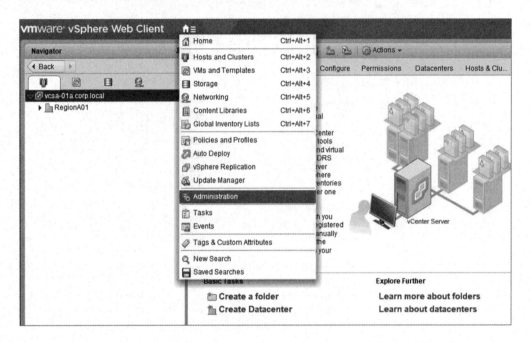

3. The first step in this lab is to create a new user. To create the user, begin by selecting Users And Groups in the Navigator pane, then click the New User Action icon (the plus symbol)/

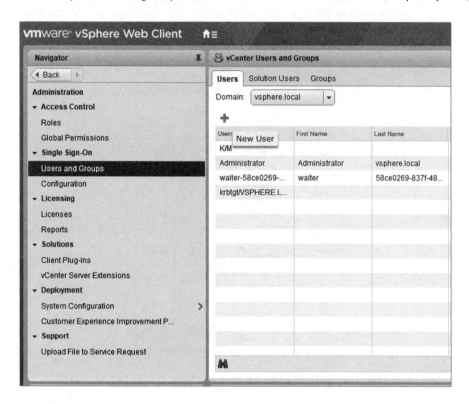

4. The **New User** window is displayed.

5. Enter the information shown in the following screen shot. Our new user, Susan Richards, will be a Datastore Administrator. For the password, use VMware1!. Click OK to add the user.

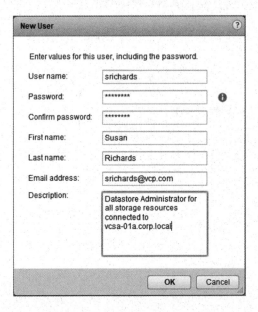

6. If the user has been successfully added, they will appear on the main users list.

7. Susan will be assigned the Datastore Administrator role on the vCenter appliance so that any datastore resources added to the server will automatically inherit permissions. To do this, click the Home icon, then click Hosts And Clusters.

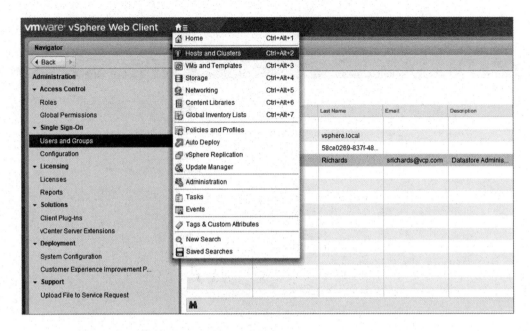

8. Ensure that the vCenter appliance is highlighted in the Navigator pane, then click the Permissions tab.

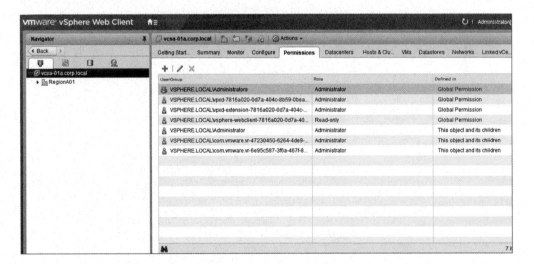

9. Click the plus sign to open the Add Permission window.

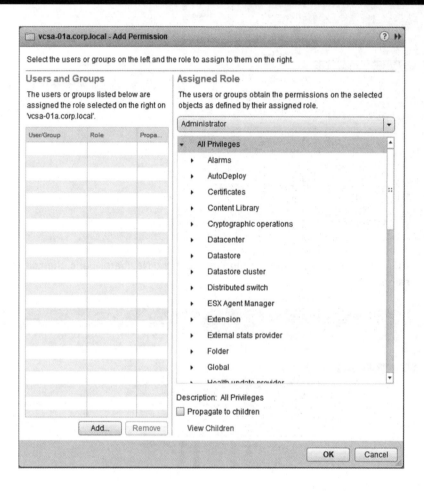

10. Select the Datastore Administrator role from the Assigned Role drop-down.

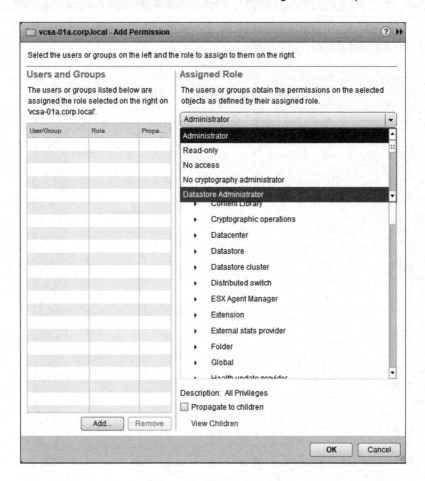

11. The Select Users/Groups window appears. Locate Susan Richards, then click Add. Click OK to assign the user to the role.

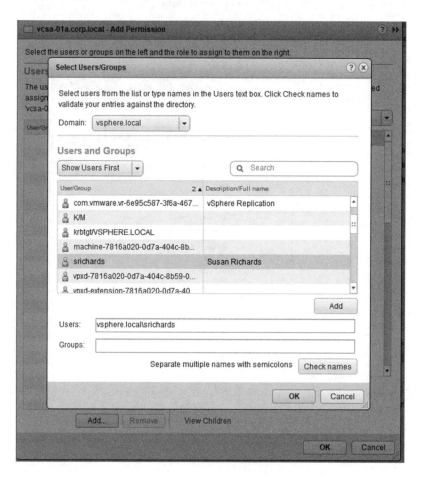

12. The display should now show the user on the left side and the assigned role on the right. Click OK to assign this user with this role to the vCenter appliance object.

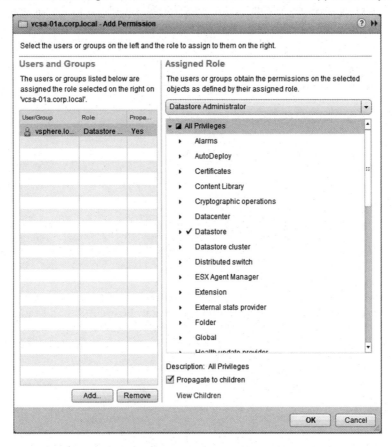

13. The Permissions list for the vCenter appliance should now show Susan and the role she has been assigned on this object.

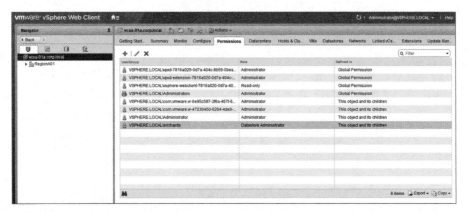

Viewing and Exporting Group and User Permissions

To see the current permission settings on an object, select the object in the navigator and click the Permissions tab. The current list of users and groups that have permissions on the object and the role they have been assigned on the object are displayed. Figure 2.7 is an example.

FIGURE 2.7   Viewing permission assignments on an object

In the Flash-based client at the bottom of this screen, there is a button that can be used to export the list. The list will be exported in CSV format. Figure 2.8 is an example.

FIGURE 2.8   Exporting permission assignments to a file

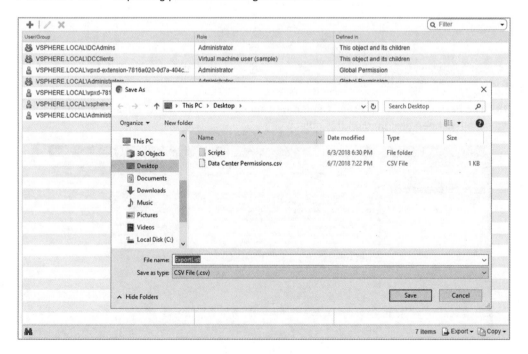

Validating Users and Groups

Before a user is assigned permissions on objects in vCenter Server, they must first be validated. Validation is done against the selected identity source. For more on identity sources, see the section "SSO and Identity Sources" later in this chapter.

vCenter Server periodically reviews current user and group lists and compares them to information in the user directory. Any users or groups that no longer exist are removed. This is done to maintain security in the environment and can be customized as needed. First, it is possible (though not recommended) to disable validation entirely. This may be something that is considered in a large, enterprise implementation, since the validation process has to search the user directory, which may consist of multiple domains and thousands of users or groups.

Rather than disabling validation entirely, consider modifying the validation period so that validation is not done as often. You can even limit the scope of the queries performed. In this way, you can maintain a high level of security while maintaining a reasonable level of performance on the vCenter Service system.

To make these adjustments, highlight the vCenter server in the navigator, click the Configure tab, then click the Edit button. The Edit vCenter Server Settings window is displayed. Click User Directory on the left, then make changes to the settings as needed (Figure 2.9). The validation period is entered in minutes, with the default setting set at 1440 minutes, or 24 hours.

FIGURE 2.9   Adjusting the validation period for users and groups

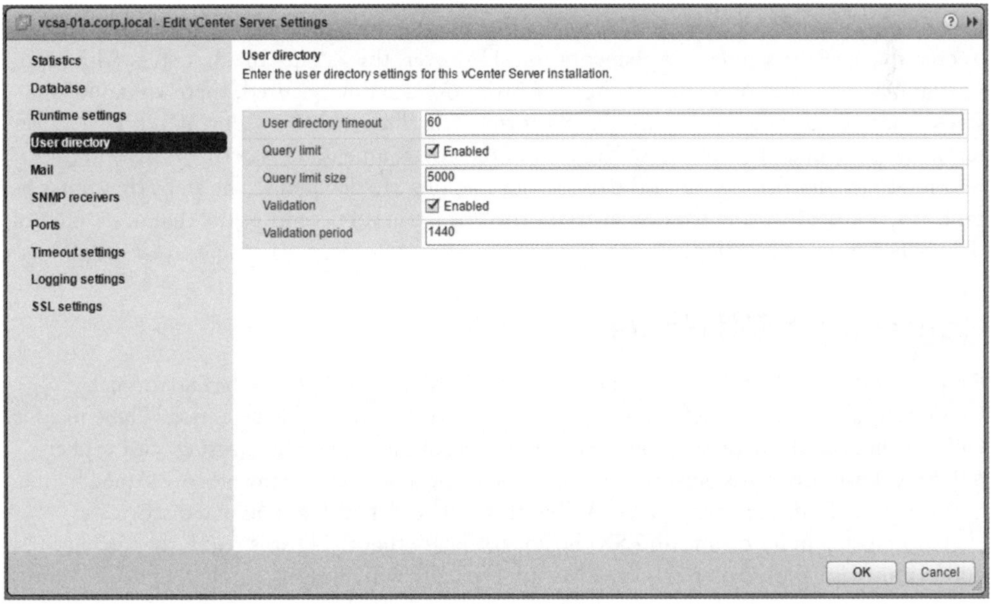

 **Real World Scenario**

How a Simple Mistake Exposed Major Security Issues

An organization has recently run into an issue where a mission-critical virtual machine was deleted. As the security team began investigating, they found several problems. First, administrative-level access to vCenter Server was distributed to a much larger audience than necessary. Similarly, several administrators had privileges on virtual machines that they didn't even directly manage. This led to a much larger review of security within the virtualized infrastructure.

The resulting report recommended restricted administrator access, more granular access to virtual machines, and an overall hardening of the infrastructure itself. The implementation of these recommendations resulted in fewer security incidents and a much smaller attack surface for the datacenter.

Securing ESXi Hosts and the vCenter Server

Establishing security on specific objects in your vCenter Server inventory is the first step to creating a secure vSphere implementation. However, this is only the first step. Although virtual machines and other objects in your inventory are now secured, there are additional steps that must be taken to secure the platform itself. This includes securing both the vCenter Server system and all of the ESXi hosts in the environment. This activity is commonly referred to as "hardening," and the following sections are devoted to the steps that must be taken to "harden," or improve, security of the infrastructure components that are a part of the vSphere implementation.

Hardening ESXi Hosts

First, let's take a look at the process needed for hardening ESXi hosts in the environment. Certain steps are taken by default to provide a basis for a secure implementation. These include CPU, memory, and device isolation as well as a robust firewall. Finally, starting with vSphere 6.0, ESXi hosts are provisioned with certificates. By default, these certificates are signed by the VMware Certificate Authority (VMCA), but this can be changed, as you will discover.

The first step in hardening an ESXi host is to ensure that the host is regularly patched. If a vulnerability is exposed on the host, VMware typically will release a patch designed to eliminate or at least mitigate that vulnerability. If a vulnerability becomes known and your hosts are not properly patched, they become an easy vector for attackers to take advantage of.

Next, you should regularly audit your hosts for any changes that might compromise security. Two areas that should be regularly audited are exception users and the host's SSH configuration. Beginning with vSphere 6.0, users can be added to an Exception Users list via the vSphere Web Client. These are users who would continue to have permissions even after the host enters Lockdown Mode. This is sometimes necessary for things like service accounts but should be an exception for user accounts and should be regularly monitored to ensure that only authorized users are on the list.

SSH provides a means to access the host but is disabled by default. However, it is possible to enable this service and open up a possible means of compromising the host. Unless absolutely necessary, this service should remain disabled. If the service is intended to be disabled, regular audits may be needed to ensure that the state remains unchanged.

Certain configuration steps should be completed to ensure that if an intrusion occurs, it can be easily tracked down. These include the configuration of NTP, SNMP, and persistent logs. Configuring NTP ensures that all hosts are using an agreed-upon time source and that time is accurate across all hosts. If an intrusion occurs, this will make it easier to track the incursion down using a specific time frame. With regard to SNMP, ensure that the service remains disabled if you do not intend to use it, and if you are using it, ensure that the proper trap destination is set. Otherwise, information regarding the host could be sent to an unwanted and potentially malicious destination.

By default, ESXi hosts store logs to an in-memory file system. In this configuration, only a single day's worth of logs are stored at any given time. Not only that, if the host is rebooted, those logs are lost. To avoid this, go into the Advanced System settings for each host and configure the `Syslog.global.logDir` parameter to point to a desired datastore path.

So far, we have looked at patching, auditing, and service configuration. Next, we should look at settings that may need to be either enabled or disabled. Enabling certain services or settings can increase security, while disabling others can make it more difficult for the host to be compromised. Let's start by looking at disabling unneeded components.

The first component to look at is the Managed Object Browser (MOB). The good news is that this is disabled by default beginning with vSphere 6.0. When enabled, it provides a means of debugging the vSphere SDK. The other component to look at is TLS. Transport Layer Security, or TLS, is a protocol designed to provide privacy and security during a connection to the host. By default, the host is enabled to use versions 1.0, 1.1, and 1.2. Whenever possible, it is recommended to disable older versions, provided no third-party tools require an older protocol version. To configure, select a host using the web client, go into the Advanced System settings, then edit the `UserVars.ESXiVPsDisabledProtocols` value to disable the desired versions. You can also use the TLC Reconfiguration Utility.

Moving on, let's take a look at enablement. There are six components that can be enabled in order to further harden the host, starting with enabling Active Directory authentication. By joining hosts to the domain, you can avoid the creation of local accounts. This reduces the means of accessing the host and also reduces administrative overhead. Furthermore, you can enforce password policies configured with AD, such as complexity and reuse. Finally, you can use the AD group ESX Admins to centralize your admin users to a single permission assignment. To enable AD authentication, select a host using the web client, go into the Authentication Services, then click Join Domain.

If you decide to use Active Directory authentication and you are configuring your hosts using Host Profiles, AD credentials are saved as part of the profile and as a result can be transmitted across the network. This can be avoided by using the vSphere Authentication Proxy. The easiest way to set this up is to follow the instructions in the previous paragraph, selecting the Using Proxy Server radio button.

EXERCISE 2.3

Hardening an ESXi host

1. Connect to a vCenter Server using the vSphere Web Client.

2. Click the Home button, then click Hosts And Clusters on the drop-down menu.

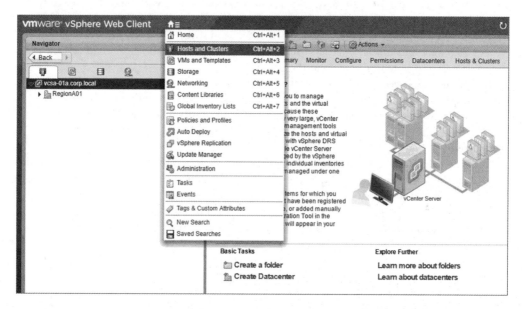

3. There are a number of actions needed to properly harden an ESXi host. This exercise will focus on two of these actions, creating a global syslog folder and disabling older protocols. To begin, select a host to perform these actions on, in this case, esx-01a .corp.local.

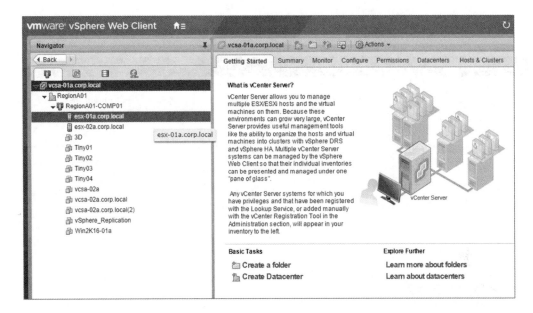

4. Click the Configure tab.

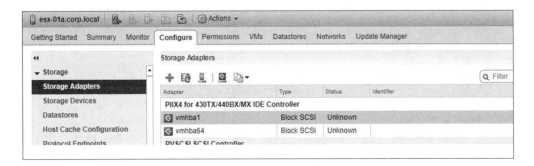

5. Click Advanced System Settings in the Navigator pane.

EXERCISE 2.3 *(continued)*

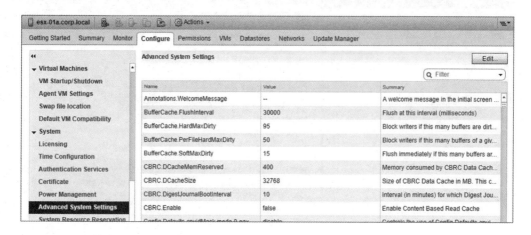

6. Click the Edit button. The Edit Advanced System Settings window opens.

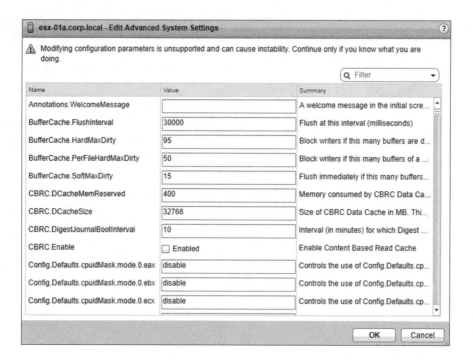

7. Because there are a large number of settings that can be manipulated, use the Filter functionality to drill down to the settings that need to be edited. In this case, you are configuring syslog, so type syslog into the Filter box. Notice that now only settings related to syslog are displayed.

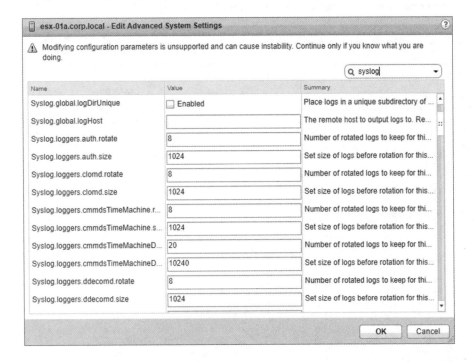

8. This is still a fairly large group of settings, so filter down further by typing `syslog`
    `.global` into the Filter box. Notice that now only a few settings are shown that are
    directly related to global syslog configuration.

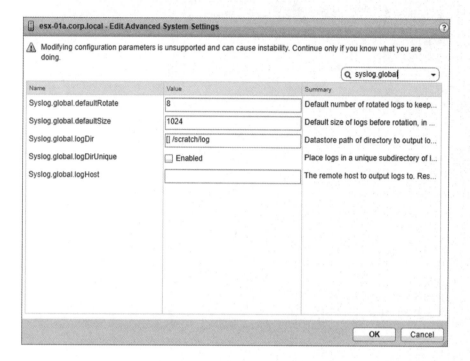

9. Enter a fixed, shared location for syslog files. In this case, use the `iSCSI-Datastore` datastore and a folder called `/FixedLog`.

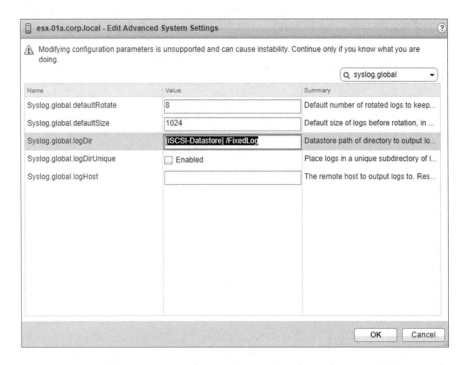

10. Click OK to apply the configuration changes. You will be returned to the Advanced Systems Settings section of the Configure tab. Filter down to `syslog.global` to verify that the change has been applied.

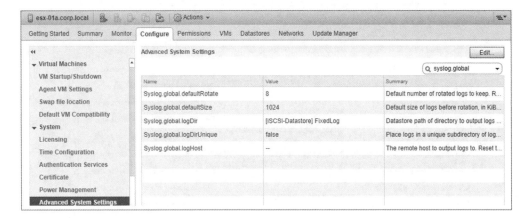

11. Now, click Edit again to return to the Edit Advanced System Settings window. You will now disable a couple of legacy protocols so that they cannot be used as attack vectors.

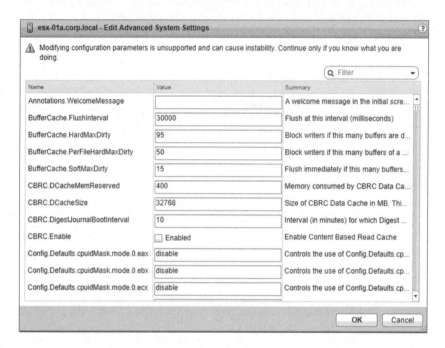

12. Filter down to the appropriate section by typing **uservars** in the Filter box.

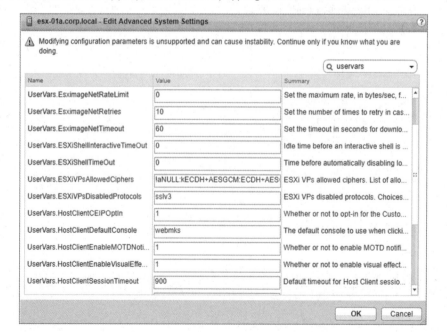

13. Locate the `UserVars.ESXIVPsDisabledProtocols` configuration item, then add **tls1.0** and **tls1.1** to any existing protocols in the box.

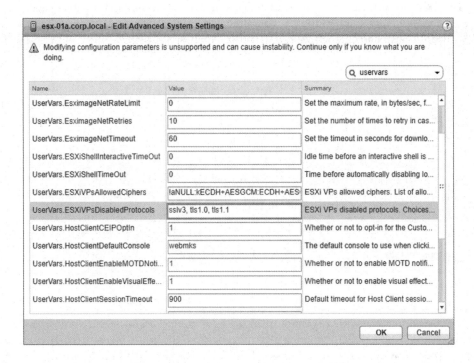

EXERCISE 2.3 *(continued)*

14. Click OK to apply the configuration changes. You will be returned to the Advanced Systems Settings section of the Configure tab. Filter down to uservars to verify that the change has been applied.

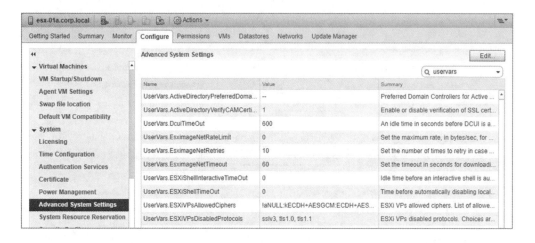

ESXi hosts also come with a feature called Lockdown Mode. This feature is designed to limit access to the host directly, forcing all connectivity to the host to pass through vCenter Server. Since the only method of accessing a host is via vCenter, an administrator can more easily ensure that the roles and permissions implemented through vCenter are adhered to. There are two settings for Lockdown Mode, Normal and Strict. In both cases, direct access to the host is disabled, but with Normal mode, the Direct Console User Interface (DCUI) is left operational, allowing users who are placed on the DCUI.Access list to override the lockdown and access the console. By default, only root is placed on the DCUI.Access list. Strict mode disables the DCUI service, eliminating the possibility of accessing the host using the console.

EXERCISE 2.4

Enabling Lockdown

1. Connect to a vCenter Server using the vSphere Web Client.

2. Click the Home button, then click Hosts And Clusters from the drop-down menu.

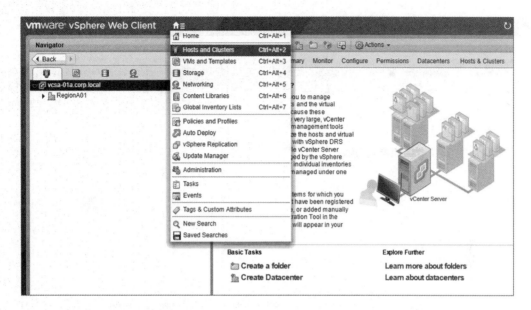

3. Enabling Lockdown Mode on managed ESXi hosts is an essential part of the hardening process. To begin, select a host to perform these actions on, in this case, esx-01a.corp.local.

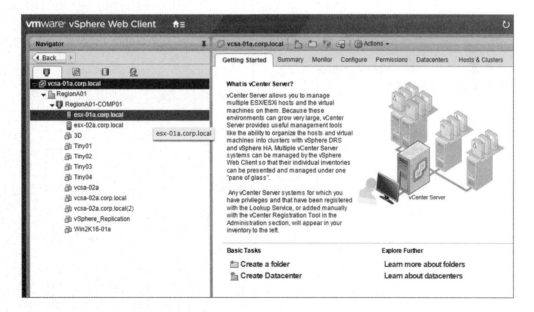

4. Once the host has been selected, a series of tabs becomes available that allow you to manage various aspects of the host.

EXERCISE 2.4 *(continued)*

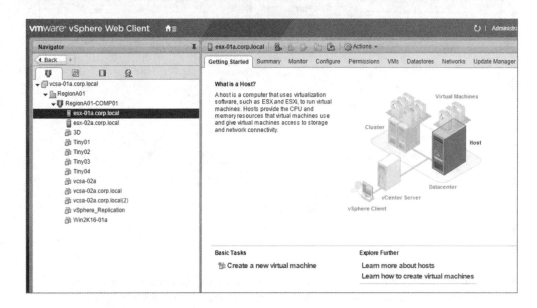

5. Click the **Configure** tab.

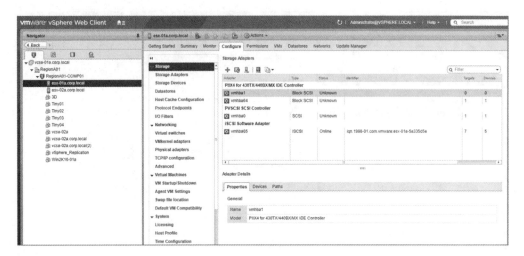

6. In the Navigation pane, click Security Profile.

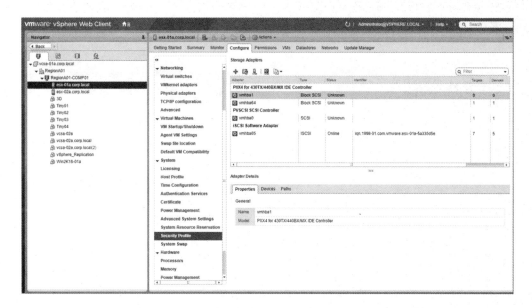

7. A number of security settings are displayed, along with their current configuration. Scroll to the section titled Lockdown Mode.

8. Click Edit. The Lockdown Mode window is displayed. By default, Lockdown Mode is disabled, meaning that the host can be accessed from vCenter, from the DCUI, or remotely via SSH.

EXERCISE 2.4 *(continued)*

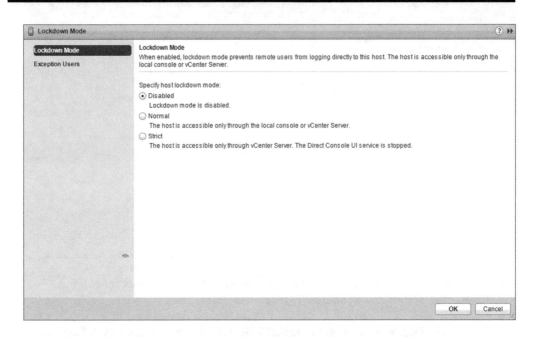

9.   At a minimum, remote access should be locked down. In some cases, you may wish to also lock down access via the DCUI. For this exercise, select Normal.

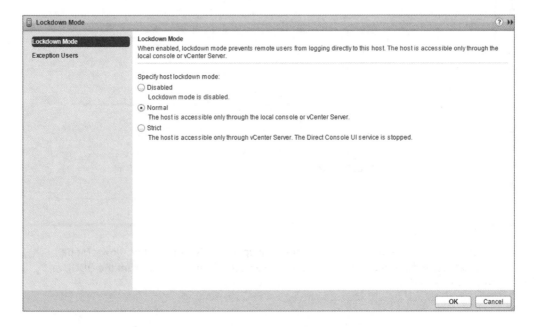

10. Click OK to apply the configuration changes. You will be returned to the Security Profile section of the Configure tab. Verify that the change has been applied by examining the Lockdown Mode section.

Lockdown Mode	Edit...
When enabled, lockdown mode prevents remote users from logging directly into this host. The host will only be accessible through the local console or an authorized centralized management application.	
Lockdown Mode:	Enabled (Normal)
Exception Users:	User
	This list is empty.

The last two areas of hardening that should be examined on the host are the password policy and firewall settings. The ESXi host has settings related to the maximum number of login attempts before an account is locked, how long an account should remain locked before it is unlocked, and of course, password strength and complexity. These should all be set, particularly if the host is joined to an Active Directory domain.

As for the firewall, the ESXi host includes a robust firewall, but some settings are not limited out of the box for functionality purposes. One of these settings is restricting access through the firewall to only authorized networks. To enable this, deselect the Allow Connections From Any IP Address check box, then add to the whitelist the network/IP ranges that you want to allow access to services. The two primary services this should be configured for are SSH and vSphere Web Access.

Hardening vCenter Server

When it comes to hardening vCenter Server, congratulations, you just completed the first step! Since the vCenter server will invariably run on an ESXi host, that host should be hardened before any steps are taken on the vCenter server itself. We have also discussed practices for setting up access through the server to objects in the inventory, another key to securing this system. Part of that process was determining who has administrator-level privileges and assigning them via an admin group. If vCenter Server has been installed on a Windows VM, it is possible that the local Windows administrator account has the Administrator role on vCenter Server. This used to be the default setting but was changed starting with vSphere 6.0. If this account does have access, it should be removed, restricting access to the accounts you have already placed in the admin group. You can further mitigate security risks by using a service account to install vCenter Server and ensuring that applications connecting to vCenter Server are also using unique service accounts. You should also restrict access to the virtual machine running vCenter Server so that only administrative personnel charged with maintaining the virtual machine or managing the database can access the system.

Since vCenter Server is running off a vDisk on a datastore, you should also make sure that access to the datastore is limited. This can be done by limiting the assignment of the Database.Browse datastore privilege to only those users that need to manage the datastores in the environment. Also, any user with the vCenter Server Administrator role can also administer the guest OS on the vCenter Server VM. This can be limited if need be by creating a custom role with the same privilege minus the Guest Operations privilege.

What remains is ensuring that password policies are properly configured and conform with the standards for your organization. By default, the vpxuser account password is set to expire every 30 days. This can be easily modified using the vSphere Web Client. The password for the administrator of vCenter Single Sign-On, `administrator@vsphere.local` by default, also has a specified password policy. By default, this password must meet the following requirements:

- At least 8 but not to exceed 20 characters
- At least one lowercase character
- At least one numeric character
- At least one special character

The password is set by default to expire every 90 days. As with the vpxuser account, this policy can also be modified. To do so, use the vSphere Web Client and navigate to the vCenter Single Sign-On configuration UI. The password policies are located on the Policies tab.

When operating vCenter Server, there are different security measures to take if the software is running on a Windows VM or if the vCenter Server Appliance is being utilized. Naturally, if the software is running on a Windows VM, the Windows OS should be regularly patched, protected by antivirus software, and secured just as any other Windows VM would be, in addition to the measures taken to harden vCenter Server itself. If the vCenter Server Appliance (VCSA) is being utilized, it is critical that NTP is set up properly. This is because proper certificate validation relies on synchronized servers. Furthermore, if an attack occurs, having properly time-stamped logs will make it much easier to perform an audit and identify the source of the attack.

Configuring and Enabling SSO and Identity Sources

One of the key parts of administering a vSphere infrastructure is the ability to administer, secure, and control permissions for vSphere resources. This administration could potentially become complicated when dealing with a vSphere infrastructure containing several components that each require account login and permission configurations. To centralize this administration and to simplify the login process, vSphere utilizes vCenter Single Sign-On (SSO). With vCenter SSO, a user logs in to the vSphere Web Client. The user is first authenticated against an identity source and is then issued a token that represents the user from this point on. The token is then used to validate the user, granting them access to the objects that the user's role had permissions for. The token is also used when the user needs to connect to other VMware or third-party components that are a part of the vSphere infrastructure.

vCenter Single Sign-On

When a user logs in to the vSphere Web Client with a user name and password (Figure 2.10, step 1), their information is passed on by the client to the vCenter Single Sign-On service (step 2). The service checks to make sure that the vSphere Web Client has a valid SAML token, then checks the user's credentials against the configured identity source, such as Active Directory. If the user's credentials are successfully authenticated against the identity source, the service returns a token to the vSphere Web Client (step 3). This token represents the user from this point on. Next, the token is passed to vCenter Server (step 4), which checks with the vCenter Single Sign-On service to make sure the token is valid and hasn't expired (step 5). Finally, the token is returned to vCenter Server and the user is allowed access to the objects they have permissions to utilize (step 6).

FIGURE 2.10   The Single Sign-On process

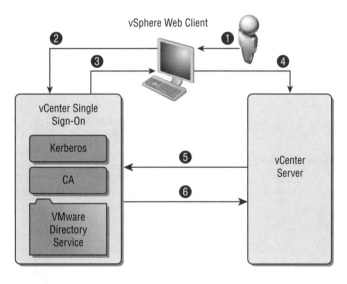

This methodology provides benefits beyond centralized administration and a simplified login process. Consider a situation where a vSphere infrastructure consists of multiple sites (Figure 2.11).

FIGURE 2.11   vCenter SSO domains and sites

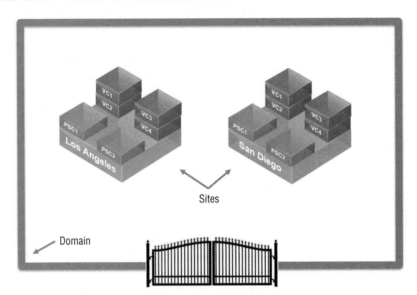

With SSO, access to each site and their related components is restricted to a single access point, represented in the graphic as the gate into the domain. Authentication data for the domain is shared between the domain and each of the sites. Furthermore, instead of login and password information being passed around, the token is used. This results in a more tightly controlled, more secure environment.

vCenter Single Sign-On actually consists of multiple components, as shown in Figure 2.12.

FIGURE 2.12   vCenter SSO Components

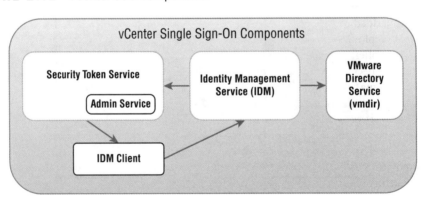

The first of these components is the Security Token Service (STS). This service issues tokens, or more specifically, Security Assertion Markup Language (SAML) tokens. These are the tokens that represent the identity of a user once the user has been authenticated against a supported identity source. Once a user has a token, the token allows the user to access any vCenter service, including VMware and third-party extensions, without authenticating again to each service. All tokens are signed with a signing certificate, which is stored on disk along with the certificate for the service itself. Next is the Administration Service, shown here running as a service within the STS. This service allows users with administrator privileges to configure the vCenter Single Sign-On server and manage users and groups from the vSphere Web Client. By default, the only admin user is administrator@vsphere.local, but beginning with vSphere 6.0, you can change the vSphere domain during installation. The next component is the VMware Directory Service (vmdir). This service is a multi-tenanted, multi-mastered directory service that provides an LDAP directory that, effective with vSphere 6.0, stores both Single Sign-On and certificate information. The information stored in the directory is propagated to other SSO instances, should they exist. The service uses port 389 and can also use port 11711 to communicate with earlier vSphere versions. The final component is the Identity Management Service. This service handles identity sources and is used to respond to STS authentication requests by communicating with LDAP or Active Directory.

Platform Services Controller

Services such as vCenter Single Sign-On, licensing, and certificate management are pervasive throughout a typical vSphere infrastructure deployment. As a result, effective with vSphere 6.0, these services have been centralized to a component called the Platform Services Controller (PSC). Because these are required services, they are embedded with every installation of the vCenter Server Appliance and vCenter Server for Windows. However, these services are also critical to the infrastructure, so vSphere also provides an external PSC that can be deployed to be highly available. There are advantages and disadvantages to embedded or external PSC, which I will review here.

deployments it makes sense to use vCenter Server with the embedded Platform roller, as shown in Figure 2.13. This is one of the simplest deployment methods because both components exist on the same virtual machine, licensing management is simplified. Furthermore, some network-based issues that due to connectivity or name resolution are eliminated in this type of installation. If you think the vSphere infrastructure might grow larger over time, keep you cannot join other vCenter servers or Platform Services Controllers to the Single Sign-On domain created on the embedded PSC. Fortunately, if the growth is unexpected and you need to change the deployment method, it is possible to convert to an external Platform Services Controller.

FIGURE 2.13 vCenter Server with an embedded PSC

For larger deployments and/or highly available deployments, an external Platform Services Controller should be used, as shown in Figure 2.14. In this type of deployment, you have a choice of creating a new vCenter Single Sign-On domain or joining an existing domain. Joined PSC instances replicate data between each other and can even span multiple sites. Once the external Platform Services Controller has been deployed, multiple vCenter Server and/or vCenter Server Appliance instances can be registered with the PSC. Once registered, these vCenter Server instances assume the vCenter Single Sign-On site of the PSC and are connected in Enhanced Linked Mode. While you could point out that disadvantages of this deployment method include increased complexity and the need to monitor network connectivity, I would say that if you have a larger deployment or want a highly available deployment, you pretty much have to go this route. The one thing I would recommend is that if you have to separate out these services and you are going to introduce network complexity, you should just go to the next step and make the solution highly available.

FIGURE 2.14 vCenter Server/vCenter Appliance with an external PSC

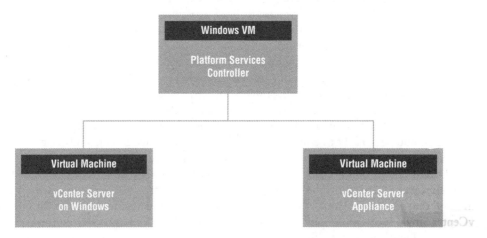

A highly available deployment would require a minimum of two external Platform Services Controllers sitting behind a load balancer, as shown in Figure 2.15. The total number of PSC instances you can have is subject to change and should be verified in the current version of the Configurations Maximums guide. This type of deployment allows for automatic failover in the event one of the PSC instances stops responding, with the load being auto-matically redistributed among the remaining instances.

FIGURE 2.15   vCenter Server/vCenter Appliance with multiple, load-balanced external PSCs

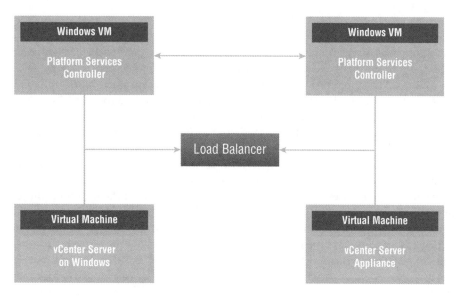

There are several other deployment types, but they are all just variations on the major themes shown here. In the end you will deploy a stand-alone model, an external model, or a highly available external model.

Configuring vCenter Single Sign-On

Once you have decided on a deployment model and deployed the PSC instances, you will need to configure vCenter Single Sign-On. The first step in configuring SSO is to configure an identity source. An identity source is a collection of user and group data stored in a database. With vCenter Single Sign-On, you can use Active Directory, OpenLDAP, or local access using the OS on the machine where SSO has been deployed. When configuring an identity source, it is possible to configure multiple identity sources and select which of these sources will be the default.

To configure an identity source, log in to the PSC instance either using the vSphere Web Client or by connecting directly to the PSC web interface. You must log in using an account that is a member of the vSphere Single Sign-On Administrators group. Next, navigate to the

SSO configuration UI. Navigate to the Identity Sources tab and click the Identity Sources icon. From here, you can add one of four different types of identity sources:

- Active Directory (Integrated Windows Authentication)
- Active Directory as an LDAP Server
- OpenLDAP
- LocalOS

If you are using Active Directory and the virtual machine running the PSC instance is connected to the domain, select the Integrated Windows Authentication option. This option uses the AD configuration information on the virtual machine. If needed, you can choose the AD as an LDAP Server option, but you will be required to manually enter all of the AD information. The LocalOS option should only be used if there is no other identity source, and even then this option would quickly become difficult to manage and is not recommended. Also keep in mind that once this step is complete, users can be authenticated but will not have any access to any objects until permissions are set within vCenter Server.

Configuring an identity source provides standard authentication into a vSphere infrastructure, but in some cases a deployment may call for stronger authentication. This can be accomplished using two-factor authentication, which was introduced starting with vSphere 6.0 Update 2. In order to use this type of authentication with vSphere, a plug-in is required. For vSphere 6.5 and up, use the Enhanced Authentication Plug-in. When using two-factor authentication, VMware supports Smart Card authentication and RSA SecurID authentication. With Smart Card authentication, a user swipes or inserts a physical card, typically a Common Access Card (CAC), into a card reader attached to the machine they log in to. The card, along with a PIN code, is matched against a smart card certificate, allowing the user to log in. RSA SecurID authentication requires a correctly configured RSA Authentication Manager and a token, which can be either a hardware token or delivered using a SmartPhone app. Only a user with the correct username and token number can successfully log in. Examples of the physical components used in two-factor authentication are shown in Figure 2.16.

The next step in configuring vCenter Server Single Sign-On is to replace the STS Signing Certificate, if required by your organization. By default, this is a self-signed certificate generated by the VMware Certificate Authority (VMCA), which resides on the PSC. If your organization's security policy prevents the use of self-signed certificates, you can configure the VMCA to act as a subordinate CA, or you can bypass it entirely. In these cases, you will be using a certificate generated by an in-house or commercial certificate authority. Once you have generated the certificate, you use the `certificate-manager` utility (see Figure 2.17) to replace the default certificate with the custom CA certificate.

The final step in configuring vCenter Server Single Sign-On is setting the policies that will be used in the environment. There are three policies that must be configured: the Password policy, the Lockout policy, and the Token policy. Keep in mind that these policies are only used with the SSO accounts and do not have any impact on accounts added by integrating an identity source like Active Directory.

FIGURE 2.16   Examples of a Common Access Card and a SecurID hardware token

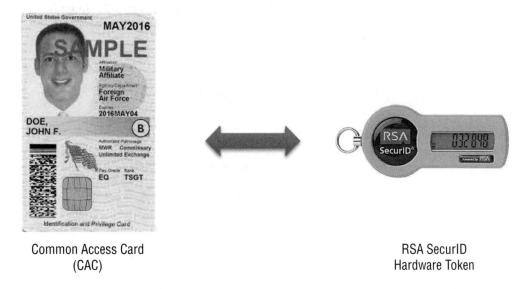

Common Access Card
(CAC)

RSA SecurID
Hardware Token

FIGURE 2.17   The Certificate Manager utility listing the various certificate replacement options

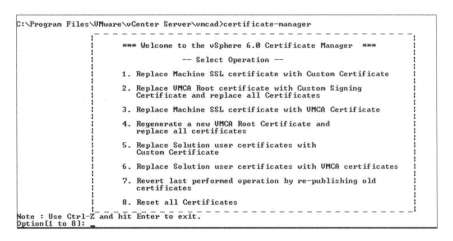

```
C:\Program Files\VMware\vCenter Server\vmcad>certificate-manager

                *** Welcome to the vSphere 6.0 Certificate Manager  ***

                            -- Select Operation --

                1. Replace Machine SSL certificate with Custom Certificate

                2. Replace VMCA Root certificate with Custom Signing
                   Certificate and replace all Certificates

                3. Replace Machine SSL certificate with VMCA Certificate

                4. Regenerate a new VMCA Root Certificate and
                   replace all certificates

                5. Replace Solution user certificates with
                   Custom Certificate

                6. Replace Solution user certificates with VMCA certificates

                7. Revert last performed operation by re-publishing old
                   certificates

                8. Reset all Certificates

Note : Use Ctrl-Z and hit Enter to exit.
Option[1 to 8]: _
```

The default vCenter SSO password policy is set to expire passwords after 90 days. This setting can be changed, along with additional parameters, including password reuse and minimum and maximum length and character requirements.

The vCenter SSO lockout policy is designed to lock out a user who enters incorrect login information. By default, a user is locked out if they enter invalid information 5 times within 3 minutes, and the account is reset after a 5-minute lockout period. This behavior can be changed by altering any of these three variables.

Finally, the vCenter SSO token policy specifies how tokens behave. In many cases, you may want to adjust these settings to conform to your organization's security standards. These settings include clock tolerance, maximum token renewal and delegation counts, and maximum bearer token and holder-of-key token lifetime.

Securing Virtual Machines

The final critical step in securing a vSphere infrastructure is the hardening and securing of virtual machines. A virtual machine should be secured in much the same way a physical server would, and the operating system running on a virtual machine is subject to the same security risks as an operating system running on a physical machine. The following sections will primarily focus on the steps needed to harden the virtual machine itself. In most cases, an organization already has a methodology for patching and securing the various operating systems running in its infrastructure, and those steps can be directly applied to the virtual environment.

Secure Boot

First, let's take a look at any bootable virtual machines that might exist in a vSphere deployment. Bootable virtual machines can be hardened using UEFI Secure Boot. UEFI Secure Boot is a security standard designed to ensure that a system boots using only trusted software. This is validated using certificate signing against the bootloader, the OS kernel, and OS drivers. vSphere 6 virtual machines also include certificates for Windows and Linux bootloaders and for booting ESXi inside a VM. To support UEFI Secure Boot, virtual machines must be running VMware Tools version 10.1 or later.

To enable Secure Boot, first verify that the virtual machine's OS supports UEFI boot, that you are using EFI firmware, and that the VM has been built on virtual hardware version 13 or later. Next, while the VM is powered down, enable UEFI Secure Boot by editing the VM's settings using the vSphere Web Client and clicking the Enable Secure Boot check box. Please note that you must have `VirtualMachine.Config.Settings` privileges in order to modify this setting.

Virtual Machine Encryption

When we look at securing a virtual machine, one of the key concepts to remember is that a virtual machine exists as a series of files. Someone with the proper level of access could make a copy of these files, place them in another vSphere infrastructure, and bring up the virtual machine, potentially allowing access to sensitive data. In fact, it wouldn't even be necessary to boot up the virtual machine if the guest OS is known, since one could simply attach the VMDK file to a virtual machine running the same OS. Another similar concern appears when a virtual machine is migrated from one storage location to another, since at that time the entire contents of the virtual machine traverses the network and is vulnerable to anyone that could tap into the network during this operation.

Until the release of vSphere 6.5, these security challenges were mitigated through the use of various encryption methods, each of which came with its own challenges. Take, for example, the use of in-guest encryption. This methodology involves using a custom preboot partition that uses keys to verify authenticity prior to allowing the encrypted partition to boot. There are two main issues with this method. First, it is guest-OS specific and most vSphere infrastructures run virtual machines with a variety of operating systems. Second, this method injects a high degree of overhead into the management process.

As an alternative, it is possible to use infrastructure-based encryption, either using self-encrypting drives (SEDs) or deploying encryption at the storage array level or even the fabric level. Unfortunately, when using SEDs or storage array level encryption, data still traverses the network as plain text. Fabric level encryption solves this problem but introduces potential portability issues. And in all of these cases, specific hardware is required.

Effective with vSphere 6.5, these issues are largely mitigated. That's because vSphere 6.5 introduced virtual machine encryption. vSphere's virtual machine encryption is centrally managed through vCenter, requires no specific hardware, and is not tied to any specific guest operating system. In addition, because data is encrypted at the virtual machine, any VM traffic that traverses the network is also encrypted. When a virtual machine is encrypted, its VMDK files, snapshot files, core dump files, swap files, and NVRAM are encrypted. Some files, such as the VM's config file, log files, and the virtual disk descriptor files, are not encrypted but do not contain any sensitive data. It is important to note that most encryption has a certain level of resource overhead. When you're enabling virtual machine encryption on a VM, additional storage capacity is consumed. This is particularly true when encrypting an existing unencrypted VM, which requires double the capacity of the VM. VMware recommends encrypting VMs at creation, whenever possible.

There are three main components involved in virtual machine encryption: the vCenter Server, the ESXi host(s) running the encrypted or to-be-encrypted virtual machines, and a Key Management Server (KMS). It is important to note that VMware does not supply a KMS. Instead, VMware provides a list of supported KMS products from a number of security and cloud vendors. It is the role of the KMS to generate and provide keys to vCenter Server, which are then handed off to the ESXi host running the encrypted virtual machine. The vCenter Server centralizes a number of administrative features, including who is allowed to access the KMS. Because of this, an added layer of security would be to ensure that the KMS and the vCenter Server are never running on the same physical machine. The vCenter Server also provides events that can assist with auditing and adds storage policies that can be used to control encryption on the virtual machines and disks. The ESXi host running the virtual machine is responsible for the actual encryption, which ensures that any data leaving the host and traversing the network is encrypted. Each ESXi host has a host encryption mode setting, which is typically enabled by default. The current setting can be checked and/or modified using the vSphere Web Client. The steps and flow involved in encrypting a virtual machine are shown in Figure 2.18.

FIGURE 2.18 The process used to encrypt a vSphere virtual machine

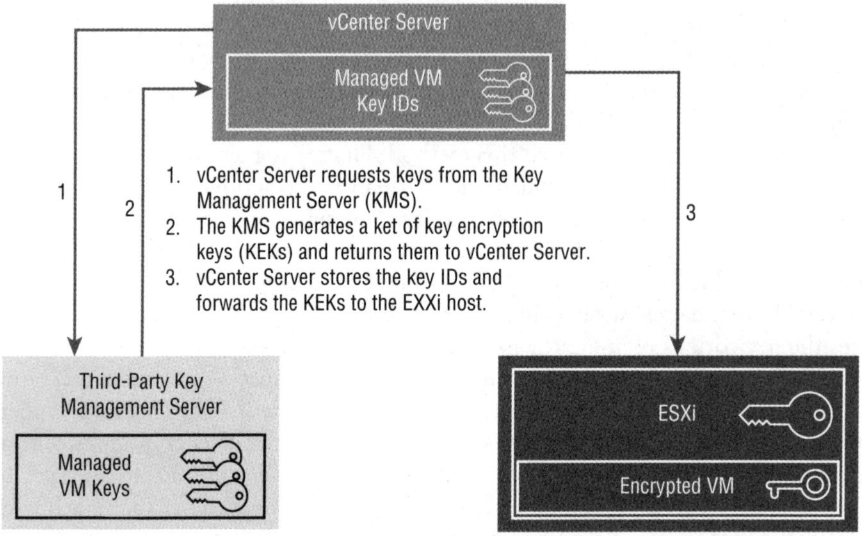
vCenter Server
Managed VM
Key IDs
1
2
3
1. vCenter Server requests keys from the Key Management Server (KMS).
2. The KMS generates a ket of key encryption keys (KEKs) and returns them to vCenter Server.
3. vCenter Server stores the key IDs and forwards the KEKs to the EXXi host.
Third-Party Key
Management Server
Managed
VM Keys
ESXi
Encrypted VM

One final piece to discuss regarding encryption is encrypted vMotion. The first thing to know is that if you are migrating an encrypted virtual machine using vMotion, the migration is encrypted by default and no additional action is required. The encryption used during migration ensures that data transmitted across the network is encrypted and not sent in plain text. But what if you wanted to migrate a virtual machine that is not encrypted but you want the migration activity to be encrypted? The good news is that this is entirely possible in vSphere and can be easily configured by editing the settings of the unencrypted VM. There are three settings: Disabled, Opportunistic, and Required. By default, unencrypted virtual machines are set to Opportunistic, which means that they will use encrypted vMotion as long as both the source and destination ESXi hosts support it. This setting can be changed to Disabled, in which case vMotion can be used but is not encrypted. The other option is Required, which requires encrypted vMotion and will not allow a vMotion to be performed if encrypted vMotion cannot be used.

EXERCISE 2.5

Configuring Encrypted vMotion

1. Connect to a vCenter Server using the vSphere Web Client.
2. Click the Home button, then click VMs And Templates on the drop-down menu.

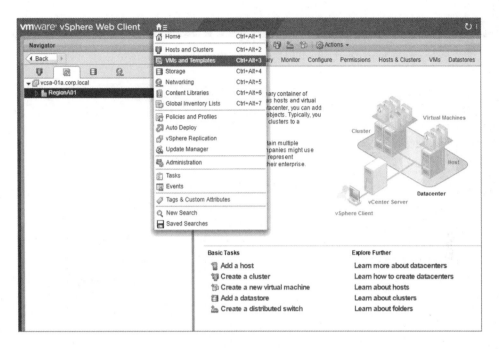

3. Encrypting vMotion traffic ensures that virtual machine data cannot be tapped as it is traversing the network, or at least that the data will not be usable. To begin, select a virtual machine to configure, in this case, `Win2K16-01a`.

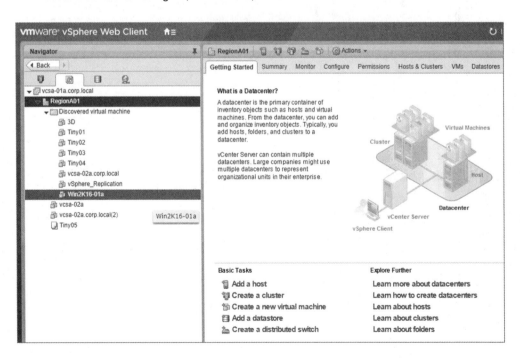

4. Click the Actions icon, then select Edit Settings from the drop-down.

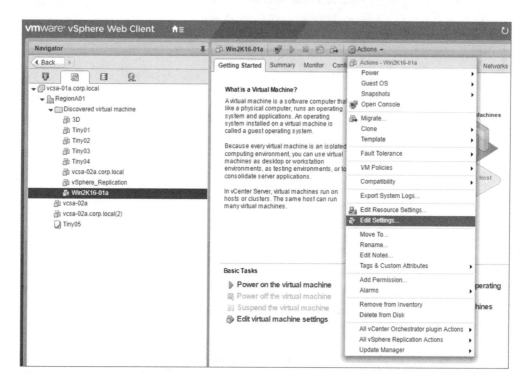

5.   The Edit Settings window is displayed.

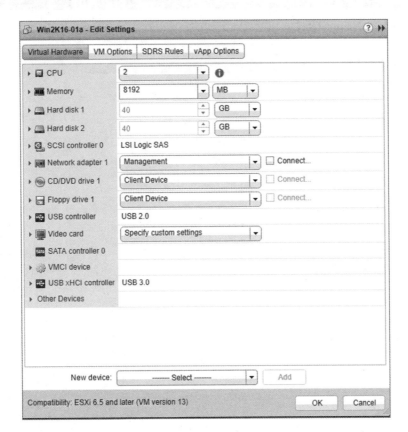

6. Click the VM Options tab.

7. Click Encryption in the navigation pane to expand the available options.

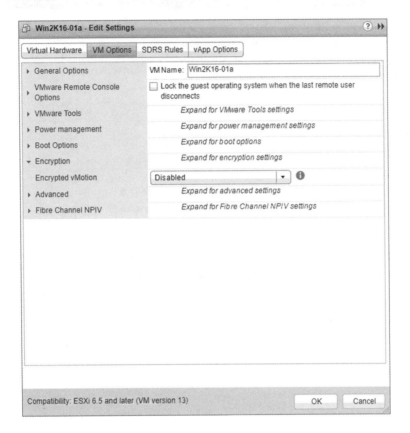

8. Encryption is set to Opportunistic by default if the VM was created with vSphere 6.5. This setting uses encryption when both the source and destination hosts support encryption. To ensure that encryption will always be used on this VM (or vMotion will not be allowed), change this setting to Required.

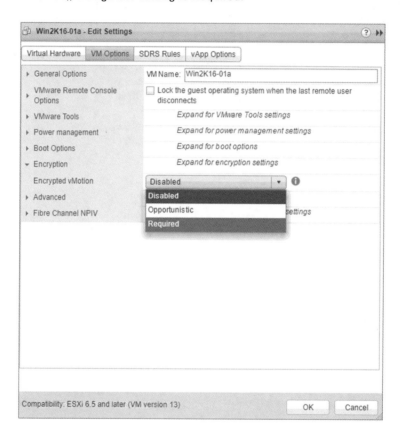

9. Verify that the setting has been changed, then click OK.

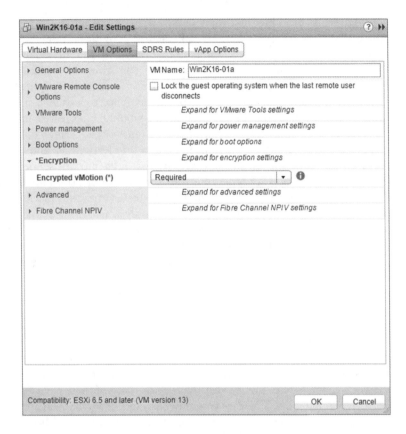

10. You will be returned to the Configure tab for the VM, which should now display the updated setting.

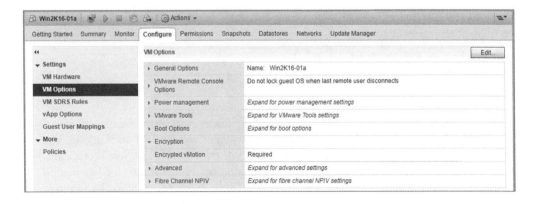

Virtual Machine Hardening

One step in securing virtual machines in a vSphere infrastructure is hardening the VM by tightening the controls governing various virtual machine activities. Tightening these controls places limits on security-sensitive actions so that only certain individuals can perform them. One way to do this would be to create a group (something like Secure Admins) and then assign privileges governing sensitive activities to this group while ensuring that these privileges are not present in any other group, or explicitly assigned to a user. A simple way to do this for administrators that do not need guest access would be to create a group (like Admins without Guest Access) and deselect All Privileges.Virtual machine.Guest Operations. Many of the more sensitive actions fall into a set of privileges known as Virtual Machine Interaction privileges. The first activity that falls into this set of privileges is the installation of VMware Tools. In order to install VMware Tools, the administrator must have the Virtual machine.Interaction.VMware Tools install privilege. Tightening this control ensures that VMware Tools is installed only where needed and makes it easier to audit this activity. Also, the installation of VMware Tools enables some security-sensitive activities. Restricting the activity can help ensure that the admins performing the installations can follow up the install by configuring the usage of the activities enabled by VMware Tools. Other privileges in this group that may need to be limited are console interaction, drag and drop of files between the VM and a remote client, and the ability to perform wipe or shrink operations on a virtual machine.

The next step in hardening a virtual machine is to disable any unnecessary functionality in the VM. Unneeded services or devices on a virtual machine are potential vectors for attack. Removing these services and devices reduces the attack surface. Begin by removing any unneeded virtual hardware devices, such as serial ports, parallel ports, CD/DVD drives, network adapters, etc. In the event that one or more of these devices cannot be removed from the virtual machine, VMware recommends that the virtual machine be modified to prevent users from changing the device status. This can be done by editing the VM and adding the settings shown in Figure 2.19.

FIGURE 2.19   The settings required to prevent users from changing the device status in a virtual machine

Name	Value
isolation.device.connectable.disable	true
isolation.device.edit.disable	true

Next, remove any unused or unexposed features. These include unused display features (like 3D functionality), features needed only when running a VM on Workstation or Fusion, and the HGFS file transfer capability. While the first two of these vectors are fairly self-explanatory, HGFS requires further explanation. HGFS stands for Host Guest File System, which is used for automated VMware Tools upgrades and some VIX commands. However, it also presents a vector that could potentially be used to transfer files to and from the guest OS. This particular feature should be evaluated by your security team because the efficiencies gained from automated upgrades may outweigh the potential security concern.

Another security concern is the ability to copy and paste data between the guest OS in a virtual machine and the remote console. In fact, the threat with this feature is high enough that this functionality is disabled by default. This is because not only could sensitive information be copied out of a virtual machine, but when the console window gains focus during the operation, processes running in the VM and even nonprivileged users could potentially access the clipboard. If sensitive information was copied to the clipboard before you used the console, now it's exposed. So even though the feature is disabled by default, VMware recommends explicitly disabling it by modifying the settings shown in Figure 2.20. Explicitly disabling this functionality ensures that any virtual machines that had enabled this feature are discovered and mitigated, and that the status of the feature can be audited moving forward.

FIGURE 2.20   The settings required to explicitly disable copy-paste operations in a virtual machine

Name	Recommended Value
isolation.tools.copy.disable	true
isolation.tools.paste.disable	true
isolation.tools.setGUIOptions.enable	false

When hardening a virtual machine, it is possible to modify a couple of settings and by doing so greatly reduce the possibility of a denial of service (DoS) attack. Since a virtual machine is essentially a collection of files, a DoS can occur if the files manage to consume all available space in the datastore they are located in or if a file becomes unavailable. There are two cases where this can happen that can be easily mitigated. The first case is related to the VMX file. Virtual machines send informational messages to the VMX file. This file starts out very small but can grow in size as these messages are added to the file. If a size limit was not enforced, it is possible for VMware Tools in the guest OS to send a large, continuous data stream to the host, which could cause the VMX file to consume all remaining space in the datastore it is located in, resulting in a DoS. Because of this, the file is limited to 1 MB by default. The file can be explicitly set to a certain size by editing the VM and adding the `tools.setInfo.sizeLimit` setting and selecting the appropriate size limit. The other activity that can lead to a DoS is virtual disk shrinking. This activity is typically used to recover unused space on a virtual disk, but repeated shrinking can cause the disk to become unavailable. This function can be disabled in a virtual machine by editing the VM and adding the parameters shown in Figure 2.21.

FIGURE 2.21   The settings required to disable virtual disk shrinking in a virtual machine

Name	Value
isolation.tools.diskWiper.disable	TRUE
isolation.tools.diskShrink.disable	TRUE

EXERCISE 2.6

Hardening a VM

1. Connect to a vCenter Server using the vSphere Web Client.

2. Click the Home button, then click VMs And Templates on the drop-down menu.

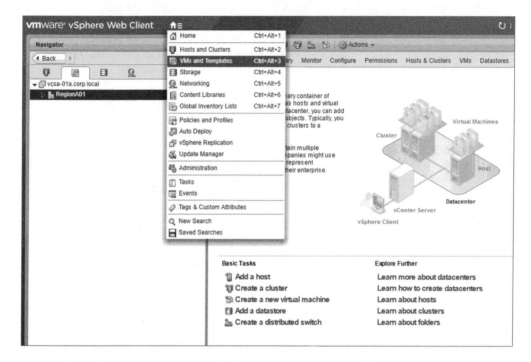

3. As with ESXi host hardening, there are a number of actions needed to properly harden a virtual machine. This exercise will focus on two of these actions: setting a maximum size for the VMX configuration file, and ensuring that users cannot move data back and forth between a VM console and the local desktop. To begin, select a virtual machine to perform these actions on, in this case, Win2K16-01a.

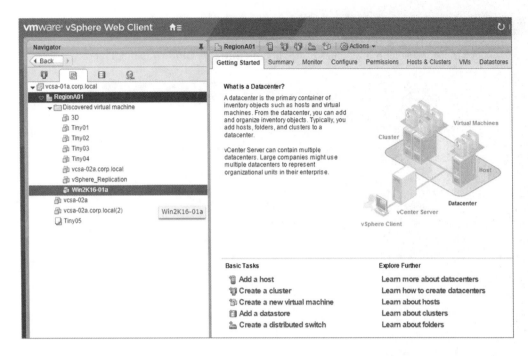

4. Click the Configure tab, then select VM Options in the navigation pane.

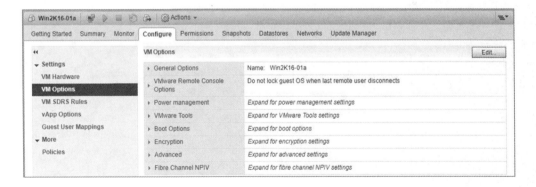

5. Click the Actions icon, then click Edit. The Edit Settings window is displayed.

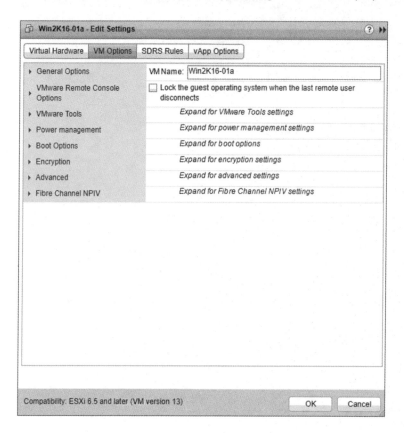

6. Click Advanced to expand the section containing advanced configuration options.

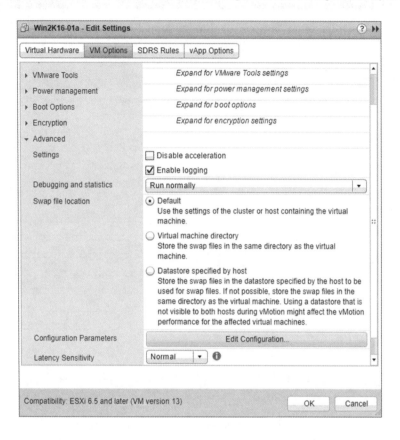

7. Click the Edit Configuration button. The Configuration Parameters window is displayed.

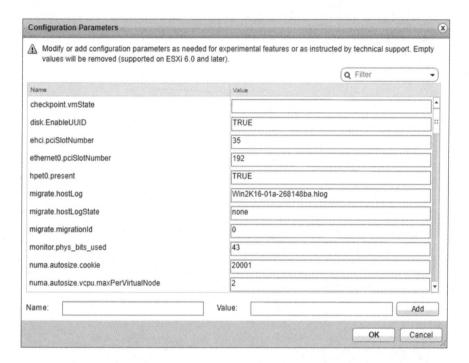

8. Similar to ESXi hosts, virtual machines also have a large number of settings. Filter down to the parameters related to tools by typing `tools` in the Filter box. Notice that the parameter that needs to be configured, `tools.setInfo.sizeLimit`, is not present.

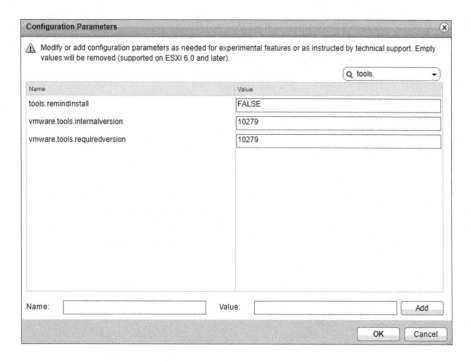

9. Parameters that are not already listed can be added by entering the parameter name
    and setting. Enter `tools.setInfo.sizeLimit` for the parameter name and `1048576`
    for the parameter value.

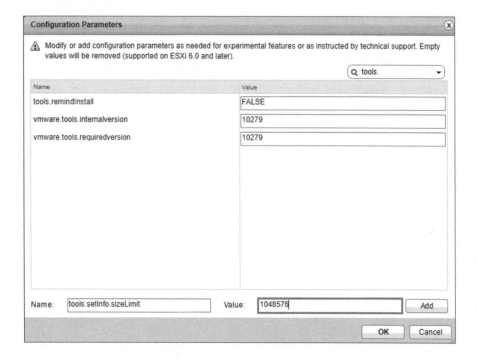

10. Click Add to add the new parameter. Notice that the parameter and its value are now displayed in the tools section.

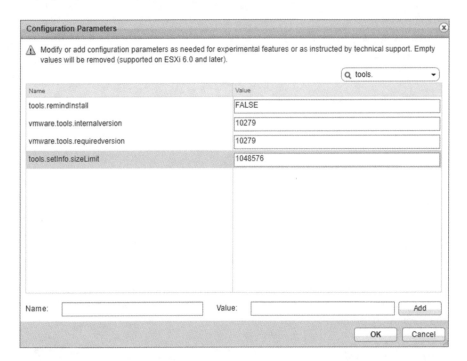

11. Click OK to return to the unfiltered version of the Configuration Parameters window. Next, you will add the parameters necessary to ensure that copy and paste operations are disabled between the VM console and the local machine. These parameters do not already exist, so add each one using the same method you just used. The first parameter is `isolation.tools.copy.disable` and the value is TRUE.

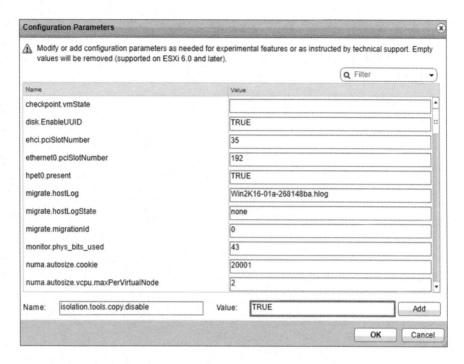

12. The next parameter is `isolation.tools.paste.disable` and the value is TRUE.

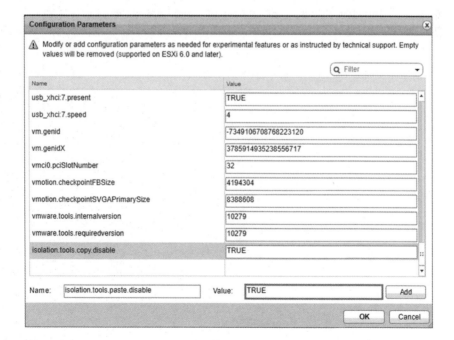

13. The final parameter is `isolation.tools.setGUIOptions.enable` and the parameter is FALSE.

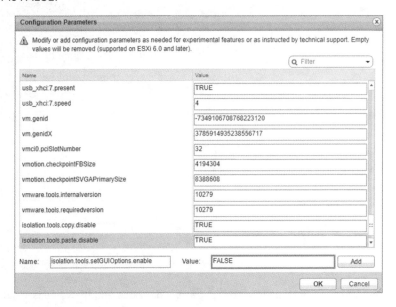

14. Verify that all three parameters are displayed and that they all have the correct values, then click OK.

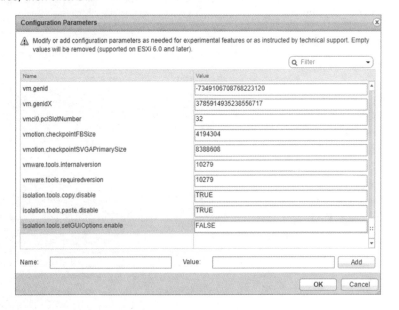

vSphere Network Security

A final area of concern regarding security is the network. Much of the configuration involved in securing a vSphere network surrounds the physical switch, VLANs, and firewalls. These components are covered in the networking section of this book. That being said, there is one area of security that is policy based and directly tied to vSphere Standard Switches and vSphere Distributed Switches, and we will focus on those settings here.

When working with vSphere Standard Switches or vSphere Distributed Switches, there are three security policies that can be configured. These are MAC address changes, Promiscuous mode, and Forged transmits. For vSphere Standard Switches, these policies can be configured on the VMkernel port group and on virtual machine port groups. For vSphere Distributed Switches, these policies can be configured on Distributed Port Groups and on the ports themselves. Each of these policies can be modified to help guard against several types of network-based attacks.

When a network adapter is created on a virtual machine, it is given a MAC address, referred to as the initial MAC address. Because this address is assigned to the virtual hardware itself, it cannot be modified by the guest OS. However, the guest OS uses its own address, referred to as the effective MAC address. While it is true that the guest OS typically assigns the initial MAC address to the effective MAC address, the guest OS can alter the effective MAC address at any time. In some cases, there is a legitimate need for the guest OS to do this, such as, for example, when using an iSCSI initiator or when working with Microsoft Network Load Balancing (NLB) in unicast mode. For this reason, the MAC address changes policy is set to Accept by default. However, this capability can also be used to impersonate a MAC address that would be recognized and authorized on the network, which could then allow a user to stage malicious attacks on devices on the network. The ability to impersonate a MAC address is also known as MAC spoofing. This capability can be disabled by setting the MAC address changes policy to Reject.

The second security policy, Forged transmits, works in concert with the MAC address changes policy. Both policies are there to ensure that the effective MAC address does not diverge from the initial MAC address, with the difference between the two policies centering on the direction of traffic. The MAC address changes policy is concerned with traffic coming into the virtual machine from the network, while the Forged transmits policy is concerned with traffic leaving the virtual machine destined for the network. If you do not have specific use cases for altering the effective MAC address on a virtual machine's adapter, you set both policies to Reject.

The final security policy to review is the Promiscuous mode policy. If this policy is set to Accept, the virtual machine is capable of seeing all of the network traffic on the wire. This would allow a user to capture potentially sensitive data destined for other devices. The only legitimate reason for enabling this policy is if the virtual machine is running network intrusion detection software and needs to see all of the traffic on the network. Even if this setting is intentionally enabled, keep in mind that leaving it enabled can impair network performance and should only be done during the time it is actively used.

Summary

Security is a key component of any system, and the more critical the system, the more secure it needs to be. A vSphere infrastructure typically hosts a large number of virtual machines, and since access to the vSphere platform grants access to those virtual machines, making sure vSphere is only accessed by authorized users is paramount.

There are several areas to cover when configuring vSphere security: permissions to users, securing the management components, identifying users, and encrypting virtual machines.

When granting permissions to users, you need to identify the privileges needed, group those into roles, and assign the roles appropriately in the infrastructure to the correct users. There are default roles included, some of which can be modified to fit your needs.

Hosts can be secured using Lockdown Mode to limit who can directly access them. You can also configure hosts to send logs to a syslog server and use advanced system settings for things like limiting the access protocols used. The vCenter can be secured by limiting user access, changing the password policies, and limiting access to the disks used by the server.

User access can be made more secure by using a central identity platform such as Active Directory. Configuring the Single-Sign On service to use an identity server prevents you from creating local users and provides easy user tracking across platforms.

Finally, virtual machine security can be enhanced with Secure Boot where the guest OS can be validated before booting and by using virtual machine encryption, which will prevent the virtual machine from being read if accessed outside its vCenter server.

Security is a priority for most environments and VMware provides several tools to ensure that your environment is secure.

Exam Essentials

Understand privileges and roles. Know that privileges are rights and they are collected in roles to be assigned to components for users. Be able to list and differentiate the default system and sample roles.

Know how to assign permissions. Be able to track permissions assigned in a hierarchy and the resulting effect on subordinate objects.

Know Lockdown Mode. Ensure that you know which mode does what and what types of access are limited and to whom.

Understand local users and passwords. Both ESXi hosts and VCSA use local users. Know the default local users and how to change the password settings.

Know how to configure Active Directory integrations. Be able to configure ESXi and SSO with Active Directory. Be aware of OpenLDAP and AD as an LDAP server as well.

Understand virtual machine security. Be able to explain Secure Boot and VM encryption. Also know how to harden a virtual machine.

Review Questions

1. What is the difference between a privilege and a role?

    A. A privilege is an action that can be taken in a vSphere environment; a role is a collection of privileges.

    B. A privilege is a duty a user has to perform as part of their job; a role is a collection of privileges.

    C. A privilege is an action that can be taken in a vSphere environment; a role is a duty a user has to perform as part of their job.

    D. A privilege is a duty a user has to perform as part of their job; a role is an action that can be taken in a vSphere environment.

2. What two types of roles are provided with vSphere by default? (Choose two.)

    A. System roles

    B. Sample roles

    C. Custom roles

    D. Host roles

3. A user belongs to two groups. One group has been granted the Virtual Machine Power User role and the other group has been granted the Read Only role. What permissions will this user have?

    A. A union of the privileges granted by both roles

    B. The most restrictive set of privileges granted by both roles

    C. The Virtual Machine Power User role

    D. The Read Only role

4. What two security concerns should be regularly audited on an ESXi host? (Choose two.)

    A. Exception users

    B. Datastore access

    C. SSH configuration

    D. Guest operations

5. What setting should be configured in order to ensure that logs on an ESXi host remain persistent, without impacting the output of any other diagnostic data?

    A. `ScratchConfig.ScratchDir`

    B. `Syslog.global.logHost`

    C. `ScratchConfig. ConfiguredScratchLocation`

    D. `Syslog.global.logDir`

6. What version of TLS (Transport Layer Security) does VMware recommend using with vSphere 6?

A. 1.0

B. 1.1

C. 1.2

D. 1.3

7. What does the enabling of Lockdown Mode using the **Strict** option change in regard to how the ESXi host is accessed?

A. Users can only access the ESXi host directly from the console.

B. Users can only access the ESXi host via vCenter Server.

C. Users can only access the ESXi host if they are on the **Exception Users** list.

D. Users can only access the ESXi host if they use SSH with a valid certificate.

8. Which vCenter Single Sign-On component stores both Single Sign-On and certificate information?

A. Security Token Service (STS)

B. Administration Service

C. VMware Directory Service (vmdir)

D. Identity Management Service

9. What are two major restrictions when using the embedded version of the Platform Services Controller? (Choose two.)

A. Additional Platform Services Controllers cannot be joined to the vCenter Single Sign-On domain.

B. Additional load balancers cannot be joined to the vCenter Single Sign-On domain.

C. Additional vCenter Server instances cannot be joined to the vCenter Single Sign-On domain.

D. Additional ESXi hosts cannot be joined to the vCenter Single Sign-On domain.

10. What is the minimum number of PSC instances required to create a highly available deployment?

A. One

B. Two

C. Three

D. Four

11. What role can be assigned to junior administrators to prevent them from accessing certain parts of the hierarchy?

A. No Cryptography Administrator

B. Read Only

    C. No Access

    D. Tagging Admin

12. What would prevent an administrator from being able to encrypt a virtual machine?

    A. The No Cryptography Administrator Role is assigned to the virtual machine.

    B. The virtual machine is version 14.

    C. No KMS server has been created.

    D. The No Cryptography Administrator Role is assigned to the administrator.

13. What service port by default would need manual intervention for firewall access for ESXi servers?

    A. 22 (SSH)

    B. 80 (HTTP)

    C. 902 (vSphere Web Client)

    D. 53 (DNS)

14. What two methods are required for nonroot DCUI access to a host with normal lockdown enabled? (Choose two.)

    A. A local user account

    B. A vCenter Server administrator account

    C. DCUI.Access configured

    D. Active Directory enabled on vCenter

15. What lockdown method can be used to block local console access for an ESXi host?

    A. Local

    B. Normal

    C. Embedded

    D. Strict

16. What two identity sources are available for Single-Sign On? (Choose two.)

    A. Active Directory (Integrated Windows Authentication)

    B. OpenLDAP

    C. LDAPS

    D. SAML

17. What would prevent virtual machine Secure Boot from being enabled?

    A. Virtual machine hardware version 12

    B. No operating system installed

    C. The No Cryptography Administrator role assigned to the administrator.

    D. No VMDK assigned

18. What two versions of Transport Layer Security (TLS) should be disabled with advanced settings? (Choose two.)

   A. 1.0

   B. 1.1

   C. 1.2

   D. 1.3

Chapter

3

Networking in vSphere

2V0-21.19 EXAM OBJECTIVES COVERED IN THIS CHAPTER:

✓ **Section 1 – VMware vSphere Architectures and Technologies**

- Objective 1.1 – Identify the pre-requisites and components for vSphere implementation
- Objective 1.8 – Differentiate between VDS and VSS

✓ **Section 2 – VMware Products and Solutions**

- Objective 2.1 – Describe vSphere integration with other VMware products

✓ **Section 4 – Installing, Configuring, and Setting Up a VMware vSphere Solution**

- Objective 4.2 – Create and configure vSphere objects
- Objective 4.5 – Configure virtual networking

✓ **Section 7 – Administrative and Operational Tasks in a VMware vSphere Solution**

- Objective 7.1 – Manage virtual networking
- Objective 7.8 – Manage resources of a vSphere environment
- Objective 7.11 – Manage different VMware vCenter Server objects

This chapter addresses how ESXi hosts and the virtual machines running on them communicate with other systems. While vSphere hosts require networking for management and monitoring, the hosts also utilize networking for key functions, including fault tolerance and vMotion. Virtual machines require networking to exchange information with other clients, servers, and other resources both on the same host and outside the host.

vSphere enables host and virtual machine networking by creating virtual network interfaces for the host and virtual machines and then providing virtual network switches to connect them with the physical network. This network virtualization allows multiple network needs to be met by limited hardware. The exam (and this chapter) will assume you know basic networking concepts such as TCP/IP (including addresses and ports), switching (including VLANs), routing, and an understanding of the network OSI model. If these concepts are new or unfamiliar you might consider a basic networking book or training course.

Understanding vSphere Networking

One ESXi host with a single physical network connection can provide virtual machines access to thousands of separate networks. By adding virtual machines with routing capabilities, you can create complex networks inside of a single physical server.

The ability of vSphere to create virtual network objects includes a variety of options and choices for connectivity, performance, reliability, and security. vSphere networks can be designed to avoid single points of failure or prioritize the network performance of some virtual machines. While vSphere networking provides limited security options, other products—such as VMware NSX—add considerable security capabilities to vSphere virtual networking.

vSphere natively only provides switching functions; it provides no routing capabilities natively. For two virtual machines on different VLANs on the same host to communicate, the traffic must leave the host, get routed to the destination network, and return to the host.

vSphere networking utilizes virtual switches to connect a virtual machine's virtual network interface cards (vNICs), the host's physical network interface cards (pNICs), and the host's *VMkernel ports*, which are used for ESXi management.

A VMkernel port is a virtual network adapter used by the host. At least one VMkernel port is required for host management, which includes vCenter, SSH, DNS, and NTP services for the host. The virtual adapters can also be used for some storage types (iSCSI, NFS, FCoE). Multiple VMkernels can be used to separate optional host functions such as vSAN, vMotion, and fault tolerance onto separate networks.

vSphere offers two types of virtual network switches: *vSphere Standard Switches (vSS)* and *vSphere Distributed Switches (vDS)*; the latter is also sometimes also called distributed virtual switch (DVS). Standard switches offer basic functionality in all license levels of vSphere (including the free vSphere Hypervisor version of ESXi) and are created and managed on each host. vSphere virtual distributed switches provide advanced functionality and are created and managed by vCenter. Figure 3.1 shows a simple standard switch and a slightly more complex distributed switch.

FIGURE 3.1   Standard switch vs. distributed switch

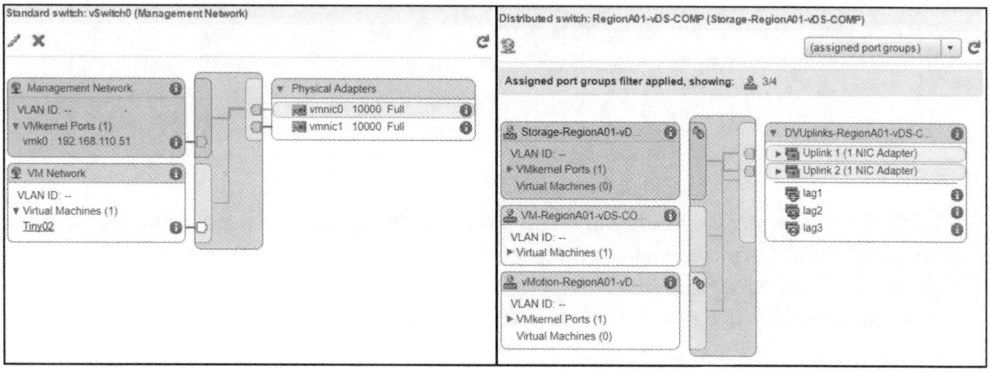

Standard Switches

While standard switches are addressed by the vSphere Foundation exam and do not appear directly on the VCP6.5-DCV exam, we will cover them briefly for completeness.

A newly built ESXi host will have a standard switch created with vmnic0 (what ESXi determines is the lowest-numbered physical network adapter) and a VMkernel port set to use DHCP. When you use the host console to change the management interface, these are the components you are changing. This is the configuration the ESXi console is manipulating in the management interface configuration—and the configuration it will revert to if you choose Restore Network Settings in the ESXi console.

Standard switches and distributed switches vary in a few key ways:

- Standard switches and the port groups using them are created and configured on each host while distributed switches and port groups are created and configured on the vCenter server.

- Operations such as vMotion depend on the port groups having the same name on each host. Distributed switches and port groups are identically maintained on the hosts by vCenter while standard switches require either carefully creating the identical port group on each host or using an automated creation method such as host profiles or scripting. See Figure 3.2 for the Network tab's Networks view, which is useful for verifying port group names.

FIGURE 3.2   Viewing standard switches in the vSphere client

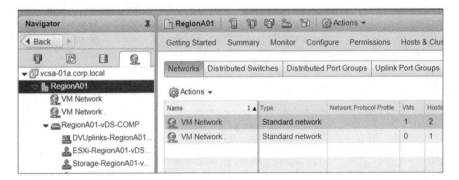

- With the standard switches being created on each host, vCenter is not required to create or maintain standard switches. However, since standard switches and their port groups are created separately on each host, their settings (such as VLAN tags and teaming) can vary from host to host. These settings are kept in sync with vDS.

- Port statistics for a standard switch (available via API or command line) are reset when a virtual machine is moved to another host using vMotion. These statistics are maintained per port in a vDS, as shown in Figure 3.3.

FIGURE 3.3   Distributed switch port statistics

Port ID	N...	Connectee	Runtime MAC Address	Port Group	D...	State	V...	Time Statistics Updated	Broadcast - Ingres...	Broadcast - Egress...
44		Tiny01	00:50:56:94:75:2d	VM-RegionA01-v...	I.	Link Up	V	11:49:18 PM	364.44	7,696.49
45		--	--	VM-RegionA01-v...	-.	--	V	--	--	--
46		Tiny04	00:50:56:94:e3:75	VM-RegionA01-v...	I.	Link Up	V	11:49:18 PM	28.05	75.80
47		--	--	VM-RegionA01-v...	-.	--	V	--	--	--
48		--	--	VM-RegionA01-v...	-.	--	V	--	--	--

When you add a VMkernel port to a standard switch, it creates a new dedicated port group. No other VMkernel port or virtual machine can connect to that dedicated port group. For distributed switches, VMkernel ports connect to an existing port group.

Standard switches lack many advanced options available to virtual distributed switches. including NetFlow, PVLAN, NIOC, and the ability to export and restore their configuration.

vDS are available in the vSphere Enterprise Plus and vSphere Remote Office Branch Office licenses. Some VMware products such as NSX include a license for distributed switches, which are required for *opaque networks*— virtual network objects created by other products such as NSX. They may be fully or only partially visible when using the vSphere client and in most cases will be managed by the product that created them.

Virtual Distributed Switches

Virtual switches in vSphere are separated into two logical components: the management plane, where the configuration is created and maintained, and the data plane, where the traffic carried by the switch flows and is manipulated, such as with filters or VLAN tags. For standard switches, both management and data planes exist on the host the switch is created on. With distributed virtual switches, the management plane is located on the vCenter server and the data plane is spread across all the hosts that are attached to that switch. This means virtual machine traffic only travels from the host the VM is running on through the *proxy switch* (what VMware calls the host's instantiation of the distributed switch) to the physical network switches connected to that host. Virtual machine traffic never flows to the vCenter server.

While the distributed switch is a datacenter-level object that spans hosts, VMware refers to the individual instance of a distributed switch on a host as a proxy switch.

With the vCenter server holding the management plane for distributed switches, it must be available for changes to be made to the virtual distributed switch. However, once changes are made, the configuration is pushed to each host. If the vCenter server becomes unavailable, hosts will continue to use the last vDS configuration they received but new hosts cannot be added to the vDS and no changes can be made to the vDS or its port groups. However, virtual machines and VMkernel ports can be added to and removed from vDS port groups using the VMware Host Client as shown in Figure 3.4.

Port groups are logical groupings of ports for a virtual switch and are the logical network component that virtual machines and VMkernel ports connect to. Most often used to manage VLAN tagging, there are a number of settings available for port groups that will be discussed in the coming pages.

FIGURE 3.4   ESXi host client network view

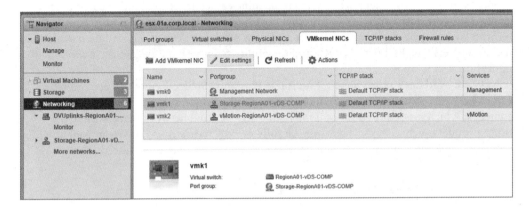

Creating Distributed Switches

There are several reasons to create distributed switches, including to take advantage of the many features available compared to standard switches, to satisfy the desire for centrally managed network configurations, or to take advantage of a separate product such as NSX or vRealize Network Insight.

> Remember that to create a distributed switch, you need to have a vSphere license that includes the feature or a separate vDS license such as the one included with NSX.

Distributed switches are created at the datacenter level, and any host in that datacenter can be connected to the same distributed switch, regardless of cluster configuration. Clusters are usually created to consolidate workloads or similarly equipped hosts, and in most cases you would want to ensure that all hosts in a cluster are connected to the same distributed switch(es). Having identical network configurations simplifies host management, but more important, it ensures that virtual machines can be run from any host in the cluster. If a cluster has four hosts and only three are connected to a distributed switch, the host that does not connect to the vDS will not support the same virtual machines as the other three.

Spanning a distributed switch across clusters is a way to ensure a consistent network configuration for networks used by both clusters. However, if the virtual machines in the clusters do not share the same network(s), then we would recommend using a separate distributed switch for each cluster. Basic security principles include limiting access to only what is needed and following the Keep It Simple philosophy; it is preferred for all objects grouped together to be as identical as possible. Those two ideas combine to suggest that clusters with different network requirements use separate distributed switches (Figure 3.5).

FIGURE 3.5   A shared vDS for the infrastructure with all hosts connected and separate vDS for the virtual machines in each cluster

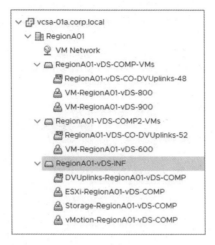

Configuring all of the hosts with similar network configurations (Figure 3.6) requires all hosts to have access to the same networks even if they are not used. However, if some networks are shared, for example the infrastructure networks for host management, then a shared distributed switch could be created for those networks and separate switches for the networks unique to the cluster.

FIGURE 3.6   A separate vDS created for each cluster with infrastructure and virtual machine traffic

Either of these configurations allows similar physical network configurations for the hosts in each cluster while limiting them to just the networks they require.

Creation of a distributed switch is accomplished from the Networking tab of the vSphere web client. As shown in Figure 3.7, you can create a new vDS using the New Distributed Switch wizard or by using the Import Distributed Switch wizard with a previously saved backup file. The backup file can also be used to reset an existing vDS by using the Restore Configuration Wizard.

FIGURE 3.7   Combining Distributed Switch ➢ New/Import with Settings ➢ Restore

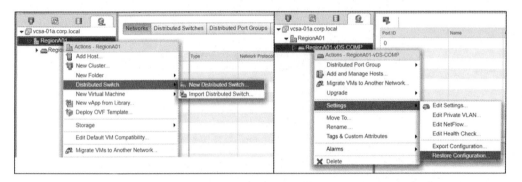

To restore the settings of a distributed switch to a previous backup, use the Restore Configuration option from the distributed switch's Actions menu. To create a copy of an existing distributed switch, use the Import Distributed Switch options from the Datacenter Actions menu and do not check Preserve Original Distributed Switch and Port Group Identifiers. There are only a few settings available in the New Distributed Switch configuration wizard and all can be changed later. The settings are as follows:

Name   The name displayed in the GUI for the virtual distributed switch.

Version   Tied to major vSphere releases, this determines what features are available for the switch and the minimum version of ESXi a host can be running to connect to the distributed switch.

Number of Uplinks   Maximum number of physical network adapters any configured host can connect to this switch.

Network I/O Control   The ability to determine bandwidth availability for different traffic types on the switch. See "Understanding Network I/O Control" later in this chapter.

You also have the option of creating and naming an initial distributed port group for the distributed switch. After a distributed switch has been created, there are a few general distributed switch settings that can be changed, including the number of uplinks (see the section "Adding and Removing Uplink Adapters") and whether Network I/O Control (NIOC) is enabled (see "Understanding Network I/O Control").

The following distributed switch settings are also available from the Advanced section of the Settings wizard for a vDS:

MTU (Bytes)   The maximum transmission unit, or MTU, is the largest packet size allowed on the switch. Most often increased to support VMware NSX or to meet network storage requirements, this setting defaults to the industry standard of 1500 bytes.

Note that any virtual machine or VMkernel port needing an increased MTU would also need to be changed. MTU is set at the switch and VMkernel or VM, not at the port group.

Multicast Filtering Mode   Distributed virtual switches default to the Basic multicast filtering mode, where any virtual machine connected receives all multicast packets for the destination MAC address of the multicast group. You could also configure multicast snooping, which, if your virtual machines are configured for it, would restrict the multicast packets they receive to just those destined for their multicast group. Per the VMware documentation, "This mode supports IGMPv1, IGMPv2, and IGMPv3 for IPv4 multicast group addresses, and MLDv1 and MLDv2 for IPv6 multicast group addresses." This is most likely to be changed to meet a specific application's or vendor's stated needs.

Discovery Protocol   This is a very useful setting that pulls configuration information from the physical switch connected to the vDS. When this setting is enabled to match the configuration of the physical switch connected, each NIC will report information such as the port the NIC is connected to and the name and IP address of the switch as well as other information.

This setting defaults to Cisco Discovery Protocol (CDP) if you are using Cisco switches but can be changed to Link Layer Discovery Protocol (LLDP) for switches that support LLDP. It can also be set to Disabled, which could be required by your security team.

Operation   This changes how the discovery protocol in use works; by default it only listens for information from the physical switch, but you could also set it to only tell the physical switch the settings of the vDS (using Advertise) or set it to Both.

Administrator Contact   This information is passed along if the discovery protocol is set to Advertise or Both.

Upgrading and Deleting Distributed Switches

If you have a vDS in your environment that is not the most recent version, you can use the Upgrade wizard available from the actions menu of the distributed switch. Note that you will not be able to upgrade a switch to a version above the highest-level host connected. So a distributed switch with 31 ESXi 6.5 hosts and 1 6.0 host will only be able to be at vDS version 6.0.

If you decide to upgrade, make sure you back up the switch first. If the upgrade fails, you will be able to quickly recover, and if you change your mind, you will be able to roll back—you cannot downgrade a switch version.

Deleting a distributed switch is accomplished by right-clicking the switch and choosing Delete. (In my experience, the Flash-based web client is more reliable when deleting distributed switches.) However, be aware that you will not be able to delete a virtual switch until all virtual machines and VMkernel ports are disconnected from the port groups on the switch. If you see an error status similar to "The resource '14' is in use" (Figure 3.8), you will need to check what is connected to the virtual switch port (in this case, switch port 14) listed in the error message, which is achieved by selecting the Ports tab of the distributed switch (Figure 3.9) and scrolling down the list.

FIGURE 3.8 Port group delete error

Recent Tasks	Alarms			
Task Name	Target	Status		Initiator
Remove vSphere Distributed Switch	RegionA01-vDS-COMP	ⓘ The resource '14' is in use.		VSPHERE.LOCAL\Administr...
Delete Distributed Port Group	DPortGroup	✓ Completed		VSPHERE.LOCAL\Administr...
Delete Distributed Port Group	vMotion-RegionA01-vD...	ⓘ The resource '30' is in use.		VSPHERE.LOCAL\Administr...
Import configuration of the entity		✓ Completed		VSPHERE.LOCAL\Administr...

FIGURE 3.9 List of ports by port number

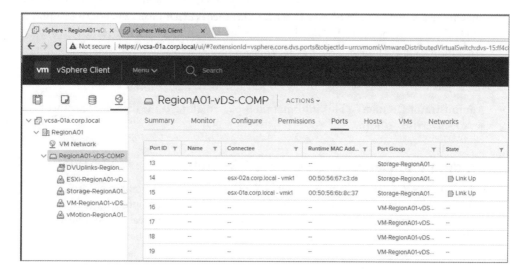

The object connected to the port could be either a virtual machine or a host's VMkernel port, and the name of the object will be listed in the Connectee column. A VMkernel port will have the name of the port listed after the hostname; in the example in Figure 3.9, the hostname is esx-02a.corp.local and the VMkernel port is vmk1.

 Real World Scenario

The Importance of Physical Network Configurations

Proper physical network configurations are crucial when configuring vSphere networking. An improper physical network switch configuration can cause all kinds of issues with a vSphere environment.

I once installed a new vSphere host with two network uplinks using the default load balancing of Route Based on Originating Virtual Port, which uses a calculation to determine which switch port sends traffic out of which uplink. This generally distributes the virtual machines (VMs) evenly between uplinks. However, as virtual machines were migrated to the host, some VMs using that switch worked (were available on the network) and some VMs did not.

When troubleshooting virtual networking, one of the first steps is to determine if traffic flows between VMs on the same host, which in this case worked fine—traffic was just not leaving the host for some VMs. I tried migrating machines around and found that every other machine I migrated to the host would not send traffic out—but if I took a VM that was not working and migrated to another switch and then migrated it back to the malfunctioning switch, then it might start working.

As it turned out, the physical network ports were not configured identically—one of the ports was not configured for the proper VLANs, and any switch port that used the uplink connected to the misconfigured physical port was not passing traffic.

In the host's Physical Adapters tab, the CDP/LLDP information and the Observed IP Ranges are useful from the vSphere side to start troubleshooting physical network issues, but the physical switches should be checked carefully for configuration issues during implementation.

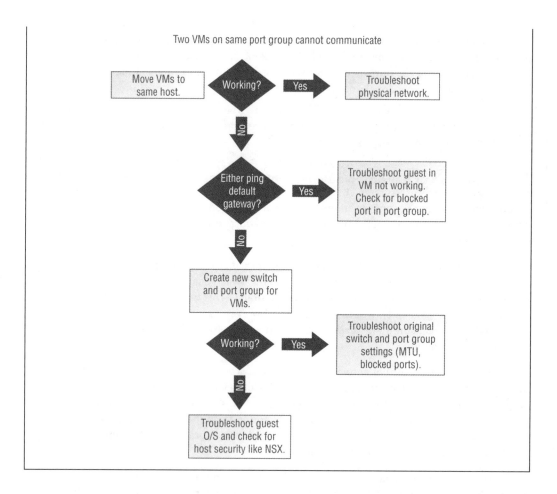

Adding and Removing Hosts from a vDS

When a distributed switch is created, no hosts are connected to it. You are not required to add hosts; however, a virtual machine cannot be connected to the vDS until the host the VM is assigned to has been added to the vDS. Note that when a host is added to a distributed switch, it is not required to connect physical adapters on the host to the switch. However, any VMkernel port or virtual machine on that host would not be able to send traffic outside the host.

Hosts can be added to a distributed switch using the Add and Manage Hosts wizard (Figure 3.10) from the action menu of the switch. The first option of the Add and Manage Hosts wizard is Add Hosts, which allows new hosts to be connected to the vDS, and (optionally) their physical adapters, VMkernel adapters, and virtual machines can be configured when the hosts are added to the switch.

FIGURE 3.10   Add and Manage Hosts wizard

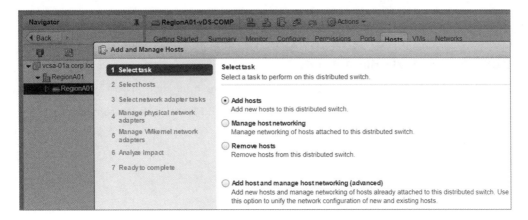

The second option, Manage Hosts Networking, allows you to manage physical adapters, VMkernel adapters, and virtual machine connectivity for hosts already connected to the switch.

Hosts can be removed from the virtual distributed switch using the third option (Remove Hosts) or from the Hosts tab of the switch (Figure 3.11).

FIGURE 3.11   Removing the host from the distributed switch

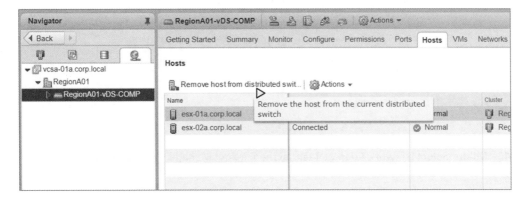

The host must have its VMkernel adapters and any virtual machines on the host disconnected from the distributed switch before it can be removed from a vDS.

The fourth option, Add Host and Manage Host Networking, allows you to add hosts and modify the new and existing hosts' physical adapter, VMkernel adapters, and virtual machine connectivity all in the same wizard.

EXERCISE 3.1

Add a host to a distributed switch.

1. Connect to the host using the vSphere web client and open the Networking view.

2. Right-click the distributed switch and choose Add and Manage Hosts from the Actions menu.

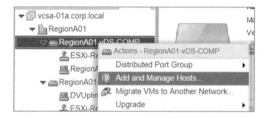

3. Using the Add hosts task, on the Select Hosts screen select the host to be added to the switch.

4. On the Select Network Adapter Tasks screen, select Manage Physical Adapters.

EXERCISE 3.1 *(continued)*

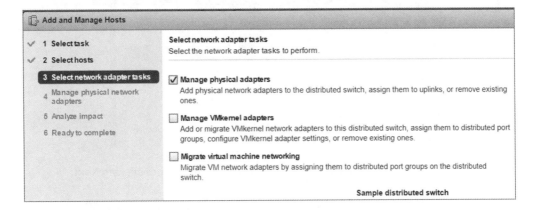

5. On the Manage Physical Network Adapters screen, select an unused adapter on the host and click Assign Uplink.

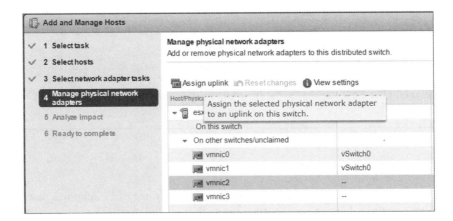

6. On the Select an Uplink screen, make sure each physical adapter has an uplink selected. (In a production environment, you will want to make sure all hosts are configured identically, including which pNIC is associated with which uplink.)

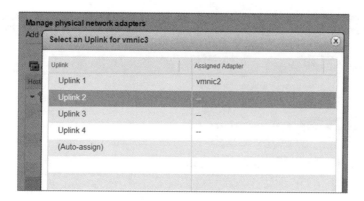

7. Ensure that the uplinks and pNICs are associated correctly before clicking Next.

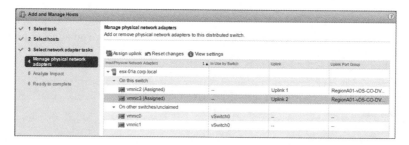

8. Click Next on the Analyze Impact screen and Finish on the Ready screen to complete the wizard.

Using dvPort Groups

Distributed virtual port groups, or *dvPort groups*, are collections of switchports that share the same settings. Port groups are the objects that virtual machines and VMkernel ports connect to—when you look at a virtual machine's network adapter in the vSphere web client, it will list the port group connected. Port groups are most often used to enable VLAN usage by VMs and VMkernel ports, which can improve security by preventing snooping—for instance, by ensuring that vMotion traffic is separate from virtual machine traffic.

Creating and Configuring dvPort Groups

Distributed virtual port groups are created on a distributed virtual switch and only exist on that virtual switch. With standard switches, virtual machines will vMotion between identically named port groups on different switches when changing hosts since each host creates and manages its own switches. However, with distributed switches, the virtual machine remains on the same port in the same distributed port group and distributed switch during vMotion since all of the network objects are created and maintained by vCenter.

Port groups can be created using the New Distributed Port Group option on the Distributed Port Group action menu item of the switch. Note that port group names must be unique among port groups in the datacenter, not just the distributed switch on which you are creating the port group.

After a port group is created, you can edit its settings by right-clicking the port group and choosing Edit Settings. To easily configure identical settings for multiple port groups on a vDS, choose the Manage Distributed Port Groups option on the Distributed Port Group action menu item of the switch (Figure 3.12).

FIGURE 3.12   Launching the Manage Distributed Port Groups wizard

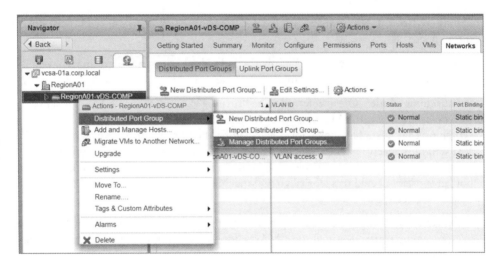

This wizard is especially useful to make sure all of your port groups have identical security and failover settings.

Removing a distributed port group is as simple as right-clicking on the distributed port group in the Networking view and choosing Delete. However, all VMkernel ports and virtual machine adapters must be disconnected before the distributed port group can be deleted.

Port group configuration options include the following:

Port Binding   The default setting is Static, which assigns a virtual machine to a specific port when the VM is connected to the vDS. Dynamic binding has been deprecated (meaning VMware intends to remove the setting in a future release) and assigns the port when the VM first powers on. Ephemeral binding doesn't permanently assign a port; the VM is given a port when it turns on and the port is unassigned when the

VM powers off. This setting has implications at scale because there is a maximum of 4096 network ports per host and 60,000 ports per vCenter. A large number of powered-off virtual machines (static binding) could theoretically max out one of those numbers.

Port Allocation Leaving the Port allocation default of Elastic will allow the port group to automatically adjust the number of ports based on the connected adapters. If Port allocation is set to Fixed, the Number of ports setting becomes a hard limit on how many connections (virtual machines and VMkernel ports) can be attached to that port group.

Number of Ports Defaulting to 8, this number adjusts automatically if Port allocation is set to Elastic. If Port allocation is set to Static, then this represents the maximum number of adapters that can connect to it.

Network Resource Pool This can be set if NIOC is configured (see "Understanding Network I/O Control").

Configure Reset at Disconnect Per-port settings (if overridden) are reset if the port is disconnected.

Override Policies These options allow the individual ports in the group to have a different setting than the group setting.

Promiscuous Mode Often referred to as "turning the switch into a hub." If set to Accept, this allows all VMs on a port group to receive all packets handled by the switch on that host. This behavior is affected by the port group VLAN settings as a VM will only receive packets for the VLAN configured on the port group unless the port group is set to VLAN Trunking. Promiscuous mode is usually only configured for port groups connected to security virtual machines as directed by the vendor, or for nesting hypervisors.

MAC Address Changes Defaulting to Reject, this setting prevents a virtual machine from *receiving* traffic destined for a MAC address not set in the virtual machine configuration. This would be set to Enabled if the operating system of the VM will need to change the MAC address in the OS.

Forged Transmits Defaulting to Reject, this setting prevents a virtual machine from *sending* traffic from a MAC address not set in the virtual machine configuration. This would be set to Enabled if the operating system of the VM would need to change the MAC address in the OS.

Traffic Shaping Ingress and egress traffic shaping can be set on a per-port group basis. Separate from NIOC, the average, peak, and burst values are set for each port in the group. This is useful for limiting chatty virtual machines.

VLAN There are four settings:

> **None:** Also called External Switch Tagging (EST) mode. This requires an access port on the physical switch. Any traffic outbound from the port group will not receive a VLAN tag.

VLAN: Virtual Switch Tagging (VST) mode, which requires a VLAN number to be set on the port group. Any traffic outbound from the port group to the physical network will receive this VLAN tag. Any traffic inbound from a physical switch with the same VLAN tag will be passed to this port group after the VLAN tag is removed. A VLAN trunk port is required on the physical switch.

VLAN Trunking: Virtual Guest Tagging mode (VGT). A VLAN range or VLAN set is also configured with this option. Inbound traffic tagged with any VLAN ID in the set will be passed to this switch and the port group will not manage any VLAN tags. This mode is usually used for security virtual appliances along with Promiscuous mode. A VLAN trunk port is required on the physical switch.

Private VLAN: See the section "Network Isolation" later in this chapter.

Load Balancing   See the section "Load Balancing and Failover Policies" later in this chapter.

Network Failure Detection   Defaults to Link Status Only, which detects only if there is any signal on the network cable but won't detect physical switch issues or configuration problems. Beacon probing will send beacon probes out every second to help determine if valid connections are available between the network adapters. However, there must be at least three active or standby NICs on the port group to ensure accurate response; if there are only two NICs and the beacon fails, it can't determine which uplink is the problem.

Notify Switches   This will alert the connected switch if a failover occurs. This setting defaults to Yes but should be changed to No if directed by an application vendor to support a specific application.

Failback   Defaults to Yes; this will allow an Active NIC that failed to be immediately used when it comes back up. You might change this to No during testing or troubleshooting to avoid "flapping," where the adapter is repeatedly going up and down.

NetFlow   NetFlow is a monitoring protocol used to send traffic metadata to a monitoring tool such as vRealize Network Insight. Disabled by default, this would be set to Enabled when the NetFlow settings on the vDS are edited to send the flows to the monitoring tool.

Traffic Filtering and Monitoring   This is configured when you need network packets dropped or tagged for QoS or need the QoS packets retagged. It can be set for specific MAC or IP addresses or ranges or even different types of host traffic such as vMotion and vSAN. Traffic can be ingress, egress, or both.

Block All Ports   This setting will stop all traffic in and out of all of the ports on the distributed port groups.

Adding and Removing Uplink Adapters

Physical NICs on each host connect to the distributed switch using uplinks. On the distributed switch itself, a special group called a dvUplink group exists to manage the global settings for the host uplinks. Only one dvUplink group can exist per distributed switch, and it is primarily used to set the maximum number of physical connections a host can have to that distributed switch as well as a few other optional settings.

By default, a dvUplink group has four connections, so any host could connect four physical NICs or link aggregation groups (which are covered in the section "Link Aggregation" later in this chapter). Hosts are not required to associate any physical connections to the vDS, but no local traffic would be able to leave the host and no external traffic would be delivered to the host's proxy switch. This would result in an outage if a functioning virtual machine connected to the distributed switch was migrated to the host.

The number of uplinks should be adjusted to your environment to meet the maximum number of connections required. Products such as VMware NSX will make configuration settings based on the number of uplinks set for a dvUplink group. Note that the number of uplinks is adjusted on the vDS settings, not on the dvUplink group.

The Add and Manage Hosts wizard and the distributed switch configuration on the host will allow you to add, change, or remove physical NICs associated with a vDS. Care should be taken when migrating NICs for networks that are in use to ensure that outages do not occur. Best practice would ensure two physical connections per switch, which for a migration would allow one to be moved at a time to avoid an outage. Migrate one physical NIC, migrate the VMkernel adapters or virtual machines using the networks carried by the physical NIC, then move the second NIC.

The Add and Manage Hosts wizard in the Flash client has an Add Host task, which is useful for ensuring that all hosts have the same configuration. The Manage Host Networking task provides similar capabilities—without the option of adding new hosts at the same time. Using either task, you can either visually compare the hosts or enable template mode by checking Configure Identical Network Settings on Multiple Hosts (Template Mode) on the Select Hosts tab (Figure 3.13).

After this option is selected, an additional step appears in the task list: Select Template Host (Figure 3.14), allowing you to pick the host with the optimal configuration—or the host you are going to configure and have all other hosts match. Note that you can use the template host to set physical connection (dvUplink), VMkernel ports, or both.

FIGURE 3.13   Configuring identical network settings on multiple hosts

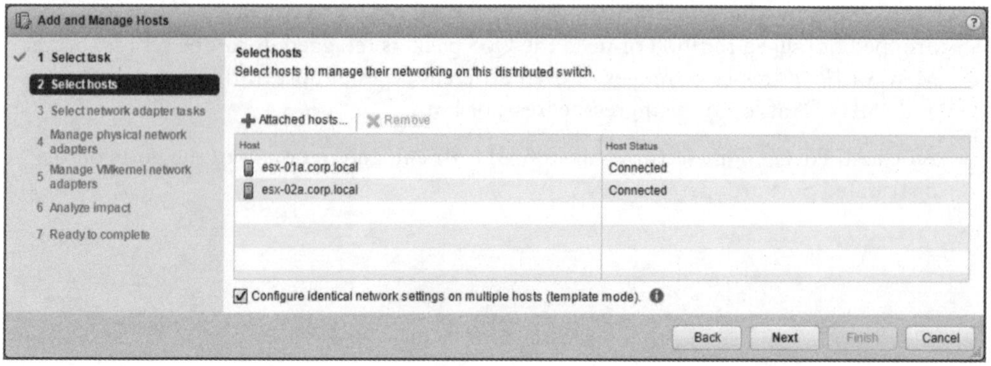

FIGURE 3.14 Select Template Host

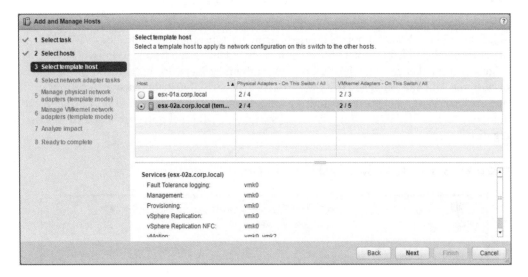

Once Select Template Host is selected, you can approve the template host's configuration or change it and apply that setting to all hosts attached to the vDS (Figure 3.15).

FIGURE 3.15 Manage Physical Network Adapters (Template Mode)

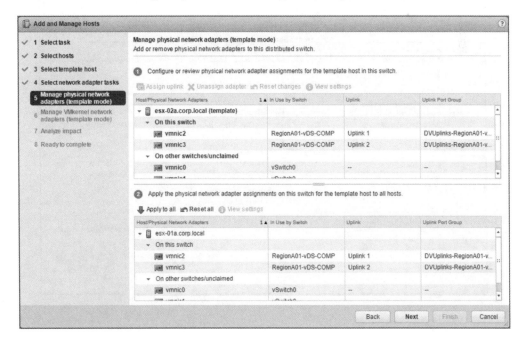

Working with Virtual Adapters

While an initial VMkernel port is created during host installation, additional VMkernel ports can be added to isolate host traffic. Host adapters can be added in two ways (Figure 3.16): either from the host's Configure tab under Networking ➢ VMkernel adapters or with the Add and Manage Hosts wizard from the virtual distributed switch action menu. When VMkernel ports are added to standard switches, a dedicated port group is created, but when added to distributed virtual switches, VMkernel ports are assigned to existing distributed port groups.

FIGURE 3.16   Two ways to add host adapters

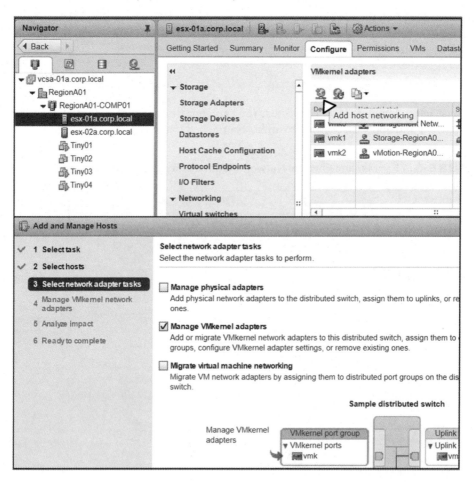

During the creation of the VMkernel adapter, you have the option of choosing IPv4, IPv6, or both to meet your network configuration. You can also choose a TCP/IP stack. There are three stacks initially: Default, Provisioning, and vMotion. The default stack carries all host TCP/IP traffic until you assign traffic to other stacks. If you create a VMkernel adapter and assign it to the vMotion stack, only VMkernel ports assigned to that stack can be used for vMotion. The same is true of the Provisioning stack and Provisioning traffic. These settings are used to ensure that those traffic types are completely separated from other host traffic. If needed, you can create custom TCP/IP stacks to separate other management traffic such as replication.

The following host traffic types can be assigned to VMkernel adapters:

vMotion   Each host that will participate in a vMotion virtual machine move (including DRS) requires a VMkernel port to be flagged for vMotion traffic.

Provisioning   This includes the traffic for cold (virtual machine powered off) migrations, cloning, and snapshot migrations.

Fault Tolerance Logging   Only one VMkernel adapter can be flagged to carry the traffic required to keep fault-tolerant virtual machine instances in sync.

Management   The only required traffic type. The first VMkernel adapter created is tagged for management traffic. Traffic types include vCenter, fat client, and SSH.

vSphere Replication/vSphere Replication NFC   These two options handle incoming and outgoing replication data when vSphere Replication is in use on the host. The NFC (Network File Copy) traffic type is for incoming replication traffic.

vSAN   Each host participating in a virtual storage area network (vSAN) cluster must have a VMkernel port flagged for vSAN.

An additional traffic type that cannot be specifically assigned using the VMkernel settings is TCP/IP storage—both NFS and iSCSI. NFS traffic will typically use the lowest-numbered VMkernel port that can access the NFS file server. If you want to dedicate a VMkernel port to NFS, make sure it is on the same VLAN as the NFS server because the host will use IP-adjacent VMkernel adapters before trying to route to NFS over the default TCP/IP stack's gateway. For iSCSI, there is a method covered in Chapter 4, "Storage in vSphere," that will dedicate NICs for iSCSI storage traffic.

An adapter can be configured to carry any or all of the traffic, unless it has been configured as dedicated to iSCSI traffic or unless the vMotion or Provisioning stacks have been assigned to other VMkernel adapters. However, best practice is to assign one VMkernel port per distributed port group, one type of network traffic per VMkernel port, and one type of network traffic per stack other than Default.

The default TCP/IP stack has a default gateway that is set on the host in the TCP/IP configuration section of the Networking menu. When you create a VMkernel adapter, you are given the opportunity to use the default gateway or set a custom gateway.

You might notice (see Figure 3.17) that if you set a static IP when you configure the host, vmk0 (the first VMkernel port) is set to override the default gateway for the adapter even though the same gateway IP is set for the default stack and vmk0.

FIGURE 3.17   VMkernel adapter default gateway and override option

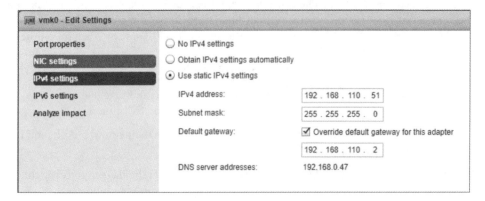

When configuring subsequent VMkernel ports, you may choose to use different default gateways to take advantage of alternate routing capabilities on your management network. You can also use the vmkping command from the command line of the host to ensure the VMkernel adapters can access their default gateways and other hosts on the same network.

The Add and Manage Hosts wizard also includes the ability to migrate VMkernel networking. Be careful during this process because migrating the VMkernel of a host to an improperly configured vDS could break connectivity to the host and thus keep vCenter from managing the host. If you lose connectivity to the host in a manner that does not trigger vDS rollback (see the section "Automatic Rollback" later in this chapter), you can use the console GUI to reset the network settings or use the console command line to move or edit the VMkernel ports.

    The Add and Manage Hosts wizard will allow you to edit VMkernel adapters on several hosts at once, which is useful for consistency in the environment.

If you move or edit a VMkernel port that is currently carrying traffic for a vMotion or provisioning activity, that activity (vMotion or provision) will complete successfully.

If the wizard detects that you are moving or changing a VMkernel port or adapter that is dedicated to iSCSI traffic, you will see a message in the Analyze Impact section of the wizard (Figure 3.18). There are three levels of messages: No Impact, Important Impact, and Critical Impact.

FIGURE 3.18   iSCSI impact warning

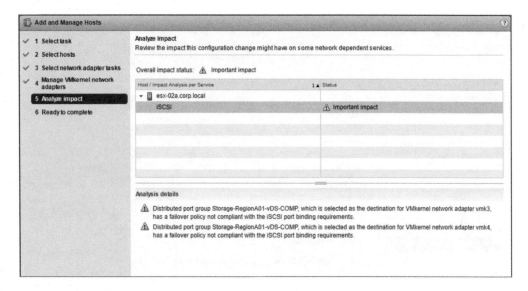

If you need to migrate a VMkernel port to a standard switch, you will need to use the VMkernel adapter tools in the host view because the Add and Manage Hosts wizard cannot move VMkernels to a vSS. Deleting VMkernel ports is pretty straightforward; just be sure you are not deleting the last management port.

Custom TCP/IP Stacks

The ability to create custom stacks is key for advanced networking, as it allows separate configurations for network types beyond the Default, Provisioning, and vMotion stacks. The ability to create custom stacks, while most commonly used by NSX for VLAN traffic, allows for advanced configurations like separate routing tables for replication traffic or a separate DNS server for NFS traffic.

Custom stacks are managed on a per-host basis, and while they are edited using the TCP/IP configuration section of the Networking menu from the Configure tab, they can only be created from the command line of the server using `esxcli network ip netstack add -N="stack_name"` as shown in Figure 3.19. You can see the new stack in Figure 3.20.

FIGURE 3.19   Adding a new TCP/IP stack from the host command line

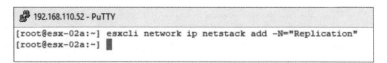

FIGURE 3.20   The new stack from the web client

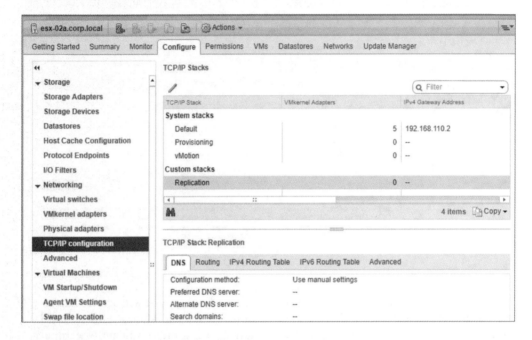

After the stack is created, you can rename it or set the DNS and routing settings as shown in Figure 3.21. If there is a VMkernel port with DHCP configured, you can use it to set the DNS settings, or you can configure then manually.

FIGURE 3.21   TCP/IP stack settings

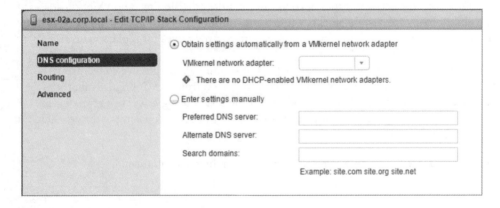

You can also change the TCP congestion algorithm between CUBIC and New Reno (New Reno is the default), but the differences are beyond the scope of this book.

EXERCISE 3.2

Create a new TCP/IP stack and create a VMkernel adapter to use it. Enable jumbo frames.

1. Connect to an ESXi host using SSH and log in as root.

2. Run the command `esxcli network ip netstack add -N="NAS"` to create the new TCP/IP stack on the host.

```
The ESXi Shell can be disabled by an administrative user. See the
vSphere Security documentation for more information.
[root@esx-01a:~] esxcli network ip netstack add -N="NAS"
[root@esx-01a:~] █
```

3. Connect to the host using the vSphere web client and open the VMkernel Adapters menu under the Configure tab.

4. Click the Add Host Networking button to launch the wizard.

5. Select the VMkernel Network Adapter on the first screen of the wizard and choose an existing network for the second screen (here we are using the port group we created in Exercise 3.1):

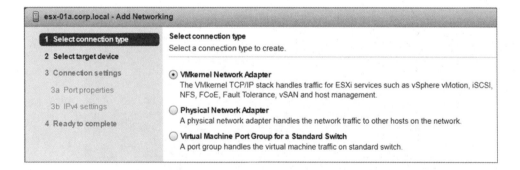

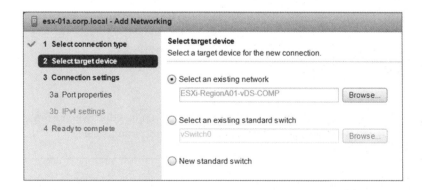

6. Under TCP/IP Stack, choose the new stack created in step 2.

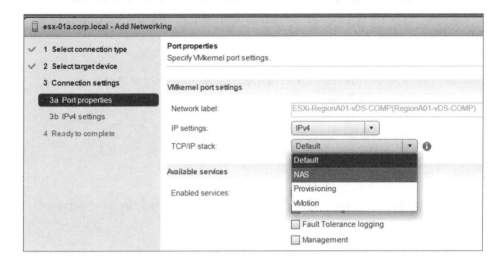

7. Leave all other settings at the default. Click Next twice, then Finish.

8. Identify the new VMkernel adapter using the custom TCP/IP stack. Click the adapter and then click Edit.

9. On the second page of the Edit wizard, set the MTU to 9000.

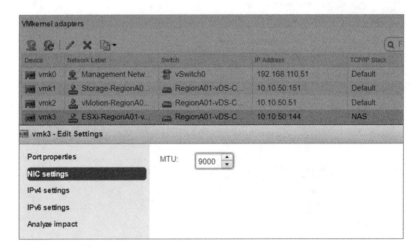

10. Click OK to complete the exercise. Note that if you do not use the switch from Exercise 3.1, you will need to set the switch to use jumbo frames also.

Long-Distance vMotion

Long-distance vMotion supports live migration across links of at least 250 Mbps and up to 150 ms of round-trip time. If the vMotion traffic needs to be routed, you should enable the vMotion TCP/IP stack for the VMkernel ports responsible for the vMotion traffic.

vCenter makes multiple checks to ensure that vMotion will work, such as, for instance, migrating to a switch without a NIC. However, vCenter doesn't check to make sure the broadcast domain in use by the virtual machine exists at the destination, so it is possible for the virtual machine to lose connectivity if you do not ensure that the destination is working on the correct network.

You cannot vMotion from a distributed switch to a standard switch, but you can always transfer to a distributed switch.

Migrating Virtual Machines to or from a vDS

Virtual machines can be migrated to or from a vDS using the Migrate VMs to Another Network or the Add and Manage Hosts wizard on the Distributed Switch action menu or on the virtual machine settings window.

The Migrate VMs to Another Network wizard can move one or many virtual machines to or from standard switches or distributed switches, but only one port group can be the source and only one port group can be the destination. This wizard is best when a single network is being moved.

The Add and Manage Hosts wizard can move any virtual machine connected to the hosts selected to any port group on the distributed virtual switch being configured. This wizard is best during the initial adoption of the distributed switch.

The virtual machine configuration window allows you to move the virtual machine to any network connected to the host. If the destination port group is configured correctly, moving it between networks will have no more impact than a vMotion of that VM.

Performance and Reliability

Distributed switches provide a couple of options for improving bandwidth and ensuring that there is no single point of failure. However, you need to make sure the hosts are configured correctly to take advantage of the distributed switch settings. Also, be aware that

LAG assignments, load balancing, and failover policies are set per distributed port group although the Manage Distributed Port Groups wizard can be used to ensure that all have the same settings.

Link Aggregation

To increase network bandwidth, multiple physical NICs can be grouped together into link aggregation groups (LAGs), which use the Link Aggregation Control Protocol (LACP) to manage load balancing and dynamic handling of the links making up the LAG. In an actual production environment, you would use your switch manufacturer's documentation to configure LAGs because their naming conventions and settings could differ from VMware vendor-agnostic guides.

 Virtual distributed switches starting with version 5.5 feature Enhanced LACP mode. If you upgrade a version 5.1 vDS that is configured with LAGs to version 6.5 or later, LAGs should be upgraded to enhanced mode during the distributed switch upgrade. There is a manual upgrade available if needed.

LAGs are created from the LACP menu found under the distributed virtual switch's Configure tab ≻ Settings section (Figure 3.22).

FIGURE 3.22 LACP menu

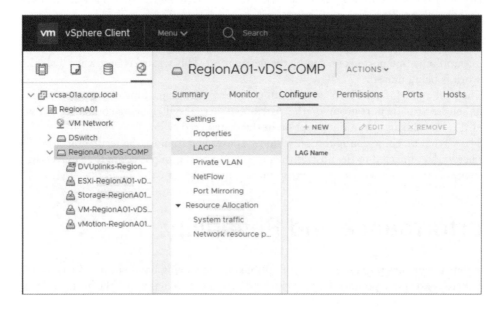

The number of ports selected for the LAG should match the ports configured on the physical switch for the LAGs and the number of NICs allocated to the LAG on each host.

A port group can only be configured to use a single active LAG (Figure 3.23); all other LAGs and stand-alone uplinks must be set to Unused. An Active LAG group will send LACP packets to the switch for negotiation while Passive will only receive LACP packets. This should be set according to the switch vendor's guidelines.

FIGURE 3.23   Single active LAG

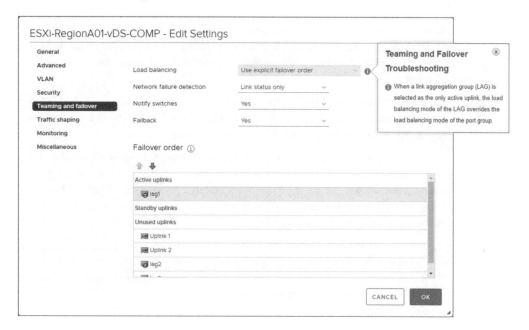

As noted in Figure 3.23, the failover settings of the LAG group override the failover settings of the port group.

A couple of important notes of caution regarding LAGs:

- LAGs are not compatible with software iSCSI initiator multipathing.
- LAGs are not compatible with host profiles and thus are not available to Auto Deploy configurations.

Load Balancing and Failover Policies

There are five load balancing options for distributed virtual switches, configured on each port group (Figure 3.24). These settings determine which uplink is used for each virtual machine's traffic—assuming there is more than one uplink.

FIGURE 3.24   Load balancing choices

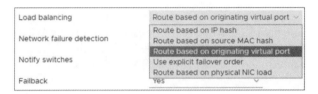

Route Based on IP Hash   This hashes the source and destination IP addresses of each packet, which could send packets for the same virtual machine out several uplinks. This load balancing method requires your physical switch to be configured for Ether-channel or IEEE 802.3ad and should be configured according to your switch vendor's documentation.

Route Based on Source MAC Hash   The switch uses the MAC address of the VM and the number of uplinks to calculate which port to use. If the VM changes switch ports, it will still use the same uplink as the MAC doesn't change.

Route Based on Originating Virtual Port   The default load balancing algorithm. The virtual switch uses the port ID to determine which uplink is used. This generally provides a round-robin effect, distributing the ports evenly between the uplinks. However, actual traffic or load is not taken into account and you could find that the uplinks vary greatly in the volume of traffic they handle.

Use Explicit Failover Order   Most commonly used for iSCSI port binding, this setting allows you to manually determine which uplinks are active, passive (only used if no active uplinks are available), or standby (not used at all). If your server had mismatched NICs (for instance, 10 GB, 1 GB) available, you could assign the faster NICs to active and the slower NICs to standby.

Route Based on Physical NIC Load   The switch tests the actual load on the physical NICs on each host every 30 seconds to determine virtual machine uplink usage. If a physical NIC's usage exceeds 75%, the uplink for the virtual machine using the most traffic is changed.

Traffic Shaping

When configuring port groups, you can enable Traffic shaping, which allows either ingress or egress network traffic limits to be set. Note that the average, peak, and burst values are per port, not for the whole port group. If you want to limit a virtual machine that is sending (or receiving) too much traffic, this is one option to restrict it. (Since ingress happens after traffic has already been received at the host, you're only saving the virtual machine from being swamped with packets; the host still has to process the incoming packets and restrict those over the caps you have set.) The Ingress setting could help virtual machines struggling to keep up with traffic, the Egress for VMs that send too much traffic, and both could be configured to mimic a restricted environment, such as replicating a 1 GB connection when your host has 10 GB uplinks.

TCP Segmentation Offload

TCP segmentation offload (TSO) is a way to push some network tasks (the breaking up of large packets into smaller ones) onto the physical network card, reducing the CPU load of the host. Both virtual machines and VMkernel ports can take advantage of TCP segmentation offload.

The physical NICs installed in the host must be capable of TSO and be configured to use TCP Offload (Figure 3.25). This can be checked on the host with the `esxcli` command.

FIGURE 3.25   Checking TSO status using `esxcli`

```
[root@esx-02a:~] esxcli network nic tso get
NIC     Value
------  -----
vmnic0  on
vmnic1  on
vmnic2  on
vmnic3  on
[root@esx-02a:~]
```

By default, hosts will use TSO if it is supported by the physical adapters. TSO is enabled on VMkernel ports by default and is also enabled on VMXNET 2 and 3 adapters connected to virtual machines. Note that this requires VMware Tools to be installed on the guests. Windows guests can disable TSO by disabling Large Send Offload V2 (IPv4) and Large Send Offload V2 (IPv6) from the Advanced setting of the VMXNET adapter. Linux guests can disable TCP Offload by running `ethtool -K eth0 tso off`.

Jumbo Frames

The default MTU size on a network is 1500 bytes. Packets larger than 1500 bytes are considered "jumbo." Jumbo frames are used to improve network efficiency by reducing overhead—each packet has the same header size (the part of the packet before the data), so increasing the amount of data reduces the ratio of data-to-header. However, not all workloads support or take advantage of jumbo frames. Jumbo frame sizes are most often configured for IP-based storage, backups, and network products such as VMware NSX.

All devices that handle traffic on the network must be configured for jumbo frames for proper functionality. Common settings for jumbo frames are 1600 and 9000. Whoever is requesting jumbo frame support—your storage team, network admin, or application owner—should provide the proper value for the MTU.

To enable jumbo frames for VMkernel ports, the MTU size must be set in the port properties of the VMkernel port (Figure 3.26).

FIGURE 3.26   VMkernel MTU

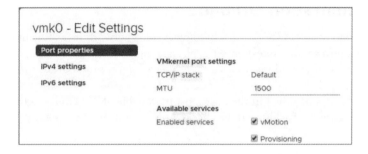

To enable jumbo frames for virtual machines, the MTU must be set in the properties of the network adapter. The virtual switch that the VMkernel port and/or virtual machines connect to must also be configured for jumbo frames. This configuration can be found in the Advanced settings of the switch (Figure 3.27).

FIGURE 3.27   MTU switch

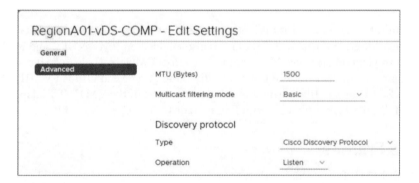

Create a new distributed switch and enable jumbo frames.

1. Connect to the host using the vSphere web client and open the Networking view.

2. Right-click the datacenter and choose New Distributed Switch under Distributed Switch in the Actions menu.

EXERCISE 3.3 *(continued)*

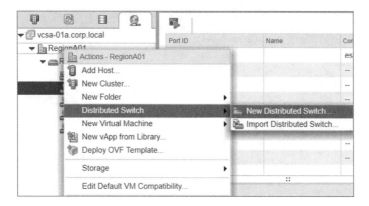

3. Enter a name for the new distributed switch and click Next. On the third screen, enter a port group name and click Next.

4. Verify the settings and click Finish.

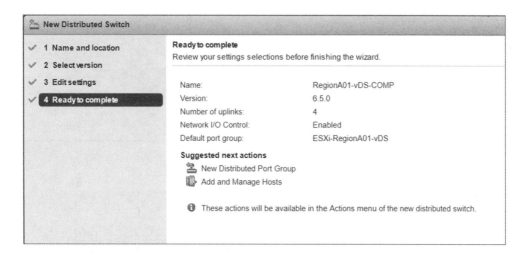

5. Right-click the new switch and choose Settings ➢ Edit Settings.

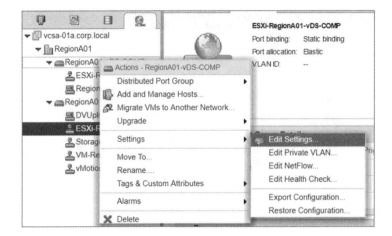

6. On the Advanced page, change the MTU (Bytes) to 9000 and choose OK.

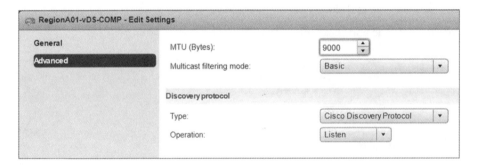

Network Isolation

Virtual local area networks (VLANs) and private virtual local area networks (PVLANs) are methods to isolate different networks that are utilizing the same network switches. When VLANs and PVLANs are implemented with distributed virtual switches, it is critical to have the physical switches configured properly to ensure traffic is handled properly.

When VLANs are used on a physical switch, the switch generates a table listing the ports that are participating in each network. The ports in each network are configured with the same VLAN ID and traffic is allowed to pass between them on the switch. If other ports on the same switch are configured with different VLAN IDs, traffic would need to be routed by a network device with access to both VLANs in order to flow between the two VLANs.

When the switch needs to connect to another network device, it can use a trunk connection and send the traffic for multiple VLANs on the same wire. To ensure that the traffic is handled properly, each Ethernet frame has a VLAN ID appended at the beginning of it. This way the destination device knows which network each packet belongs to and will handle them appropriately. Only packets traveling between trunk connections receive the VLAN tag.

Private VLANs add an additional level of information, where one VLAN is configured with one or more secondary VLAN IDs. While all of the VLANs (primary and secondary) are considered part of the same network, the network devices will treat the packets differently. Secondary PVLANs can be configured as Community or Isolated, while the primary PVLAN is always promiscuous. Ports tagged with a Community secondary PVLAN can communicate with other ports with the same secondary PVLAN or any port configured with the primary PVLAN ID. Ports tagged with an Isolated secondary PVLAN ID can only communicate with ports tagged with the primary PVLAN ID.

VLANs are configured on port groups so that VMs can participate on the proper networks. PVLANs must be defined on the vDS before they can be configured on port groups to provide additional VLAN isolation. To define the private VLANs, select the vDS, click Configure, and select Private VLAN. When creating private VLANs, keep these guidelines in mind:

- Only one secondary PVLAN can be set as Isolated. Only one is needed since each port associated with that PVLAN is isolated to only talking to primary VLAN ports.

- Community PVLANs are useful for VMs that will communicate with each other; isolated PVLANs are useful for VMs that do not need to communicate with any other VM on the same network.

- The router for the private VLAN must be connected to the primary VLAN so that it can route traffic to/from all VMs on the network, regardless of their community or isolated membership.

Again, it is critical to have the physical switches configured properly to ensure that traffic is handled properly. Note that this only provides VLAN isolation, not true security.

Automatic Rollback

If a network change is made to a host that disrupts the host's ability to communicate with vCenter, the host should automatically roll back the last change to the VMkernel ports. Changes include MTU sizes, VLAN settings, physical NIC speed or duplex, VMkernel IP settings, default gateway changes, and removing the VMkernel port or physical adapters.

After a host detects a vCenter connection loss and rolls back the last change (which usually happens very rapidly), you might see a few alerts to let you know what happened (Figure 3.28).

FIGURE 3.28   A few variations of rollback alerts

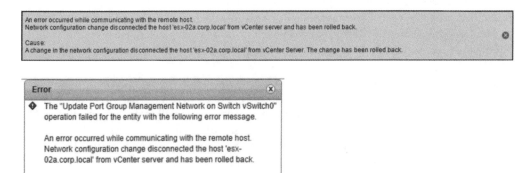

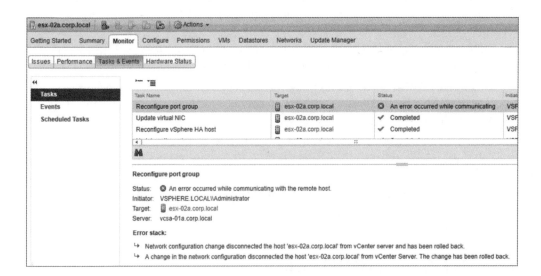

Distributed switches also have rollback mechanisms in the case of changes such as teaming, MTU, or VLAN causing problems.

If the rollback mechanism does not correct the problem, you may need to restore the vDS from an earlier version or update the network settings directly on the host using the

Direct Console User Interface (DCUI) or ESXi shell—or both if you find that the vDS doesn't realize it needs to roll back and continues to push the change to the host, while the host initiates a rollback. In that scenario, the host will be out of sync with the vDS (Figure 3.29).

FIGURE 3.29   Out of sync error

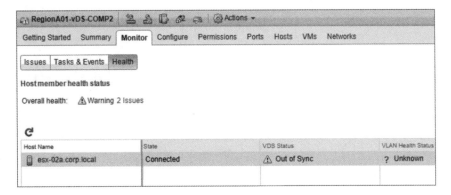

If you enable the health check routines for the distributed switch as shown in Figure 3.30, you can get more information on what went wrong (Figure 3.31).

FIGURE 3.30   Configuring the vDS health check

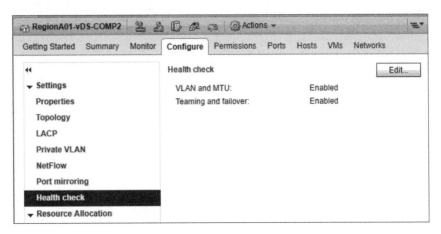

From the host's virtual switch menu, you can use the rectify option to resolve this (Figure 3.32).

FIGURE 3.31   Monitoring the health of a vDS

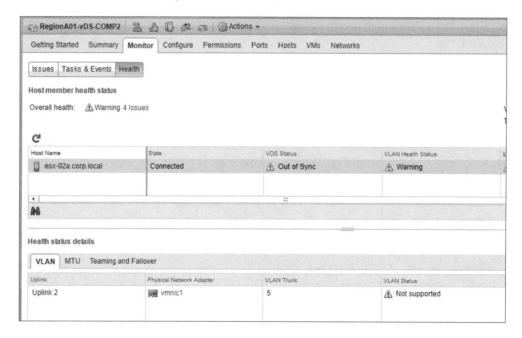

FIGURE 3.32   Rectify a vDS from a connected host

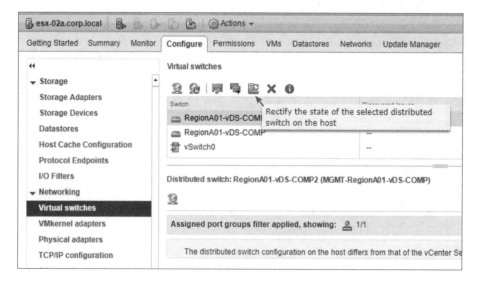

Monitoring and Mirroring

VMware distributed switches include the capability of mirroring traffic from one port to either another port on the vDS or a remote destination. This is useful for security purposes, but also to examine packets with a utility such as Wireshark for application troubleshooting.

Encapsulated Remote Switched Port Analyzer (ERSPAN) is a means of delivering mirrored traffic to a remote destination, which VMware implements as Encapsulated Remote Mirroring (L3) Source.

To configure port mirroring, in the Port Mirroring section of the virtual distributed switch's Configure tab, select New ➤ Encapsulated Remote Mirroring (L3) Source (Figure 3.33). This will allow sending traffic to an ERSPAN destination.

FIGURE 3.33   Configuring port mirroring

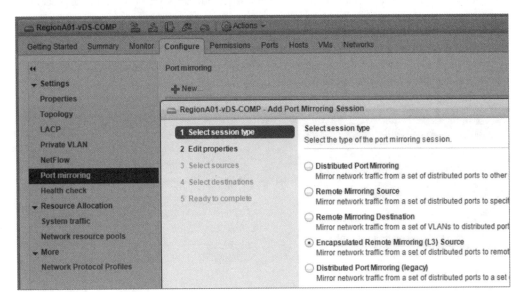

Name the session as desired and make sure you set the status to Enabled. You can change the other settings if required by your ERSPAN destination. Note that the default is to send every packet, but the sample rate can be adjusted as needed.

Select the specific ports (VMkernel or virtual machine) you wish to monitor (Figure 3.34), or enter a range of ports.

The ports will default to sending both egress and ingress traffic to the destination, but you can change that on a per-port or per-range basis.

FIGURE 3.34   Selecting the source distributed ports

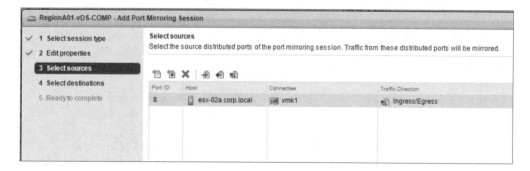

Using NetFlow

One of the advanced settings available on virtual distributed switches is NetFlow. NetFlow is metadata about the traffic on the switch, which is very useful for traffic analysis and is used by utilities such as vRealize Network Insight. To configure NetFlow on your vDS, use the NetFlow section of the switch's Configure tab (Figure 3.35).

FIGURE 3.35   Configuring NetFlow

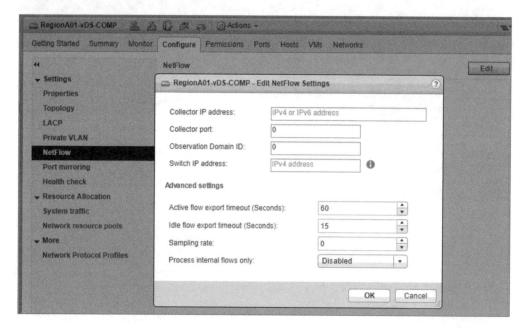

Here you set the IP address of the network analysis tool that will be receiving the Net-Flow statistics. The port, domain ID, and advanced settings, if needed, should be obtained from the tool. The switch IP address option is important as it allows all of the data from the switch to be grouped together.

Understanding Network I/O Control

Enabling vSphere Network I/O Control (NIOC) lets you can set shares, reservations, and limits on network bandwidth for system traffic and/or virtual machines. NIOC is enabled by default when you create a distributed virtual switch, and the values are set on a per-distributed-switch basis.

The shares, limits, and reservations work much the same as they do with memory, CPU, and storage settings. However, while the system traffic settings are on a per-host basis, virtual machine settings (specifically, reservations) have implications across hosts. Virtual machine reservations (if configured) are used for Distributed Resource Scheduler virtual machine migration decisions and for HA placement decisions.

All calculations for shares, limits, and reservations are on a per-adapter basis, and between system traffic and virtual machine traffic, you can only reserve a maximum of 75 percent of the bandwidth of the slowest physical NIC connected.

System traffic setting are configured in the Resource Allocation menu on the Configure tab of the vDS (Figure 3.36).

FIGURE 3.36   NIOC system settings

RegionA01-vDS-COMP							
Getting Started	Summary	Monitor	Configure	Permissions	Ports	Hosts	VMs	Networks

0 Gbit/s	7.50 Gbit/s	10.00 Gbit/s

Network I/O Control:	Enabled
Version:	3
Physical network adapters:	4
Minimum link speed:	10,000 Mbit/s

Total bandwidth capacity	10.00 Gbit/s
Maximum reservation allowed ⓘ	7.50 Gbit/s
Configured reservation	4.00 Gbit/s
Available bandwidth	6.00 Gbit/s

Settings
- Properties
- Topology
- LACP
- Private VLAN
- NetFlow
- Port mirroring
- Health check
- Resource Allocation
  - **System traffic**
  - Network resource pools
- More
  - Network Protocol Profiles

Q Filter

Traffic Type	1 ▲ Shares	Shares Value	Reservation	Limit
Fault Tolerance (FT) Traffic	Normal	50	0 Mbit/s	Unlimited
Management Traffic	Normal	50	0 Mbit/s	Unlimited
NFS Traffic	Normal	50	0 Mbit/s	Unlimited
Virtual Machine Traffic	High	100	4,000 Mbit/s	Unlimited
iSCSI Traffic	Normal	50	0 Mbit/s	Unlimited
vMotion Traffic	Normal	50	0 Mbit/s	Unlimited
vSAN Traffic	Normal	50	0 Mbit/s	Unlimited
vSphere Data Protection Backup Tr...	Normal	50	0 Mbit/s	Unlimited
vSphere Replication (VR) Traffic	Normal	50	0 Mbit/s	Unlimited

WARNING   Only configure the settings for the system traffic that will actually be carried on this vDS. If the distributed switch has no VMkernel adapters connected to it, you should not change the system settings at all. Reservations set for system traffic can only be used by that type of system traffic, so setting a reservation for vSAN at 1000 Mbit/s on a switch with no VMkernel adapters connected puts an artificial limit on the virtual machine traffic it can carry.

System traffic shares are used to determine how bandwidth is allocated on saturated links. (See the next section, "Configuring NIOC Reservations, Shares, and Limits," for more details.) Reservations set a guaranteed amount of network bandwidth per adapter for that traffic type. Limits set a maximum amount of bandwidth that a specific traffic type can consume.

Reservations are useful to guarantee a performance level, shares are good for adjusting the balance between traffic types during contention, and limits can be used to address chatty VMs or reduce traffic for known issues—such as replication traffic causing WAN issues when it hits a certain throughput.

vSphere 6.0 introduced Network I/O Control version 3, which allows for bandwidth settings per VM. If you have a vDS created with version 2, you can upgrade it to version 3, but settings such as user-defined network resource pools and CoS tagging for system traffic will be removed. Note that virtual machines connected to a vDS with NIOS v3 cannot use SR-IOV.

Configuring NIOC Reservations, Shares, and Limits

To apply network I/O control to virtual machines, you first need to set a reservation for virtual machine traffic. By default the reservation is 0.

- If there will not be any system traffic on the vDS, set the reservation to the max (75 percent of the slowest physical link).

- If there will be system traffic, you will need to decide how much bandwidth you would like to guarantee to virtual machines. The value needs to be at least the total amount you would like to reserve to individual virtual machines.

- If you will not be reserving bandwidth for individual virtual machines, set the reservation to 1 Mbit/s (Figure 3.37), which is enough to enable network resource pools.

Once the virtual machine traffic reservation is set, you can create network resource pools. These pools will then be assigned to distributed port groups on the vDS to set a reservation quota (really, a limit on the total reservations) for the VMs connected to the port group and to enable the VMs to set individual limits and *shares*. Multiple port groups can be assigned to the same network resource pool, but all VMs assigned to the pool will share the same reservation quota.

FIGURE 3.37   Virtual Machine Traffic set to 1 Mbit/s

RegionA01-vDS-COMP 🔍 🔍 🔍 🔍 🔍 🔍 Actions ▾					
Getting Started Summary Monitor **Configure** Permissions Ports Hosts VMs Networks					

◀◀	0 Gbit/s 7.50 Gbit/s 10.00 Gbit/s	Network I/O Control:	Enabled
▾ **Settings**		Version:	3
Properties	Total bandwidth capacity	10.00 Gbit/s	Physical network adapters: 4
Topology	Maximum reservation allowed ⓘ	7.50 Gbit/s	Minimum link speed: 10,000 Mbit/s
LACP	▨ Configured reservation	0.00 Gbit/s	
Private VLAN	▢ Available bandwidth	10.00 Gbit/s	
NetFlow			
Port mirroring			Q Filter ▾
Health check			
▾ **Resource Allocation**			

Traffic Type	1 ▲ Shares	Shares Value	Reservation	Limit
Fault Tolerance (FT) Traffic	Normal	50	0 Mbit/s	Unlimited
Management Traffic	Normal	50	0 Mbit/s	Unlimited
NFS Traffic	Normal	50	0 Mbit/s	Unlimited
Virtual Machine Traffic	High	100	1 Mbit/s	Unlimited
iSCSI Traffic	Normal	50	0 Mbit/s	Unlimited
vMotion Traffic	Normal	50	0 Mbit/s	Unlimited
vSAN Traffic	Normal	50	0 Mbit/s	Unlimited
vSphere Data Protection Backup Tr...	Normal	50	0 Mbit/s	Unlimited
vSphere Replication (VR) Traffic	Normal	50	0 Mbit/s	Unlimited

(Resource Allocation sidebar items: **System traffic**, Network resource pools, ▾ **More**, Network Protocol Profiles)

> **NOTE**   Shares give you a way to allocate resources during times of contention. Objects allocated more shares receive more resources when the resources are overallocated. Only unreserved resources are shared. The default setting of Normal provides a value of 50; other settings are Low with 25 and High with 75, or you can set a custom share setting of 1–100.

For shares, there are two stages of calculation when an adapter is saturated: the traffic type share and the virtual machine share. First, the shares for the traffic types carried on the adapter have their share values added and each traffic type share setting is divided by the total number of shares in play. By default, each system types has 50 shares and VM traffic has 100 shares. Here are three examples of share calculations:

- If a 10 Gbit/s adapter is carrying vSAN and virtual machine traffic and the adapter is saturated with traffic and no reservations are set, the virtual machines would be allocated 2/3 of the bandwidth. (50 shares for vSAN plus 100 shares for virtual machines equals 150 shares total. Virtual machines are granted 100 shares of the 150 total shares, 100 / 150 = 2/3 of the shares and thus 2/3 of the traffic under contention.)

- If a 10 Gbit/s adapter is carrying vSAN with a 1 Gbit/s reservation and virtual machine traffic with no reservation and the adapter is saturated with traffic, the virtual machines would be allocated 2/3 of the bandwidth available after the reservation, or about 6 Gbits/s.

- If a 10 Gbit/s adapter is carrying vSAN with a 1 Gbit/s reservation and virtual machine traffic with a 4 Gbit/s reservation and the adapter is saturated with traffic, the virtual machines would be allocated 2/3 of the bandwidth available after the reservation, or about 3.3Gbit/s plus the 4 GB reservation for a total of 7.3 Gbit/s to share among the virtual machines.

In each of these examples, each virtual machine has 50 shares by default and thus would share equally in the traffic available to virtual machines.

If a virtual machine has a reservation set, that VM will receive a guaranteed amount of traffic, and traffic sent over the reservation will contend using the share setting. In the last example, if there were a virtual machine with a 1 Gbit/s reservation that was trying to use 1.2 Gbit/s of bandwidth, the last 0.2 Gbit/s would be allocated using the shares and receive equal priority if all VMs have the default of 50 shares.

A virtual machine that only requires 1000 Mbit/s can have a limit set, and the vDS will ensure that the VM only consumes that amount of bandwidth.

Set limits and reservations sparingly. The reservation will be permanent for system traffic or take effect as long as the VM is powered on for virtual machines and will reduce the bandwidth available to other VMs and system resources. Limits set an artificial performance cap on the resource and if not documented could cause troubleshooting headaches later on.

Determining NIOC Requirements

Network I/O Control requires only a distributed virtual switch. For best results, all hosts should have identical NICs and the same number of NICs connected to the vDS. NIOC v3 requires a VDS of version 6.0 or higher.

Traffic shaping settings take precedence—if traffic is restricted to 1000 Mbit/s on a port group where a VM has a reservation of 1500 Mbit/s, it will be limited to 1000 Mbit/s.

Network I/O Control is best monitored from the Resource Allocation menu, where you can see the bandwidth settings under System Traffic and the virtual machines in the resource pools (refer back to Figure 3.36).

EXERCISE 3.4

Configure Network I/O Control on a distributed switch.

1. Connect to the host using the vSphere web client and open the Networking view.

2. Select the distributed switch and choose System Traffic from the Configure menu.

EXERCISE 3.4 *(continued)*

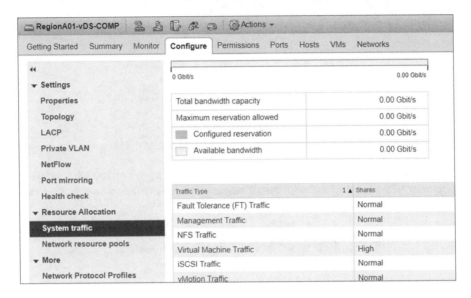

3. Select the Virtual Machine Traffic type and click the edit icon.

4. Enter a reservation of 1000 Mbit/s and click OK (this will give virtual machines at least 10 percent of each pNIC's bandwidth to share).

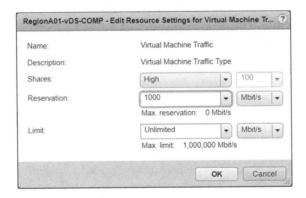

5. Select the vMotion traffic and set the shares to High and the reservation to 500 (this will give vMotion at least 5 percent of each pNIC and higher priority during contention).

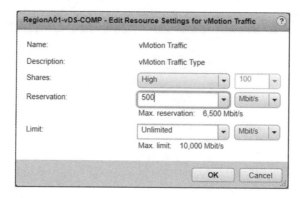

6. Select the NFS Traffic type and set the shares to Low and a limit of 200 Mbit/s (this will restrict NFS access to no more than 2 percent of each pNIC and de-prioritize even that amount during contention).

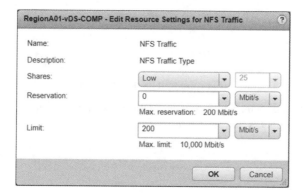

Summary

This chapter has covered host and virtual machine networking, including advanced host network settings, vSphere Distributed Switches, and network I/O control. Host networking using VMkernel adapters has a variety of options available to meet the networking requirements of the modern datacenter, including allowing multiple default gateways on the same network and providing the host with multiple TCP/IP stacks. VMkernel adapters are configured per host, requiring care to be taken during configuration to ensure that all hosts are set up correctly.

Distributed switches offer an extensive list of enhancements over standard switches, including centralized management, the ability to mirror ports or forward port traffic to a remote destination, the ability to load balance across physical NICs based on the load, and network I/O control.

NIOC brings the concepts of shares, reservations, and limits to networking, allowing you to guarantee bandwidth to some virtual machines or types of host networking and guarantee that during contention, network I/O is distributed evenly—or not, depending on your use case.

Exam Essentials

Know how vSphere Distributed Switches are different from standard switches.   Know how the control plane and data plane are different and how the distributed switch model makes management easier. With most settings moved to vCenter control, you can be sure the switch and port group implementation is the same on all hosts. However, uplink and VMkernel ports are configured per host, so be sure to understand where to look to make changes or troubleshoot those components.

Understand how VMkernel adapters are configured for different traffic types.   While one VMkernel adapter can carry all of the different traffic types, know how to create a VMkernel adapter for each type of traffic for security and performance and know how to create new TCP/IP stacks and use multiple default gateways for different networking design considerations.

Know how to add hosts to or remove hosts from a vDS.   Know how you can manage hosts with the wizard in the Networking view, or manage the hosts' uplinks and VMkernel in the Hosts view or use the Host Client to manage the host components if vCenter is unavailable.

Know the different load balancing options, including LAGs.   Know that port groups have four load balancing options, and understand the difference. Also be able to create LAGs using the switch's LACP menu and know the limitations of LAGs.

Understand how automatic rollback works.   An automatic rollback will attempt to keep incorrect switch changes from affecting host connectivity. Be aware of what can trigger an automatic rollback and how to identify when it has occurred.

Know how Network I/O Control works and is configured.   Network I/O Control adds the concepts of shares, reservations, and limits to host and virtual machine networking. Understand how to configure NIOC, how shares are calculated, and why shares only matter during times of contention.

Review Questions

The answers to the chapter review questions can be found in the Appendix.

1. A virtual distributed switch with two 10 GB NICs per host has the default system traffic settings set and a resource pool with a quota of 500 Mbit/s. There is one virtual machine in the resource pool with network shares set to Low, reservation set to 250 Mbit/s, and a limit of 500 Mbit/s. What change would improve network performance for that virtual machine at all times?

   A. Set the Virtual Machine Traffic type reservation to 1000 Mbit/s.

   B. Set the Limit on the virtual machine to 1000 Mbit/s.

   C. Set the Reservation Quota on the resource pool to 1000 Mbit/s.

   D. Set the Reservation on the virtual machine to 1000 Mbit/s.

2. What is the simplest way to restrict the traffic for a collection of virtual machines that are all on the same VLAN?

   A. Network I/O Control

   B. Distributed Port Group traffic shaping

   C. Network Protocol Profiles

   D. Traffic filtering and marking

3. What could account for a virtual machine dropping off the network after moving to a new host via DRS? (Choose two.)

   A. Improper VLAN configuration on the distributed port group

   B. No NIC configured on the virtual machine

   C. Improper VLAN configuration on the physical switch

   D. No NIC configured on the host

4. What can be used to prevent a virtual machine from communicating with other virtual machines on the same broadcast domain but allow its traffic to route to virtual machines? (Choose two.)

   A. Private VLAN

   B. Virtual switch with no uplinks

   C. Traffic filtering and marking

   D. Network I/O Control

5. A virtual distributed switch with two 10 GB NICs per host has the default system traffic settings set, a resource pool with a quota of 500 Mbit/s. There is one virtual machine in the resource pool with network shares set to Low and a reservation set to 250 Mbit/s. What two changes would improve network performance for that virtual machine at all times? (Choose two.)

   A. Set the Virtual Machine Traffic type reservation to 1000 Mbit/s.

   B. Set the Limit on the virtual machine to 1000 Mbit/s.

   C. Set the Reservation Quota on the resource pool to 1000 Mbit/s.

   D. Set the Reservation on the virtual machine to 1000 Mbit/s.

6. Which are valid services you can enable for a VMkernel adapter?

   A. NFS

   B. iSCSI

   C. vSAN

   D. NIOC

7. Which VMkernel service is responsible for incoming vSphere replication traffic?

   A. Management

   B. vSphere Replication

   C. vSphere Replication NFC

   D. vSphere Replication Appliance

8. What can be used to ensure that a host with two NICs has the proper connectivity? (Choose two.)

   A. LLDP

   B. vmkping

   C. Beacon probing

   D. NetFlow

9. An administrator wishes to improve the performance of virtual machine cloning. Which option could be one step in improving that performance?

   A. Configure traffic shaping on the VM's port group.

   B. Create a new VMkernel adapter for Provisioning traffic.

   C. Upgrade the distributed switch to version 6.5.0.

   D. Set the virtual machine traffic to High in NIOC.

10. Which load balance option is not available when using software iSCSI initiator multipathing?

    A. Route Based on IP Hash

    B. Explicit

    C. Route Based on Physical NIC Load

    D. LACP LAG

11. A datacenter has separate networks for management, iSCSI, and Network Attached Storage (NAS) traffic. Both management and NAS traffic requires routing to remote networks, but those networks do not route to each other. What option would allow an ESXi host to use these networks?

    A. Custom TCP/IP stacks

    B. Override default gateway

    C. NIOC

    D. Traffic filtering and marking

12. Consider the figure here. A datacenter has separate networks for management and Network Attached Storage (NAS) traffic. Both management and NAS traffic requires routing to remote networks, and both have gateways on the same network. What option would allow an ESXi hosts to use these networks with the fewest steps possible?

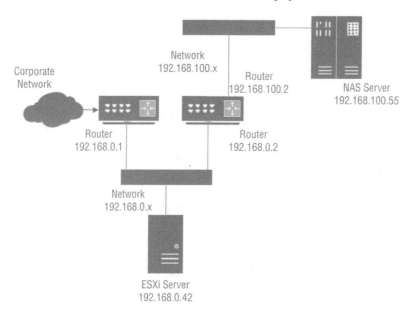

A. Custom TCP/IP stacks

B. Override default gateway

C. NIOC

D. Traffic filtering and marking

13. Which object sets the maximum number of uplinks a host can use for a virtual distributed switch?

A. Port group on the vDS

B. Virtual switch on the host

C. Uplink group on the vDS

D. vSphere Distributed Switch (vDS)

14. Which port group mode should be used for a network-monitoring virtual appliance that needs access to Ethernet frames with VLAN headers?

A. External Switch Tagging (EST)

B. Virtual Switch Tagging (VST)

C. Virtual Guest Tagging (VGT)

D. Private VLAN (PVLAN)

15. Which port group option should be used when the pNIC is connected to an access port?

    A. External Switch Tagging (EST)

    B. Virtual Switch Tagging (VST)

    C. Virtual Guest Tagging (VGT)

    D. Private VLAN mode (PVLAN)

16. Which port group settings should be enabled to allow any VM in the port group to receive packets not intended for it?

    A. Traffic filtering and marking

    B. Promiscuous mode

    C. Virtual Guest Tagging (VGT) mode

    D. Private VLAN (PVM) mode

17. If you want a particular port group to only use one NIC regardless of fail conditions, which object and setting would you choose?

    A. Uplink group, Use Explicit Failover Order

    B. Port group, Use Explicit Failover Order

    C. Port group, Route Based on Physical NIC

    D. Uplink group, Route Based on Physical NIC

18. Several VMs on different hosts connected to the same port group lose connectivity during a network test. All hosts have two NICs connected to the switch. What setting could cause the problem?

    A. Route Based on IP Hash with the switches in Etherchannel mode

    B. TSO Offload not enabled on all hosts

    C. Explicit Failover configured using Unused

    D. Jumbo frames enabled on the physical switches but not the vDS

19. What would prevent you from setting the Virtual Machine Traffic reservation above 0 Mbit/s?

    A. NIOC not enabled

    B. NIOC version 2

    C. No pNICs connected

    D. No port groups created

20. Which settings on the physical switches could cause VMs to behave differently on different hosts? (Choose two.)

    A. Jumbo frames

    B. CDP/LLDP

    C. VLAN tagging

    D. NetFlow

Chapter

4

Storage in vSphere

2V0-21.19 EXAM OBJECTIVES COVERED IN THIS CHAPTER:

✓ **Section 1 – VMware vSphere Architectures and Technologies**

- Objective 1.3 – Describe storage types for vSphere
- Objective 1.4 – Differentiate between NIOC and SIOC
- Objective 1.6 – Describe and differentiate among vSphere, HA, DRS, and SDRS functionality
- Objective 1.10 – Describe virtual machine (VM) file structure
- Objective 1.11 – Describe vMotion and Storage vMotion technology

✓ **Section 4 – Installing, Configuring, and Setting Up a VMware vSphere Solution**

- Objective 4.2 – Create and configure vSphere objects

✓ **Section 7 – Administrative and Operational Tasks in a VMware vSphere Solution**

- Objective 7.2 – Manage datastores
- Objective 7.3 – Configure a storage policy
- Objective 7.6 – Configure and use vSphere Compute and Storage cluster options
- Objective 7.8 – Manage resources of a vSphere environment
- Objective 7.11 – Manage different VMware vCenter Server objects
- Objective 7.13 – Identify and interpret affinity/anti affinity rules

Storage is one of the basic requirements for ESXi—along with compute and memory. You can have a complete, air-gapped virtual datacenter with no physical networking, but there will be no persistent virtual machines without somewhere to store them. VMware has slowly been adding features and capabilities to the storage stack over the years, and today a host can connect to local disks, remote file or block storage with physical and virtual adapters, plus share out its local disks as file- or block-level storage. It can even host storage for physical servers.

Note that this chapter focuses on connecting to shared storage arrays and network-attached storage and configuring local storage to become shared storage. There is no coverage of local disks for booting or virtual machine storage.

Managing vSphere Integration with Physical Storage

We will start with the basic ways to connect ESXi hosts to shared storage. Shared storage takes two basic forms: block-level and file-level, which essentially comes down to where the file table is maintained.

 NOTE Absent using host profiles, all physical storage access is configured separately on each host.

With block-level storage, an array presents unformatted raw storage identified by a unique logical unit number (LUN) to an ESXi host using either iSCSI or Fibre Channel protocols. The host then formats the storage for use with the VMware File System (VMFS) and creates a file table to track folders, filenames, and storage blocks in use by files. With file-level storage, a network-attached storage (NAS) server (or any server with the capability) formats its local storage and shares out folders using the Network File System (NFS) protocol.

The question of which datastore type to use has a great many variables—what storage technologies are currently in use and what technologies are the staff knowledgeable and comfortable with? What are the future storage needs for the datacenter? What vendors are preferred? While the current trend is toward a Software-Defined Data Center (SDDC) using software-defined storage such as vSAN, there are still plenty of reasons to purchase physical arrays, including supporting separate physical equipment or features such as datastore-level snapshots.

One of the traditional standards was using block storage for virtual machines and a low-cost NFS server for templates and ISOs. The idea of multiple levels of storage, usually differentiated by cost and performance, is still very valid and can be easily implemented, as we will see later, by storage profiles. While the Keep It Simple philosophy would suggest only maintaining one type of storage, you may find cost, performance, features, or availability reasons to maintain multiple arrays.

Adding an NFS Datastore

ESXi hosts support connecting to file-level storage using either NFS version 3 or version 4.1. NFS version 4.1 adds Kerberos for authentication and data integrity assurance, some multipathing capabilities via session trunking, and support for server-side locking. However, NFS 4.1 is not currently supported for Storage DRS, Storage I/O Control, or Site Recovery Manager.

For setting up an ESXi host to connect to NFS, version 3 has a very simple add wizard; there are multiple possible steps for NFS v4.1. For NFS v3, you will provide a datastore name, the share name as it is configured on the server, and the IP address or DNS name of the NAS. For version 4, you can specify multiple DNS names or IP addresses if your NFS server supports multipathing (see your vendor's documentation for best practices) and then configure Kerberos for security and data integrity.

As Figure 4.1 shows, you need to have the host added to Active Directory and have a Kerberos user added to the host configuration before you can enable Kerberos for the NFS 4.1 datastore.

Kerberos credentials are set once per host, so if you have multiple NFS 4.1 servers, they all need to use the same credentials because only one set of credentials can be set on a host.

As shown in Figure 4.1, the Kerberos credentials are set in the Authentication Services menu on the host, the same menu page where the Active Directory settings are located.

FIGURE 4.1   Configuring Kerberos credentials

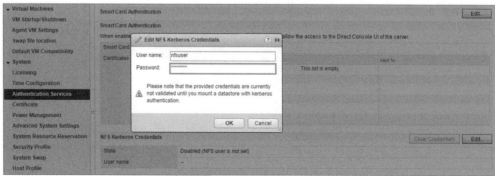

Once the datastore is created on one host, you can use the Mount Datastore to Additional Hosts wizard to ensure that the configuration matches on your hosts. This is important as advanced features such as vMotion and HA require the datastore to be named identically on each host.

FIGURE 4.2　Unmounting an NFS datastore

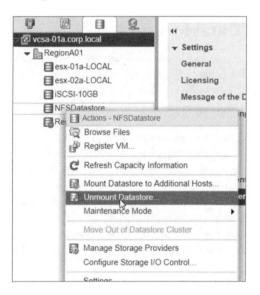

You can remove an NFS datastore from an individual host or from all hosts using the Storage view. Right-click the datastore and choose Unmount Datastore (Figure 4.2). You will see a list of hosts with the datastore currently mounted.

If there are virtual machines running on the datastore, you will not be able to unmount it from the hosts running those VMs. Figure 4.3 shows an error message resulting from trying to unmount an NFS datastore on a host with virtual machines present on the datastore.

FIGURE 4.3　Error when removing a datastore that's in use

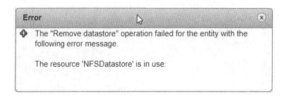

EXERCISE 4.1

Add an NFS v3 datastore.

Requires a NAS providing an NFS v3 share.

1. Connect to vCenter using the vSphere web client, open the Host and Cluster view, and click an ESXi host.

2. Open the Datastores tab, click the Create a new datastore icon, and choose NFS from the first screen of the wizard.

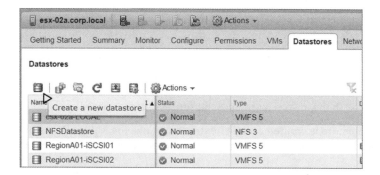

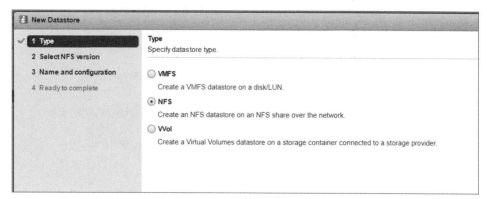

3. On the second screen, pick NFS v3.

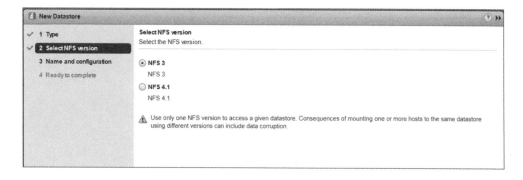

4. For NFS version 3, provide a datastore name for how the NFS share will appear in the GUI. Enter the share name as it is configured on the server, along with the IP address or DS name of the server.

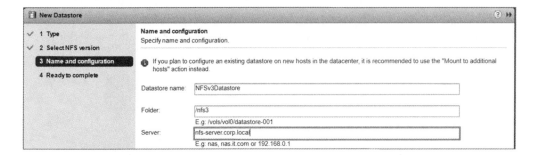

5. Click Next and then Finish to complete the Add Datastore wizard.

6. Once the datastore is created on one host, you can use the Mount Datastore to Additional Hosts wizard to ensure that the configuration matches on your hosts.

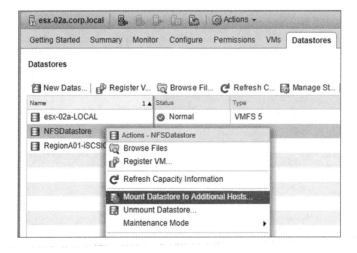

Add an NFS v4.1 datastore

Requires a NAS with an NFS v4.1 share and Kerberos credentials set.

1. Connect to vCenter using the vSphere web client, open the Host and Cluster view, and click an ESXi host.

2. Open the Authentication Services menu on the host and set the Kerberos credentials.

3. Open the Datastores tab, click Add Datastore, and choose NFS from the first screen of the wizard.

4. On the second screen, pick 4.1 for the version of NFS your server is using to present the share.

5. With NFS version 4.1, you can specify multiple DNS names or IP addresses if your NFS server supports multipathing (see your vendor's documentation for best practices). Here you will enter your NAS IP address(es).

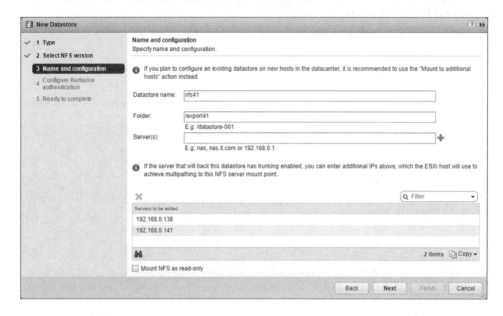

6. You can then configure Kerberos for security and data integrity. You will see an error if you skipped step 2.

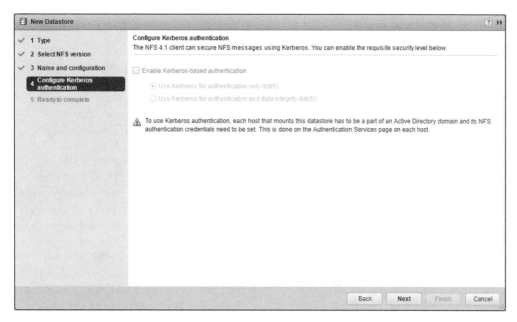

7. Once the datastore is created on one host, you can use the Mount Datastore to Additional Hosts wizard to ensure that the configuration matches on your hosts:

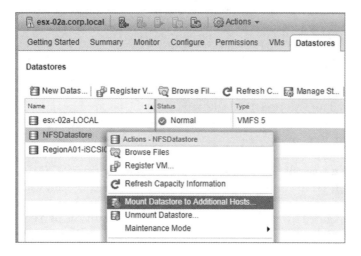

Using Block Storage

Block-level shared storage accessed using the iSCSI and Fibre Channel protocols can be accessed using either physical adapters—host bus adapters (HBAs) or converged network adapters (CNAs), where the physical card handles most of the I/O and communication with the storage server—or network interface cards (NICs) that may or may not provide hardware assistance for some of the I/O- and storage-related communication tasks.

For Fibre Channel arrays, the communication path between the ESXi hosts and the storage arrays can be either dedicated Fibre Channel fabrics with HBAs in the host connected to Fibre Channel switches using special cables or Fibre Channel over Ethernet (FCoE), where the cables and switches are regular network cables. With FCoE, the Fibre Channel protocol is encapsulated in Ethernet frames (not TCP/IP packets)—which requires an extra step when sending or receiving data from the array. There is a variety of hardware choices available for the hosts, ranging from CNAs that will handle the I/O and network encapsulation duties to NICs that support FCoE but require the host to do most of the work. If you want to boot your host using FCoE, you will need either an HBA or a network card that supports FCoE Boot Firmware Table (FBFT) or FCoE Boot Parameter Table (FBPT). The trade-off is generally the more expensive the adapter, the lower the CPU load on the host. Which adapter to choose is really a conversation to explore with your storage vendor if you are considering FCoE.

Fibre Channel fabrics use the concept of *zoning* to determine what hosts have access to what storage arrays. Usually created and maintained at the Fibre Channel switch, zones are created between host ports and array ports to ensure that hosts have access to only what they need. Normally, groups are created to reduce the number of objects maintained—for example, all host ports needing to connect to a specific set of array ports are grouped together and then a zone is created to allow access to the correct group of array ports. Once a zone is created to allow communication from a host port to an array port, a LUN map is created to allow access from the host to the specific LUNs created on the array. For shared storage (as required for vMotion, HA, DRS), the same LUNs need to appear identically to all required hosts. However, when booting a host from an array, the boot LUN should only be mapped to the host booting from it.

With iSCSI storage, the communication path is over regular network cables and switches. However, you still have a choice of adapters ranging from iSCSI HBA to normal network cards. The HBAs available for iSCSI can be either Independent, where the adapter has a more sophisticated chipset and has a BIOS-level configuration, or Dependent, where the adapter is configured from ESXi. Network card options available to iSCSI implementations include the ability to take some of the load off the CPU by handling TCP packet processing using a TCP/IP offload engine, or TOE. You can also use a network card that offers an iSCSI Boot Firmware Table (iBFT), which will let you boot from the SAN without the expense of an iSCSI HBA.

To boot a host from a storage array, you need a LUN created and presented to the host (usually using zoning and mapping for Fibre Channel and sharing for iSCSI—but see your vendor's documentation), and then you need to configure the storage adapter on the host. Each of the options (Fibre Channel HBA, FCoE HBA, network card with FBFT or FBPT, network card with iBFT) requires you to access the adapter during the boot process of the host. The parameters you set might vary depending on the vendor, but generally a Fibre Channel HBA will provide a list of arrays and LUNs that it finds and you select the LUN to boot from, while a FCoE adapter requires VLAN and IP settings for the adapter and IP or DNS name for the array before providing a list of available LUNs. Booting from an iSCSI array is similar to FCoE, where you need to specify network parameters for the adapter and array, but you may also need to add credentials if your array has Challenge Handshake Authentication Protocol (CHAP) configured for security.

Configuring the Software iSCSI Initiator

If you are accessing iSCSI storage using a NIC instead of an HBA, you will need to enable and configure the software iSCSI initiator (sometimes also called the iSCSI adapter) on each host. As shown in Figure 4.4, the software iSCSI adapter can be added from the Storage Adapters option of the host's Configure tab. Only one software iSCSI adapter can be added per host.

FIGURE 4.4   Adding an iSCSI initiator

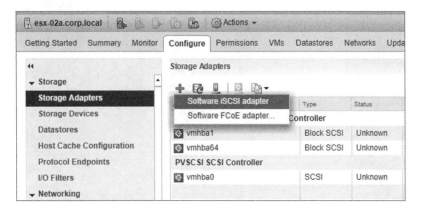

Once the iSCSI software initiator appears in the adapters list, you can start configuring it. iSCSI hosts are identified by a iSCSI qualified name (IQN), which in the GUI is referred to as ISCSI name. This is used by the iSCSI array to identify hosts and map them to allowed LUNs. By default the IQN for a host is `iqn.1998-01.com.vmware:<hostname>-<random 8 character hex string>`, which can be modified if needed.

> If a host is rebuilt, the random part of the IQN will change. You can either make a note of the IQN before rebuilding and reset it after the update (Figure 4.5) or update the array with the new IQN.

If your array has CHAP configured for security, you can set the credentials for the host either for the adapter (so all arrays receive the same credentials) or per array. When setting the credentials, you have four options (Figure 4.6).

FIGURE 4.5   Changing the IQN for a host

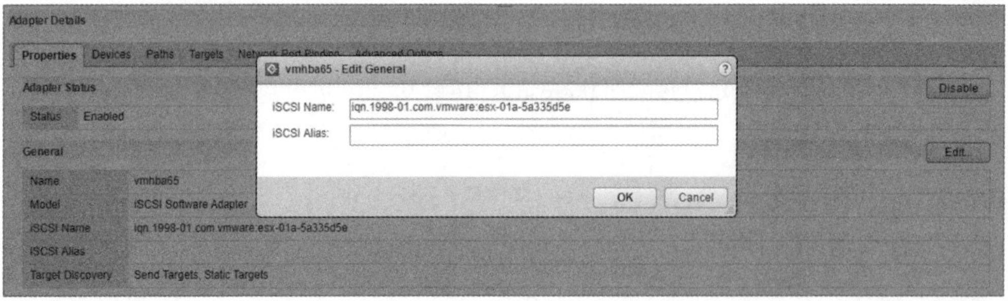

FIGURE 4.6   CHAP options

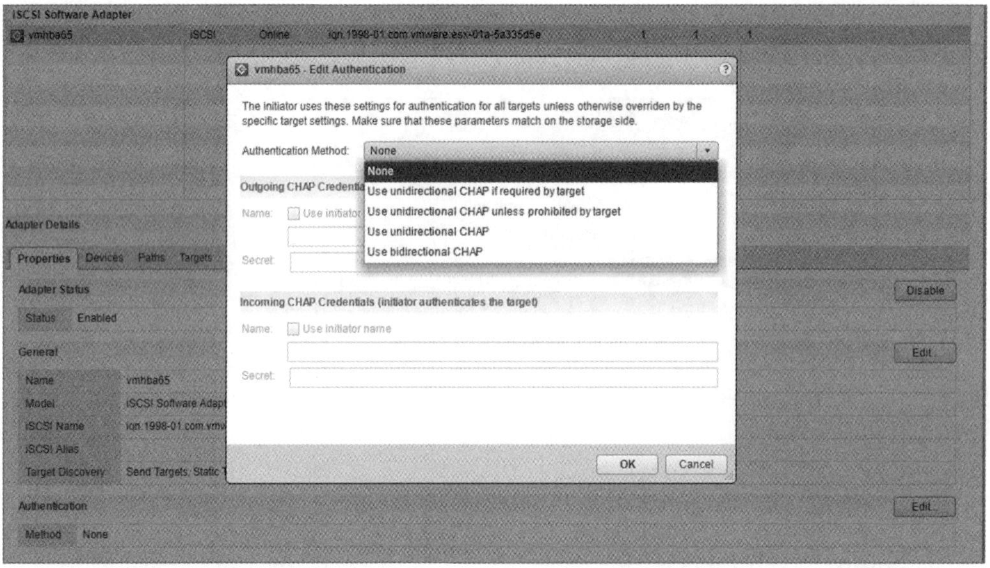

Unidirectional means the array checks the credentials the host sends (Outgoing). *Bidirectional* means the array will check the credentials of the host (Outgoing) and reply with credentials for the host to verify (Incoming). Unidirectional has three versions: use "if required," use "unless prohibited," and simply "use." Refer to your vendor's documentation for which options it supports and which it recommends.

To add an array, open the Targets tab of the iSCSI and click Add with Dynamic Discovery selected (Figure 4.7).

If your array requires CHAP and you did not set the credentials at the adapter level as described earlier, you can add them here by unchecking Inherit Settings from Parent (Figure 4.8).

The difference between Dynamic and Static refers to whether the array dynamically populates the Static page with all the LUNs the host is mapped to or if the LUN information needs to be entered annually. Refer to your array's documentation to see which method is supported.

FIGURE 4.7   Adding an iSCSI target

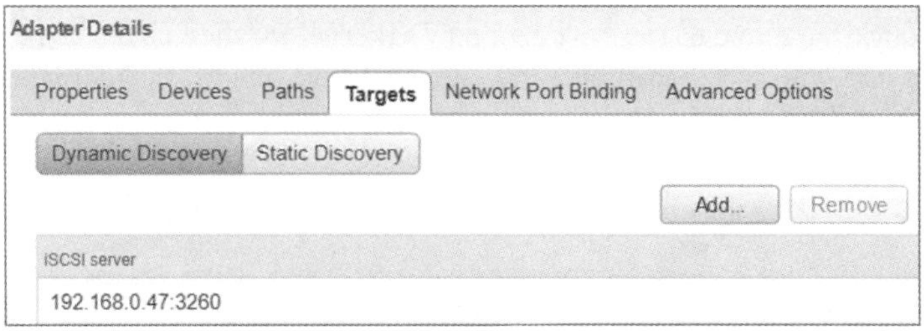

FIGURE 4.8   Setting CHAP on a target server

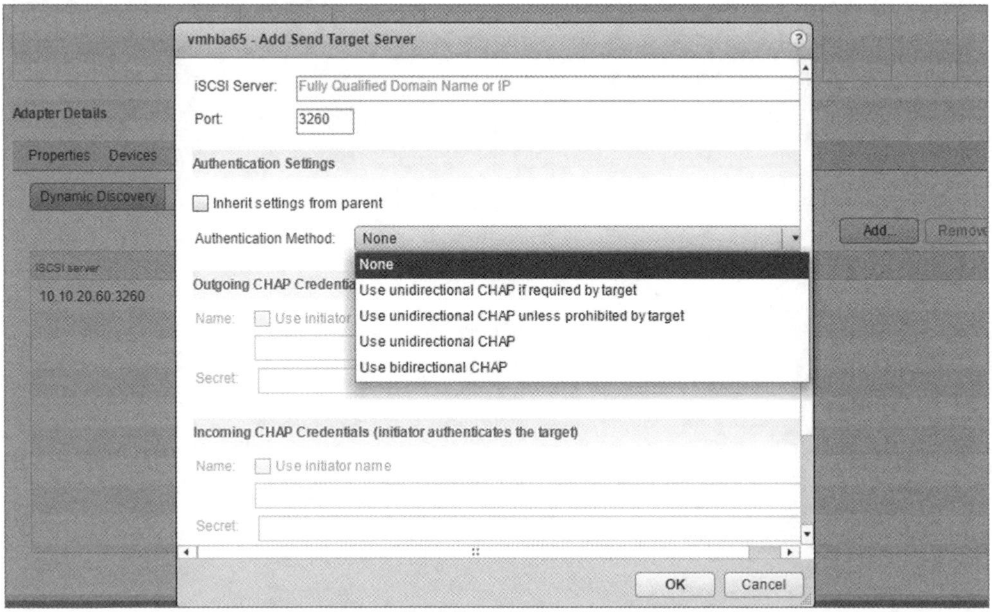

Binding VMkernels to the Software iSCSI Initiator

The final step for software iSCSI configuration is to ensure that there are multiple paths to the storage array. You need to ensure that there are at least two VMkernel adapters and that the adapters are "bound," or configured to use distinct physical NICs. This ensures discrete paths for the storage traffic. Preferably the NICs will connect to different physical switches, but that is not a requirement.

You will need to create two new VMkernel adapters that can be dedicated to iSCSI storage. They can be created on two switches, which guarantees different network cards, or both can be created on a single switch with two NICs. The example shown in Figure 4.9 assumes one switch with two NICs and two VMkernel ports.

The steps to dedicate one NIC per VMkernel will vary depending on if you are using a distributed switch (vDS) or a standard switch (vSS), as the setting is at the port group level.

Port group settings are configured on each host for a vSS as opposed to just once at the switch for vDS.

For a vSS, click the name of the port group (VMkernel *x*), then click the pencil icon to edit the port group, and pick Teaming and Failover. Leave one of the adapters as Active and move the others to Unused (Figure 4.9).

FIGURE 4.9   Getting a standard switch ready for iSCSI binding

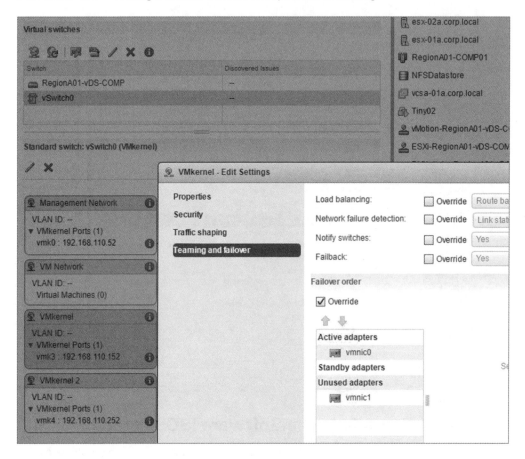

For a vDS, use the Networking view to find and select the port group the VMkernel port is connected to. Also, with vDS you need two different port groups, one for each VMkernel port. In the Configure tab of the port group, pick the Policies menu and then click Edit. On the Teaming and Failover section, leave one Uplink or Link Aggregation Group (LAG) in the Active group and move all others to Unused (Figure 4.10). Link aggregation groups are discussed in further detail in Chapter 3, "Networking in vSphere."

With either vSS or vDS, you need to repeat the process for each VMkernel (vSS) or port group (vDS), picking a different NIC/Uplink/LAG to be active for each.

FIGURE 4.10   Setting up iSCSI binding on a vDS

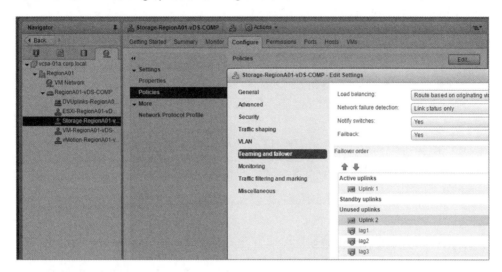

After configuring the VMkernel ports to have distinct network adapters, you are ready to "bind" them to the iSCSI initiator. On each host, select the iSCSI software adapter from the Storage Adapters menu. In the Adapters Details pane, select the Network Port Binding menu and click the green plus sign.

In the Bind wizard, select the appropriate network adapters (Figure 4.11). You will only be able to select adapters with unique NIC/Uplink/LAGs, so if the appropriate adapters don't show up, double-check your work.

FIGURE 4.11   Binding VMkernel adapters

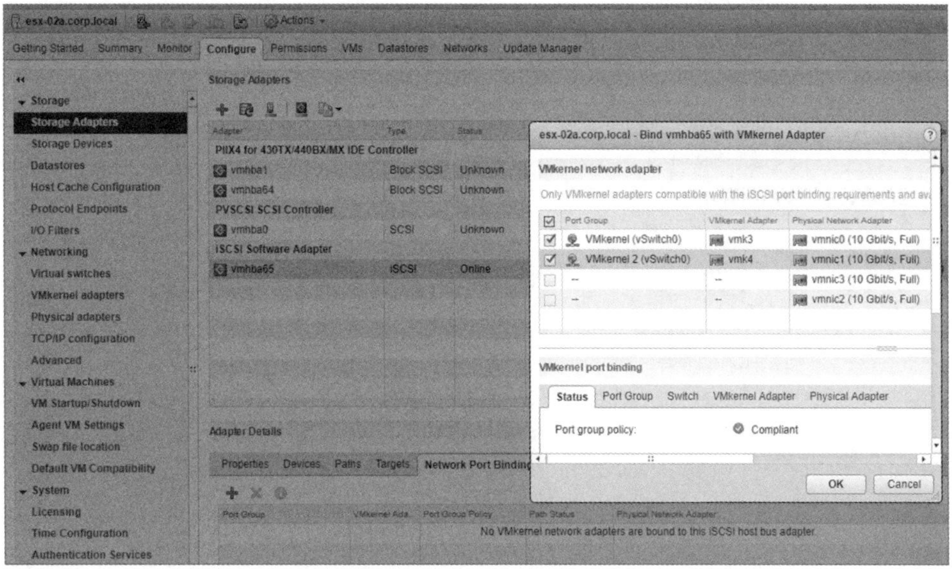

You will then see the bound ports. If there are no datastores created yet, then Path Status will be set to Not Used (Figure 4.12).

FIGURE 4.12 Path status is Not Used when no datastores are in use.

Port Group	VMkernel Ada...	Port Group Policy	Path Status	Physical Network Adapter
VMkernel (vSwitch0)	vmk3	⊘ Compliant	◇ Not used	vmnic0 (10 Gbit/s, Full)
VMkernel 2 (vSwitc...	vmk4	⊘ Compliant	◇ Not used	vmnic1 (10 Gbit/s, Full)

*(Adapter Details — Properties, Devices, Paths, Targets, **Network Port Binding**, Advanced Options)*

Scanning for Changes

After configuring your iSCSI software adapter or making any other changes in the storage configuration, you can use the Scan function to look for new storage devices or new datastores. You can scan either all of the storage adapters (Figure 4.13) or just the adapter you have selected (Figure 4.14). If you have several adapters, just scanning one may save you some time.

FIGURE 4.13 Scan all

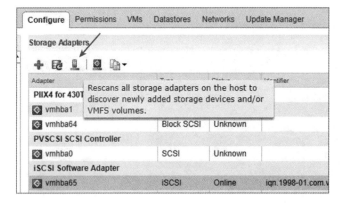

FIGURE 4.14   Scan one

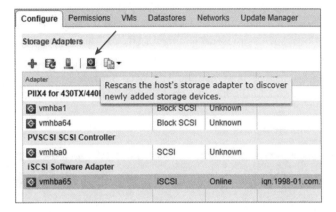

If you decide to scan all adapters, you can also choose to scan for new storage devices, new datastores, or both (Figure 4.15).

FIGURE 4.15   Rescan storage options

Storage Filters

When using storage arrays, not all possible LUNs are presented to your hosts at all times. The vCenter server uses four filters to restrict certain operations to help prevent corruption:

- The VMFS filter prevents adding an existing datastore as an RDM disk for a virtual machine.
- The RDM filter prevents formatting a virtual machine's RDM for VMFS.

- The Same Host and Transports filter filters for incompatibilities such as preventing iSCSI LUNs from displaying when you want to add an extent to a local VMFS volume.

- The Host Rescan filter turns off the automatic rescan when you're performing certain storage operations, such as presenting a new LUN to a host or cluster.

These filters are set at the vCenter server level and do not appear in the settings list by default. If you want to disable them, use the Advanced Settings menu of the Configure tab on the vCenter server and add the filter by name with a value of false (Figure 4.16).

FIGURE 4.16   Modifying storage filters

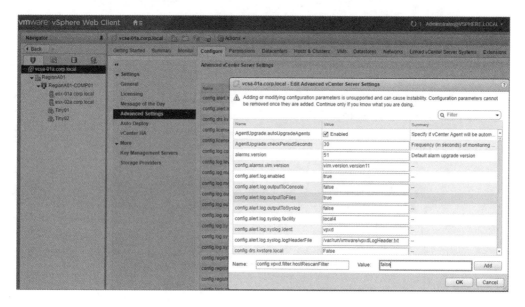

The full names of the filters are as follows:

- `config.vpxd.filter.vmfsFilter`

- `config.vpxd.filter.rdmFilter`

- `config.vpxd.filter.SameHostsAndTransportsFilter`

- `config.vpxd.filter.hostRescanFilter`

It is suggested that you only change these filters after consulting with VMware support.

Thin Provisioning

Many storage arrays offer *thin provisioning* functionality. In Chapter 11, "Administer and Manage vSphere Virtual Machines," we will also cover thin provisioning for virtual machines. In both cases, the full storage quota specified is not allocated up front. The primary benefit to thin provisioning is cost savings through increased efficiency; effectively, your storage is now pay-as-you-go. An environment that typically uses 50 percent of the allocated storage would cut the storage cost in half.

For storage arrays, this means that while a host might see a 500 GB iSCSI LUN and format it as a 500 GB VMFS volume for virtual machine storage, the LUN on the actual array might not take up any space at all on the physical disks of the array until virtual machines start being created on it or copied to it. With thin-provisioned LUNs, you can then overallocate the storage on your array. If you are planning on 500 GB LUNs and project them to only be 50 percent used, you could create three of them on a 1 TB array. While ESXi would be seeing 1.5 TB of total VMFS datastores, your array would only have 750 GB of space actually in use.

With virtual machine thin provisioning, the VMDK (virtual machine disk) "disks" start very small and grow as data is written to them. A thin-provisioned VMDK for the 60 GB C: drive of a new Windows 2016 virtual machine will be 0 KB before the OS is installed and 9 GB after the install (which would include any Windows swap files stored locally). With your VMs taking up less space than they are allocated, you can then overallocate the space in your VMFS volume. On a 100 GB VMFS datastore, you could create eight Windows 10 virtual machines with thin-provisioned 60 GB C: drives. While the operating systems would report 480 GB total (eight 60 GB C: drives), there would only be 72 GB (eight 9 GB VMDK files) used on the datastore for those virtual machines. Keep in mind that this is a simplified example that ignores Virtual Machine Swap (.vswp) files.

If you are thin-provisioning virtual machines and decide to thick-provision critical machines to ensure that they will not run out of space, make sure those machines are monitored for snapshots. Creating a snapshot on a thick-provisioned VMDK effectually makes it thin-provisioned because the snapshot VMDK files are written to as blocks change. If the VMFS volume runs out of space, that thick-provisioned-with-a-snapshot virtual machine will halt along with the thin-provisioned VMs.

The primary detriment to thin provisioning is the increased administrative overhead from monitoring the environment. A virtual machine with thin-provisioned disks on a VMFS datastore that runs out of room will not be able to write changed blocks to its disks. This might crash the OS, or stop applications, databases, and certainly local logs for that VM. Any thin-provisioned virtual machine on that VMFS volume would encounter problems. A thick-provisioned VM would continue to run with no problems, but a thick-provisioned machine that was powered off would not be able to be started if its swap file could not be created. Fortunately, only thin-provisioned VMDKs of running virtual machines on the VMFS that ran out of space would be affected.

For an overallocated storage array that runs out of space, all virtual machines on all thin-provisioned LUNs would be affected. However, running out of space isn't the only concern as some arrays will see significant performance issues when they start to run out of space.

In either scenario, the solution is careful monitoring, usage projections, and a set plan to remediate the issue. For thin-provisioned VMFS volumes, you can ensure that there is sufficient space to expand on the array and expand the VMFS on-the-fly. For storage arrays, you can either ensure that there is extra space or plan ahead to purchase the extra space when needed. This is where accurate projections come into play so you can have plenty of lead time to obtain the storage. Part of monitoring will include tracking anomalies—changes that are outside the norm that could affect your projections.

As with many storage topics, check with your particular vendor for its best practices on thin provisioning, monitoring, and remediating.

Storage Multipathing and Failover

A constant mantra in datacenter reliability is "no single point of failure." The idea is to ensure there is no one "thing," one Achilles' heel, that can take components down. To that end, servers have redundant power supplies, databases have clusters, and storage has *multipathing*. Multiple paths ensure that there is no single point of failure that can prevent access to the storage. Multipathing can also provide a performance boost when more than one of the paths is used.

Multipathing requires software and hardware components. Regardless of the technology, you need at least two physical components on the server (HBA, NIC, etc.), at least two cables leading to a distribution component (network or Fibre Channel switch), two cables to the storage array, and two discrete components on the storage array, often called a head or node or processor, to receive and process the I/O. While the hardware is out of the scope of this guide, make sure you work with your vendor to ensure that there is no single point of failure for the hardware.

 **Real World Scenario**

Redundancy in Duplicate

In my time as a consultant, I have seen more than one company with a dual-head Fibre Channel array and two FC HBAs in each host, with only one switch connecting the hosts to the array. Two of the times I was in a datacenter with a setup like this, they actually owned a second FC switch and had it either in a box or mounted next to the working switch but powered off. Staff at both companies said the second switch was there in case the first switch failed—but they had no idea they could have both switches configured, connected, and running at the same time.

You need to work with your various vendors to ensure that you have redundant paths for all storage and no single point of failure for any mission-critical function. Different vendors will take different paths, so you might need two discrete IP networks for iSCSI or just one with multiple IPs and all redundant hardware. Be sure you understand the different options your vendor has and the pros/cons of all requirements.

Also make sure you have redundant power, sufficient cooling, and physical security and that your critical functions are monitored and logged. The software components on an ESXi host that manages multiple hardware paths are a collection of APIs called the Pluggable Storage Architecture (PSA). The PSA manages multipathing plug-ins such as the Native Multipathing Plug-in (NMP) that is included with ESXi or multipathing plug-ins (MPPs) obtained from a storage vendor. VMware's NMP comprises two parts, the Path Selection Plug-in (PSP) and the Storage Array Type Plug-in (SATP). Your storage vendor might provide a replacement for one of those plug-ins or provide its own MPP to use instead of the NMP.

The Storage Array Type Plug-in provides array-specific commands and management. ESXi ships with a variety of SATPs for specific vendors and models as well as generic SATPs for Asymmetric Logical Unit Access (ALUA) and active-active storage arrays. An active-active array will provide multiple paths to its LUNs at all times, while an ALUA array will report paths through each head but only one head will be active for the LUN at a time.

You must use an SATP that is compatible with your array, and you should check your array documentation for the preferred SATP—whether default or available separately from your vendor. ESXi should choose a working SATP for any array on the Hardware Compatibility List using the claim rules (which we'll discuss later in this section), but changes to your array (such as enabling ALUA) could result in unexpected behavior.

The Path Selection Plug-in chooses which path for storage I/O to take. ESXi ships with PSPs for three path algorithms. The PSPs can be differentiated by what happens before and after a path failure.

Most Recently Used (VMW_PSP_MRU)   The most-recently-used (MRU) plug-in selects one path and uses it until it fails and then chooses another. If the first path comes back up, the PSP will not revert to the old path but will continue to use the most-recently-used path. The MRU plug-in is the default for active-passive arrays.

Fixed (VMW_PSP_FIXED)   The fixed PSP uses one path until it fails and will choose another path if the first fails. With fixed, you can manually set a preferred path, and if that path fails, the PSP will pick another working path. If the preferred path comes back up, the PSP will switch back to using the preferred path. This PSP is usually the default for active-active arrays.

Round Robin (VMW_PSP_RR)   The round robin PSP is the only load-balancing PSP that ships with ESXi. For an active-passive array, it will rotate between active paths and will rotate between available paths for an active-active arrays.

You should work with your array vendor to choose the correct PSP for your array. You can set the PSP per LUN or per SATP—however, setting it per SATP will set it for any array using that SATP.

     Changing the PSP for the SATP will affect only new datastores created—
existing datastores will not receive the policy.

When choosing paths, some SATPs like the included ALUA SATP will report paths as active or inactive and optimized or unoptimized as determined by the array and path. While the PSPs will always use an active path, they will default to using an optimized path if available. This includes the MRU PSP; while it will continue to use its most-recently-used, it will switch from unoptimized to optimized when it can.

The PSP for a datastore can be viewed and changed using the Storage view in the web client. Look for the Connectivity and Multipathing menu under the Configure menu for the datastore you would like to change. Select the host to view and edit the settings for how that datastore is accessed on that host (Figure 4.17).

FIGURE 4.17 Viewing a datastore's PSP for a specific host

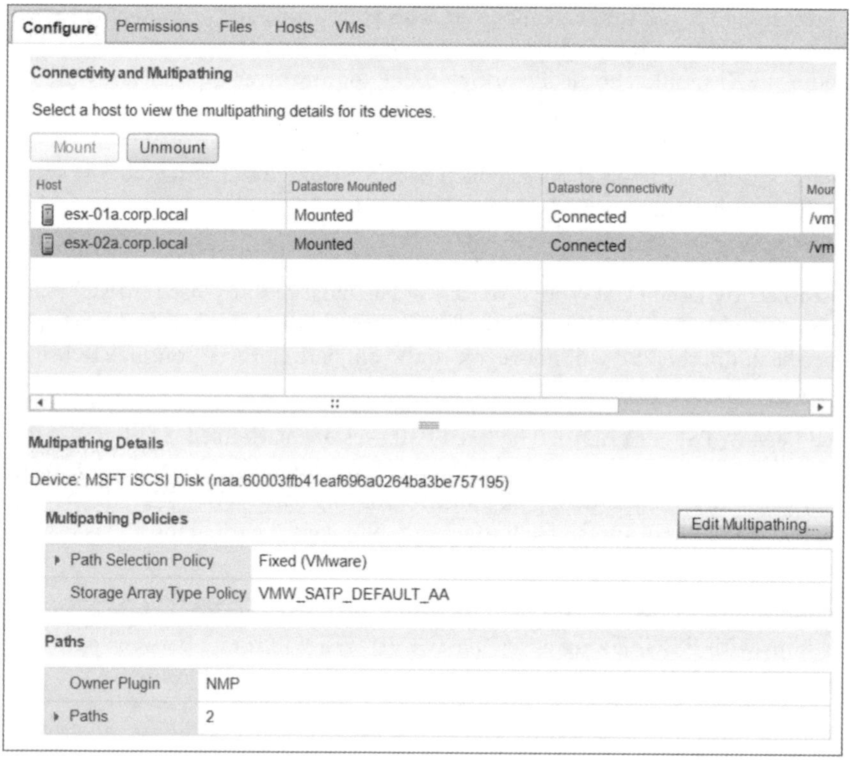

Here you can make a change to the PSP in use for that datastore on that host or set the preferred path if available (Figure 4.18).

You can change the default PSP for a given SATP, which affects all future datastores created on arrays using that SATP; however, that must be done from the vSphere CLI and is outside the scope of the VCP-DCV 6.5 exam.

FIGURE 4.18   Setting the path selection policy

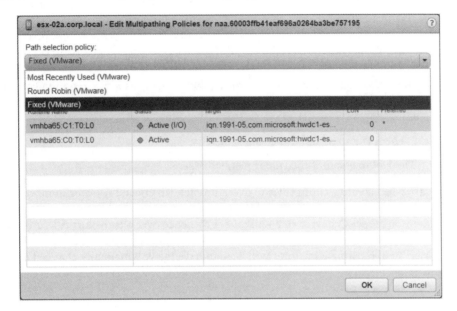

ESXi uses *claim rules* to determine which MPP and/or which SATP is used for a given device. Claim rules are a series of requirements for an array to meet. When new physical storage is detected, the host will run through MPP and SATP claim rules from the lowest-numbered rule to the highest and assign the MPP, SATP, and PSP for the first rules that match. The order of rules is driver rules, vendor/model, then transport. If no match occurs, the NMP will be used with a default SATP and a PSP will be assigned. For iSCSI and FC arrays, the default SATP is VMW_SATP_DEFAULT_AA with the VMW_PSP_FIXED PSP. The default PSP for devices using the VMW_SATP_ALUA SATP is VMW_PSP_MRU.

Best practice is to work with your array vendor to install its preferred MPP, SATP, and PSP on each host and ensure that the correct claim rules are created. You can see the default claim rules in Figure 4.19.

FIGURE 4.19   Default claim rules

```
[root@esx-02a:~] esxcli storage core claimrule list
Rule Class   Rule   Class    Type        Plugin     Matches
----------   -----  -------  ---------   ---------  --------------------------------------
MP              50   runtime  transport   NMP        transport=usb
MP              51   runtime  transport   NMP        transport=sata
MP              52   runtime  transport   NMP        transport=ide
MP              53   runtime  transport   NMP        transport=block
MP              54   runtime  transport   NMP        transport=unknown
MP             101   runtime  vendor      MASK_PATH  vendor=DELL model=Universal Xport
MP             101   file     vendor      MASK_PATH  vendor=DELL model=Universal Xport
MP           65535   runtime  vendor      NMP        vendor=* model=*
[root@esx-02a:~]
```

The following types of claim rules can be used:

Vendor/Model   The device driver returns a string identifying the vendor and model of the array.

Transport   The type of array or data access, including USB, SATA, and BLOCK.

Device ID   You can set a device ID returned by the array as a rule requirement. This is most useful when using the MASK_PATH plug-in to prevent a path or device from being used.

SATP   The SATP to assign if the rule is met.

PSP   The PSP to assign if the rule is met.

Take care when creating claim rules to avoid unintended effects. A lower-numbered rule created with just a vendor name will take precedence over a higher-numbered rule with vendor and model. A device rule will take precedence over a transport rule. Also, a rule assigning a specific PSP will only take effect for datastores created or discovered after the rule is created. Existing datastores will need to have the PSP manually changed on each host.

When a host loses connectivity to a particular storage device, it will try to determine if the device will become available again. A device that should become available again will be flagged as All Paths Down (APD), meaning the host has no access currently. If an array responds on a path but rejects the host or sends SCSI sense codes indicating that the device requested is no longer available, the host will flag the storage device as Permanent Device Loss (PDL).

For a device to be flagged as PDL, the host must receive the codes on all paths for the device.

A host will continue to try to communicate with a datastore flagged as APD for 140 seconds by default. After this period, if the device is not responding, the host will stop non-virtual machine I/O but will not stop VM I/O. VMs can be migrated to a different host that is not experiencing the problem. If a datastore is flagged as PDL, the host will stop all virtual machine I/O and power off the VMs. vSphere HA (if configured) will try to migrate and start the VMs on a host that is not showing PDL for that device, if a host is available.

Storage policies and VASAStorage policies can be created for virtual machines to provide a set of rules to govern the storage that virtual machines are placed on. Storage policies are created and managed under the Policies and Profiles view from the Home menu. These policies can leverage host-based "common rules" or datastore-based rule sets. Common rules pertain to services offered by the host, such as encryption and Storage I/O Control, while datastore rules can include datastore tags, VSAN, and VVol settings. Storage policies will be covered in more detail in the section "Configuring Software-Defined Storage" later in this chapter.

Storage arrays can communicate with vSphere using vSphere APIs for Storage Awareness, or VASA. While vSphere includes some APIs, many storage vendors have additional APIs available. Using VASA, arrays can report on their performance characteristics and health and pass events back to vCenter. In return, vCenter can use VASA to determine if the storage array meets the requirements of a particular storage policy. Storage arrays using VASA are registered as storage providers on the Configure tab of each vCenter Server (Figure 4.20).

FIGURE 4.20   Storage providers

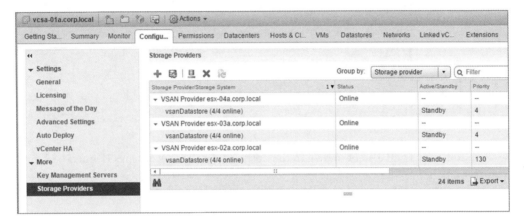

If a path to a device is lost, it will be shown as dead on the host and on the datastore (Figure 4.21 and Figure 4.22).

FIGURE 4.21   Dead path as seen on the host adapter

Adapter Details				
Properties Devices **Paths** Targets Network Port Binding Advanced Options				
Enable Disable				
Runtime Name	Target		LUN	Status
vmhba65:C1:T0:L0	iqn.1991-05.com.microsoft:hwdc1-esxi-02a-target:10.10.50.130:3260		0	◉ Active (I/O)
vmhba65:C0:T0:L0	iqn.1991-05.com.microsoft:hwdc1-esxi-02a-target:10.10.50.130:3260		0	◇ Dead

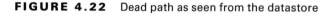

FIGURE 4.22 Dead path as seen from the datastore

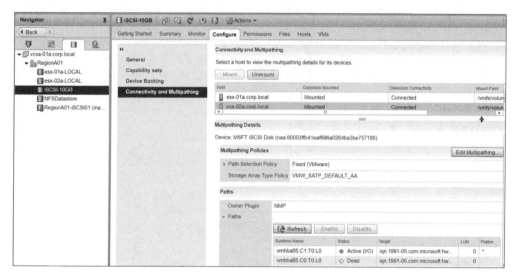

Relevant events will also be shown in the host and datastore event logs (Figure 4.23 and Figure 4.24).

FIGURE 4.23 Path messages in the host events

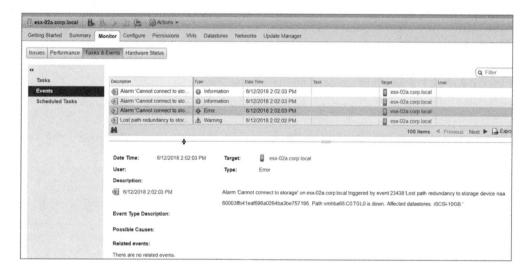

FIGURE 4.24   Path messages in the datacenter events

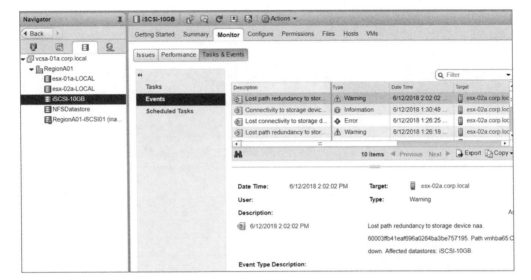

Configuring and Upgrading VMFS and NFS

VMware vSphere starting with version 4.1 offers a set of instructions to offload some operations to the storage array. The Storage APIs - Array Integration (VAAI) depend heavily on support from the storage vendors. While vSphere ships with many VAAI "primitives," or commands, some arrays may provide limited or no support any of the included primitives and might require software installation from the vendor. Some arrays might require a configuration on the array before responding to any primitives also.

The VAAI operations for block storage include Atomic Test & Set (ATS), which is called when a VMFS volume is created and when files need to be locked on the VMFS volume; Clone Blocks/Full Copy/XCOPY, which are called to copy or move data; Thin Provisioning, which instructs hosts to reclaim space on thin-provisioned LUNs; and Block Delete, which allows the SCSI command UNMAP to reclaim space. When VAAI is available and working, the hosts will demonstrate slightly lower CPU load and less storage traffic. For example, without VAAI, copying a VMDK requires each block to be read by the host, then written back to the array. The Full Copy primitive will instruct the array to manage the copy process—and no I/O for the copy will be sent to the host.

The VAAI primitives are enabled by default, but they can be disabled (Figure 4.25) from the client using the Advanced System Settings menu on each host.

FIGURE 4.25   Disabling VAAI primitives

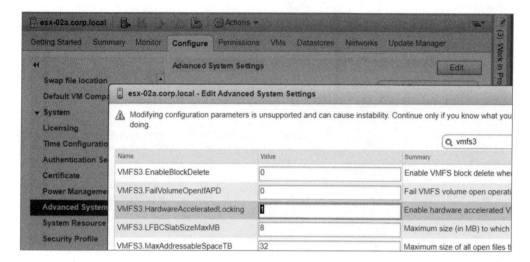

In the Advanced System Settings, you need to set a value of *0* for three options:

- VMFS3.HardwareAcceleratedLocking
- DataMover.HardwareAcceleratedMove
- DataMover.HardwareAcceleratedInit

This should only be performed after talking with VMware and your storage vendor's support teams. There may also be updated primitives available from your storage vendor to be installed on each host.

There are no included primitives for NAS servers, but there is a framework in place to support vendor-supplied primitives, including Full File Clone (similar to the block copy, but NFS servers copy the file instead of block by block), Reserve Space, and a few others. Reserve Space is useful as NFS servers typically store VMs as thin-provisioned on the actual array, regardless of VMDK settings. When the Reserve Space primitive is used, the array will allocate the space for the VMDK at creation.

The NAS primitives need to be obtained from the storage vendor. You should follow their instructions for installing, but typically there will be a vSphere Installation Bundle (VIB) to install on each host using the following command:

```
esxcli --server=server_name software vib install -v|--viburl=URL
```

You cannot typically disable the VAAI VIB, but you can remove it if needed by using this command on the host command line:

```
esxcli --server=server_name software vib remove --vibname=name
```

Once you are connected to an array and have an MPP, SATP, and PSP selected and VAAI in use, you are ready to create a VMFS datastore on one of the LUNs presented by the array. VMFS is VMware's file system, created to allow multiple hosts to have access to the same block storage. Once you format the LUN on one host, rescanning the storage on the other hosts in the cluster will allow them to see and access the new datastore.

Once a VMFS datastore is created, it can be resized in one of two ways, either by adding an additional LUN as an "extent" or by changing the size of the underlying LUN and using an "extend" operation to resize the VMFS datastore. An extend operation is preferred as keeping a 1:1 relationship between LUNs and datastores is simpler. However, if your storage array does not support changing the size of a LUN on-the-fly or has a LUN size limitation, then extents might make more sense. VMFS supports datastores of up to 64 TB. If your storage array only supports 32 TB LUNs, you would need two LUNs to make a maximum-size datastore. If you do use extents, it is important to ensure that the LUNs used are as identical as possible for performance and reliability, and in addition, all LUNs for a datastore must have the same sector format, either 512e or 512n. Note that losing one of the LUNs that is an extent of a datastore will prevent access to the datastore.

 VMware has periodically updated VMFS over the years. New with vSphere 6.5 is the most recent update, VMFS6. Regardless of the naming convention, vSphere 6.0 is not compatible with VMFS6; only vSphere 6.5 and later can use VMFS6. The two previous versions, VMFS5 and VMFS3, are also compatible with vSphere 6.5, but vSphere 6.5 can only create VMFS5 or VMFS6 datastores. VMFS3 can be accessed but a new VMFS3 datastore cannot be created.

The new VMFS6 datastore offers several improvements over VMFS5, including automatic space reclamation (using the VAAI UNMP primitive), SEsparse snapshots for all VMDK files, and support for 4k storage, but only in 512e mode. Upgrading a VMFS5 datastore to VMFS6 consists of creating a new VMFS6 datastore and copying the virtual machines over. There is no in-place upgrade to VMFS6.

If your environment is only vSphere 6.5, create VMFS6 datastores. If you are still using previous versions of vSphere and might have 6.0 or 5.5 ESXi servers accessing the datastore, then create VMFS5 datastores. If you still have VMFS3 datastores in your environment, you should replace them with VMFS6 datastores unless there are 6.0 or 5.5 ESXi servers accessing the datastore; then you should upgrade the VMFS3 datastore to VMFS5.

To upgrade a VMFS3 datastore to VMFS5, take the following steps:

1. Open the upgrade wizard from the Datastore view or by right-clicking the datastore and choosing Upgrade to VMFS-5 (Figure 4.26).

FIGURE 4.26   The Configure tab of a VMFS3 datastore

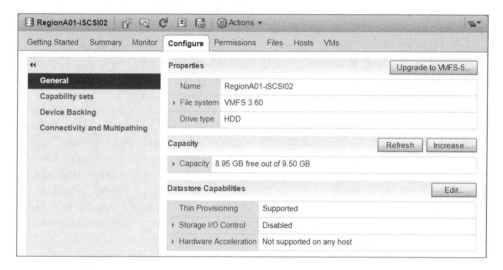

2. Select the datastore to upgrade and click OK (Figure 4.27).

FIGURE 4.27   Upgrading to VMFS5

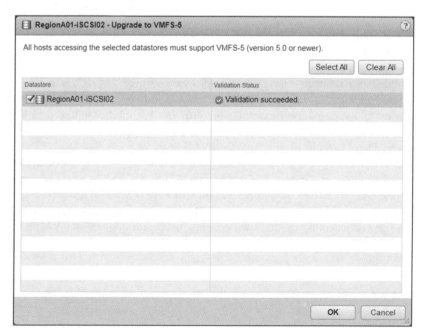

3. Verify that the update was successful on the Summary tab of the datastore (Figure 4.28).

FIGURE 4.28   Verifying VMFS5 conversion

Configuring VMFS Datastores

VMware vSphere allows for the creation of datastore clusters to provide pooling of storage resources. Storage DRS, which allows for VMDK files to be migrated between datastores automatically to balance space and storage I/O, requires the use of datastore clusters. When creating a datastore cluster, you should ensure that the datastores' characteristics are similar. All hosts should have access to all datastores in the cluster, and the performance (latency, spindle speed) and reliability characteristics (RAID, multipathing) should match. While both VMFS and NFS are supported for datastore clusters, you cannot mix and match VMFS and NFS datastores in one cluster.

You can create a datastore cluster from the Datastore view by right-clicking the data center object and choosing Storage\New Datastore Cluster. Please note that Storage DRS is enabled by default, and on the Automation screen you will see that the level is set to manual by default.

As with compute DRS, this means recommendations will be made but no VMDKs will move without user intervention. You can change this to Fully Automated if you would like the VMDKs to be migrated according to the settings and rules you create individual automation levels for: space balance, I/O balance, rule enforcement, policy enforcement, VM evacuation. So with a cluster default of No/Manual, you can set changes to happen automatically when an I/O imbalance is detected on the datastores but only recommend or alert for any other trigger.

The third screen of the New Datastore Cluster wizard lets you set the I/O and space triggers for the automation, which defaults to 80 percent for space used (Figure 4.29). When a datastore hits 80 percent utilization, Storage DRS will either recommend or start moving VMDKs to free up space on the datastore.

The default I/O trigger is 15 ms latency before moves are triggered. This figure is taken from the VMObservedLatency performance value, which measures round-trip I/O. Storage DRS I/O has no direct relationship with Storage I/O Control (SIOC), which will be covered

FIGURE 4.29 Storage DRS default settings

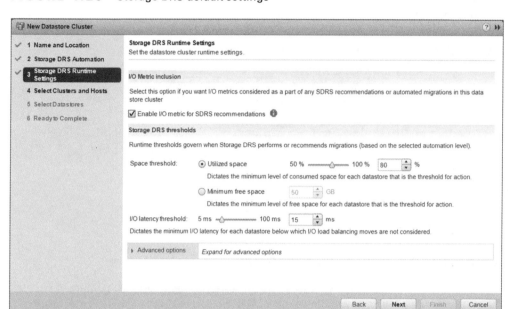

in more detail later. While SIOC is responsible for the individual performance of VMs and how the available performance is distributed between VMs on a datastore, Storage DRS I/O is responsible for maintaining performance balance between datastores in a datastore cluster. Storage DRS latency settings are intended to provide a balance over time; SIOC is there to adjust real-time performance storage I/O of virtual machines.

Once the datastore cluster is created, you can edit these settings from the Storage DRS menu of the Configure tab for the VM, including virtual machine rules. If a virtual machine has multiple VMDKs, Storage DRS will attempt to keep them together. However, you can use the VM Overrides to keep a VM's VMDKs together or apart. You can also disable Storage DRS for a VM.

Under the Rules menu, you can create VMDK anti-affinity rules to keep two VMDKs from being stored on the same datastore (such as the data drives for two clustered database servers) or VM anti-affinity rules to prevent virtual machines from being placed on the same datastore.

Datastore clusters also enable the ability for datastores to be place in maintenance mode, which can be performed from the actions menu of the datastore (Figure 4.30). Maintenance mode can be used when replacing a datastore, changing the multipathing, or performing any other potentially disruptive maintenance. When a datastore is placed in maintenance mode, Storage DRS can automatically move affected VMs and VMDKs off the datastore using the same rules or the files can be manually moved. All registered VMs and VMDKs must be moved off the datastore before it will enter maintenance mode.

FIGURE 4.30   Placing a datastore in maintenance mode

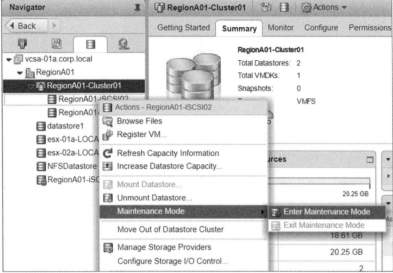

Create and configure a new datastore cluster.

Requires two identical LUNs and a VM on one of them.

1. Connect to the host using the vSphere web client and open the Datastore view.

2. Create a datastore cluster from the Datastore view by right-clicking the data center object and choosing Storage ➢ New Datastore Cluster.

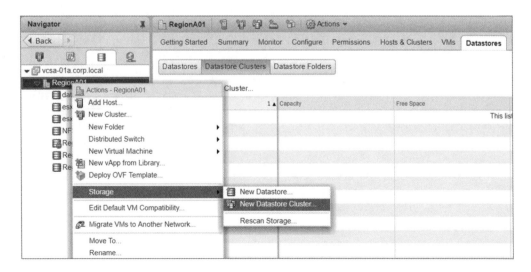

EXERCISE 4.3 *(continued)*

3. Set a name for the new datastore cluster and leave Storage DRS On.

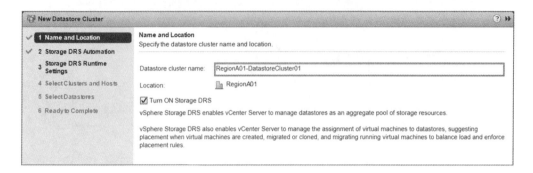

4. Leave Storage DRS set for manual mode.

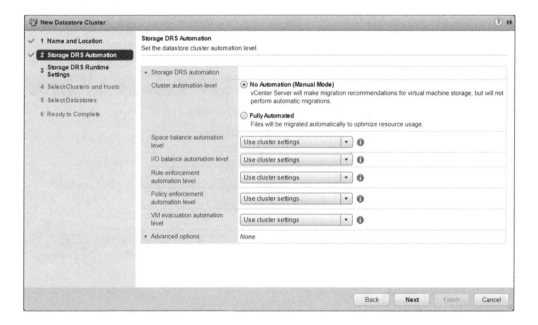

5. The third screen of the New Datastore Cluster wizard lets you set the I/O and space triggers for the automation. Set these to 90% and 10 ms.

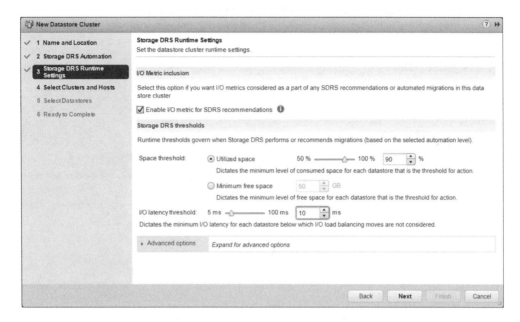

6. Select the cluster your hosts are in.

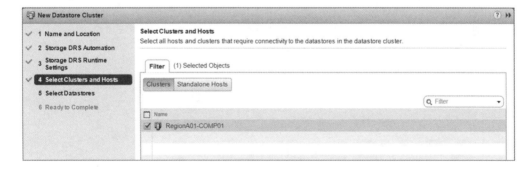

7. Pick your two identical datastores to add to the cluster. Click Next and then Finish.

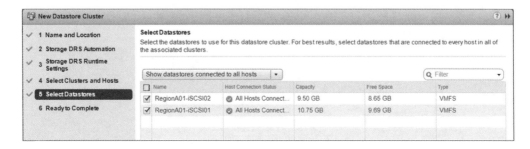

8. Edit the new cluster and set the rule enforcement automation level to Fully Automated. This will automatically move VMs when a rule is triggered.

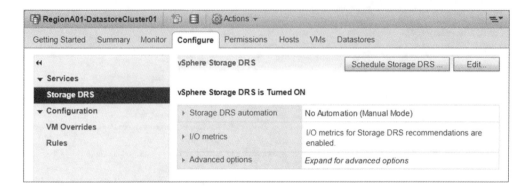

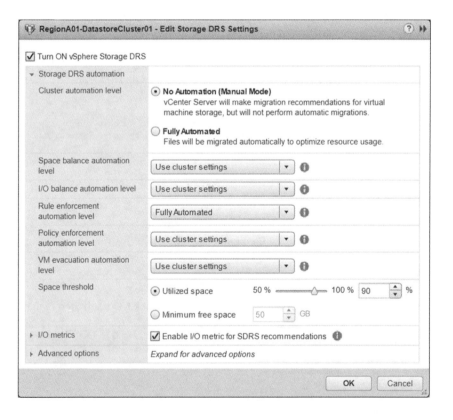

9. Add a VM override for one of the virtual machines, choosing the Keep VMDKs Together option. This will allow Storage DRS to move one VMDK at a time for that virtual machine.

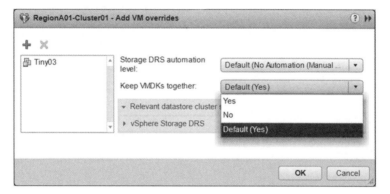

10. Set one of the datastores of the cluster to Maintenance Mode.

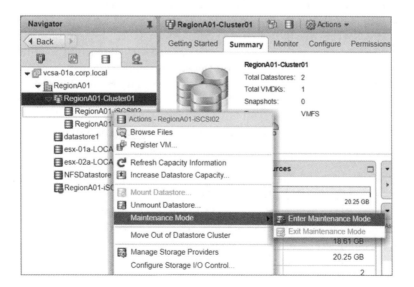

11. Apply the recommendations.

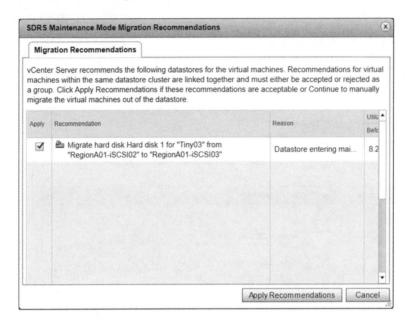

Raw Device Mapping and Bus Sharing

Host storage is not the only use for LUNs; virtual machines can be provided direct access to LUNs also using raw device mapping (RDM). RDMs are used for some clustering solutions such as MSCS where one of the cluster nodes will be either physical or on a separate host. RDMs are also used where tools or applications in a virtual machine require direct access to the underlying storage, such as taking advantage of array-based snapshots.

When an RDM is attached to a virtual machine, the vCenter storage filters prevent that LUN from being available to hosts for a VMFS datastore. The RDM is dedicated to the virtual machine it is assigned to—but all hosts the virtual machine can run on still need access to the LUN so that the virtual machine can migrate to (vMotion) or restart on (HA) different hosts. There are two modes for RDMs to use: physical mode, where SCSI commands from the VM are passed directly to the storage, and virtual mode, which provides functionality such as vSphere snapshots and advanced file locking. Either mode requires a VMFS volume to hold a mapping file for the RDM.

When adding an RDM, you can change the location of the mapping file, which is useful if the virtual machine is on an NFS datastore. The sharing options (Figure 4.31) will enable or disable multi-writer, or simultaneous write protection. This protects against data corruption by default by blocking virtual machines from opening and editing the same file. Change this setting if directed to by your application vendor.

FIGURE 4.31 VMDK sharing options

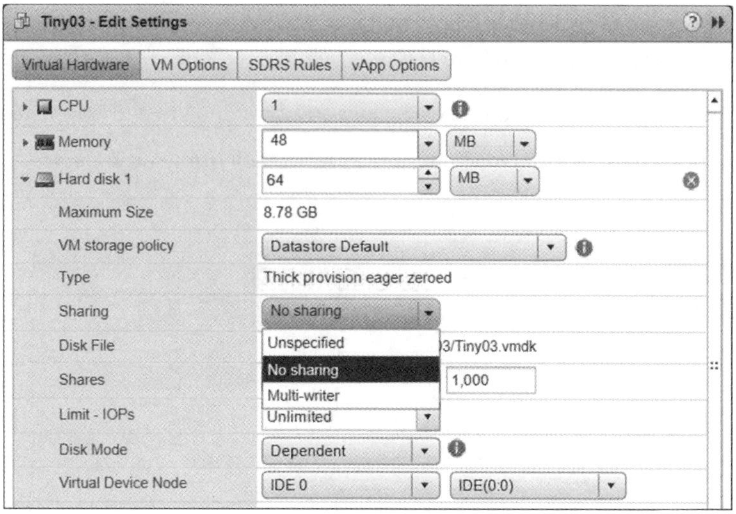

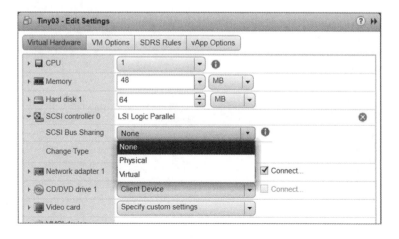

Virtual machines can also have access to the same VMDK files using SCSI Bus Sharing. You can enable or prohibit multiple virtual machines writing to the same VMDK by combining VMDK sharing and SCSI Bus Sharing options.

SCSI Bus Sharing has two options (Figure 4.32): Virtual, where VMs must reside on the same host to share VMDKs, and Physical, where VMs on different hosts can share VMDKs. Each virtual machine needing to access the same VMDK needs the same Bus Sharing and VMDK sharing options. Make sure the shared VMDK is Thick Provisioned Eager Zeroed, and please note that snapshots are not supported for VMs configured for Bus Sharing. If you use Bus Sharing with RDMs for Windows Server Failover Clustering solutions, you will be able to vMotion clustered VMs.

FIGURE 4.32 Setting the SCSI Bus Sharing property

EXERCISE 4.4

Add an RDM to a virtual machine.

Requires a virtual machine and an unused LUN.

1. Connect to vCenter using the vSphere web client and open the VM and Templates view.

2. Open the settings of the virtual machine, select RDM Disk from "New Device," and click Add.

3. Select the correct LUN from the list.

4. Set the RDM to use virtual mode.

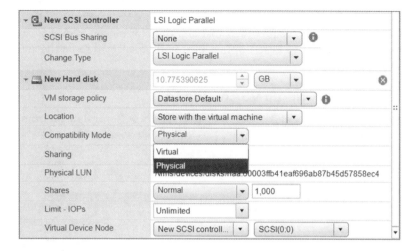

5. Click OK to complete.

Configuring Software-Defined Storage

A key component of VMware's Software Defined Data Center (SDDC) vision is virtualized storage, which for vSphere takes the forms of virtual storage area network (vSAN) and Virtual Volumes (VVols). VMware's vSAN technology uses local SSD and (optionally) HDD storage to create a distributed storage pool available to all the hosts in a cluster. VVols is a software layer to abstract existing physical arrays and create a framework for ESXi hosts that is optimized for virtual workloads. While vSAN is VMware software to aggregate local host storage, VVols is a framework that requires support from the array vendor to implement. Both solutions provide storage profiles to allow virtual machines a set of rules to determine where they should be placed.

Virtual Storage Area Network

For a working vSAN cluster, you need at least three ESXi hosts managed by vCenter with dedicated local storage consisting of at least one SSD and one HDD, or two SSD drives. Each host needs to have a VMkernel adapter enabled for Virtual SAN traffic, and vSAN needs to be licensed. The licenses for vSAN are purchased separately from vSphere, and there are currently five versions (Standard, Advanced, Enterprise, ROBO Std, ROBO, Adv). The important differences between the license levels is that while all levels offer all-flash storage capabilities, Advanced adds deduplication and compression and RAID-5/6 erasure coding, and Enterprise adds stretched clusters and data at rest encryption.

Each host in the vSAN cluster will have a storage provider created for it and added to vCenter. This allows vCenter to communicate with the vSAN components, receive the capabilities of the datastore, and report virtual machine requirements. However, vCenter will only use one storage provider/host at a time for a given vSAN cluster. If something happens to the active host, another host will be selected to be the active storage provider.

Creating and Configuring a vSAN Cluster

You create a vSAN cluster by configuring it under the vSAN ➢ General menu from the Configure tab of the cluster (Figure 4.33).

FIGURE 4.33 Creating a vSAN datastore on a cluster

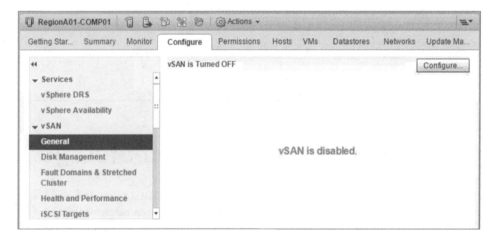

The first screen of the Configure vSAN wizard (Figure 4.34) has you configure the basic capabilities of the vSAN, including Services (Deduplication and Compression, and Encryption) and Fault Domains and Stretched Cluster. You can also configure a two-host vSAN cluster, which is intended for remote offices; however, it actually still requires three hosts—two hosts contributing storage at the remote office and a witness host at the main site.

The second screen of the wizard (Figure 4.35) lets you check the hosts in the cluster to verify that they have VMkernel ports configured for vSAN traffic.

Once the network settings have been verified, you can set the local hosts disks to use for vSAN. The Claim Disks screen (the third one of the wizard) will try to allocate disks by speed (SSD/HDD) and size. Hosts will need one SSD claimed for cache and at least one disk (SSD or HDD) claimed for capacity. Once claimed, the drives will not be available for anything else—which means you can't boot from a disk used for vSAN. Disks need to be identified by the host as SSD to be used for cache and as local to be used by vSAN at all.

FIGURE 4.34   Configuring vSAN capabilities

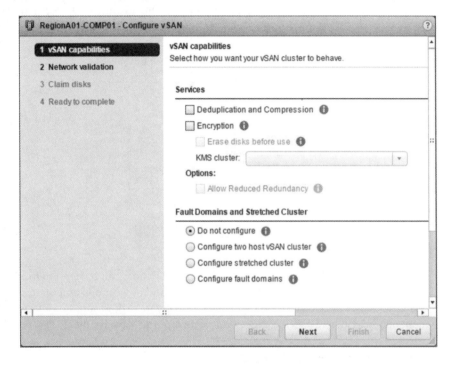

FIGURE 4.35   vSAN network validation

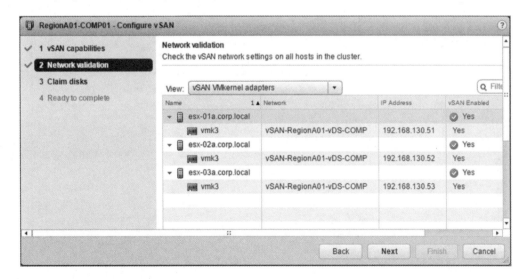

If a disk is not being properly identified as local or SDD (or both), you can use the All Actions menu for that disk in the Storage Devices menu of the host to set the local and/or SSD flags it as local or SSD (Figure 4.36).

FIGURE 4.36 Changing the local and/or SDD flags for a datastore

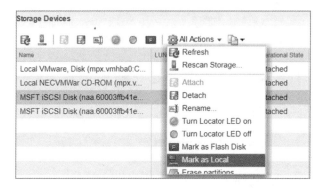

Host disks claimed by vSAN are formed into groups. Each host can have up to five disk groups, and each group must have one SSD disk for cache and at least one and up to seven capacity disks. You have the option of allowing vSAN to create disk groups automatically, or you can manually associate specific cache disks with specific capacity disks (Figure 4.37).

FIGURE 4.37 Claiming disks for the vSAN cluster

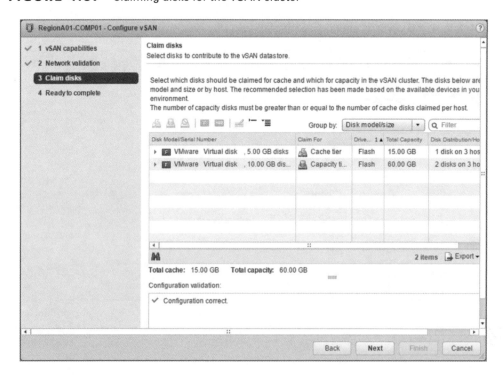

After claiming disks, make sure all settings are correct (Figure 4.38) before clicking Finish.

FIGURE 4.38   Ready to complete the vSAN configuration

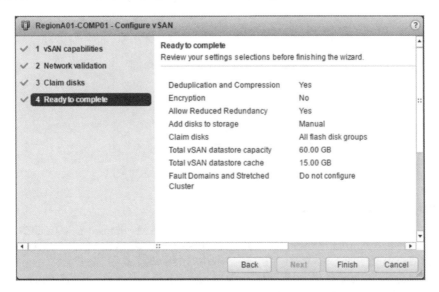

After your vSAN cluster is configured, you can use the Configuration Assist tab (Figure 4.39), which is also available from the Configure tab of the cluster, to check the configuration, display warnings, and troubleshoot issues. Configuration Assist even includes the ability to change host networking and claim disks from within the assistant.

FIGURE 4.39   Configuration Assist

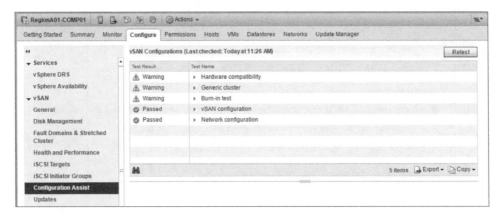

You can configure fault domains (Figure 4.40) to define blade chassis, rack boundaries, or any other grouping of hosts. Hosts in the same fault domain will not receive duplicate data, so loss of the entire fault domain will not affect integrity.

FIGURE 4.40 VSAN fault domain setup

Fault Domains
Configuration can tolerate maximum
1 fault domain failures
Fault Domain/Host
Rack1 (2 hosts)
esx-01a.corp.local
esx-04a.corp.local
Rack 3 (2 hosts)
esx-03a.corp.local
esx-06a.corp.local
Rack 2 (2 hosts)
esx-02a.corp.local
esx-05a.corp.local

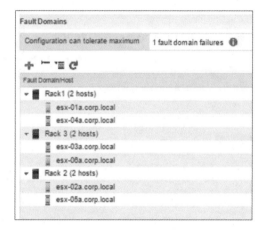

Creating an iSCSI Target from vSAN

A new feature of vSAN is the ability to present part of the vSAN datastore as an iSCSI target to physical servers. Similar to other iSCSI target services, you set aside part of the vSAN storage to serve as a LUN, then provide access to the LUN via one of the vSAN cluster hosts. The LUN receives a storage policy just like a VM and can use all of the vSAN capabilities.

During configuration (Figure 4.41), you choose the VMkernel port that will be responding to iSCSI requests. You can use an existing VMkernel adapter, but a better practice would be creating a new, dedicated VMkernel with a VLAN dedicated to iSCSI.

FIGURE 4.41 Enable vSAN iSCSI target

RegionA01-COMP01 - Edit vSAN iSCSI Target Service
Enable vSAN iSCSI target service
Select a default network to handle the iSCSI traffic. You can override this setting per target.
Default iSCSI network:
vmk3
Default TCP port:
3260
Default authentication:
None
When you enable iSCSI target service, vSAN creates a home object that stores metadata for iSCSI target service (similar to the VM Home object of a virtual machine). The vSAN iSCSI home object contains critical vSAN iSCSI configurations, and therefore the highest primary level of failures to tolerate (storage policy) is strongly recommended to be applied to the home object. The space and the storage IO used by this object is minimal, so a higher level of failures to tolerate doesn't cause a significant cluster cost.
Storage policy for the home object:
vSAN Default Storage Policy
OK
Cancel

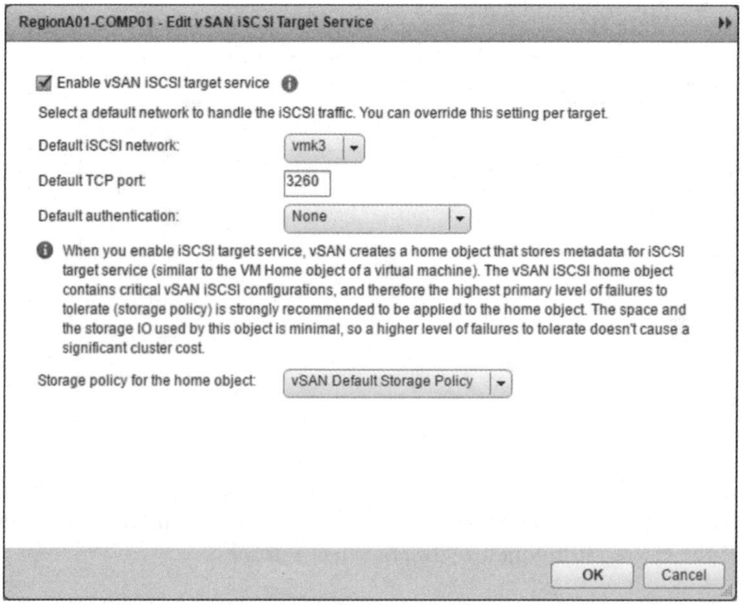

To provide multipath access, use the IP address of multiple vSAN hosts when configuring the initiator. CHAP support is provided for authentication if needed. You will need to create an initiator group containing the IQN of the iSCSI initiators and associate the initiator group with the LUN it will be accessing.

Important iSCSI Target Terminology

iSCSI target service   Provides the ability for a vSAN cluster to serve part of its data as a LUN to iSCSI initiators on physical servers

iSCSI initiator   Client of an iSCSI target

initiator group   List of server IQNs that can access the iSCSI target service

iSCSI target   Part of vSAN datastore presented as an iSCSI LUN

Monitoring vSAN

Monitoring of vSAN can be accomplished from the Monitor tab of the vSAN cluster. Monitoring options include Health, Capacity, Resyncing Components, Virtual Objects, and Physical Disks. There are also proactive tests you can run on your vSAN cluster.

Health   Similar to Configuration Assist, this reports the results of the Health Service, which periodically runs tests on the vSAN cluster.

Capacity   The capacity overview (Figure 4.42) shows the total amount of space used on the drive and the overhead consumed. You can also see deduplication and compression statistics, including overhead, saved percentage, and ratio.

FIGURE 4.42   vSAN capacity overview

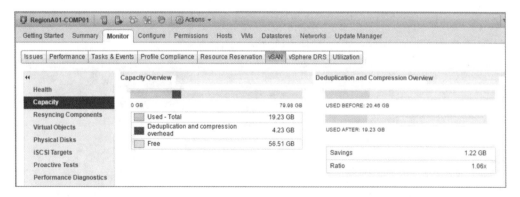

The capacity screen will also display object information about the datastore by object type or data type, including total storage used and percentage of the total by type (Figure 4.43).

FIGURE 4.43 vSAN capacity by object

Used Capacity Breakdown

Breakdown of the used capacity before it was deduplicated and compressed.

Group by: [Object types ▾]

0 GB		21.28 GB
■ Virtual disks		72.00 MB (0%)
■ VM home objects		1.45 GB (7%)
■ Swap objects		16.38 GB (77%)
□ Performance management objects		724.00 MB (3%)
■ File system overhead		1.64 GB (8%)
■ Checksum overhead		1.03 GB (5%)

Resynching Components   Displays the progress of cluster changes, including changing the storage policy used by a virtual machine, hosts going into maintenance mode, and recovering a host from a failure.

Virtual Objects   Lets you view virtual machines on the vSAN and details of their vSAN usage.

Physical Disks   Lets you view statistics and properties of the physical disks in use by the vSAN.

The Performance tab of the vSAN cluster reports the results of the Virtual SAN performance service. This service is disabled by default and can be enabled using the Health and Performance menu of the Configure tab (Figure 4.44). With the service enabled, you can report on IOPS (input/output operations per second), throughput, and latency for the cluster, virtual machines, and hosts.

FIGURE 4.44 Enabling the vSAN performance service

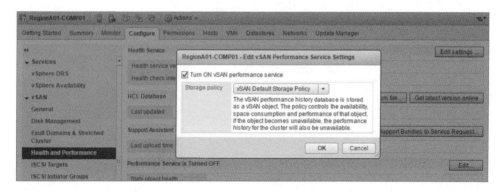

For advanced performance analysis and monitoring of vSAN, you can use Ruby vSphere Console (RVC) on your vCenter server, which enables you to utilize the VMware Virtual SAN Observer. The Observer provides advanced details about disk groups, CPU, and memory usage. When working with VMware technical support, you can export a log bundle from vSAN Observer using the following on a single line.

```
vsan.observer <cluster> --run-webserver --force
        --generate-html-bundle /tmp --interval 30 --max-runtime 1
```

Or you can create a full raw statistics bundle using

```
vsan.observer <cluster> --filename /tmp/vsan_observer_out.json
```

Virtual Volumes

VMware's Virtual Volumes implementation requires one host managed by vCenter, a storage array or NAS that is compatible with Virtual Volumes, and the storage vendor's VASA storage provider added to vCenter. After the array is configured to present a storage container to the host, the ESXi host can then create a Virtual Volumes datastore for that storage container (Figure 4.45).

FIGURE 4.45   Creating a Virtual Volumes datastore

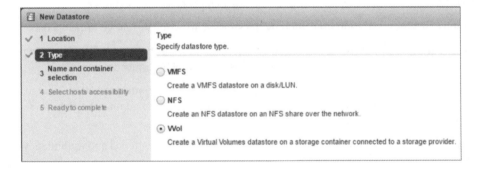

The storage presented is not formatted with VMFS; rather data is stored directly on the storage array.

The storage container can be configured to present a variety of features and performance tiers that can be grouped by Virtual Volumes into different storage profiles. Using Storage Policy-Based Management (SPBM), virtual machines can be configured to consume the storage resources they need.

When a virtual machine is created on or migrated to a VVol datastore, there are multiple VVols created:

- A *Config VVol* will hold the VMX (.vmx) file, log files, and virtual disk descriptor file.
- A *Data VVol* will be created for each virtual disk (the -flat file).

- A *SWAP VVol* will be created for the VM swap file at power on.

- If the VM has snapshots, there will be a *Data VVol* for each snapshot VMDK.

- If the VM has snapshots, there will be a *Mem-VVol* for each memory snapshot.

Snapshots for virtual machines stored on a VVol datastore are still created by the vSphere client, but the snapshots are managed by the storage provider, not by the host running the virtual machine.

These VVols are just constructs for the storage server or array to use when storing those file types; a VVol is not an object you can view in the vSphere GUI. Virtual machines still see the VMDK as a local SCSI disk; there is no change from the virtual machine's point of view. Similarly, the vSphere UI, host CLI, and PowerCLI all see the virtual machine and its files the same way as a virtual machine stored on any other datastore type. The key differences of how the files are stored are all handled by the storage array or storage server.

Key VVols Terminology

VASA storage provider   The API mechanism for vSphere and the storage array to manage the storage consumption for Virtual Volumes. vSphere 6.5 introduced support for VASA 3.0, which includes data protection and disaster recovery capabilities.

storage container   Storage presented by the storage array for Virtual Volumes usage.

Virtual Volumes datastore   Datastore framework used by vSphere to access the storage container. There is a 1:1 ratio of storage container to Virtual Volumes datastore.

protocol endpoint   The Virtual Volumes equivalent of mount points and LUNs. Created on a storage array, protocol endpoints provide an access point to administer paths and policies from the host to the storage system.

storage profile   Collection of storage capabilities such as performance and redundancy used to allocate virtual machines the storage they need.

Virtual volumes are not compatible with RDMs, and vSAN cannot provide a storage container for Virtual Volumes. While a single array can provide block and NFS storage containers, one storage container cannot span array types. For instance, you cannot have NFS and iSCSI storage in the same storage container.

To create a VVol datastore, you need to be sure your storage array has presented a storage container and has protocol endpoints configured. You also need to deploy the vendor's VASA storage provider in vCenter. See the storage vendor's documentation for more information.

EXERCISE 4.5

Configure VVols provider.

Requires an array or server that supports Virtual Volumes. If you're using an array, the LUNs must be available on the hosts.

1. Connect to vCenter using the vSphere web client, open the Host and Cluster view, and click the vCenter server.

2. Click the Configure tab, select Storage Providers, and click the green plus sign. Enter the information for your new storage device.

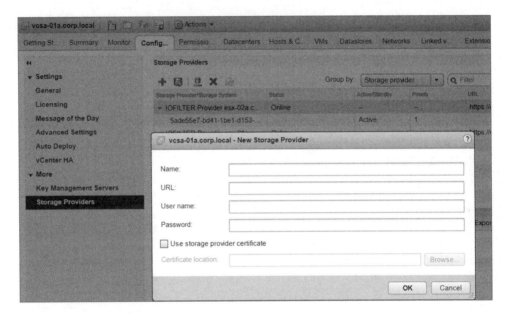

3. Once the provider is added, you can create VVol datastores for the storage containers presented. Use the cluster's Actions menu to add a datastore.

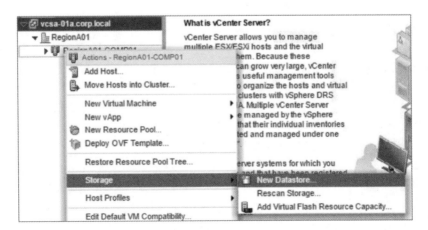

EXERCISE 4.5 *(continued)*

4. Choose VVol.

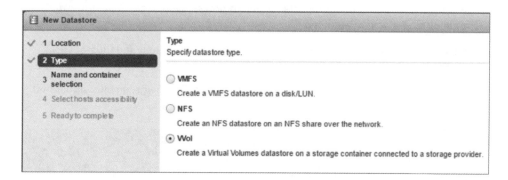

5. Name the new datastore and choose the correct container.

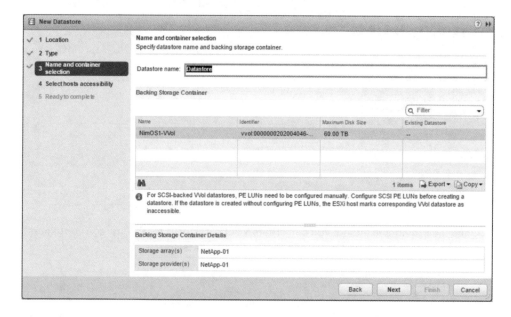

6. Choose the hosts that will access the datastore. You should include all the hosts in a cluster to ensure the most flexible virtual machine placement.

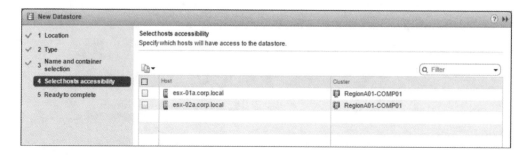

7. The newly created VVol datastore will appear in any of the relevant datastore lists
    with a type of VVol.

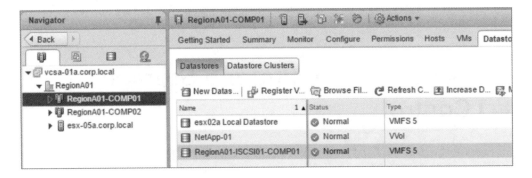

Storage Policy–Based Management

Storage Policy–Based Management (SBPM) is a method of providing storage capabilities
to virtual machines. By creating storage policies that link to different capabilities of the
underlying storage, administrators can then attach the storage policies to virtual machines,
ensuring that those VMs have the capabilities they need.

Storage policies can include tags applied to datastores, vSAN capabilities, configuration
settings, VVol storage capabilities, and other capabilities as passed along by VASA storage
providers. Datastore tags are useful for traditional storage that does not interact deeply
with vSphere. As datastores are created, they can be tagged with RAID level, relative
performance level, or replication level. Storage policies can then be created to leverage
those features.

If you create a tagging system with performance levels of Gold for SSD-backed LUNs,
Silver for 10K SCSI-backed LUNs, and Bronze for 5400RPM HDDs and further tag any
LUNs replicated offsite as Replicated, you can then create storage policies to reflect those
capabilities. You might have a storage policy of Fast, Replicated for any datastore tagged
with Gold, and Replicated. If you then attach that storage policy to a virtual machine,
vSphere will ensure that virtual machine disks always reside on datastores with the appropriate tags and will alert if the VM is moved to an inappropriate datastore.

Storage policies used with vSAN and Virtual Volumes capabilities do not depend on
a vSphere administrator to manually assign and maintain the correct tags to a datastore.
Rather, the capabilities are supplied using Storage API calls and available to choose when
creating policies.

Tag-based storage policy rules are created by virtualization administrators to differentiate datastores, and VVol storage policy rules pull available capabilities from the storage array. However, vSAN-based storage policy rules create the capabilities when the storage policies are applied to virtual machines.

Enabling and Configuring Storage I/O Control

Storage I/O Control (SIOC) provides mechanisms to decide how storage I/O is allocated to virtual machine VMDKs, especially in times of contention. Storage I/O Control can be used to limit the IOPs available to specific VMDKs at all times and to prioritize VMDKs when resources are scarce. Without SIOC, one machine can grab an excessive amount of IOPs and starve any other VMDK on the datastore. With SIOC enabled (and not other settings), just prior to the IOPs maxing out, the virtual machines on the datastore would begin receiving equal access to the storage, reducing the impact of any "noisy neighbor."

Storage I/O Control is disabled by default and needs to be enabled for each datastore you would like to use it on using the Configure Storage I/O Control wizard (Figure 4.46). The wizard can be launched with the Edit button under Datastore Capabilities in the General section of the Configure tab of the datastore.

FIGURE 4.46 Enabling Storage I/O Control

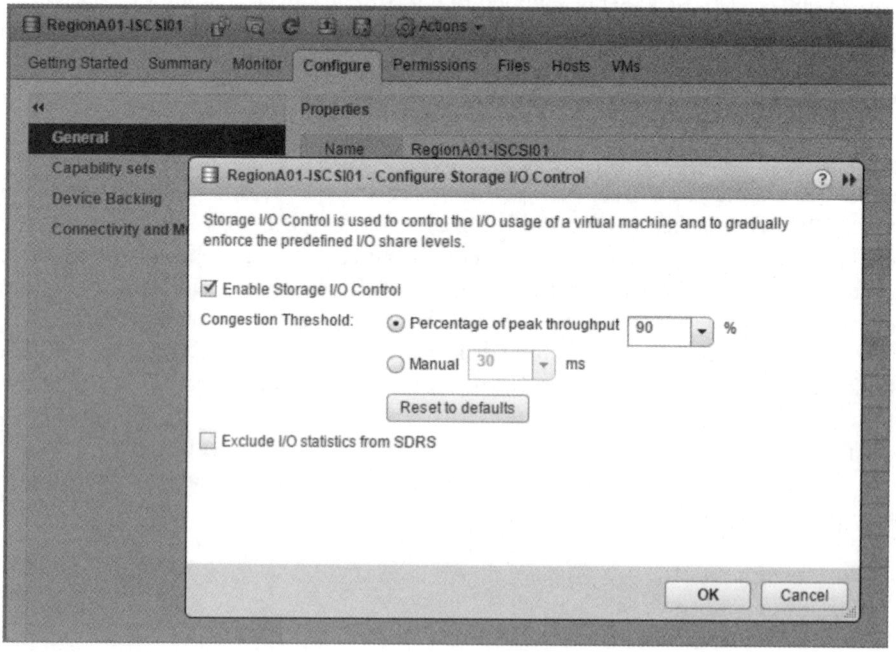

![Screenshot of the Configure Storage I/O Control dialog for RegionA01-ISCSI01. The dialog reads: "Storage I/O Control is used to control the I/O usage of a virtual machine and to gradually enforce the predefined I/O share levels." A checked checkbox labeled "Enable Storage I/O Control" is shown. Congestion Threshold options: selected radio "Percentage of peak throughput" set to 90 %, unselected radio "Manual" set to 30 ms, a "Reset to defaults" button, and an unchecked "Exclude I/O statistics from SDRS" checkbox. OK and Cancel buttons at the bottom.]

SIOC defaults to the Congestion Threshold triggering at 90 percent of peak throughput, or you can choose to set a millisecond threshold (which defaults to 30 ms). When the congestion threshold is reached, the datastore will evenly distribute storage I/O between the VMDKs on it, unless the default shares for the VMDK are modified. With the I/O being balanced between VMDKs and not virtual machines, a VM with two VMDKs on the same datastore will get twice the I/O of a single-VMDK VM.

When you enable Storage I/O Control, you have the option of excluding I/O statistics from Storage DRS (SDRS). This is useful if you have SDRS configured but your storage array automatically adjusts VMs or LUNs for performance and you would like the stats used for SIOC for performance throttling but not for virtual machine placement.

If you are using SDRS for VM relocation for performance and SIOC, you should consider how they work together. Storage DRS is intended to work over a longer period of time, gradually ensuring a balance of I/O, while SIOC is intended for short-term fixes. We would suggest setting the Storage DRS performance limit below that of SIOC so that gradual imbalances are corrected before contention is reached and SIOC steps in.

Using the setting of the VMs, you can adjust the shares and set an IOPs limit for each VMDK (Figure 4.47). These settings only take effect when the VMDK is on a datastore with Storage I/O enabled, and the shares setting will only take effect when the congestion threshold is reached.

FIGURE 4.47   Setting the shares and limits for a VMDK

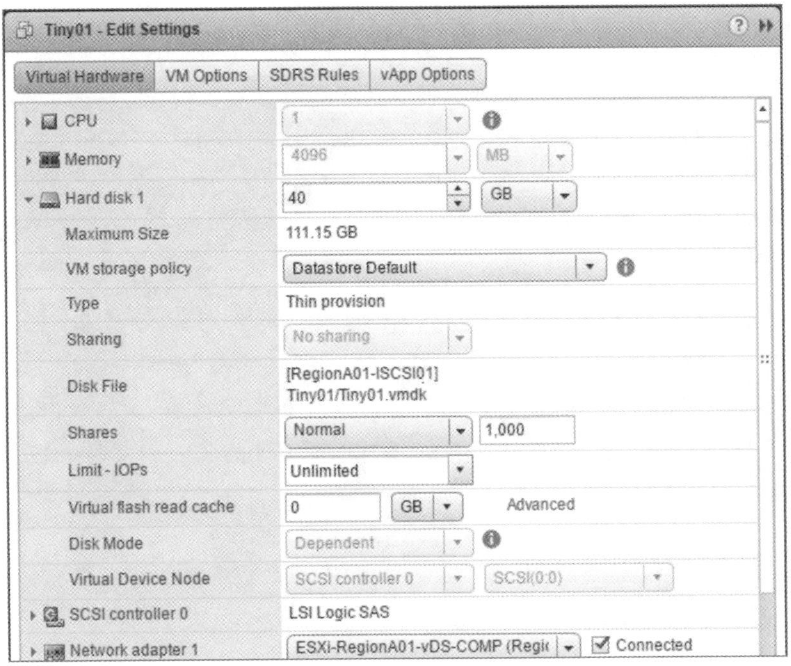

The virtual machine must be powered off to change either setting or you will see the error shown in Figure 4.48.

FIGURE 4.48 Power state notification

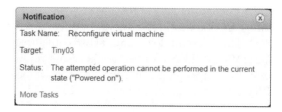

You can view the storage shares and IOPs from the VM tab of the datastore.

You can also create storage policies to apply limits and shares to VMs. There are three default storage policy components you could create a storage policy with, or you can create a custom one. Each of the default storage policy components includes an IOPs limit—and using the storage policy enables an IOPs Reservation value (Figure 4.49) that is not available from the virtual machine settings in the GUI.

FIGURE 4.49 Storage policy showing storage I/O reservations

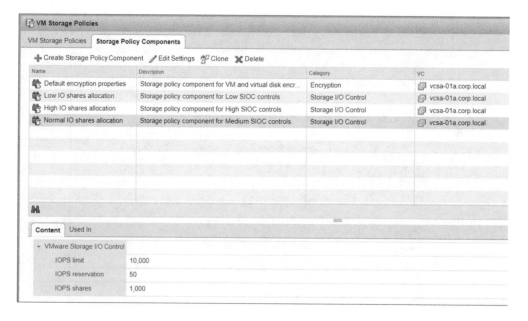

Even when using storage policies, a virtual machine needs to be power cycled when changing limits or IOPs for the new values to take effect.

Storage I/O Control uses the shares assigned to the virtual machines and the total number of shares allocated to VMDKs on the datastore to set the queue slots for the virtual machines.

SIOC also adjusts the I/O queue depth for the hosts to balance the I/O available for each host to be proportional to the VM shares available on that host.

For example:

Datastore: iSCSI01 with Storage I/O control enabled at 90 percent

Host A:

- Virtual machine Tiny01 with one VMDK on iSCSI01with 1000 shares

Host B:

- Virtual machine Tiny02 with one VMDK on iSCSI01 with 500 shares

- Virtual machine Tiny03 with one VMDK on iSCSI01 with 1500 shares

Host A shares for iSCSI01:1000

Host B VM shares for iSCSI01: 2000

Total shares: 3000

When the IOPs for iSCSI01 hit 90 percent, SIOC will adjust the I/O queue depth of the hosts until the ratio between the hosts is 1:2. On Host B, the virtual machines will have their queue slots adjusted until the ratio of slots is 1:3.

SIOC's queue depth adjustment is done proactively at the threshold limit set by the SIOC, and it has an effect on the host relative to the VM shares in play. Hosts also have a feature called Adaptive Queuing that will cut the queue depth of the storage in half if the storage reports that it is busy or has a full queue. The limit set by SIOC is enforced per VM by an I/O filter.

Summary

There are many options for storing vSphere virtual machines, from local disks to traditional arrays. With vSphere 6.5, you can add modern twists to those options with vSAN and Virtual Volumes bringing new capabilities and introducing the ability to set storage policies on your VMs to set the capabilities they will consume.

With vSAN, VMware has given vSphere environments the ability to have shared storage without adding third-party hardware or software and features such as deduplication and compression to ensure that you are making the most efficient use of your hardware. With Virtual Volumes, traditional arrays and storage servers have a much more flexible way of presenting storage to ESXi hosts. With all of these options, you want to make sure there is no single point of failure to ensure reliability.

Exam Essentials

Understand VMware vSAN and how it is implemented. One of VMware's flagship features for vSphere, vSAN keeps adding features. You should be aware of the requirements both for vSAN and features such as deduplication and compression and All-Flash.

Know vSAN terminology and configuration settings. Know how RAID5/6 Erasure Encoding differs from RAID-1, how each is implemented, and the capacity implications of each. You should know how and why to create disk groups and fault domains. You should be able to create an iSCSI target and know the requirements for them.

Describe networking and multipathing for block and NFS storage. You need to know the PSA framework, what each component does, and how to configure the different settings. You should be able to describe how vSphere networking supports the different block and file storage technologies and know how to configure vSphere networking to support storage.

Understand policy-based storage management. Know why storage policies are used and how to create them for the different types of storage. Know when and how to apply different policies to different VMs.

Know how to add an RDM to a virtual machine. Be able to add an RDM to a virtual machine and know the difference between physical and virtual mode. Also be able to share VMDKs between virtual machines and know the different options for that.

Understand VVols and their requirements. Know how to create a Virtual Volume datastore for a host and the requirements. Understand how a storage array stores the files and the benefits of doing so.

Be able to describe the differences between NFS v3 and NFS v4.1. Be able to add NFS datastores to many hosts and know the requirements. Be able to configure Kerberos for the host and datastores.

Review Questions

The answers to the chapter review questions can be found in the Appendix.

1. What should be considered before creating a shared VMFS6 datastore?
   A. Number of cache disks.
   B. VASA support for the array.
   C. All hosts are on version 6.5.
   D. NFS 4.1 support on the NAS.

2. Which is the simplest method to upgrade a VMFS3 datastore to VMFS6?
   A. Create a new VMFS6 datastore and use Storage vMotion to move the VMs.
   B. Upgrade the VMFS3 datastore to VMFS5, then upgrade the datastore to VMFS6.
   C. Upgrade the VMFS3 datastore to VMFS6.
   D. Create a new VMFS6 datastore and use SIOC to move the VMs.

3. Which storage technologies require ESXi hosts to maintain the file and folder structure? (Choose two.)
   A. VVol
   B. iSCSI LUN
   C. Local disks
   D. NFS

4. Which options allow boot from SAN over FCoE? (Choose three.)
   A. FBFT
   B. FBPT
   C. iBFT
   D. HBA
   E. IQN

5. What is required to support iSCSI storage arrays?
   A. HBA
   B. CNA
   C. CHAP
   D. IQN

6. Where should CHAP be configured if you have multiple arrays with multiple capabilities?
   A. FCoE target settings
   B. iSCSI initiator adapter settings
   C. iSCSI target settings
   D. FCoE initiator adapter settings

7. Which would prevent the use of deduplication and compression on a vSAN cluster? (Choose two.)

    A. SIOC

    B. Network card with iBFT

    C. Disk Format 2

    D. Hybrid

8. Which storage option doesn't support Storage DRS?

    A. NFS v3

    B. NFS v4.1

    C. iSCSI with HBA

    D. iSCSI with software initiator

9. Which options require multiple vSAN disk groups? (Choose two.)

    A. Two SSD drives and ten HDD drives

    B. Fourteen SSD drives

    C. One SSD drive and seven HDD drives

    D. Seven SSD drives

10. Which option requires multiple vSAN disk groups to utilize all of the disks?

    A. Eight SSD drives

    B. One SSD drives and seven HDD drives

    C. Three SSD drives and ten HDD drives

    D. Seven SSD drives

11. Which storage technology uses only local ESXi disks?

    A. NFS

    B. vSAN

    C. FCoE

    D. iSCSI with software initiator

12. Which storage technology can vSphere leverage to supply storage to physical servers?

    A. NFS

    B. vSAN

    C. FCoE

    D. iSCSI with software initiator

13. What security options are available for TCP/IP-based storage? (Choose two.)

    A. CHAP

    B. Kerberos

    C. TACACS

    D. SSO

14. Which storage technology can be configured in vSphere to ensure data integrity?

    A. NFS

    B. vSAN

    C. FCoE

    D. iSCSI with software initiator

15. Which storage technology can vSphere configure to encrypt data at rest?

    A. NFS

    B. vSAN

    C. FCoE

    D. iSCSI with software initiator

16. Which storage profiles method creates the capabilities on the datastore when the storage policy is applied?

    A. Tagging

    B. VVol capabilities

    C. vSAN capabilities

    D. SIOC components

17. What storage supports VVols? (Choose two.)

    A. vSAN

    B. NFS

    C. iSCSI

    D. Local disks

18. What components are required in vCenter to use VVols? (Choose two.)

    A. Storage profile

    B. iSCSI LUN

    C. VMFS datastore

    D. Storage provider

19. Which step could be taken to improve performance for virtual machines on an NFS v3 datastore during off-peak hours?

    A. Enable SIOC and increase the shares

    B. Increase the write percentage of the cache drive

    C. Enable Storage DRS

    D. Replace the datastore with an NFS 4.1 datastore

20. Which technologies are supported for booting a host? (Choose two.)

    A. vSAN

    B. iSCSI

    C. TRoE

    D. Fibre Channel

Chapter

5

Upgrading a vSphere Deployment

2V0-21.19 EXAM OBJECTIVES COVERED IN THIS CHAPTER:

✓ **Section 1 – VMware vSphere Architectures and Technologies**

- Objective 1.1 – Identify the pre-requisites and components for vSphere implementation

✓ **Section 4 – Installing, Configuring, and Setting Up a VMware vSphere Solution**

- Objective 4.6 – Deploy and configure VMware vCenter Server Appliance (VCSA)

✓ **Section 5 – Performance-tuning and Optimizing a VMware vSphere Solution**

- Objective 5.2 – Monitor resources of VCSA in a vSphere environment

✓ **Section 7 – Administrative and Operational Tasks in a VMware vSphere Solution**

- Objective 7.15 – Utilize VMware vSphere Update Manager (VUM)

Keeping your vSphere environment up-to-date is important in order to have the latest features and improvements that typically provide improved performance and stability. It is also important to ensure compatibility with new industry changes such as hardware and operating systems. VMware has a prescriptive "top down" upgrade path for its products that has not changed much over the years.

Following a carefully planned upgrade strategy will ensure consistency and reliability during the transition. It will also allow you to recover smoothly from issues encountered during the upgrade process. Key components of the upgrade path will be backing up your current environment, checking the compatibility guides, and deciding if your deployment topology will need to change.

An additional consideration will be whether to move a Windows-based vCenter to the vCenter Server Appliance (VCSA). VMware vSphere 6.5 does not have a Windows requirement for any of its components, and VMware suggests you migrate to the appliance. However, the Windows-based vCenter is still supported for 6.5.

VMware provides tools such as vSphere Update Manager (VUM) to automate some of the processes and help you implement a reliable upgrade path. Following the steps outlined by VMware will ensure that you have a consistent and safe upgrade.

Upgrading from vSphere 5.5

This section will list the specific issues with upgrading from vCenter 5.5 to vCenter 6.5.

In an effort to not repeat content, upgrading and migrating that is not specific to 5.5 will be covered along with the 6.0 content in the sections "Upgrading a vCenter Server on Windows" and "Migrating to the vCenter Server Appliance."

Upgrading to vCenter 6.5 from vCenter 5.5 is fully supported, but mixed-version environments are only supported during the transition period.

There are several considerations to address depending on your topology.

- If you have a simple vSphere 5.5 installation with all v5.5 components, then the upgrade is straightforward.

- However, if you have deployed your 5.5 environment in a fully distributed deployment, you will need to manage those separate components because they are decentralized during the upgrade.

- Also, if you are using a now-deprecated topology, such as linked, embedded Single Sign-On (SSO), you will need to move to a supported topology before the upgrade. See KB Article 2147672 for supported and unsupported topologies.

With vSphere 5.5, there were multiple components that could be installed either on the vCenter server or on separate servers. With vSphere 6.x, only the Platform Services Controller (what the Single Sign-On server evolved into for version 6) can be installed separately from vCenter. For the other distributed services, the upgrade process will migrate the responsibilities, configuration, and possibly the data from the distributed services to the new vCenter 6.5 server as described in the following list:

vCenter Inventory Service   Data from the service will be copied to the vCenter Content Library.

vSphere Web Client   Any data will be copied to the vSphere web client on vCenter 6.5.

vSphere Auto Deploy   Data will be copied to the new vCenter 6.5 service. The old service will not be shut down. You will need to change your DHCP options to point to the new vCenter server.

vSphere Syslog Collector   The configuration is retained but not the data. You will need to repoint your hosts to the new vCenter server.

vSphere ESXi Dump Collector   No data is kept. You will need to repoint hosts to the new vCenter server.

vSphere Update Manager   Configuration and data will be copied to the new vCenter 6.5 server. Make sure you run the migration assistant on the host running VUM before you start the migration.

Regardless of how many different servers were used to distribute the 5.5 services, the end result will be one 6.5 vCenter server for each v5.5 vCenter server. You will also have one 6.5 Platform Services Controller for each v5.5 Single Sign-On service, which will be either stand-alone or embedded with vCenter depending on how your v5.5 environment was deployed. See Figure 5.1 for the upgrade diagram of a basic vCenter installation with an embedded Single Sign-On service.

FIGURE 5.1   Basic vCenter 5.5 upgrade with embedded Single Sign-On

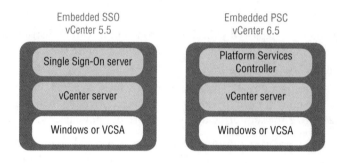

If you used an external Single Sign-On server for vCenter 5.5, the upgraded environment will have an external Platform Services Controller (PSC) as shown in Figure 5.2. Note that in this diagram the Auto Deploy server was also deployed on the SSO server; however, with 6.5 the Auto Deploy service is only available on a vCenter server. Only the Platform Services Controller can be installed on a separate instance.

FIGURE 5.2   vCenter 5.5 upgrade with external Single Sign-On

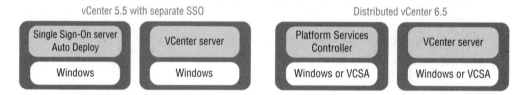

If you have a fully distributed vCenter 5.5 instance, where every possible service was deployed on its own server, the end state will still be one PSC and one vCenter server, with all of the services installed on the vCenter server as shown in Figure 5.3.

If you are currently using an unsupported topology, or one that would be unsupported in vSphere 6.5 such as linked embedded SSO services, VMware suggests you migrate to a supported topology as shown in Figure 5.4 before starting the 6.5 upgrade. See VMware Knowledge Base article 2130433 for more information.

Before the vCenter 6.5 migration can start, you need to make sure all components are at least version 5.5. This includes any ESXi hosts, vCenter servers, and SSO servers in the environment. Since vCenter 6.5 cannot be used with ESXi hosts before version 5.5, any that are version 5.0 or 5.1 will need to be upgraded or decommissioned. This may add an interim step to the 6.5 migration, similar to what is shown in Figure 5.4.

FIGURE 5.3   Fully distributed vCenter 5.5 upgraded to distributed vCenter 6.5

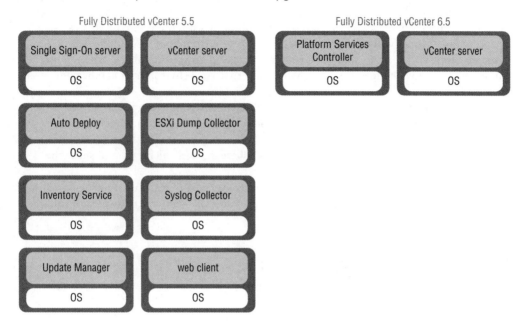

FIGURE 5.4   vCenter 5.5 topology migration and 6.5 upgrade

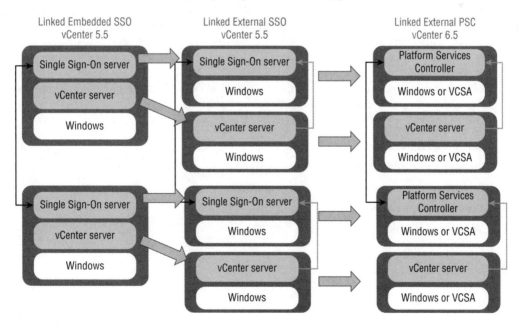

Before migrating a vCenter 5.5 database, there are cleanup scripts you can run to prepare the database. There is a separate script for MS SQL databases and Oracle databases: `cleanup_orphaned_data_MSSQL.sql` and `cleanup_orphaned_data_Oracle.sql`. These cleanup scripts will remove any unnecessary data from your vCenter server database. The appropriate script should be run after backing up your database. Backing up the database before any changes are made will ensure that your environment can be completely recovered.

If your topology includes a distributed linked mode environment, the distributed linked mode will not work during the transition period when both vCenter 5.5 and vCenter 6.5 servers are in use. However, the upgraded vSphere 6.5 client will show the 6.5 and 5.5 vCenter servers during the transition. The vSphere 5.5 web client will not show the 6.5 servers.

After your migration has completed and you have verified that the upgraded environment is working properly, make sure you decommission any services that were consolidated to the vCenter server.

Upgrading a vCenter Server on Windows

There are essentially two options for upgrading a Windows-based vCenter server from either 5.5 or 6.0: GUI or command line (CLI). This is because changing the topology during an upgrade is not supported (refer to the preceding section) and there are no options for a distributed installation. You *can* migrate a Windows-based vCenter server to a vCenter Server Appliance (VCSA); that will be covered in the section "Migrating to the vCenter Server Appliance."

Before upgrading your environment, there are several tasks that should be addressed. In the vSphere 6.5 Upgrade documentation, VMware has broken these out as follows:

1. Verify basic compatibility.
2. Download the vCenter Server Installer.
3. Prepare a vCenter Server database for upgrade.
4. Prepare for upgrading the Content Library.
5. Verify network prerequisites.
6. Verify load balancer.
7. Prepare ESXi hosts.
8. Verify that preparations are complete.

Verify Basic Compatibility and Download the Installer

As mentioned in the previous section, upgrading from a deprecated topology is not supported. Make sure your topology and all of the components are supported with 6.5 before you start the upgrade process. You should also verify that all of your components are compatible with vSphere 6.5 on the VMware Compatibility Guide at www.vmware.com/ resources/compatibility. In case you have multiple VMware components in your environment, VMware has a prescribed upgrade path available in Knowledge Base article 2147289. If you have any of these components in your environment, this is the order in which VMware suggests they be upgraded. (Note that most of the topics listed here are outside the scope of this book/the exam.)

1. vRealize Automation

2. vRealize Orchestrator, vRealize Business

3. vRealize Operations, vRealize Log Insight

4. vRealize Log Insight Agent, vRealize Operations Manager End-Point Operations Agent

5. vStorage APIs for Data Protection–based backup solution

6. NSX for vSphere

7. External PSC/SSO

8. vCenter Server

9. vSphere Update Manager

10. vSphere Replication, SRM

11. VMware Update Manager Download Service

12. ESXi

13. VMware Tools

14. Virtual hardware

15. vSAN, VMFS

Once your environment and topology are known to be compatible with vSphere 6.5, you can continue preparing for the vCenter upgrade. The second step in the VMware list is to download the binaries for vCenter 6.5. You will need to have a current support license for vSphere in order to download the files.

Prepare the Database for Upgrade

Before any changes to the environment are made, you should back up the database by either using a database backup tool or making a backup of the entire virtual machine. See VMware Knowledge Base article 2091961 for steps on backing up the PostgreSQL database. You can also make a backup of the vCenter SSL certificates by copying the C:\Users\ All Users\VMware\VMware VirtualCenter\SSL directory to a safe location.

Once an upgrade is completed, you cannot revert to an earlier version; you must instead restore the earlier state. The simplest backup method would be to make a clone of the

VM(s) related to the upgrade. The vCenter 6.5 installer will require you to check a box stating that you have backed up the environment prior to starting the upgrade, as shown in Figure 5.5.

FIGURE 5.5   Verify that you have backed up the vCenter instance.

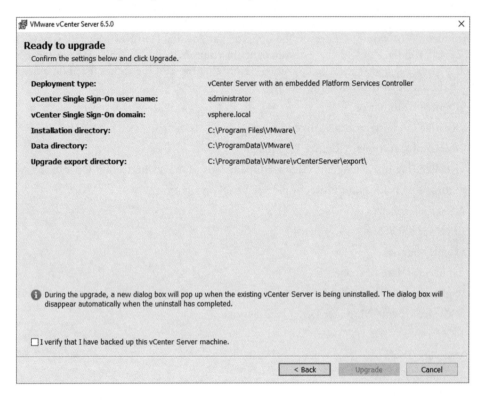

With vCenter version 6.5, the embedded database used is PostgreSQL. If you are currently using the embedded Microsoft SQL Express database installed with earlier versions, it will be replaced with PostgreSQL during the upgrade. If you do not want to use PostgreSQL, you can migrate your SQL Express database to a full SQL database (see Knowledge Base article 1028601) or change your embedded SQL Express so it will not be converted to PostgreSQL (see Knowledge Base article 2109321).

If you are using an external database (either Microsoft SQL or Oracle), make sure the version is compatible with vSphere 6.5. If the database is not compatible, it will need to be upgraded before vCenter is upgraded. With either external database, you should verify that the correct permissions are assigned. See the section "Database Permission Requirements for vCenter Server" in the vCenter Server Upgrade guide. For Oracle, also verify the Oracle instance using the SERVICE_NAME and check that the CLASSPATH variable includes the JDBC driver. If you are using an external SQL database, make sure JDK 1.6 or later is installed, the CLASSPATH variable includes sqljdbc4.jar, and you are using Microsoft SQL Server Native Client 10 or 11.

Prepare for Upgrading the Content Library

If you are using the vSphere Content Library, there are a few things to check before the upgrade. You must be using Remote File Systems or Datastores for the libraries. If you have any libraries using the local disks of a vCenter, they need to be migrated to Remote File Systems or Datastores. You also need to make sure all libraries are accessible during the upgrade and no subscribed libraries are using a file-based URI.

Verify Network Prerequisites, Load Balancer, and ESXI Hosts

The VMware upgrade document lists several steps for testing network settings before the upgrade. You should check that the fully qualified domain names (FQDNs) of your vSphere components resolve to the IP address configured for each component and the IP addresses of your vCenters and SSO servers (if used) will return the correct FQDN when queried. If you use DHCP, make sure the DNS records are updated if the IP addresses change. Also, make sure each component has the correct DNS servers entered. If you are using Active Directory (AD), make sure it is configured properly and that all components use the same time source as the Active Directory servers.

The VMware upgrade guide provides a list of services that must be running before an upgrade is started:

- The vCenter Single Sign-On instance to which you are registering vCenter Server
- VMware Certificate Authority
- VMware Directory Service
- VMware Identity Manager Service
- VMware KDC Service
- `tcruntime-C-ProgramData-VMware-cis-runtime-VMwareSTSService`

The list of tasks provided in the vCenter Server Upgrade guide includes checking the load balancer and ESXi hosts, but the steps you are expected to take have already been covered by verifying that "all components" and the topology are compatible with vSphere 6.5. Those compatibility checks should include verifying that the load balancer and its topology are compatible and that all ESXi hosts are at least version 5.5.

Starting the vCenter on Windows Upgrade

Once the compatibility checks and prerequisite steps are done and the environment is backed up, you can proceed with upgrading the environment. Assuming you have already updated any other products mentioned in Figure 5.5, your first step will be to upgrade your Single Sign-On servers. If you are using a simple installation with embedded SSO, then there will be only one wizard to run through that will update the embedded SSO to an embedded PSC and upgrade vCenter at the same time.

To start the upgrade, launch autorun.exe from the ISO image (either extracted or mounted on your Windows desktop). The wizard will identify upgrading an external PSC compared to upgrading an embedded 6.0 PSC (Figure 5.6) or an embedded 5.5 SSO service (Figure 5.7).

FIGURE 5.6   Upgrading an external (left) or embedded (right) PSC instance

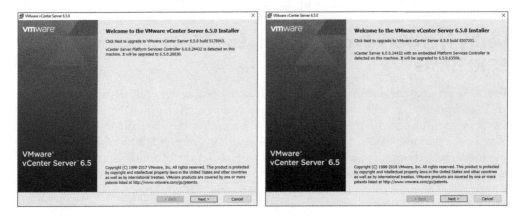

FIGURE 5.7   Upgrading vCenter with an embedded PSC instance

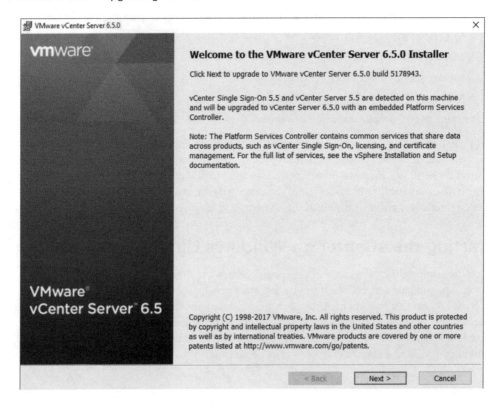

You will need to make sure you are executing the upgrade in the correct order, upgrading the SSO or PSC first (if separate) and then vCenter followed by hosts and virtual machines. During the vCenter migration, you will be prompted to migrate data from the old installation (Figure 5.8). You will not see this option if you are upgrading an external SSO or PSC.

FIGURE 5.8   Upgrade options for vCenter

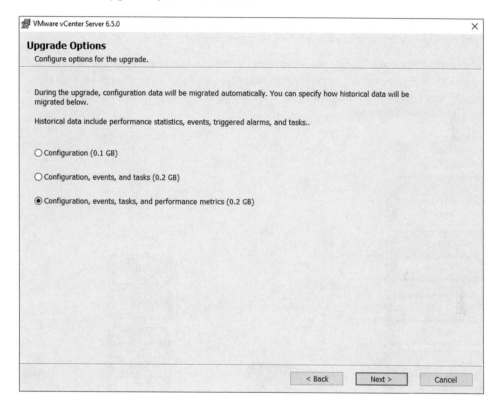

This allows you to choose how much old data to bring forward from the previous version, and you are given size estimates for the data. While we would suggest bringing over all of the data, this is a very useful option if you are doing a test migration.

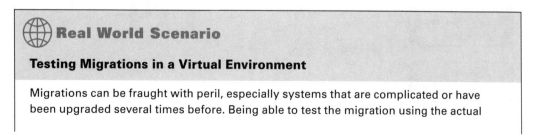

Real World Scenario

Testing Migrations in a Virtual Environment

Migrations can be fraught with peril, especially systems that are complicated or have been upgraded several times before. Being able to test the migration using the actual system can be very beneficial—and in a virtual environment might not be that hard to do. Using the vSphere clone feature (or any feature you have that can duplicate a VM, including backup utilities or storage array features like LUN cloning), you can create exact copies of your systems that can then be experimented on without consequence.

You will need a copy of any dependent component, including perhaps a time server, DNS server, Active Directory, and of course copies of the SSO/PSC and vCenter servers. If some of these components are not available as virtual machines, you might need to create temporary virtual facsimiles that will provide the same functionality—just make a careful note of which components were not actually tested.

One vSphere host that is large enough to hold all of the required components and does not participate in the production environment is ideal as it reduces network complications—simply create port groups without physical NICs for any networking required, as shown in the following image.

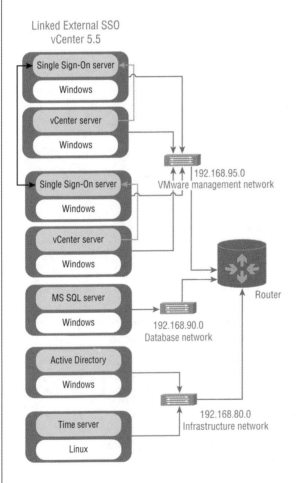

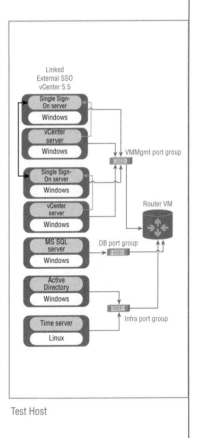

It also reduces the risk of accidentally making changes to the production environment. For access into the test environment, either use the consoles for the VMs or add a virtual machine to the host with connections to the test environment and the normal environment.

This method can be used for testing many scenarios, not just vCenter upgrades. We have used this to walk through Active Directory topology changes and renames, Exchange migrations, and database migrations.

If the migration fails at a later step, you will need to clean up the export directory, which is defined on the screen after you set the upgrade options as shown in Figure 5.9.

FIGURE 5.9   Setting the destination directories including the exported data

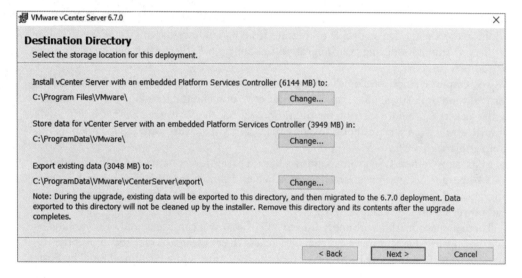

If you do not clean up the export directory between upgrade attempts, you will get the error shown in Figure 5.10.

FIGURE 5.10   Possible error message when rerunning the upgrade

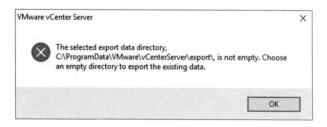

After the migration is complete, you can delete the export directory, which by default is C:\ProgramData\VMware\vCenterServer\export. Make sure the new topology is working correctly before you move on to upgrading ESXi hosts (which we'll do in the the section "Upgrading ESXi Hosts and Virtual Machines" later in this chapter); reverting to the previous version will be much more difficult if you have to restore hosts as well as the vCenter topology.

Migrating to the vCenter Server Appliance

The vCenter Server Appliance is the preferred deployment for a Platform Services Controller and vCenter Server. It doesn't require a Windows Server license and is very simple to deploy and maintain compared to having to maintain the Windows OS in addition to vCenter. If you decide to migrate from a Windows-based vCenter to the vCenter Server Appliance during your migration to vSphere 6.5, there are a few considerations to address.

You cannot change topologies during the migration, and you should not migrate a deprecated topology. You should make sure your environment and topology are compatible with vCenter 6.5 before starting the migration. Check the VMware Compatibility Guide at www.vmware.com/resources/compatibility to make sure your environment is fully compatible with VCSA 6.5

Migrating to the VCSA from Windows has an easier revert path than a Windows or VCSA upgrade because the source is untouched and simply shut down at the end of the migration. Reverting to the previous version is a matter of powering off the new appliance and powering on the Windows VM.

There are two methods of upgrading to VCSA 6.5: you can use a GUI or command-line tool. Either one requires a PC that can access the existing vCenter server and the management IP of the host ESXi server that the appliance will be deployed on. The host ESXi will also need access to the network on which the current vCenter server is running.

You will also need to launch the migration-assistant utility on the existing vCenter server before the migration or migration prechecks start. You can find the migration-assistant in the migration-assistant directory on the VCSA 6.5 install .ISO you download from VMware.

Upgrading Using the Command Line

Using the command-line version requires some prework to create the required JSON template file. You can find sample files in the installation media at vcsa-cli-installer/templates/migrate to migrate from 5.5 or 6.0 with embedded or external databases and stand-alone or embedded SSO/PSCs. For authentication, there is an Active Directory section in the JSON templates, or you can use the `migration.ssl.thumbprint` key in the JSON, which uses the key provided by the `migration-assistant` utility on the vCenter server.

After the file is created, you can verify it by using the `--verify-template-only` parameter. If a problem is found in the JSON file, you will need to resolve the issue before the verification will complete. If the JSON file is OK, it will start a limited version of the prechecks and prompt you to run the full version of the prechecks.

You can initiate the precheck sequence using the `--pre-check-only` parameter and the JSON file. Additional tests include space required and the `ovftool`.

Once the checks have completed successfully, you can initiate the migration using the `vcsa-deploy` command in the `migrate` mode with the JSON file. You will also need the `--acknowledge-ceip` and `--accept-eula` parameters.

You will need to execute the CLI from a server other than the existing vCenter server since the vCenter server will be shut down during the migration process.

Upgrading Using the Graphical Interface

The GUI version of the migration can be found on the VCSA ISO downloaded from VMware in the `vcsa-ui-installer` directory. As with the command-line version, there are 32-bit Windows, 64-bit Linux, and Mac versions of the GUI installer. Upon launching the installer utility, click Migrate to start the migration process.

The GUI version detects the vCenter version and type (SSO/PSC-only or SSO/PSC embedded), as shown in Figure 5.11 and Figure 5.12.

FIGURE 5.11   Migrate a Platform Services Controller

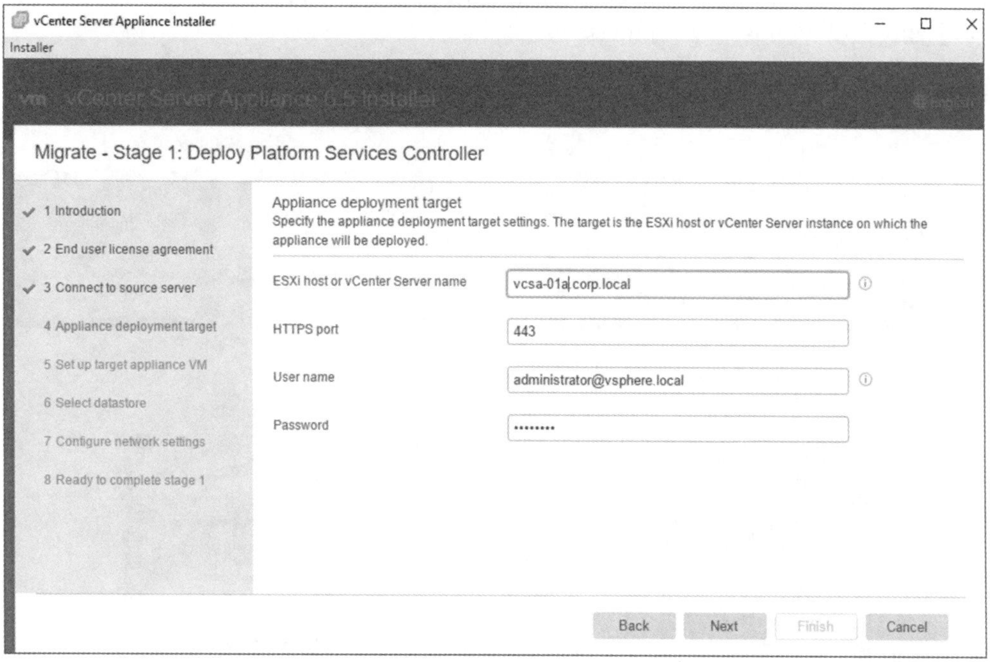

FIGURE 5.12 Migrate vCenter with an embedded PSC

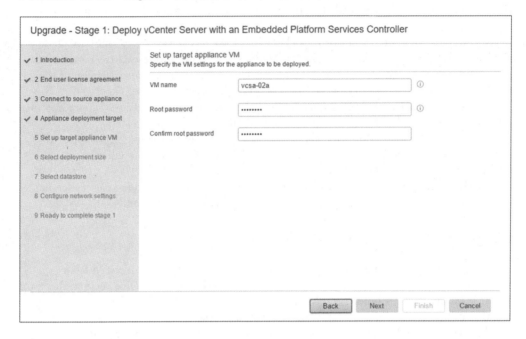

The CLI and GUI migration paths can migrate an external SSO server to a version 6.5 VCSA Platform Services Controller or a version 6.0 PSC to a version 6.5 VCSA Platform Services Controller. The tools can also migrate a 5.5 vCenter with an embedded SSO or a 6.0 vCenter with embedded PSC with vCenter to a version 6.5 VCSA with embedded PSC. See Figure 5.13 for migration options.

FIGURE 5.13 Migrate vCenter with an embedded PSC

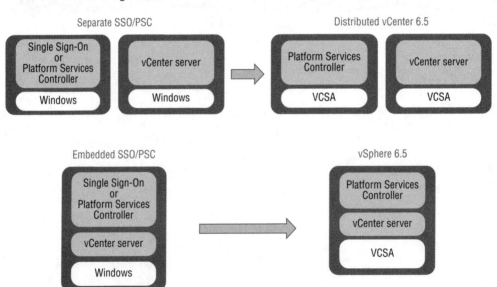

During the migration option, you assign a temporary IP to the VCSA appliance in either the JSON file or the GUI. This IP is used to initially stand up the appliance so that it can receive the file transfer containing the configuration and exported data from the source appliance. When the migration is complete, the VCSA appliance should have the same configuration, including name and IP address as the source server. However, if the temporary IP address is not on the same network as the source server, the temporary IP address will be retained by the VCSA appliance at the end of the migration. This is to ensure that the VCSA server has network access at the end of the migration but will require additional work to change any other components referencing it. As with the CLI version, you need to execute the GUI from a server other than the existing vCenter server since the vCenter server will be shut down during the migration process

EXERCISE 5.1

Upgrade a VCSA 6.0 server with embedded PSC to VCSA 6.5

1. From a Windows desktop, mount the VCSA ISO, and with the autorun utility, start the Deploy process.

2. Click Upgrade.

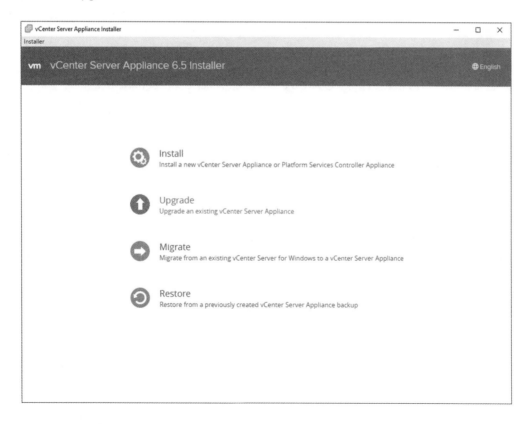

3. Click Next on the Introduction screen.

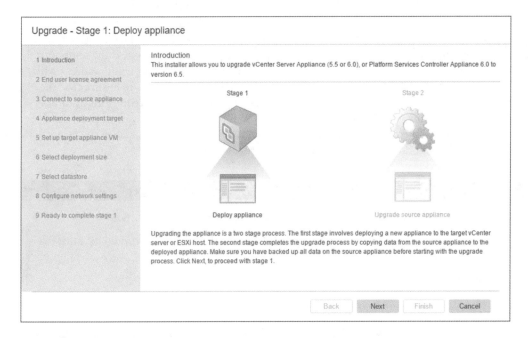

4. Accept the EULA and click Next.

5. Enter the FQDN or IP of the vSphere 6.0 server and click Connect to Source.

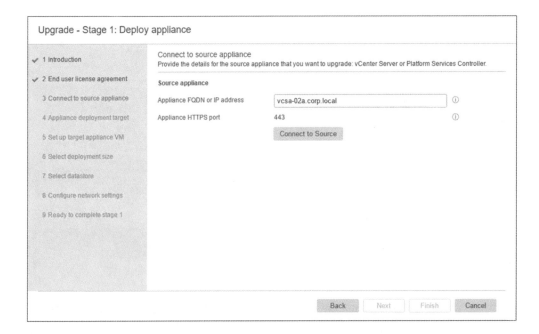

EXERCISE 5.1 *(continued)*

6. Enter the credentials for SSO and the host of the source appliance and click Next.

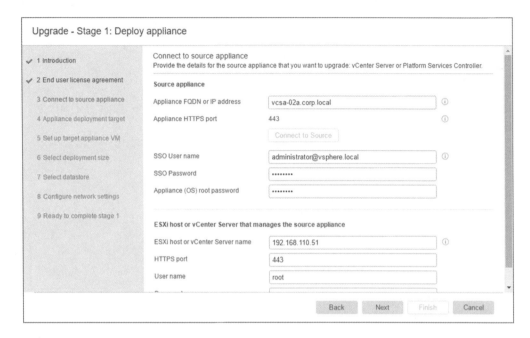

7. Enter the FQDN or IP and credentials for the vCenter or host that the new VCSA appliance will be deployed to.

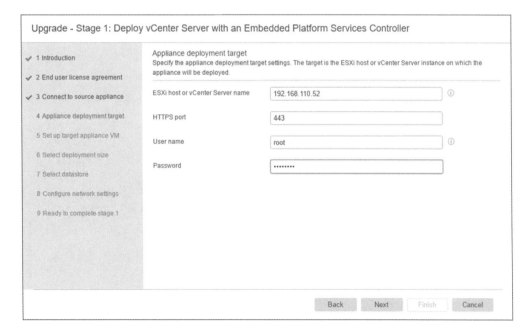

8. Enter the name (for the vSphere inventory) and root password for the new appliance.

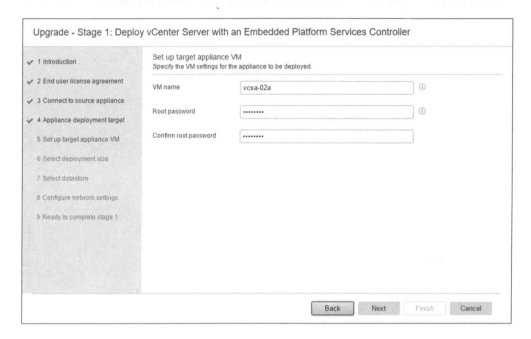

9. Select the deployment size of the new appliance.

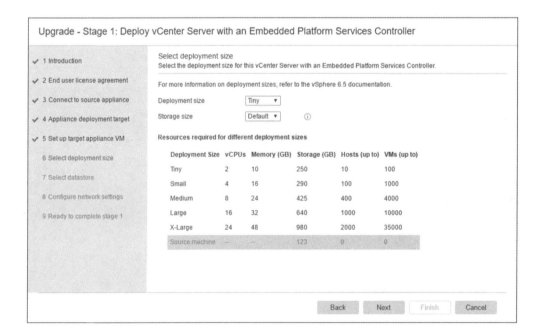

10. Select the datastore for the new appliance.

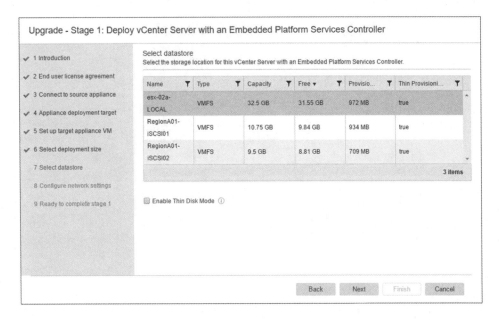

11. Configure the network and temporary IP settings for the appliance. The network should be the same one the current VCSA appliance is on, and the IP address should be an unused address on the same network.

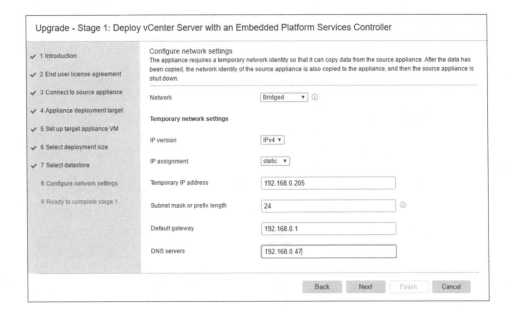

12. Monitor the deployment.

13. Verify the completion of Stage 1 and click Finish.

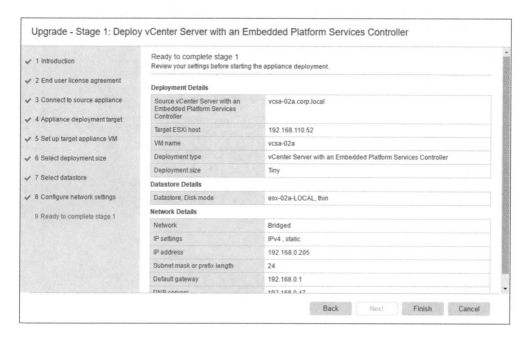

14. Click Continue to start Stage 2.

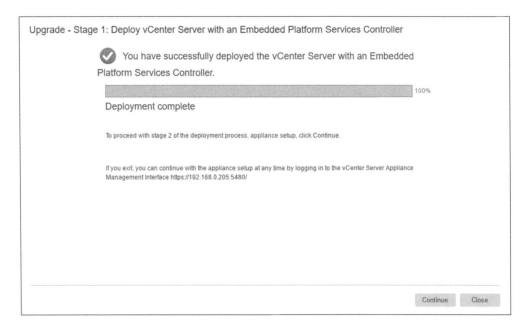

Upgrade - Stage 1: Deploy vCenter Server with an Embedded Platform Services Controller

✓ You have successfully deployed the vCenter Server with an Embedded Platform Services Controller.

100%

Deployment complete

To proceed with stage 2 of the deployment process, appliance setup, click Continue.

If you exit, you can continue with the appliance setup at any time by logging in to the vCenter Server Appliance Management Interface https://192.168.0.205:5480/

Continue   Close

15. Click Next.

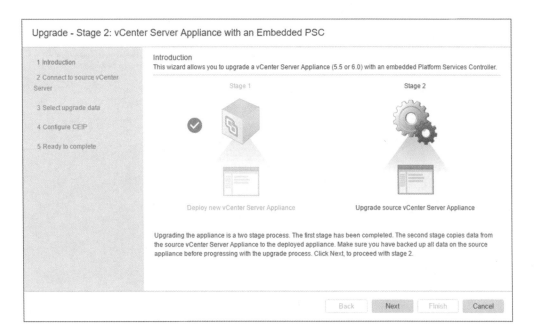

Upgrade - Stage 2: vCenter Server Appliance with an Embedded PSC

1 Introduction

2 Connect to source vCenter Server

3 Select upgrade data

4 Configure CEIP

5 Ready to complete

Introduction
This wizard allows you to upgrade a vCenter Server Appliance (5.5 or 6.0) with an embedded Platform Services Controller.

Stage 1   Stage 2

Deploy new vCenter Server Appliance   Upgrade source vCenter Server Appliance

Upgrading the appliance is a two stage process. The first stage has been completed. The second stage copies data from the source vCenter Server Appliance to the deployed appliance. Make sure you have backed up all data on the source appliance before progressing with the upgrade process. Click Next, to proceed with stage 2.

Back   Next   Finish   Cancel

16. Verify the settings and click Next.

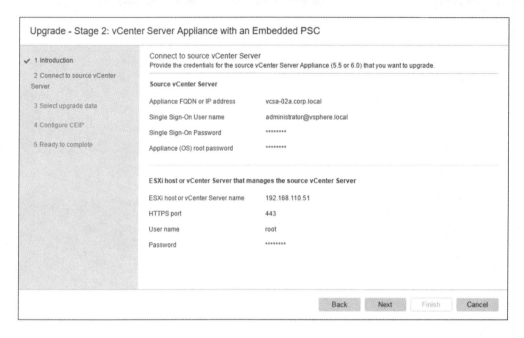

Upgrade - Stage 2: vCenter Server Appliance with an Embedded PSC

✔ 1 Introduction	**Connect to source vCenter Server**
2 Connect to source vCenter Server	Provide the credentials for the source vCenter Server Appliance (5.5 or 6.0) that you want to upgrade.

Source vCenter Server

Appliance FQDN or IP address	vcsa-02a.corp.local
Single Sign-On User name	administrator@vsphere.local
Single Sign-On Password	********
Appliance (OS) root password	********

ESXi host or vCenter Server that manages the source vCenter Server

ESXi host or vCenter Server name	192.168.110.51
HTTPS port	443
User name	root
Password	********

Back   Next   Finish   Cancel

17. Select the amount to data to include with the migration and click Next.

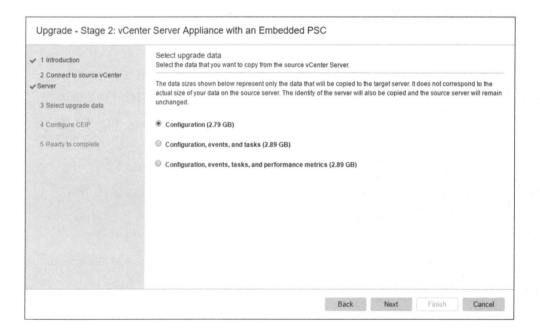

Upgrade - Stage 2: vCenter Server Appliance with an Embedded PSC

✔ 1 Introduction	**Select upgrade data**
2 Connect to source vCenter	Select the data that you want to copy from the source vCenter Server.
✔ Server	

The data sizes shown below represent only the data that will be copied to the target server. It does not correspond to the actual size of your data on the source server. The identity of the server will also be copied and the source server will remain unchanged.

- ◉ Configuration (2.79 GB)
- ○ Configuration, events, and tasks (2.89 GB)
- ○ Configuration, events, tasks, and performance metrics (2.89 GB)

Back   Next   Finish   Cancel

EXERCISE 5.1 *(continued)*

18. Join CEIP (optional) and click Next.

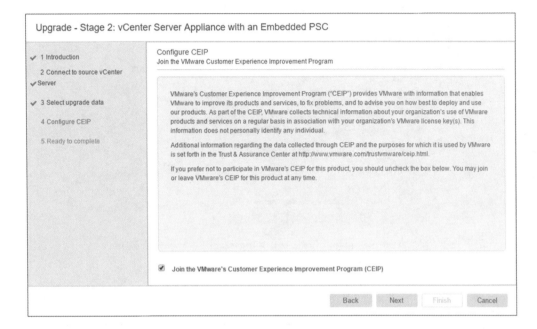

Upgrade - Stage 2: vCenter Server Appliance with an Embedded PSC

✓ 1 Introduction

2 Connect to source vCenter
✓ Server

✓ 3 Select upgrade data

4 Configure CEIP

5 Ready to complete

Configure CEIP
Join the VMware Customer Experience Improvement Program

VMware's Customer Experience Improvement Program ("CEIP") provides VMware with information that enables VMware to improve its products and services, to fix problems, and to advise you on how best to deploy and use our products. As part of the CEIP, VMware collects technical information about your organization's use of VMware products and services on a regular basis in association with your organization's VMware license key(s). This information does not personally identify any individual.

Additional information regarding the data collected through CEIP and the purposes for which it is used by VMware is set forth in the Trust & Assurance Center at http://www.vmware.com/trustvmware/ceip.html.

If you prefer not to participate in VMware's CEIP for this product, you should uncheck the box below. You may join or leave VMware's CEIP for this product at any time.

☑ Join the VMware's Customer Experience Improvement Program (CEIP)

Back   Next   Finish   Cancel

19. Acknowledge that the source appliance will be shut down by clicking OK.

Shutdown Warning

⚠ The source vCenter will be shut down once the network configuration is enabled on destination vCenter Server.

Click OK to continue, or Cancel to stop the upgrade.

OK   Cancel

20. Acknowledge that the source appliance and its data have been backed up and complete the migration by clicking Finish.

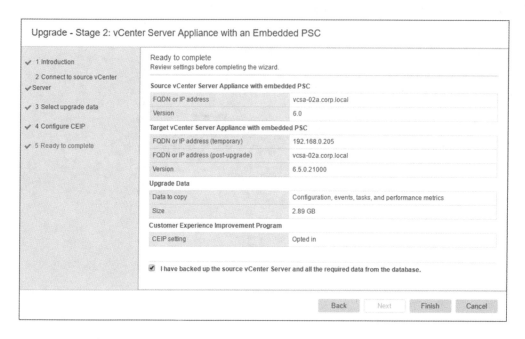

Upgrading ESXi Hosts and Virtual Machines

The VMware vSphere Update Manager is included with vSphere to help you apply patches, updates, and upgrades to hosts, virtual machines, and virtual appliances (VMs/VAs). Starting with version 6.5, you do not need a separate Windows server if you are using the vCenter Server Appliance because VUM runs as an embedded service on the VCSA. If you are not using VCSA, you will need to install VUM on either the same server as your vCenter Server or a separate Windows server.

Using the Update Manager Download Service

If the vSphere Update Manager is installed on a system that doesn't have Internet access, or you have multiple VUM servers and want to consolidate the downloads, you can install the vSphere Update Manager Download Service (UMDS) in order to download the patches and updates. You can install UMDS on a Windows or Linux-based operating system as long as it has Internet access. You cannot install UMDS on a Windows server with vSphere Update Manager installed.

If you install on a Windows server, you can manually create a database instance to use, or the installer will deploy SQL Express. On a Linux-based server, you will need to configure a PostgreSQL database prior to installing UMDS.

After UMDS is installed, you can configure it using the command-line utility vmware-umds. Some of the command-line parameters used with this utility include the set parameter -S and the --enable-host and --enable-va parameters to download host and appliance patches respectively.

The -E parameter is also important because it exports the downloaded patches for you to copy to your VUM server.

The downloaded patches can be copied to the web server acting as a shared repository for multiple VUM servers or copied onto a portable device to transfer to an air-gapped VUM server.

Using vSphere Update Manager

VMware continually makes patches and updates for ESXi hosts, virtual machines, and appliances available online. You can use VUM (or the UMDS) to download the patches and then apply the patches to your vSphere environment.

The vSphere Update Manager groups patches and updates available from VMware into *baseline objects*. These baselines can then be grouped into *baseline groups*. You attach baselines or baseline groups to vCenters, datacenters, clusters, hosts, virtual machines, appliances, or folders to scan the associated entities for compliance and remediation.

There are two types of baselines (host and VM/VA), and a baseline group can only include one type of baseline. There are predefined baselines for hosts that include Non-Critical and Critical patches as shown in Figure 5.14 and predefined baselines for VMs/VAs that include VA Upgrade to Latest, VM Hardware Upgrade to Match Host, and VMware Tools Upgrade to Match Host as shown in Figure 5.15.

FIGURE 5.14   Default baselines for hosts

FIGURE 5.15   Default VMs/VAs baselines

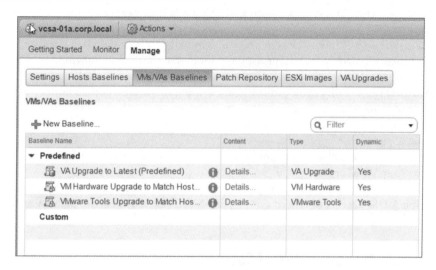

You can create your own baseline objects that only include the patches you are looking to apply to your hosts or VMs/VAs and create baseline groups to combine multiple baselines to be applied at once.

Baselines and baseline groups are then attached to vCenter objects using the Update Manager tab of that object. Some objects such as clusters and hosts can only attach host baselines and baseline groups, while virtual machines and VM folders can only attach VM/ VA baselines and groups. Other objects, including vCenter and datacenters, can have host and VM/VA baselines and groups attached (Figure 5.16) as those objects can contain hosts and virtual machines/appliances.

FIGURE 5.16   Attaching host and VM baselines

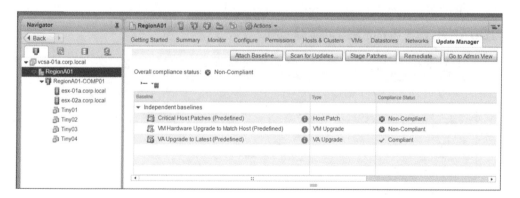

After a baseline or group is attached to a vSphere object, you can scan the objects for compliance with the baseline or group as shown in Figure 5.17.

FIGURE 5.17   Scanning for compliance

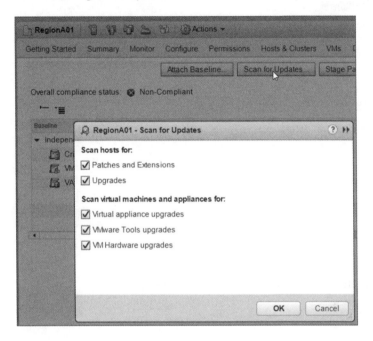

The options presented for scanning allow you to only check for a subset of the baseline or group. For hosts, you can choose to check for either patches and extensions or upgrades. Extensions are defined as "any additional software" in the Update Manager Guide, and by default VMware only has extensions for the Cisco NEXUS 1000v as shown in Figure 5.18.

For VMs/VAs, you can check for virtual appliance upgrades, VMware Tools upgrades, and VM Hardware upgrades. By default, VMware only has virtual appliance upgrades for VMware appliances as shown in Figure 5.19.

After the scan is complete, you will see in the Update Manager tab for the object which items are in compliance with the baseline or baseline group used in the scan. You are not required to scan before remediating, but it is suggested to scan so you are aware of what items will be updated and what updates they will receive. After scanning, you can click on the number of patches that are noncompliant to see the list as shown in Figure 5.20 and Figure 5.21.

FIGURE 5.18 Extensions available by default

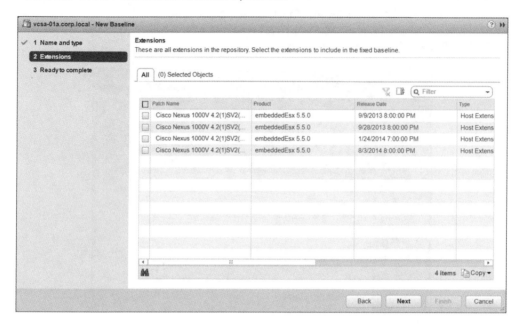

FIGURE 5.19 Appliance updates available by default

Name	Vendor	Product	Version	Release Date	1 ▼
VMware vRealize L...	VMware Inc.	VMware vRealize Suite LCM Applia...	1.3.0.14 Build ...	7/6/2018 2:23:...	
VMware vRealize L...	VMware Inc.	VMware vRealize Suite LCM Applia...	1.2.0.10 Build ...	4/11/2018 4:3...	
The GA release of ...	VMware Inc.	VMware Workbench 3.6 8230365	3.6.0.1 Build 8...	4/10/2018 7:3...	
VMware vRealize O...	VMware Inc.	VMware vRealize Orchestrator Appli...	7.4.0.23619 B...	3/23/2018 1:1...	
vRealize Business f...	VMware Inc.	vRealize Business for Cloud	7.4.0.19475 B...	3/22/2018 1:4...	
VMware vRealize A...	VMware Inc.	VMware vRealize Appliance	7.4.0.645 Buil...	3/16/2018 5:2...	
vRealize Business f...	VMware Inc.	vRealize Business for Cloud	7.3.1.14362 B...	8/21/2017 1:2...	
vRealize Business f...	VMware Inc.	vRealize Business for Cloud	7.3.0.12473 B...	6/3/2017 7:35:...	
vRealize Business f...	VMware Inc.	vRealize Business for Cloud	7.2.1.10029 B...	2/21/2017 11:...	
vRealize Business f...	VMware Inc.	vRealize Business for Cloud	7.2.0.7586 Bu...	11/11/2016 4:...	
VMware vRealize O...	VMware Inc.	VMware vRealize Orchestrator Appli...	7.2.0.19944 B...	11/10/2016 10...	
VMware vRealize A...	VMware Inc.	VMware vRealize Appliance	6.2.5.0 Build 4...	11/8/2016 8:4...	
vRealize Orchestrat...	VMware Inc.	VMware vRealize Orchestrator Appli...	6.0.5.1 Build 4...	10/26/2016 4:...	
VMware Identity Ap...	VMware Inc.	VMware Identity Appliance	2.2.5.0 Build 4...	10/25/2016 3:...	
vRealize Business f...	VMware Inc.	vRealize Business for Cloud	7.1.0.0 Build 4...	8/18/2016 2:5...	
vSphere Replication...	VMware Inc.	vSphere Replication Appliance	5.5.1.7 Build 4...	8/16/2016 11:...	
vSphere Replication...	VMware Inc.	vSphere Replication Appliance	6.1.1.13216 B...	5/5/2016 5:54:...	
vSphere Replication...	VMware Inc.	vSphere Replication Appliance	6.0.0.3 Build 3...	5/4/2016 8:57:...	
vCenter Orchestrato...	VMware Inc.	VMware vRealize Orchestrator Appli...	5.5.3.3 Build 3...	3/25/2016 12:...	

FIGURE 5.20   Click on the number of updates to view the patches that are required for compliance.

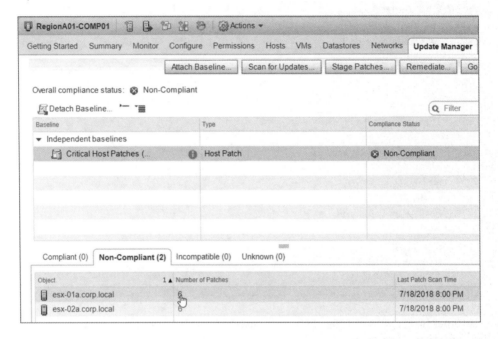

FIGURE 5.21   Required patches and their impact

esx-01a.corp.local - Patch Details for Critical Host Patches (Predefined)				
Update Name	Patch ID	Compliance Status	Severity	Impact
Updates esx-base, t-b...	ESXi650-201707201-UG	✓ Installed	Critical	Reboot, Maintenance ...
VMware ESXi 6.5 Co...	ESXi650-Update01	✓ Installed	Critical	Reboot, Maintenance ...
Updates esx-base, es...	ESXi650-201710401-BG	✗ Missing	Critical	Reboot, Maintenance ...
Updates esx-base, es...	ESXi650-201712401-BG	✗ Missing	Critical	Reboot, Maintenance ...
Updates misc-drivers ...	ESXi650-201712408-BG	✗ Missing	Critical	Reboot
Updates esx-base, es...	ESXi650-201805201-UG	✗ Missing	Critical	Reboot, Maintenance ...
Updates esx-xserver ...	ESXi650-201805223-UG	✗ Missing	Critical	
VMware ESXi 6.5 Co...	ESXi650-Update02	✗ Missing	Critical	Reboot, Maintenance ...
Updates esx-base	ESXi550-201312101-SG	-- Not Applicable	Critical	Reboot, Maintenance ...
Updates esx-base	ESXi550-201312401-BG	-- Not Applicable	Critical	Reboot, Maintenance ...

Remediating hosts requires copying the patches or upgrade to the host, placing the host in maintenance mode, and then installing the patches. You can reduce the time it takes for this sequence by copying the required patches to the affected hosts using the Stage option. During the Stage wizard, you will be given the option of staging some or all of the updates, as shown in Figure 5.22. You cannot stage VM/VA patches.

FIGURE 5.22   Staging updates

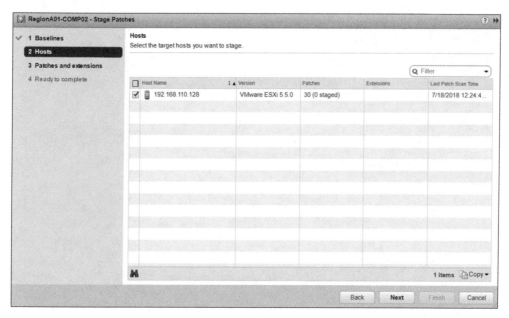

Whether or not you scan the objects or stage the hosts, you need to use the Remediate wizard to apply the patches. When remediating VM/VA baselines or groups, you have an option to schedule the update as shown in Figure 5.23 and set a pre-update snapshot that can be automatically removed as shown in Figure 5.24. Being able to automatically take a snapshot before the update allows a quick return to a known good state if there is a problem with the update; having an automatic removal of the snapshot reduces administrative overhead by not requiring an administrator to manually remove them.

When applying updates to hosts, you are presented with options including the ability to ignore warnings, as shown in Figure 5.25. While this is useful for avoiding flags for known issues, ignoring warnings would not be considered a best practice.

Other options include whether to change the power state on virtual machines on the host, which will affect how the host enters maintenance mode, and the number of retries for maintenance mode, which is useful if it takes a while to shut down VMs or evacuate the host (Figure 5.26).

If you are remediating a cluster, you will see options to disable Distributed Power Management (DPM), HA admission control, and fault tolerance (FT); see Figure 5.27. Disabling DPM (if it is enabled) will ensure that all hosts are powered on, which will make moving virtual machines around easier (as hosts are put into maintenance mode), and ensure that the hosts are available for remediation. Shutting off HA admission control will make moving virtual machines around easier as hosts will be able to hold more virtual machines without capacity being reserved. Disabling FT for VMs with FT will make moving virtual machines around easier as FT may prevent the VMs from being on hosts with different update levels, will reduce the number of VMs being moved (since the secondary will be removed), and will reduce overhead on the hosts.

FIGURE 5.23 Scheduling VM/VA updates

FIGURE 5.24 Creating snapshots and scheduling their removal

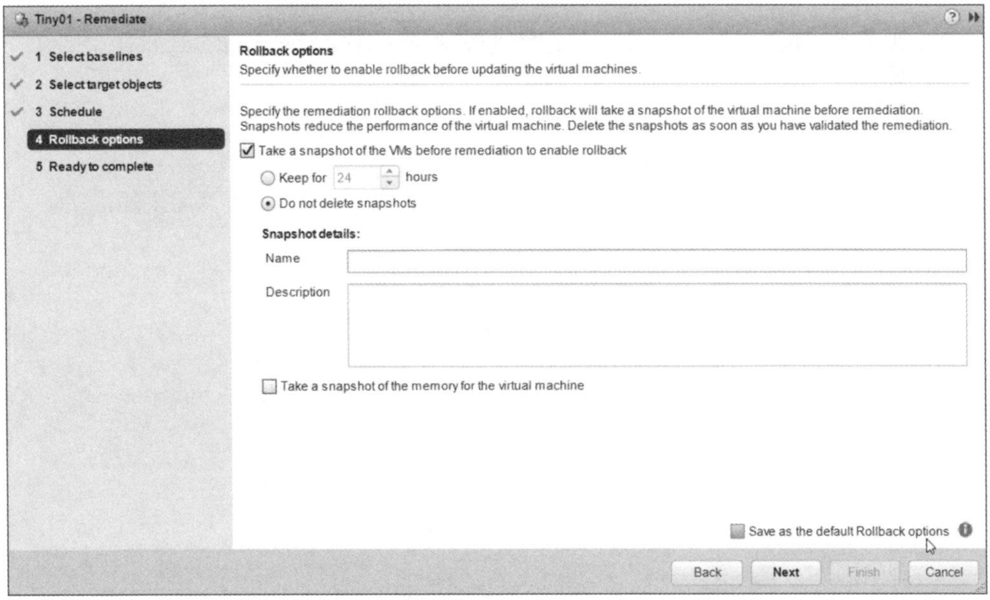

FIGURE 5.25 Scheduling host updates and choosing whether to ignore warnings

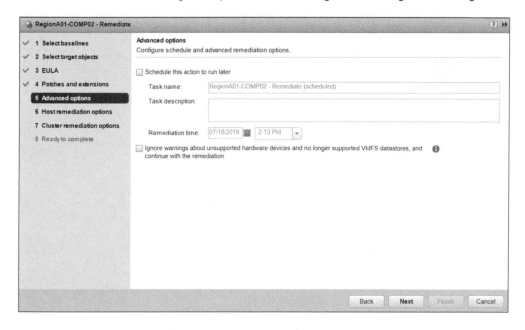

FIGURE 5.26 Changing VM power options and retry count

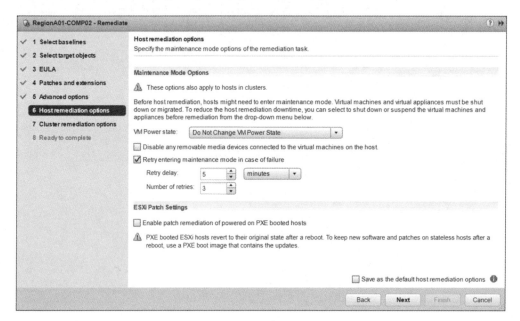

FIGURE 5.27 Change host and cluster remediation options.

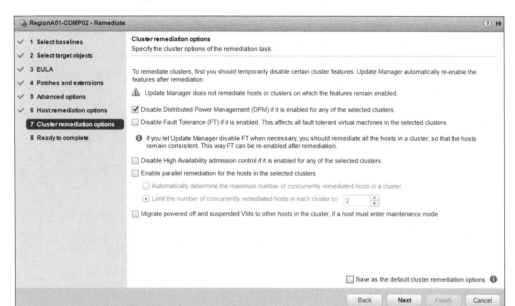

Other cluster options include the ability to update multiple hosts at a time (the default is one host at a time), and you can also manually set the max number of hosts to remediate at one time or allow VUM to decide the max. You can also choose to migrate powered-off and suspended VMs before a host is updated, which is useful if you suspect the update might make the host unavailable. These options are shown in Figure 5.27.

If you will be using VUM to upgrade your ESXi hosts as well as to apply updates, you will need to import the ESXi image to use and then use that image in the baseline. Figure 5.28 shows the import utility for ESXi images

When you create the baseline for the host upgrade, choose Host Upgrade from the first screen and then select the image you updated. If you want the upgraded host to have all the latest patches, you can create a baseline group with the upgrade and patch baselines.

You can monitor the VUM process using the Tasks & Events tab of the object being patched (Figure 5.29) or the Monitor tab of VUM (Figure 5.30).

After all of your hosts are upgraded, you can upgrade any Distributed Virtual Switch to the latest version supported by all the hosts connected. Please see the section "Upgrading and Deleting Distributed Switches" in Chapter 3, "Networking in vSphere," for more information.

FIGURE 5.28 Import ESXi image for updating.

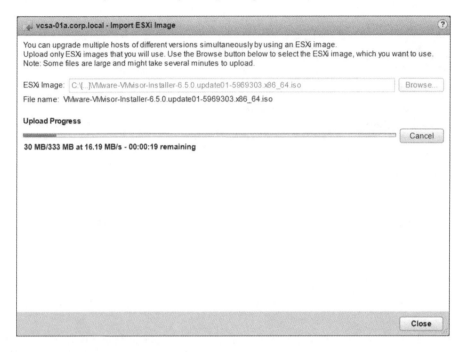

FIGURE 5.29 VUM events for a host

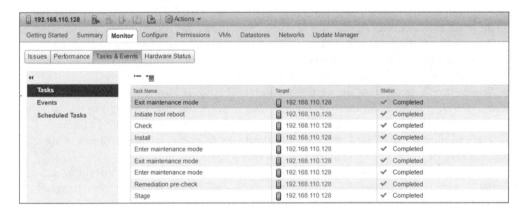

FIGURE 5.30   All VUM events

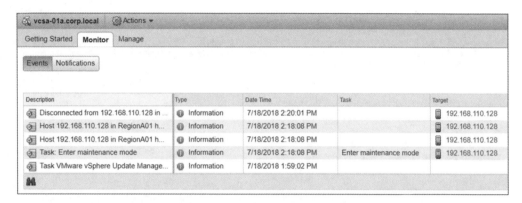

EXERCISE 5.2

Upgrade a host from 5.5 to 6.5 using VUM

Requirements: vCenter 6.5 server and one ESXi 5.5 host.

1. Download the ESXi 6.5 binaries from VMware.

2. Using the web client, start the Import ESXi Image wizard from ESXi Images in the Manage tab of the VUM view.

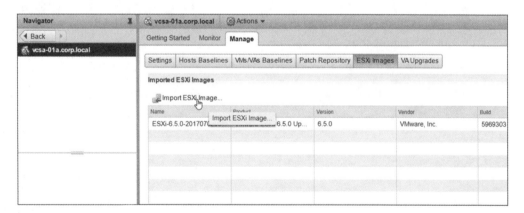

3. Select the downloaded image to start uploading it.

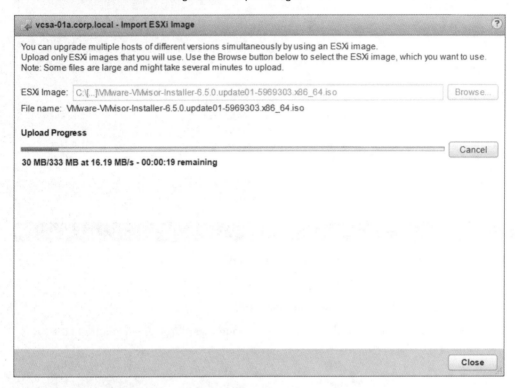

4. From Host Baselines, add a new baseline.

5. Add a name for the baseline and select Host Upgrade as the baseline type.

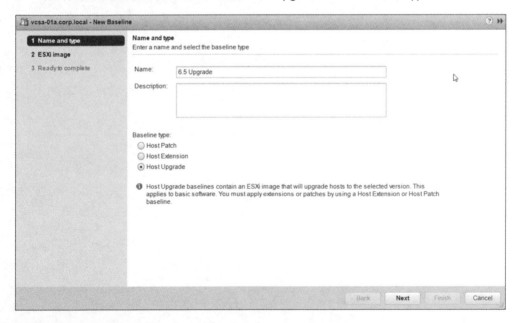

6. Select the correct upgrade image.

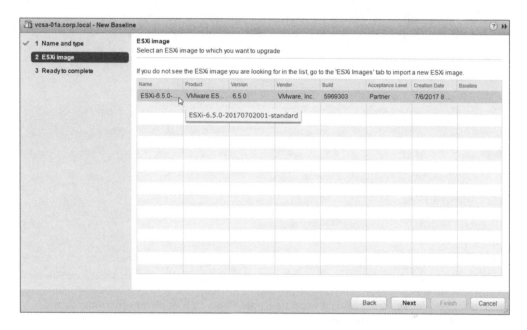

7. Click Finish to complete creating the baseline.

8. From Host Baselines, add a new baseline group.

9. Add a name for the baseline group and click Next.

10. On the Upgrades screen, select the baseline you just created and click Next.

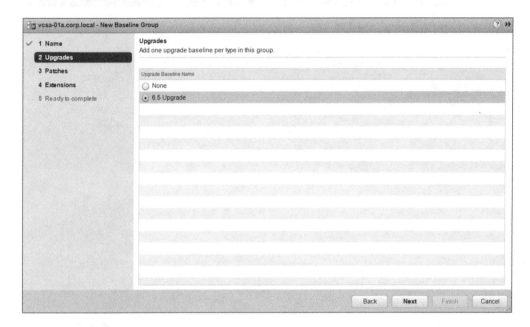

11. From the Patches screen, select the default baselines so that all current updates are applied after the upgrade and click Next.

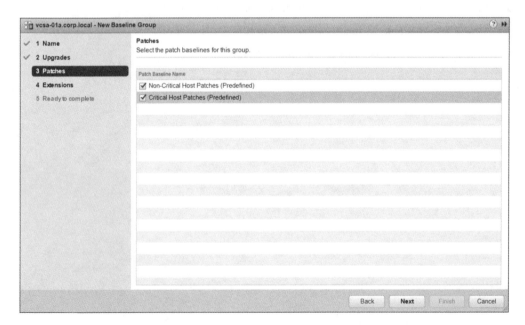

12. Click Next on the Extension screen and click Finish to complete the baseline group.

13. From the Update Manager tab of the cluster to update, click Attach Baseline to start the Attach wizard.

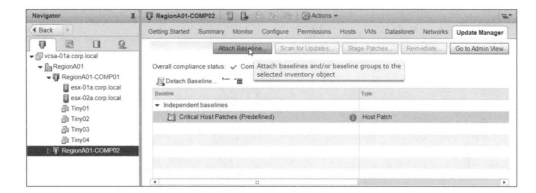

14. In the Attach wizard, select the baseline group created in step 12 and click OK.

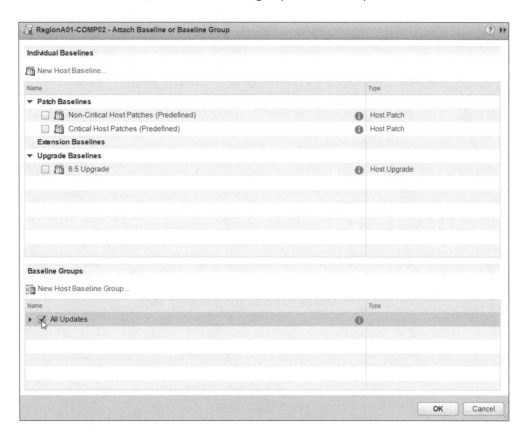

15. Click Remediate to launch the Remediate wizard.

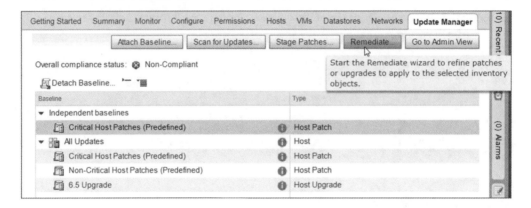

16. In the Remediate wizard, select the baseline group from step 12 and click Next.

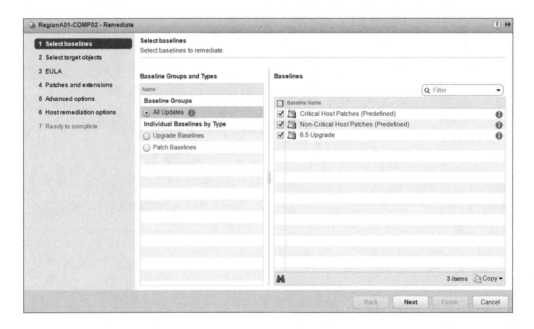

17. Select the hosts to upgrade and click Next.

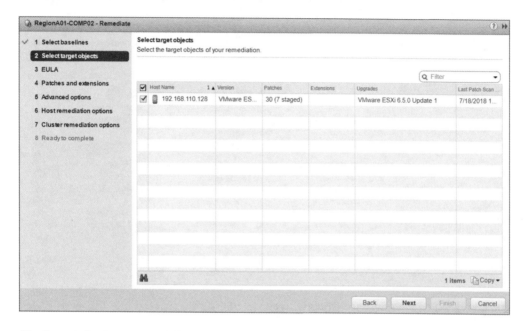

18. Accept the EULA and click Next.

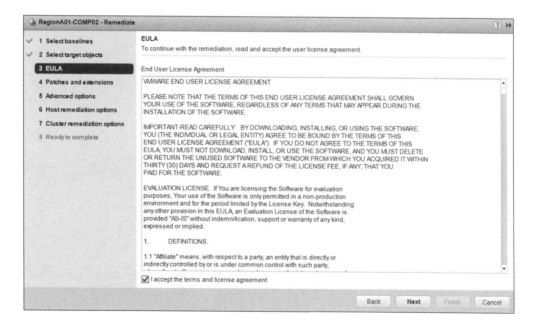

19. Verify the updates to apply and click Next.

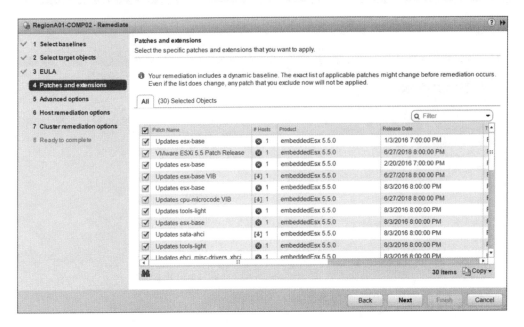

20. Click Next on the Advanced Options screen.

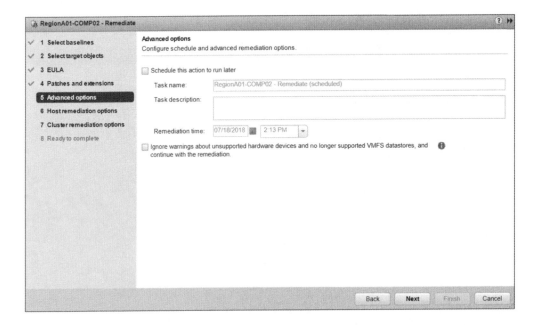

EXERCISE 5.2 *(continued)*

21. On the Host Remediation Options screen, accept the defaults by clicking Next.

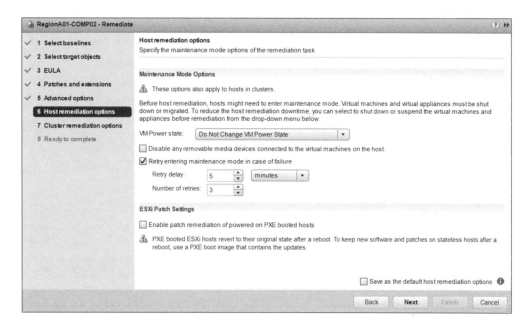

22. On the Cluster Remediation Options screen, click Next to accept the default settings.

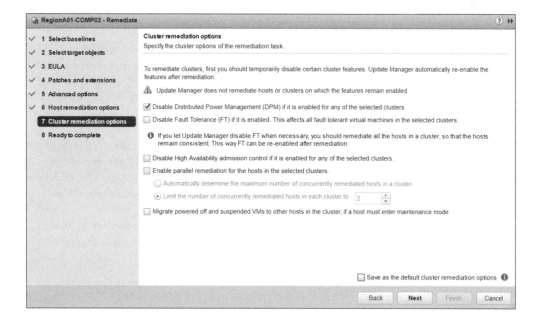

23. Verify the settings and click Finish to apply the upgrade and updates.

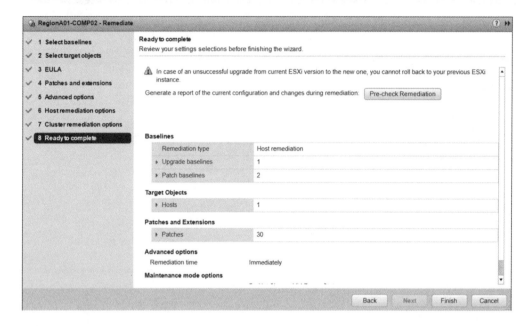

Summary

This chapter has covered upgrading a vSphere environment to version 6.5. Keeping your environment current is crucial to maintaining the best security, performance, features, and support. When migrating to 6.5, it is important to update the components in the correct order to maintain compatibility with all of the components in the environment. The upgrade order is SSO or PSC (depending on the current environment version), vCenter, hosts, and then virtual machines.

If you are currently using a Windows-based vCenter server, you have the option during the 6.5 upgrade to migrate to a vCenter Server Appliance (VCSA). This has a variety of benefits, including reducing the number of Windows licenses that are needed. The VCSA also includes vSphere Update Manager (VUM), which prior to 6.5 also required a Windows license.

After the upgrade, you can keep your hosts, VMs, and appliances up-to-date by using VUM, which allows scheduling of updates as well as choosing options such as concurrent host updates and automatic snapshot creation and removal.

Exam Essentials

Know how the upgrade changes the topology.   At the end of an upgrade, you will have either an external Platform Services Controller and vCenter server or a vCenter server with embedded PSC. While the topology can extend from there (multiple PSC and/or vCenters with or without load balancers), you can't have a distributed installation like 5.5 offered and any unsupported topology must be changed before the upgrade starts.

Understand how many Windows servers would be required.   Since your topology can't be distributed and VUM is deployed automatically on VCSA, using Auto Deploy, Inventory Service, PSC, vCenter, and VUM could use either zero, one, two or three Windows servers. Also know that VUM can't be installed on a Windows server to support VCSA, but you could deploy UMDS on a separate Windows server.

Know the upgrade order.   Know that you must update an external SSO/PSC before vCenter, update vCenter before hosts, and update hosts before VM Hardware. You need to maintain compatibility with all objects in the environment.

Know the UMDS options.   Know the main parameters for the vmware-umds.exe executable including -S, -D, -E, --enable-host, and --enable-va, and know that the UMDS can be installed on Windows- or Linux-based platforms in order to download the patches for VUM.

Understand the host and VM/VA remediate options for VUM.   Know how to configure VUM to automatically take and remove virtual machine snapshots and update concurrent hosts.

Review Questions

1. What database migration can be performed during an upgrade?

   A. Full MS SQL to PostgreSQL

   B. MS SQL Express to PostgreSQL

   C. Oracle 10 to Oracle 11

   D. MS SQL Express to full MS SQL

2. If VCSA is deployed, what function can be installed on a Windows server?

   A. Platform Services Controller

   B. Update Manager Download Service

   C. vCenter Update Manager

   D. Auto Deploy

3. If vCenter is installed on a Windows server, what other components can be installed on a separate Windows server to support it? (Choose two.)

   A. vSphere web client

   B. Auto Deploy

   C. vCenter Update Manager

   D. Update Manager Download Service

4. What vSphere objects can VUM be used to upgrade? (Choose two.)

   A. VMware virtual appliances

   B. Virtual distributed switches

   C. ESXi hosts

   D. vCenter Server

5. What virtual machine components can VUM be used to upgrade? (Choose two.)

   A. Guest OS

   B. Virtual hardware

   C. Guest applications

   D. VMware Tools

6. When you're upgrading from VCSA 6.0 to VCSA 6.5, what functions can be performed on a Windows server? (Choose two.)

   A. `vCenterServer\export`

   B. `vmware-umds`

   C. `vcsa-deploy`

   D. `migration-assistant`

7. When migrating from Windows-deployed vCenter 6.0 to VCSA 6.5, what function must be performed on a Windows server?

   A. `vCenterServer\export`

   B. `vmware-umds`

   C. `vcsa-deploy`

   D. `migration-assistant`

8. After migrating from Windows-deployed vCenter 6.0 to VCSA 6.5, what can be used to clean up the move?

   A. `C:\ProgramData\VMware\vCenterServer\export`

   B. `vmware-umds`

   C. `vcsa-deploy`

   D. `migration-assistant`

9. What is not a primary function of the `vcsa-deploy` utility?

   A. Migrate

   B. Upgrade

   C. Install

   D. Export

10. What database will be migrated to PostgreSQL during a vCenter for Windows upgrade?

   A. SQL Express

   B. MS SQL Full

   C. Oracle 11e

   D. JSON

11. What databases can be used by vCenter 6.5 on Windows? (Choose three.)

   A. SQL Express

   B. MS SQL Full

   C. Oracle 11e

   D. JSON

   E. IBM DB2

12. What is the proper upgrade order for vSphere 6.5?

   A. PSC, hosts, VMs, vCenter

   B. Hosts, PSC, vCenter, VMs

   C. vCenter, PSC, hosts, VMs

   D. PSC, vCenter, hosts, VMs

13. After several hosts were upgraded to vSphere 6.5, they are no longer available to manage in the vSphere client. What steps could be taken to resolve this? (Choose two.)

A. Revert the hosts to their previous version.

B. Upgrade the VDS to version 6.5.

C. Upgrade vCenter to version 6.5.

D. Upgrade the Web Client to version 6.5.

14. What steps should be taken after a migration of a fully distributed vSphere 5.5 environment to VCSA 6.5? (Choose two.)

A. Change DHCP to point to the new VCSA 6.5 server.

B. Shut down the Auto Deploy v5.5 service.

C. Copy the historic vCenter events to the new 6.5 vCenter.

D. Upgrade the VMware Update Manager to 6.5.

15. What data is included in a migration of a fully distributed vSphere 5.5 environment to vCSA 6.5? (Choose two.)

A. Inventory Service data

B. vSphere Syslog Collector

C. vSphere Update Manager

D. vSphere ESXi Dump Collector

16. After a migration of a fully distributed vSphere 5.5 environment to VCSA 6.5, what changes should be made manually?

A. Update vCenter to point to the new PSC.

B. Repoint ESXi Dump Log settings to the new VCSA.

C. Update hosts to point to the new Auto Deploy server.

D. Update the Auto Deploy service for the new DHCP settings.

17. Which topologies are supported for end-state of the migration of a fully distributed vSphere 5.5 environment to VCSA 6.5? (Choose two.)

A. One Windows-based vCenter server, embedded PSC

B. Two Windows-based vCenter servers, embedded PSC

C. Two VCSA, embedded PSC

D. Two VCSA, external PSC

18. By default, how many hosts will VUM update at a time?

A. One

B. Two

C. Depends on the Admission Control settings

D. Two VCSA, one external PSC, one embedded PSC

19. Which inventory objects can VUM baselines be attached to? (Choose two.)

    A. vSphere Distributed Switch

    B. Datastores

    C. Virtual machine view folders

    D. vCenter

20. Which inventory objects can VUM host and VM/VA baselines be attached to? (Choose two.)

    A. Clusters

    B. Datacenters

    C. Virtual machine view folders

    D. vCenter

21. What feature can be enabled during remediate to allow for easy rollback of changes?

    A. Export

    B. Snapshot

    C. VDP

    D. JSON

Chapter
6

Allocating Resources in a vSphere Datacenter

2V0-21.19 EXAM OBJECTIVES COVERED IN THIS CHAPTER:

✓ **Section 1 – VMware vSphere Architectures and Technologies**

- Objective 1.5 – Manage vCenter inventory efficiently
- Objective 1.6 – Describe and differentiate among vSphere, HA, DRS, and SDRS functionality
- Objective 1.7 – Describe and identify resource pools and use cases
- Objective 1.9 – Describe the purpose of cluster and the features it provides

✓ **Section 4 – Installing, Configuring, and Setting Up a VMware vSphere Solution**

- Objective 4.2 – Create and configure vSphere objects

✓ **Section 5 – Performance-tuning and Optimizing a VMware vSphere Solution**

- Objective 5.2 – Monitor resources of VCSA in a vSphere environment

✓ **Section 7 – Administrative and Operational Tasks in a VMware vSphere Solution**

- Objective 7.6 – Configure and use vSphere Compute and Storage cluster options
- Objective 7.7 – Perform different types of migrations
- Objective 7.8 – Manage resources of a vSphere environment
- Objective 7.11 – Manage different VMware vCenter Server objects
- Objective 7.13 – Identify and interpret affinity/anti affinity rules

This chapter focuses on how resources are allocated to virtual machines in a vSphere 6.7 datacenter. One of the greatest benefits of vSphere virtualization is the ability to efficiently utilize all of the physical resources in a datacenter. In fact, it is common to overcommit resources based on the assumption that in most cases the average virtual machine workload demands will fall within the available capacity of the datacenter. However, when peak conditions require that demand exceed available capacity, a number of controls exist to both manually and dynamically allocate resources to virtual machines in a manner that ensures that critical workloads are receiving the resources they require. This chapter focuses on how to administer those controls and effectively manage available resources.

When an ESXi host is added to a vSphere datacenter the resources of that host become available to virtual machines. When the datacenter consists of multiple hosts, these hosts are often grouped into vSphere clusters for both availability and load balancing purposes. The first half of this chapter will cover the creation and administration of resource pools, which can be used to distribute the aggregated CPU and memory resources of a group of ESXi hosts that have been configured as a vSphere cluster. I will cover the hierarchy that can be established with resource pools, including parent, sibling, and child pools and how their interaction with each other affects resource availability to virtual machines in the cluster. In vSphere 6.5, Custom Attributes were brought back, so we will look at how you can apply Custom Attributes to a resource pool. Since the whole purpose of setting up a resource pool hierarchy is to allocate cluster resources to virtual machines and vApps, we will look at how to create and remove resource pools and populate the pools with appropriate workloads. Finally, we will look at how to control CPU and memory distribution within a resource pool by utilizing shares, reservations, and limits.

Although one of the key concepts of a vSphere cluster is the aggregation of resources across all ESXi hosts in the cluster, a virtual machine is still only able to run on one of those hosts at any given time. To achieve the optimum balance of virtual machine performance and efficient resource utilization, vSphere Distributed Resource Scheduler, or DRS, is used. DRS was traditionally developed to handle CPU and memory resources only, much in the way that resource pools do. However, DRS functionality was applied to storage resources beginning with vSphere 5.0. It is important to note that DRS, as it relates to storage resources, is not configured or administered in a vSphere cluster. Rather, a special storage-based cluster called a datastore cluster is created that uses the storage resources of existing ESXi hosts or even vSphere clusters.

In the second half of this chapter we will focus on the creation of these clusters, beginning with how groups of hosts or virtual machines are managed within a given DRS-enabled vSphere cluster. We will then look at how to manage multi-app virtual machines and/or business-critical virtual machines using affinity and anti-affinity rules. A critical concept of DRS is how it operates depending on the level of automation configured, so we will spend some time looking at examples of this functionality. Finally, we will observe how DRS affinity and anti-affinity rules work with ESXi hosts as virtual machines are powered on in the cluster.

Administering and Managing vSphere 6.x Resources

A vSphere 6.x deployment begins with the installation and configuration of ESXi on a physical server. ESXi employs the VMkernel to virtualize the physical resources on that server. In a vSphere environment, there are four core resources: CPU, memory, network, and storage. These resources start out as physical, are virtualized by the VMkernel, and are then made available to virtual machines running on the host. As more and more hosts are brought online, a large amount of decentralized resources begins to accumulate, requiring mechanisms that can provide an efficient way to centrally manage and distribute those resources.

One of the fundamental components of this resource management methodology is the *vSphere cluster*. A vSphere cluster is a construct that aggregates a number of ESXi hosts so that their underlying resources can likewise be aggregated and distributed as needed to virtual machines and vApps running on the hosts within that cluster.

Figure 6.1 shows a vSphere cluster with two ESXi hosts viewed from a vSphere 6.7 Web Client using HTML5.

FIGURE 6.1   A vSphere 6.7 hierarchy containing a vSphere cluster, two ESXi hosts, and three virtual machines

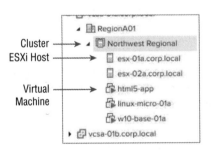

To see what resources are available within the cluster, we could take a look at the Summary page for the cluster, as shown in Figure 6.2.

FIGURE 6.2   The Summary page for a vSphere 6.7 cluster showing Free, Used, and Capacity Resources

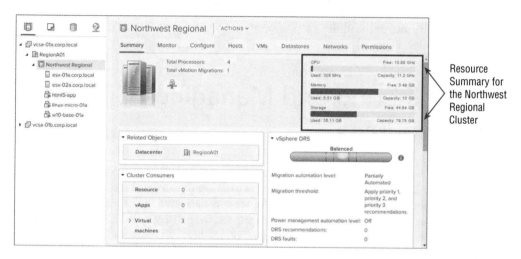

Resource
Summary for
the Northwest
Regional
Cluster

As you can see, the resources for the two ESXi hosts have been aggregated into a single block of resources that can now be monitored for utilization. However, there are many resource management use cases that cannot be met without further refinement Additionally, if multiple departments have contributed budget resources to this cluster, there is no way to ensure that any given department is guaranteed the resources they paid for. These are just a couple of cases that can be met through the use of *resource pools*.

🌐 **Real World Scenario**

Resource Pools Solve an Organization's Workload Issues

An organization has recently run into an issue where several business-critical work-loads have reported severely degraded performance. These workloads are vital to the company, and performance degradation can be directly tied to lost revenue. Upon inspection, it is determined that the affected workloads are memory intensive. There are other noncritical memory-intensive workloads that have continued to perform well during this period.

The organization decides to implement resource pools in order to resolve the problem. They create a resource pool for critical workloads and one for noncritical workloads. They utilize shares in the resource pools, setting the share value to high for the critical pool and low for the noncritical pool.

After two weeks, workload administrators report that no further performance degradation issues have been reported.

Configuring Multilevel Resource Pools

The vSphere Resource Management Guide defines a resource pool as "a logical abstraction for the flexible management of resources." The part regarding logical abstraction is another way of saying that a resource pool can be used to represent an amount of CPU and memory resources that could come from any number of ESXi hosts in a vSphere cluster, with varying amounts of resources pulled from those hosts at any time. The part regarding flexibility is an indication that a resource pool can be easily adjusted to provide more (or less) CPU and/or memory resources, as well as adjusting the priority access to those resources. When resource pools are created as child pools of existing pools, an administrator can create a guaranteed, repeatable way to allocate resources and priority access to resources across a vSphere cluster.

For example, an organization has two departments, Sales and R&D. Both departments have contributed budgetary resources for IT infrastructure. The vSphere cluster has a total available capacity of 10 GHz CPU and 8 GB memory. In real-life environments, this would be a ridiculously small amount of resources, but throughout this book I have used an environment and screen shots identical to what you would see if you go through VMware's Hands-on Labs. The small size also works to our advantage when describing how multilevel resource pools function.

Figure 6.3 displays a resource pool configuration that would meet the needs of the organization. Starting from the top down, we have the actual vSphere cluster. The cluster contains two ESXi hosts, and the resources shown are aggregated. The vSphere cluster and its available resources are referred to as the *root* resource pool. From this pool, we are able to create *child* resource pools for each department. These pools are considered child pools because they get resources from the pool immediately above them (in this case the root pool). However, these pools are also considered *sibling* pools in relation to each other. Sibling pools are at the same level in a resource pool hierarchy and are completely isolated from one another.

When we create these pools, we would allocate the resources each department has budgeted. Workloads that run within these pools are only able to use the resources provided by the pools, unless the *Expandable Reservation* option has been selected (more on this later).

Let's focus a little more on the workloads themselves. In Figure 6.3, each virtual machine in the Sales resource pool is configured with 2 GHz of CPU and 1 GB RAM. However, just because a virtual machine is configured to use resources does not mean that the virtual machine is guaranteed those resources. In order for a virtual machine to have guaranteed access to CPU and memory resources, they must be reserved. To do this, an administrator would go to the configuration settings for the virtual machine and establish reservations for CPU and memory resources. In fact, administrators have the option of setting reservations, limits, and shares for both CPU and memory resources on virtual machines, vApps, and resource pools. Before moving further, let's take some time to ensure a good understanding of these three settings.

FIGURE 6.3 A representation of a vSphere cluster with child resource pools and virtual machines

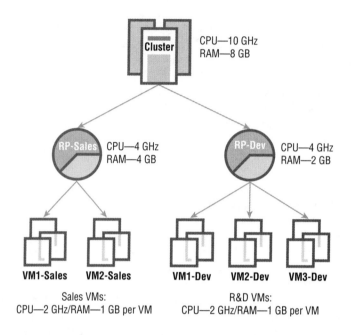

Reservations, Limits, and Shares

A *reservation* is a guaranteed amount of resources. These resources are allocated to the virtual machine when it is powered on, and the resources cannot be claimed for any other workload, even if the virtual machine is idle. By default, a virtual machine does not have a reservation. So, using Figure 6.3 as an example, let's say that none of the Development virtual machines have a reservation configured. If all three were powered on and running applications, they would likely have to compete for resources since the aggregated amount of resources for the three virtual machines exceeds the amount of resources available in the pool.

I use the term *likely* because in order for contention to occur, all three virtual machines would need to be active to the point where they exceed the resources in the pool. If one was idle, or if they were all running but using few resources, there would be no contention and no potential performance issues.

In fact, it is this functionality that allows an administrator to fully utilize all of the available resources of a vSphere cluster by overcommitting resources and assuming that not all virtual machines will operate at peak utilization at the same time. Of course, if there is high activity and virtual machine requirements exceed available resources, contention occurs and performance may be impacted. This may be OK for some virtual machines (like our Development virtual machines), but it would not be OK for more mission-critical production virtual machines.

To achieve an optimal balance between utilization and performance, it would be necessary to put some controls in place to ensure that the environment performs as expected. We have been looking at reservations, which are one type of control. We could use a full reservation for extremely mission-critical virtual machines, which would ensure that those virtual machines have complete access to resources at any time. For less critical virtual machines, it might make sense to determine average utilization and set a reservation that ensures that the average usage can be met without contention. That way, the virtual machines have the resources they need under most conditions.

To set a reservation, edit the settings of the virtual machine as shown in Figure 6.4.

FIGURE 6.4   The Edit Settings page for a virtual machine showing the configuration of CPU and memory resources

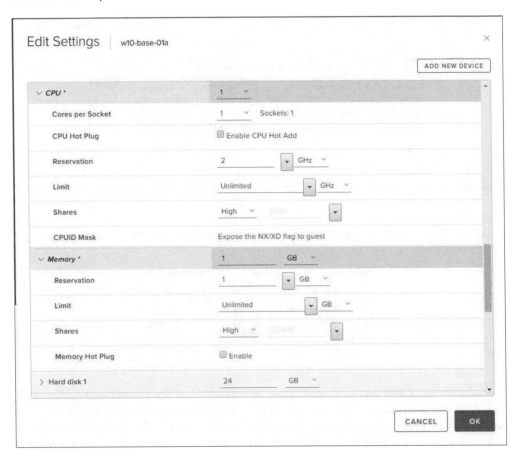

Another control that can be used with resource allocation is the *limit*. A limit establishes an upper boundary for the amount of CPU and/or memory resources a virtual machine is granted. By default, there is no defined limit, so a virtual machine is limited to the amount of resources allocated to it during initial configuration. For example, our Sales virtual machines were configured with a single CPU and 1 GB of memory. Therefore, the intrinsic limit for these virtual machines is the speed of the CPU in the ESXi host and 1 GB for memory.

The other control we want to address is *shares*. A share value determines priority access to resources during times of contention, or when virtual machines are forced to share resources. This distinction is important, because unless there is contention for resources, the share values assigned to virtual machines are not taken into consideration. There are three selectable share levels: High, Normal, and Low. These levels operate at a 4:2:1 ratio, so a single high share would provide four times more resources than a single low share. Figure 6.5 shows the default share values for virtual machine CPU and memory resources.

FIGURE 6.5 The number of shares assigned to a virtual machine depending on the share setting

Virtual Machine Share Allocation (by default)		
Setting	CPU Share Values	Memory Share Values
High	2000 Shares per vCPU	20 Shares per MB
Normal	1000 Shares per vCPU	10 Shares per MB
Low	500 Shares per vCPU	5 Shares per MB

To provide an example, let's say we had three virtual machines in a single resource pool, as shown in Figure 6.6.

FIGURE 6.6 Three virtual machines, each with one vCPU and the default share setting of Normal

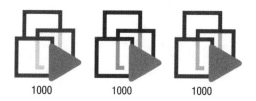

| 1000 | 1000 | 1000 |

Under normal operating conditions where no contention exists, each virtual machine would receive 100 percent of the resources it requires and share settings would not be a factor. However, when contention does exist, the share settings in this case would provide approximately 33 1/3 percent of available resources to each virtual machine. Let's further consider that one of the virtual machines is running a mission-critical application and should have higher-priority access to resources. Using the share setting of High, we change the configuration of the middle virtual machine, as seen in Figure 6.7.

FIGURE 6.7   Three virtual machines, the second of which has been elevated to a High share setting

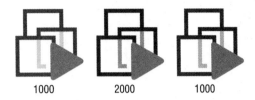

1000   2000   1000

Now, should contention occur, the mission-critical virtual machine would receive 50 percent of the available resources, and each of the other machines would receive 25 percent. Shares are dynamic by nature, so as additional virtual machines are powered on, the amount of resources would scale appropriately. An example of this is shown in Figure 6.8, where a fourth virtual machine with a Low share setting has been powered on.

FIGURE 6.8   Four virtual machines, the fourth of which has a Low share setting

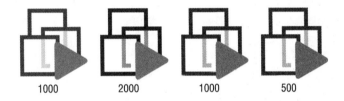

1000   2000   1000   500

In this final example, should contention occur, the mission-critical virtual machine would receive approximately 44 percent of the available resources, each of the Normal virtual machines would receive 22 percent, and the new virtual machine would receive 11 percent. These amounts would continue to adjust as other machines were powered on or off.

Taking these concepts into consideration, let's establish that each virtual machine in Figure 6.9 has been configured with reservations in the amounts shown.

If an IT administrator were to power on all three virtual machines in the Sales resource pool, they would power on successfully since the requirements of each virtual machine can be satisfied by the resources from the pool. However, if an IT administrator were to power on all three virtual machines in the Development pool, the third virtual machine would fail to power on. This would occur even though the aggregated resource requirements of the virtual machines are 3 GHz of CPU and 3 GB of RAM, and the resource pool is configured with the same amount of resources. The reason for this is that when a deployment like this is designed, an architect must take into account the memory overhead required for each virtual machine. Those requirements are shown in Figure 6.10.

FIGURE 6.9   A multilevel resource pool deployment with two pools and six virtual machines

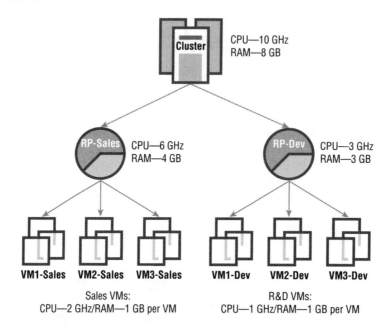

Sales VMs:
CPU—2 GHz/RAM—1 GB per VM

R&D VMs:
CPU—1 GHz/RAM—1 GB per VM

FIGURE 6.10   The memory overhead for a virtual machine based on various vCPU and memory configurations

Virtual Machine Memory Overhead				
	1 vCPU	**2 vCPUs**	**4 vCPUs**	**8 vCPUs**
256 MB	20.29 MB	24.28 MB	32.23 MB	48.16 MB
1024 MB	25.90 MB	29.91 MB	37.86 MB	53.82 MB
4096 MB	48.64 MB	52.72 MB	60.67 MB	76.78 MB
16384 MB	139.62 MB	143.98 MB	151.93 MB	168.60 MB

To resolve this issue, the resources for the pool could be increased, or the *Expandable Reservation* option could be enabled. If this option is selected and additional resources are required, they can be allocated from a higher-level resource pool if available (in this case the root pool). Since the pool only needs about 78 MB (three 1vCPU, 1 GB VMs with approximately 26 MB of overhead each as seen in Figure 6.10), the requirement could be fulfilled in this way and the third virtual machine could be powered on using resources from the root pool.

The problem with using the Expandable Reservation option is that it negates the purpose of the resource pool configuration. It allows a pool to allocate resources from an upper-level pool. Figure 6.11 shows a similar configuration as Figure 6.9 but with an additional virtual machine added to the Sales pool and with increased CPU reservations on the Development virtual machines. Both resource pools have also been configured to utilize the Expandable Reservation property.

FIGURE 6.11 A virtual machine has been added to the Sales pool, and Expandable Reservations is enabled.

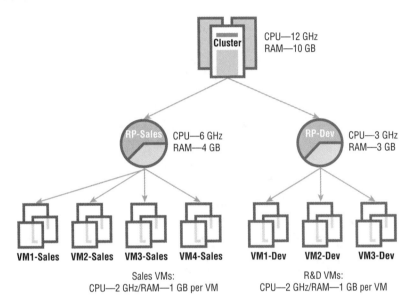

Now, an IT administrator powers on the four virtual machines in the Sales pool. Because there are insufficient resources to meet the virtual machines' requirements and the Expandable Reservation option has been enabled, the Sales pool can look to its parent pool to see if resources are available. In this case, 9 GHz of CPU resources and 7 GB of RAM have been reserved by the two pools, leaving 3 GB of CPU and 3 GB of RAM available. Since the resources are available, they are allocated from the root pool. If an administrator then attempts to power on virtual machines in the Development pool, the first virtual machine would power on. The second virtual machine requires additional CPU resources, but since the Expandable Reservation option is enabled, it can obtain the resources from its parent pool. Since the root pool has 1 GHz of CPU still available, it is allocated to the Development pool and the virtual machine is powered on. However, it is not possible to power on the final virtual machine. Even though enough memory could be allocated, there are no CPU resources available. Every time an administrator attempts to power on a virtual machine in a resource pool, or create a child pool from a resource pool, this same process is repeated. This process is known as *resource pool admission control*.

Consider the multilevel resource pool shown in Figure 6.12. An additional set of pools has been configured from the Sales parent pool to allow for virtual machines related to the organization's web storefront to have resources isolated from the rest of the Sales group's machines.

FIGURE 6.12   A multilevel resource pool deployment showing parent, child, and sibling relationships

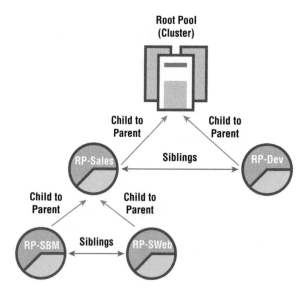

As shown in the figure, if a virtual machine in the RP-SBM pool were powered on and resources were not available in the pool, the resources could be allocated from a parent. So, the RP-SBM pool could get resources from the RP-Sales pool, which in turn could get resources from the root pool. Pools cannot attempt to obtain resources from sibling pools. If insufficient resources were available, the power operation would fail.

Now that we've had an opportunity to explore critical exam concepts around creating a multilevel hierarchical structure; dealing with shares, limits, and reservations; and looking at the impact of the Expandable Reservation property, let's turn to some of the common administrative tasks that should be mastered.

Resource Pool Administration Exercises

Now that you have learned about resource pools and resource allocation mechanisms, let's apply that knowledge in some hands-on exercises. For most of these exercises, you can use either C# or HTML5 clients. If you do not have a test environment, I would recommend using the one of the Hands-on Labs available from VMware, which can be used for free. If you are using your own environment, I would recommend at least two ESXi hosts added to a vSphere cluster with a couple of virtual machines.

In the first exercise, you are creating a resource pool hierarchy for a hospital. We are assuming a cluster has already been created, labeled Northwest Regional.

EXERCISE 6.1

Create a resource pool

1. Connect to a vCenter Server using the vSphere Web Client.

2. Right-click the Northwest Regional vSphere cluster and click New Resource Pool.

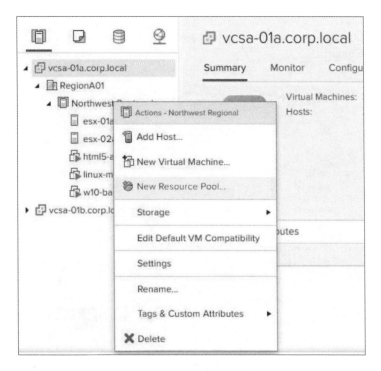

3. Name the resource pool Sales. Define a 4 GHz CPU reservation for the pool. You can choose GHz from the drop-down as shown when using larger resource quantities. Make sure to uncheck the Expandable box in the Reservation Type section.

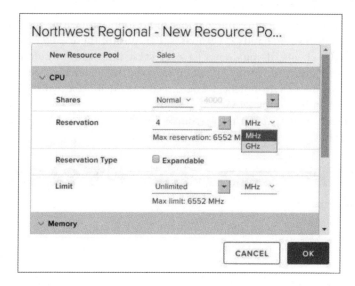

4. Define a 4 GB memory reservation in the same manner, again unchecking the Expandable box:

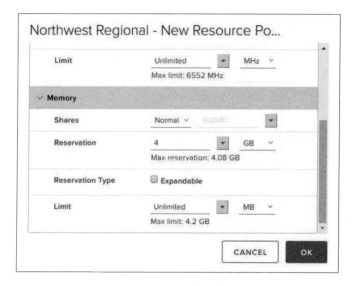

5. Click OK to complete the Sales resource pool configuration. Your resulting configuration should look like this.

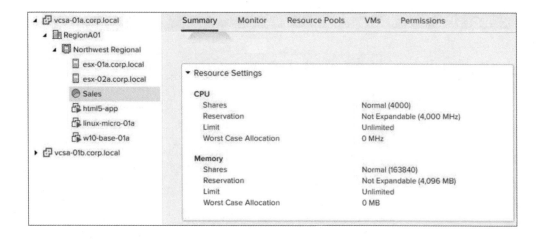

Next, you will add a virtual machine to the Sales resource pool you just created.

EXERCISE 6.2

Add a virtual machine to a resource pool

1. Connect to a vCenter Server using the vSphere Web Client.

2. Click the Sales resource pool you just created, then click the VMs tab just under the Actions drop-down. Currently, no VMs are attached to the pool.

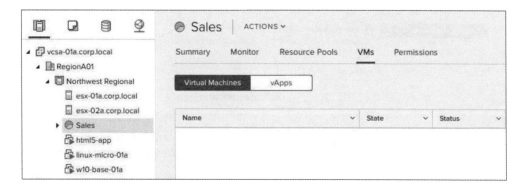

3. There are multiple methods for moving a VM into a resource pool. One method is to drag the VM into the pool. In this exercise, right-click the VM, in this case the html5-app VM, and click Migrate.

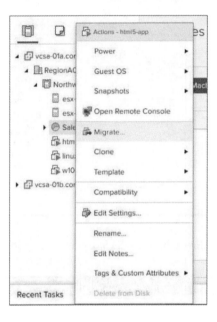

4. Click the Resource Pools filter, then choose the Sales resource pool. The Compatibility window should indicate "Compatibility checks succeeded."

5. Click Next. You will be prompted to select a vMotion priority. Since this is the Sales resource pool, leave the option set to high priority.

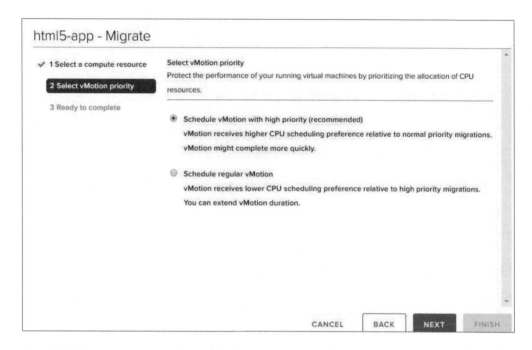

6. Click Next. A summary of your choices appears. Click Finish.

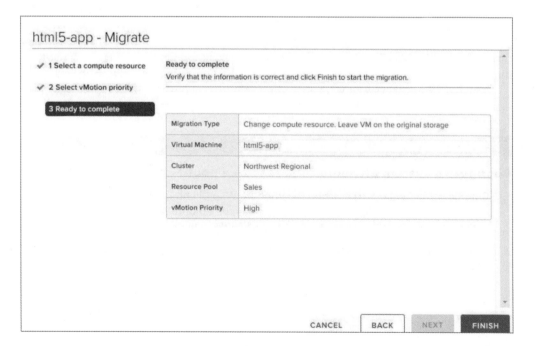

7. The VMs tab just under the Actions drop-down will now show the html5-app VM. It takes a minute or so before the resource pool information is updated.

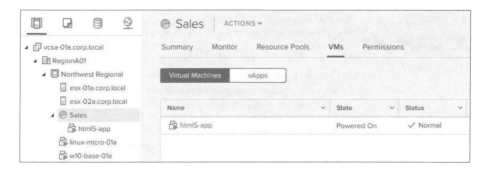

Using Tags and Custom Attributes

Before the next exercise, let's take a moment to review the concept of *tags* and *custom attributes*. A tag is a label that can be applied to many vSphere inventory objects, including a resource pool. These tags can be used to add specific metadata to an object, which could then be used to identify one or more objects that have the same tag. However, before tags debuted in vSphere 5.1, they were actually known as custom attributes. Now, as of vSphere 6.5, custom attributes are back and you are free to use both tags and custom attributes to add information to your inventory objects. The key difference between the two is that when you define a custom attribute, you can then assign a specific value for that attribute to every object. With tags, you can, for example, create a category and apply that category to one or more objects, but you cannot assign the category with a unique value to those objects.

Now that we have reviewed what a custom attribute is and what it is used for, let's assign one to our resource pool.

Configure a custom attribute for a resource pool

1. Connect to a vCenter Server using the vSphere Web Client. For this exercise, it is necessary to use the Flash Client in order to see the Custom Attributes window (although you can still set a custom attribute in either client).

2. Right-click the Sales resource pool and scroll to the Tags & Custom Attributes option. When the option expands, click Edit Custom Attributes.

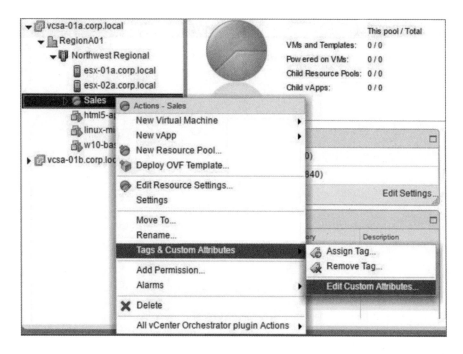

3. We will add a custom attribute that indicates who the administrator of each resource pool is. For the Sales resource pool, that individual is Jacob Barnes. Type **RP_Administrator** into the Attribute box and **Jacob Barnes** into the Value box.

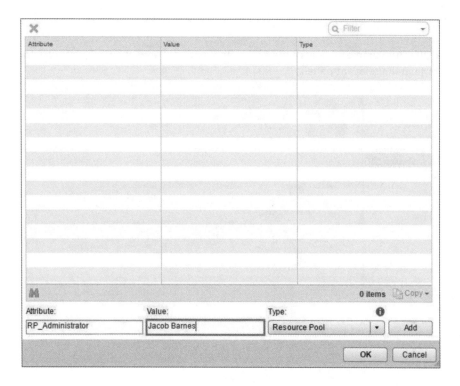

4. Click Add. Notice how the attribute and value now show in the box.

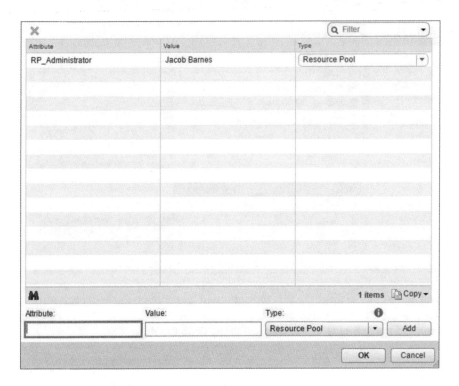

5. Click OK. The Summary page of the Sales resource pool now shows the new custom attribute in the relevant panel.

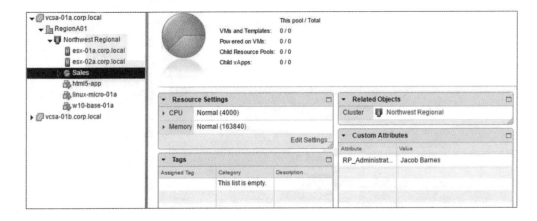

In the next exercise, you will remove a virtual machine from a resource pool. This might occur if you are moving a VM to another pool, or if you are doing development work on the VM and don't want resources in the pool impacted by the work you are doing.

EXERCISE 6.4

Remove a virtual machine from a resource pool

1. Connect to a vCenter Server using the vSphere Web Client.

2. Click the Sales resource pool you just created, then click the VMs tab. You should see the html5-app in the pool.

3. Right-click the html5-app VM and select Migrate.

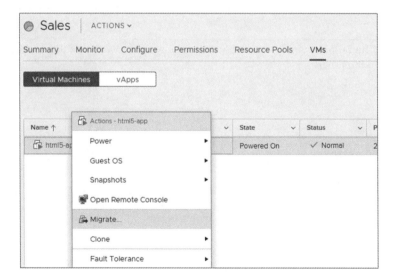

4. To remove this VM from the pool, we need to place it into another pool, or into the root pool, which in this case is the Northwest Regional cluster. Select the Clusters filter and then select the Northwest Regional cluster. Confirm that the Compatibility window indicates "Compatibility checks succeeded."

5. Click Next. You will be prompted to select a vMotion priority. Since this is the Sales resource pool, leave the option set to high priority.

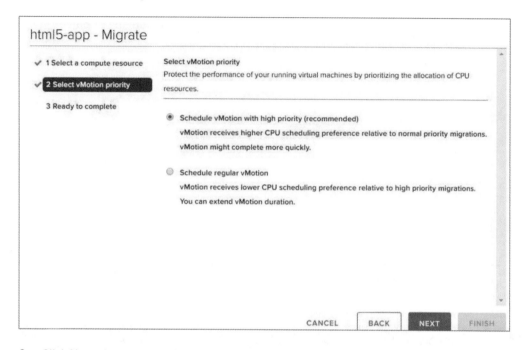

6. Click Next. A summary of your choices appears. Click Finish.

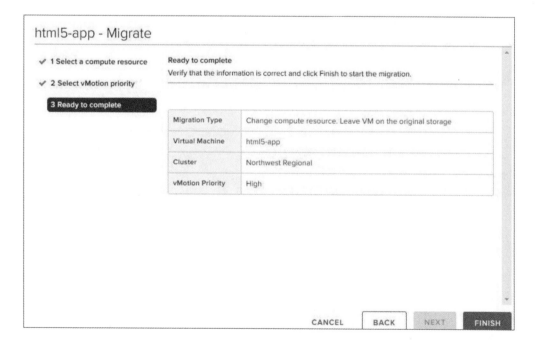

7. The VMs tab will now be empty and the html5-app VM will show in the inventory under the Northwest Regional cluster. It takes a minute or so before the resource pool information is updated.

In the next exercise, you will remove the resource pool you have created. You may need to remove a resource pool if you intend to change your resource allocation structure.

EXERCISE 6.5

Remove a resource pool

1. Connect to a vCenter Server using the vSphere Web Client.

2. Right-click the Sales resource pool you just created, then click Delete.

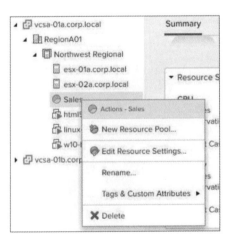

3. Confirm your selection by clicking Yes.

4. A look at the inventory should indicate that the Sales resource pool has been successfully removed.

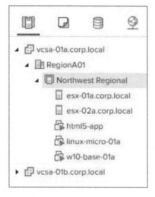

Configuring vSphere DRS and Storage DRS Clusters

With resource pools, we first gather resources from a number of ESXi hosts into a cluster, then allocate resources from that cluster to pools of virtual machines. However, this is only one method of resource management, and it does not cover all of the concerns an organization would have regarding the allocation of resources. For example, how do we prevent one of the hosts in the cluster from becoming resource constrained even though there are other hosts with available resources? Or how do we prevent a datastore from becoming I/O bound? These are just two of the concerns addressed by the use of the Distributed Resource Scheduler, or DRS. DRS comes in two flavors. The first is simply DRS, which governs CPU and memory resources. The second is Storage DRS, which governs storage I/O. Both of these are detailed in the following sections.

Distributed Resource Scheduler

Distributed Resource Scheduler, or DRS, is a technology designed to balance the distribution of resources in a cluster with the virtual machines running on the cluster. When DRS is enabled on a cluster, it becomes aware of the resources available across the cluster. DRS can then work to ensure that virtual machines are distributed across the cluster in a manner that balances resource utilization. It does this in two ways. First, DRS controls the *initial placement* of virtual machines. Initial placement involves the placement of a virtual machine on a host in the cluster based on current workloads across the cluster. When a virtual machine is first powered on, DRS looks at the available resources on the cluster as well as the individual resource utilization of each host in the cluster. Based on this information, the virtual machine is placed on the host with the most available resources. This is done for every virtual machine, balancing the resources of the hosts with the resource requirements of the virtual machines.

Next, DRS maintains the balance by monitoring resource utilization across the cluster. Should a host become resource constrained due to an uptick in utilization by the VMs running on the host, DRS is capable of migrating one or more VMs off the host and on to other hosts in the cluster. This helps to ensure that the cluster maintains a balanced load across all hosts.

Figure 6.13 shows a three-host cluster. The top part of the diagram shows the cluster before DRS load balancing is performed. After enabling DRS, migrations are made that balance out the workload, resulting in the end state shown.

FIGURE 6.13   A vSphere 6.7 cluster before and after DRS is enabled

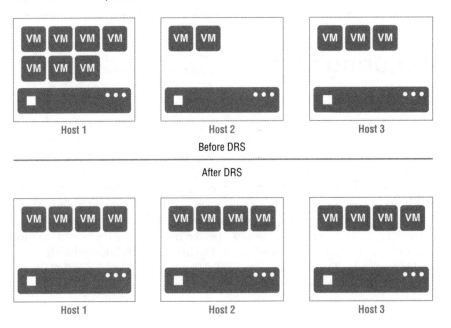

When enabling DRS, there are a number of settings to control functionality. The first is the *Automation Level* set for DRS. The DRS Automation Level is the degree to which DRS will automatically control both initial placement and load balancing across the cluster. There are three levels of automation: Manual, Partially Automated, and Fully Automated. When it's set to Manual, DRS will provide recommendations for initial placement and migration but will not take any action. If it's set to Partially Automated, initial placement is automated but migration is still manual. Finally, when it's set to Fully Automated, both initial placement and migration are automatic. These options are in place to allow an administrator to decide exactly the amount of control they wish to allow the system to have, and there are adjustable settings so that even if the system is automated, the automation can be restricted to certain levels and virtual machines.

The first step to working with DRS is to enable it on a cluster and select the level of automation, as shown in Figure 6.14.

FIGURE 6.14   Enabling DRS on a cluster and selecting the level of automation

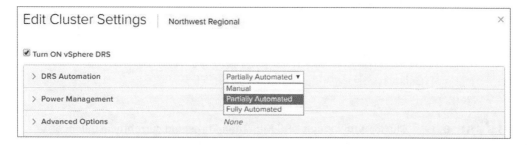

So, you are enabling DRS but have concerns about setting the automation level to Fully Automated. There are a number of logical reasons to be concerned. For example, you may be comfortable with the performance of an application on a specific host and are concerned about it being moved. Or you may have concerns that all of the migration performed to load balance may generate additional overhead. Not to worry, because there are several controls that can be adjusted to ensure that the amount of automation performed is exactly how you want it.

The first of these controls, and perhaps the most important, is the DRS *Migration Threshold*. The DRS Migration Threshold controls how aggressively migrations are performed in order to balance workloads across the cluster. The setting runs from priority 1 to 5, where 5 is the most aggressive setting. For details on each priority level, refer to the chart in Figure 6.15.

As you can see in the diagram, the default is priority level 3, which is suitable for most implementations. However, it's a good idea to monitor the balance level of the cluster to ensure that the current setting is ideal. You can view DRS status and current settings on the summary page of the cluster. A cluster with the default priority setting that is balanced would look like the image in Figure 6.16.

FIGURE 6.15   DRS Migration Threshold priorities based on criticality of recommendation

Migration Threshold	Details
Criticality of recommendation	
1	Apply only critical recommendations that must be taken to avoid violating cluster constraints like affinity rules and host maintenance.
2	Apply only major recommendations that promise a significant improvement to the cluster's load balance and priority 1 recommendations.
3*	Apply typical recommendations that promise at least good improvements to the cluster's load balance as well as priority 1 and priority 2 recommendations.
4	Apply any recommendation that would provide a moderate improvement to the cluster's load balance as well as priority 1, priority 2, and priority 3 recommendations.
5	Apply any recommendation, even those that would only provide a slight improvement to the cluster's load balance as well as all other priority recommendations.

FIGURE 6.16   Cluster with default DRS Migration Threshold currently in balance

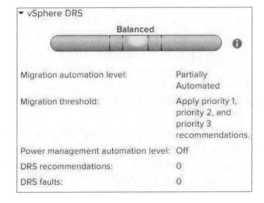

Predictive DRS

The options for configuring DRS to this point allow you to establish one of two methods for dealing with resource imbalance. The first is the *Reactive method*. The Reactive method is one in which DRS determines that a resource imbalance has occurred and supplies a recommendation but takes no action. This happens if DRS is configured for Manual mode. If in Partially Automated mode, this is the case for any migration recommendation. Finally, for Fully Automated mode, this still occurs for any recommendation below the threshold setting. While there is very little overhead associated with this method, resource imbalances are only addressed after the fact and after an administrator has acted on the recommendation.

The second method is the *Balanced method*. The Balanced method is one in which DRS determines that a resource imbalance has occurred and automatically acts to resolve the imbalance. This is the case when DRS is configured for Fully Automated mode and the recommendation is at or above the threshold setting. This method has the advantage of mitigating risk and keeping workloads balanced across hosts in the DRS cluster but has a higher overhead. In fact, it is possible to inject a large overhead into cluster operations if the DRS threshold is improperly configured. That said, this method is very effective at preventing most resource imbalances or in the very least quickly resolving those imbalances.

Effective since vSphere 6.5 is a third method, the *Predictive method*. The Predictive method is one in which DRS is able to predict future demand and identify when and where a resource imbalance is likely to occur. It then uses this information to move workloads before the affected resource is in contention. The Predictive method utilizes a new feature called Predictive DRS, which combines the abilities of DRS with another VMware product, vRealize Operations Manager (vROps). Because only the affected workloads are adjusted on the DRS cluster, this method requires minimal overhead.

Now, it is important to underscore that Predictive DRS is only possible by using vSphere in conjunction with vRealize Operations Manager. This is because Predictive DRS leverages the dynamic thresholds found in vROps, which use historical and live data to establish a baseline for the behavior of a given workload. The baseline is then combined with an upper and lower threshold for what is considered "typical" behavior. Anything that falls above or below these thresholds is anomalous.

Predictive DRS takes the information supplied by vROps and asks three simple questions. First, what resources are available on each host in the DRS cluster? Second, what VMs are powered on, and on which hosts are they running? Finally, how much of a given resource is required for each of the VM workloads over the day?

To better understand this concept, let's look at the graph in Figure 6.17.

The graph depicts the demand for a resource (like CPU or memory) by a workload over a period of time. The dotted line represents the actual utilization of the resource by the workload. The long dashed line represents the predicted utilization of the resource by the workload over the same period of time. So, for example, let's say that an accounting company performs batch operations at the same time every day, resulting in a spike in the utilization of CPU resources. Since vROps is using historical data, it is aware that this is a spike that occurs with given regularity. As a result, Predictive DRS can use this information to proactively remediate the workload to a host that has sufficient resources to handle the spike, thereby avoiding any impact to performance. This vastly reduces the likelihood that a spike in utilization will result in any noticeable impact.

FIGURE 6.17 Predictive DRS method vs. Balanced method (resource demand for a given workload over a 24-hour period recommendation)

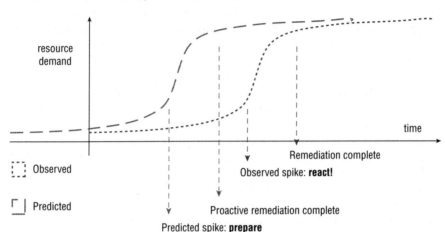

It is important to be aware that the Predictive method does not resolve every workload imbalance. This is because Predictive DRS relies on regular changes in utilization. No method can proactively resolve an unforeseen spike in utilization, which is why it is important to properly configure Fully Automated mode with an appropriate threshold. This way, Predictive DRS can proactively resolve any known utilization changes, while DRS can react and balance workloads in the event an unforeseen change occurs.

Network-Aware DRS

Traditionally, DRS has always focused on two of the four "core" resources used by virtual machines, CPU and memory, when balancing workloads across hosts in the cluster. This is because for the most part, CPU and memory resources are the most likely to experience rapid increases in utilization that could impact other workloads on the same ESXi hosts. However, there are some workloads that can have similar spikes in network and/or storage resource utilization. Fortunately, there are tools in vSphere 6.7 to help mitigate these types of spikes and ensure that all workloads perform well no matter what resource or resources might be impacted.

In earlier releases of vSphere, DRS did not analyze network utilization and did not factor this resource into consideration when migrating a workload. As a result, a workload with heavy network resource requirements could be migrated due to a CPU spike to an ESXi host that is already network saturated. Unfortunately, this means that the workload could continue to experience potential performance issues, but this time due to contention for network resources instead of CPU resources. In addition, since earlier versions of DRS didn't look at network utilization, the problem would go unnoticed by DRS and require manual, reactive intervention.

DRS became network-aware beginning with version 6 and was significantly enhanced in 6.5. This feature is known as *network-aware DRS*. Network-aware DRS monitors the network send and receive rates of the physical uplinks on ESXi hosts in the cluster and avoids placing virtual machines on hosts that are network saturated. This means that DRS now considers the network utilization of ESXi hosts in the cluster as well as the network requirements of VMs during both initial placement and load balancing.

Looking at placement first, when a user powers on a VM, DRS looks at available CPU and memory resources on hosts and the CPU and memory requirements of the VM and makes an initial determination as to which host the VM will be placed on. DRS then factors in some network heuristics and makes a final decision on where the VM should be placed.

Before discussing actions taken by DRS for workload balancing, it is important to note that DRS will *not* move a virtual machine due to a network resource imbalance. What DRS will do is make sure that when a VM is moved due to a CPU or memory imbalance, it is moved to a host in the cluster that can accommodate the VM's network requirements.

As a result, when DRS performs a load balancing check for a VM, it starts by making a list of possible migration destinations. It then eliminates from that list ESXi hosts in the cluster that are network saturated. Finally, it makes a recommendation using a host from the remaining list of destinations that both provides the best CPU and memory balancing and contributes to network resource availability on the VM's source ESXi host.

So, at what point exactly does DRS consider a host in the cluster to be network saturated? By default, DRS considers a host to be network saturated if the host network utilization reaches or exceeds 80 percent. If needed, this can be adjusted using a DRS advanced option, NetworkAwareDrsSaturationThresholdPercent. DRS advanced options can be set using the vSphere Web Client, as shown in Figure 6.18.

FIGURE 6.18   The vSphere DRS Configure tab showing the entry point for Advanced Options

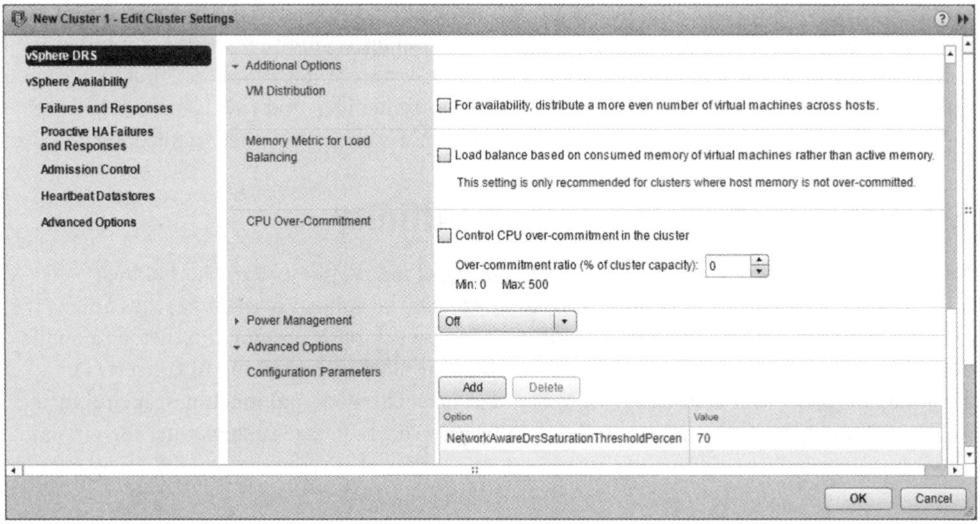

You can also view the current network utilization for the DRS cluster. The utilization is shown for each ESXi host in the cluster and is based on the average capacity across all the physical NICs (pNICs) on the host. For example, if a host has four pNICs where two are 50 percent utilized and two are 0 percent utilized, then the network utilization of the host is considered to be 25 percent. This can be seen in the vSphere Web Client, as shown in Figure 6.19.

FIGURE 6.19   The vSphere DRS Monitor tab showing network utilization for the DRS cluster

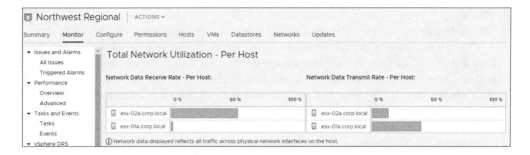

Storage DRS

The final resource that needs to be addressed when considering the load balancing of resources across a cluster is storage. Some workloads can be very storage intensive, causing a potential bottleneck for other virtual machines accessing the same storage resource. These potential bottlenecks can be mitigated using *Storage DRS*. Storage DRS allows you to create a cluster of storage resources, then monitors that collection of resources to provide recommendations for virtual machine disk placement and migration in order to balance storage capacity and I/O. Storage DRS groups storage resources into a datastore cluster, much like hosts are grouped into a DRS cluster to manage compute resources. You'll find detailed information about Storage DRS in Chapter 4, "Storage in vSphere," but as we are talking about resource allocation and consumption, remember that this is one of the core resources that must be carefully managed when administering a vSphere datacenter.

Establishing Affinity and Anti-Affinity

Now that we have discussed all of the different ways that vSphere can load balance resources across a cluster, it is important to approach the subject of *affinity rules* and *anti-affinity rules*. First, let's look at affinity. Many workloads are not confined to a single virtual machine; they may consist of multiple virtual machines working in concert. For example, a typical web application consists of at least three virtual machines, including a web server, an application server, and a database server. In a case such as this, the virtual machines pass data back and forth, so moving just one of these VMs to another host may do more harm than good in terms of performance. An affinity rule is used to keep a number of VMs together, and if a migration needs to take place, it ensures that all of the VMs in the group are moved to the same destination ESXi host.

Anti-affinity is all about availability. For example, if you had a mission-critical application or key infrastructure component that existed on multiple VMs for the sake of redundancy, the last thing you would want is for those VMs to reside on the same ESXi host. This is because if the host were to fail for some reason, the application or infrastructure component would go down as well, at least until the VMs are restarted on other hosts. An anti-affinity rule is used to ensure that a number of VMs are kept apart, and if a migration needs to take place, it ensures that the VMs do not wind up on the same ESXi host.

Affinity and anti-affinity settings can be established between individual VMs, but they can also be set up to work with groups of VMs and/or groups of hosts. This can be beneficial if you have licensing concerns that limit one or more VMs to specific hosts, or if you want to extend the capability of a standard affinity/anti-affinity rule. For example, let's say you have two domain controllers and you want to make sure they are always placed on separate hosts. You could create a VM-VM anti-affinity rule for the domain controller VMs, which would work well in a medium to large DRS cluster. However, in a small cluster a downed host might result in the need to place both VMs on the same host, which would be prevented by the rule. In a situation like this, it might be advantageous to establish groups.

The first step to using DRS groups is to create a *DRS host group*. A DRS host group is a subset of ESXi hosts in a DRS cluster that will be used in conjunction with a VM group to establish affinity or anti-affinity rules. A DRS host group is created by selecting Cluster ➤ Configure ➤ VM/Host Groups ➤ Add and selecting the host group type. Next, add the hosts in the cluster that should be part of the group. At this point, if your goal is to create rules for individual VMs within this host group, you may think you are done here. However, if you want to establish rules for even a single VM in conjunction with a host group, you will also need to create a *DRS VM group*. A DRS VM group is a collection of virtual machines that will be used in conjunction with a host group to establish affinity or anti-affinity rules. The process of creating a DRS VM group is identical to the process for creating host groups, except you are adding VMs to the group.

Once you have created the groups, the next step is to create a VM/Host rule, making sure to set type Virtual Machines to Hosts. There are additional options when creating this type of rule. These options revolve around how strict you want the rule to be. For a VM-Host affinity rule, the options are Must Run on Hosts in Group and Should Run on Hosts in Group. If you set the rule to Must Run on Hosts in Group and the selected hosts are down, the VMs will also be down and will not be restarted on other hosts. I would recommend using this option only if you have licensing requirements tied to specific hosts. In all other cases, choosing Should Run on Hosts in Group allows DRS to prefer the selected hosts but still use other hosts in the cluster should the need arise.

For a VM-Host anti-affinity rule, the options are Must Not Run on Hosts in Group and Should Not Run on Hosts in Group. Going back to the domain controller example, we saw that a simple VM-VM anti-affinity rule could result in the second domain controller remaining offline if the only option was placing both VMs on the same host. Using a VM-Host anti-affinity rule with Should Run on Hosts in Group would provide the same benefit but allow both controllers to exist on the same host if no other option was available.

DRS Cluster Administration Exercises

Now that you have learned about DRS clusters and the mechanisms that control virtual machine recommendations and migrations, let's apply that knowledge in some hands-on exercises. You can use either the Flash or the HTML5 client for most of the upcoming exercises. I recommend using the VMware Hands-on Labs environment available from VMware, which can be used for free. If you are using your own environment, I recommend at least two ESXi hosts added to a vSphere cluster with a couple of virtual machines.

In the first exercise, you will use the same cluster as you did for the resource pool exercises, labeled Northwest Regional. You will begin by enabling this cluster for DRS and configuring an automation level and threshold.

EXERCISE 6.6

Enabling a cluster for DRS

1.   Connect to a vCenter Server using the vSphere Web Client.

2. Right-click the Northwest Regional vSphere cluster and click Settings.

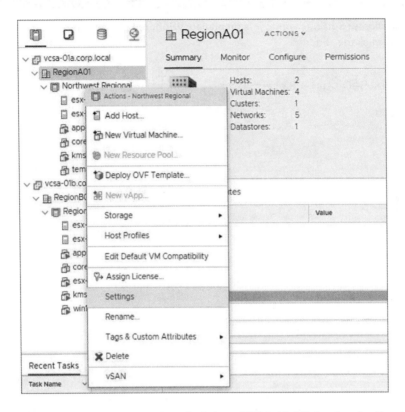

3. The Configure panel is displayed, and vSphere DRS is highlighted under Services in the navigation pane. Click the Edit button.

4.   The Edit Cluster Settings window is displayed. vSphere DRS is currently disabled. To enable it, click the slider.

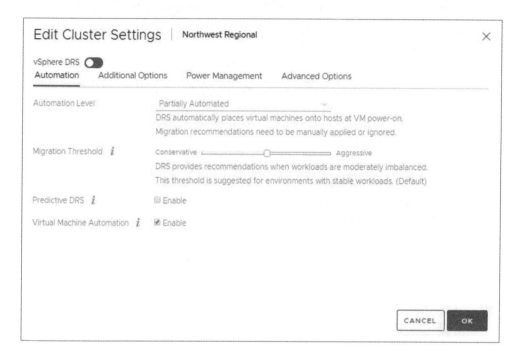

Edit Cluster Settings | Northwest Regional   ✕

vSphere DRS ⬤

Automation   Additional Options   Power Management   Advanced Options

Automation Level   Partially Automated   ⌄
                                    DRS automatically places virtual machines onto hosts at VM power-on.
                                    Migration recommendations need to be manually applied or ignored.

Migration Threshold *i*   Conservative └──────────○═══════════┘ Aggressive
                                    DRS provides recommendations when workloads are moderately imbalanced.
                                    This threshold is suggested for environments with stable workloads. (Default)

Predictive DRS *i*   ☐ Enable

Virtual Machine Automation *i*   ☑ Enable

                                                              CANCEL   OK

5. Next, to set an Automation Level, click the drop-down and select Fully Automated.

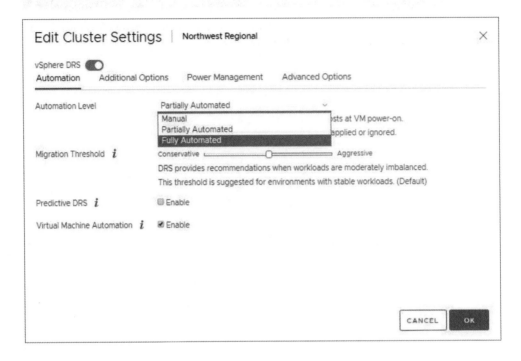

EXERCISE 6.6 *(continued)*

6. Change the Migration Threshold to level 4 by moving the slider one notch to the right. The level will momentarily highlight as shown.

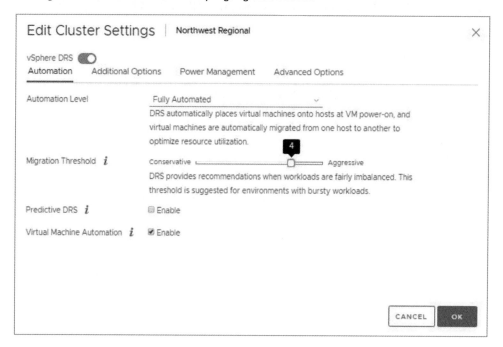

7. Click OK to return to the Configure panel. DRS will now show that it is enabled. If you want to see the specific configuration settings you set for automation, click the down arrow next to DRS Automation:

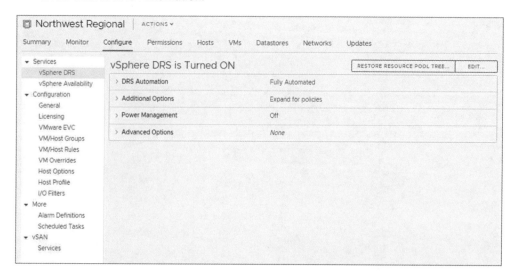

Next, you will create a host DRS group to ensure that a licensed virtual machine is not migrated off the ESXi host it is tied to.

EXERCISE 6.7

Add a host DRS group

1. Connect to a vCenter Server using the vSphere Web Client.

2. Highlight the Northwest Regional cluster and click the Configure tab.

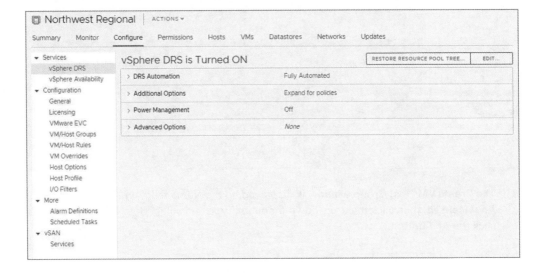

3. Next, select VM/Host Groups from the Configuration drop-down in the navigation pane, then click the Add button.

4. The Create VM/Host Group window is displayed. In the Name field, type **AppLicensed**, then click the drop-down menu for Type and select Host Group. Finally, click the Add button.

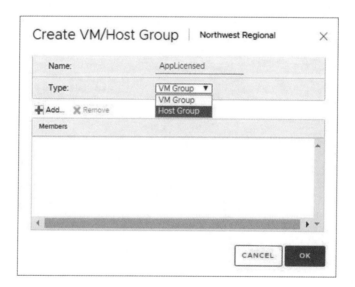

5. The Add Group Member window is displayed. Select the esx01a.corp.local host, then click OK.

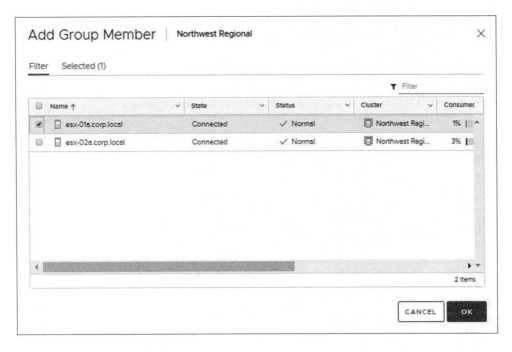

6. The Create VM/Host Group window is displayed again, this time with the selected hosts. Click OK to complete the operation.

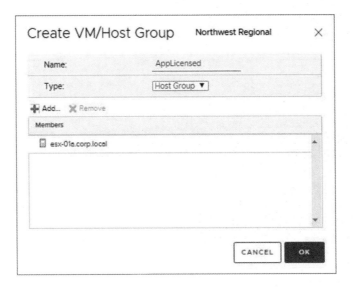

In the next lab, you need to identify which VMs will run on the host group, even if it is only a single VM.

EXERCISE 6.8

Create a VM group

1. Connect to a vCenter Server using the vSphere Web Client.

2. Highlight the Northwest Regional cluster and click the Configure tab.

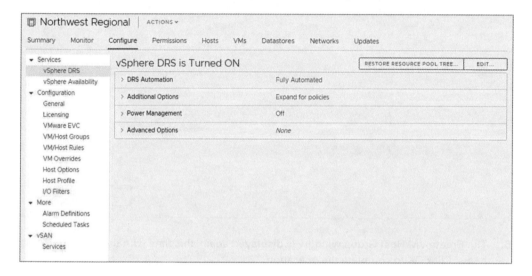

3. Next, select VM/Host Groups from the Configuration drop-down in the navigation pane, then click the Add button.

4. The Create VM/Host Group window is displayed. In the Name field, type **AppVMLicensed**, then click the drop-down menu for Type and select VM Group. Finally, click the Add button.

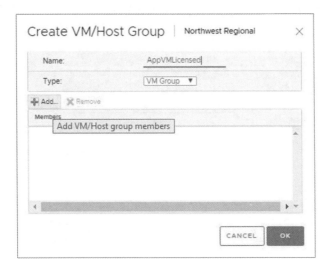

5. The Add Group Member window is displayed. Select the html5-app virtual machine, then click OK.

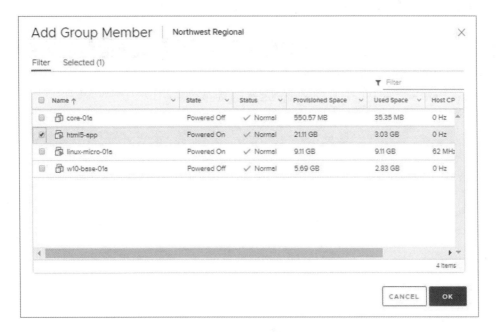

6. The Create VM/Host Group window is displayed again, this time with the selected virtual machines. Click OK to complete the operation.

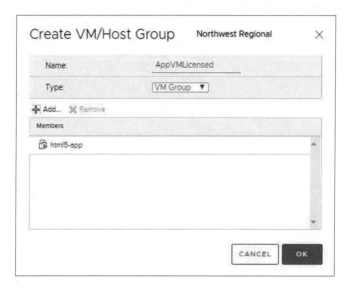

Now that we have a DRS host group and a DRS VM group, we can establish an affinity rule that ensures that the VM will only run on the licensed host.

EXERCISE 6.9

Create a VM/Host affinity rule

1. Connect to a vCenter Server using the vSphere Web Client.

2. Highlight the Northwest Regional cluster and click the Configure tab.

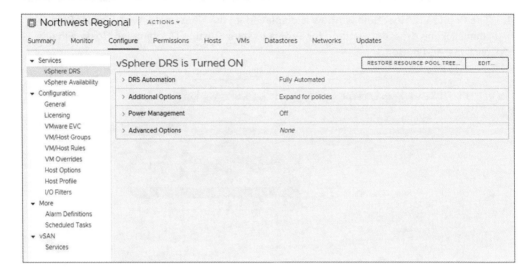

3. Next, select VM/Host Rules from the Configuration drop-down in the navigation pane, then click the Add button.

4. The Create VM/Host Rule window is displayed. In the Name field, type **LicenseRule**, then click the drop-down menu for Type and select Virtual Machines to Hosts. Finally, click the Add button.

5. Normally, you would select the VM group, the host group, and the rule type. Since you have only created one group of each type, they will automatically populate. However, you must still choose the appropriate rule, which in this case is Must Run on Hosts in Group. Select this rule, then click OK.

6. You are returned to the Configure panel, where you can now see the VM/Host rule details.

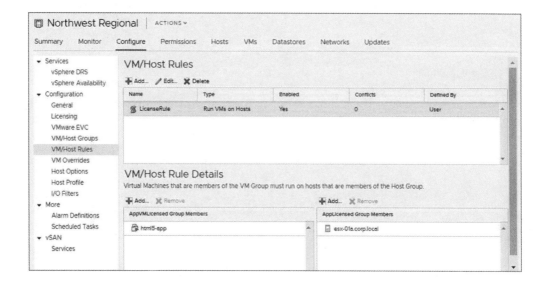

The last two exercises show how to remove the host and VM group entities. You do not have to remove associated rules first, but you will receive a warning.

EXERCISE 6.10

Remove a VM group

1. Connect to a vCenter Server using the vSphere Web Client.

2. Highlight the Northwest Regional cluster and click the Configure tab.

DRS Cluster Administration Exercises

3. Next, select VM/Host Groups from the Configuration drop-down in the navigation pane, then click the Delete button.

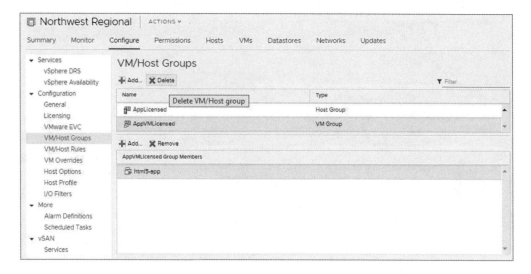

4. You will receive a warning, as there is an associated rule. Click OK to acknowledge the warning and remove the VM Group.

EXERCISE 6.10 *(continued)*

5. The VM/Host Group window is displayed again, this time showing that the group has been removed.

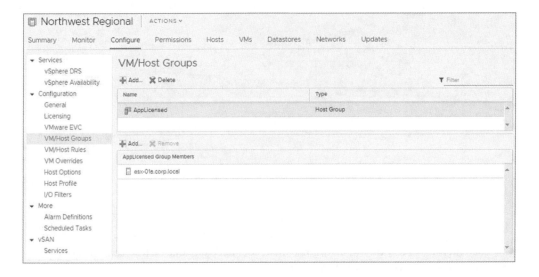

EXERCISE 6.11

Remove a host group

1. Connect to a vCenter Server using the vSphere Web Client.

2. Highlight the Northwest Regional cluster and click the Configure tab.

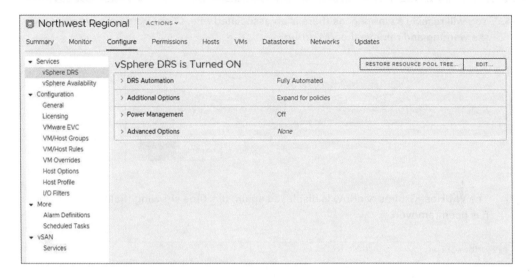

3. Next, select VM/Host Groups from the Configuration drop-down in the navigation pane, then click the Delete button.

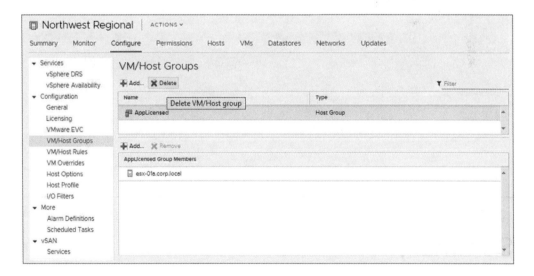

4. You will receive a warning, as there is an associated rule. Click OK to acknowledge the warning and remove the VM group.

Delete VM/Host Group   ×

Group AppVMLicensed is being used in one or more rules. Are you sure you want to delete the selected group?

CANCEL   OK

5. The VM/Host Groups window is displayed again, this time showing that the group has been removed.

Summary

Allocating resources in your vSphere datacenter is critical to ensure virtual machines perform as expected. Using the different features available in vSphere you can provide resource pools for specific workloads, ensure workloads don't use an excessive amount of resources and affect where workloads run in the datacenter.

With resource pools you can reserve resources (CPU and memory) for the virtual machines in that pool, or set limits on the pool to prevent those virtual machines from using excessive resources. By creating multilevel pools you allow for scenarios such as a department pool with specific resources shared between child pools for different projects. Child pools can also be set with expendable reservations, allowing their usage to increase - if the parent pool has available resources.

The distributed resource scheduler or DRS provides a mechanism to balance resource usage within a host. Typically used to automatically migrate virtual machines from heavily-used to lightly-used hosts, DRS can ensure resources are not starved on one host while others are unused. You can also use affinity rules to ensure certain virtual machines run on certain hosts and to ensure or prevent two virtual machines from running on the same host.

With a good understanding of how resources are shared in a vSphere environment, you can leverage these different tools to keep your datacenter balanced and efficient.

Exam Essentials

Understand how resource pools work   Know how virtual machine reservations work within resource pools. Know what expendable reservations do and how they affect parent and sibling resources.

Be able to explain reservations, limits and shares   And when each takes effect. While reservations are made as soon as the virtual machine powers on, shares only come into play during times of contention while limits prevent the virtual machine (or pool) from consuming recourse over the set amount.

Be able to calculate shares and reservations from pools   Know how shares in a pool work to determine how resources are distributed during times of contention and be able to calculate available resources in a pool hierarchy given pool and virtual machine settings.

Understand Distributed Resource Scheduler (DRS)   Know the different settings for DRS including automation level and know the migration threshold options. Know what the requirements for Predictive DRS are. Predictive DRS requires both DRS and vROPs in order to anticipate workload demands.

Know how to configure affinity rules   Affinity rules can keep virtual machines on (or off) specific hosts and either keep or prevent virtual machines from running on the same host.

Review Questions

1. Which is a valid reason for creating a snapshot of the resource pool tree?

   A. An administrator needs to disable HA for maintenance purposes.

   B. An administrator needs to disable DRS for maintenance purposes.

   C. An administrator is adding an ESXi host with resource pools to a vSphere cluster.

   D. An administrator is removing an ESXi host with resource pools from a vSphere cluster.

2. An administrator is configuring resource pools for a vSphere 6.x cluster. The cluster has these characteristics:

   - 4 ESXi 6.x hosts
   - 8 cores per host
   - 60 virtual machines with 1 vCPU each

   The administrator configures three resource pools and places the virtual machines into the pools as follows:

   Sales pool—High share value with 30 virtual machines

   Engineering pool—Normal share value with 20 virtual machines

   Test pool—Low share value with 10 virtual machines

   Given this configuration, what resources would be allotted to each pool during resource contention?

   A. The Sales pool will receive twice the amount of resources as the Engineering pool.

   B. The Engineering pool will receive twice the amount of resources as the Test pool.

   C. Each pool will receive the same amount of resources.

   D. The Test pool will perform two times as well as the Engineering pool.

3. An administrator determines that a Windows virtual machine in a resource pool called Sales is unable to power on. Which two actions might resolve this issue? (Choose two.)

   A. Increase the memory reservation of the virtual machine.

   B. Increase the CPU shares on the resource pool where the virtual machine resides.

   C. Decrease the CPU reservation of the virtual machine.

   D. Set the Expandable Reservation property on the resource pool.

4. Which element should be configured if a resource pool requires guaranteed memory resources?

   A. Shares

   B. Reservation

   C. Limit

   D. Expandable Reservation

5. Which statement best describes the Expandable Reservation parameter?

    A. The Expandable Reservation parameter can be used to allow a sibling resource pool to request resources from any other sibling.

    B. The Expandable Reservation parameter can be used to allow a child resource pool to request resources from any parent.

    C. The Expandable Reservation parameter can be used to allow a child resource pool to request resources from its parent.

    D. The Expandable Reservation parameter can be used to allow a child resource pool to request resources from a sibling.

6. Which two resources can be allocated using resource pools? (Choose two.)

    A. Memory

    B. Storage

    C. CPU

    D. Network

7. When two pools exist at the same level in the hierarchy and are completely isolated from each other, what are they called?

    A. Sibling pools

    B. Child pools

    C. Parent pools

    D. Root pools

8. What resource allocation mechanism should be used to guarantee that a virtual machine can only use the resources granted to it?

    A. Reservation

    B. Limit

    C. Shares

    D. Expandable Reservation

9. What is the ratio of resources allocated when using the High, Normal, and Low settings?

    A. 4:2:1

    B. 10:5:1

    C. 3000:2000:1000

    D. 6000:3000:1000

10. An administrator is configuring resource pools for a vSphere 6.x cluster. The cluster has these characteristics:

    ▪ 4 ESXi 6.x hosts

    ▪ 8 cores per host

    ▪ 60 virtual machines with 1 vCPU each

The administrator configures three resource pools and places the virtual machines into the pools, as follows:

Sales pool—High share value with 30 virtual machines

Engineering pool—Normal share value with 20 virtual machines

Test pool—Low share value with 10 virtual machines

Given this configuration, what resources would be allotted to each pool if no contention exists?

    A. The Sales pool will receive twice the amount of resources as the Engineering pool.

    B. The Engineering pool will receive twice the amount of resources as the Test pool.

    C. Each pool will receive as much resources as it needs.

    D. The Test pool will perform two times as well as the Engineering pool.

11. An administrator has a single VM that can only run on specific hosts due to licensing requirements. Which two steps must be taken to ensure that DRS will satisfy the requirements? (Choose two.)

    A. Create a DRS host group.

    B. Create a DRS host group and a VM group.

    C. Create a VM-VM affinity rule.

    D. Create a VM-Host affinity rule.

12. In which case would the use of VM-VM affinity rules not be supported?

    A. The cluster is configured for HA using the Cluster resource percentage option and the percentage is greater than 25 percent.

    B. The cluster is configured for HA using the Slot policy option and more than two slots are configured.

    C. The cluster is configured for HA using the Dedicated failover hosts option and multiple failover hosts are configured.

    D. The cluster is configured for HA using the Proactive HA option and the automation level is set to Manual.

13. An administrator has configured a DRS VM group containing four infrastructure VMs. The administrator removes one of the VMs from the cluster, then adds it back into the cluster at a later date. Which statement accurately explains the condition of the VM once it has been added back into the cluster?

    A. The VM is automatically added back into the DRS VM group.

    B. The VM must be manually added back into the DRS VM group.

    C. The DRS VM group was removed when the VM was removed from the cluster. It must be re-created, and all VMs must be added back into the group.

D. The DRS VM group must be deleted, then re-created, and all VMs must be added back into the group.

14. What additional VMware product must be available in order to enable Predictive DRS?

   A. vRealize Automation

   B. vRealize Orchestrator

   C. vRealize Operations Manager

   D. vRealize Code Stream

15. Which statement is an accurate description of how network-aware DRS functions?

   A. Network-aware DRS monitors the network utilization of virtual machines and takes action in the event a network resource is saturated.

   B. Network-aware DRS monitors the network utilization of ESXi hosts in the cluster and takes action in the event a network resource is saturated.

   C. Network-aware DRS monitors the compute utilization of virtual machines and takes action in the event a compute resource is saturated while taking into consideration the network utilization of the VM.

   D. Network-aware DRS monitors the compute utilization of ESXi hosts and takes action in the event a compute resource is saturated while taking into consideration the network utilization of the host.

16. Which two use cases would be reasons for implementing an anti-affinity VM-Host rule? (Choose two.)

   A. Licensing restrictions limit a VM to one or more ESXi hosts in the cluster.

   B. Two infrastructure VMs must be kept apart in a medium-sized cluster.

   C. The cluster has non-uniform hardware capabilities.

   D. Maximum availability is required for a clustered application.

17. At what point is an ESXi host with three physical uplinks considered to be network saturated?

   A. When the collective utilization of the physical uplinks reaches or exceeds 80 percent

   B. When any one of the three physical uplinks reaches or exceeds 80 percent

   C. When the collective utilization of the physical uplinks reaches or exceeds 70 percent

   D. When any one of the three physical uplinks reaches or exceeds 70 percent

18. Which three conditions would result in DRS generating a migration recommendation? (Choose three.)

   A. The DRS cluster is experiencing a CPU imbalance.

   B. The DRS cluster is experiencing a memory imbalance.

   C. The DRS cluster is experiencing a storage imbalance.

   D. A resource pool reservation must be satisfied.

   E. An ESXi host in the cluster experiences an unplanned downtime issue.

19. An administrator creates a VM-VM affinity rule for two virtual machines. Six months later, another administrator attempts to create a VM-VM anti-affinity rule for the same VMs. Which statement accurately describes the end result of this action?

    A. The older rule will remain enabled and the new rule will be disabled.

    B. The new rule will be enabled and the older rule will be disabled.

    C. Both rules will be enabled.

    D. Both rules will be disabled and an alert will be generated.

20. An administrator has established a VM-Host affinity rule using the Must Run On option on a DRS cluster. Which two actions are *not* performed in the cluster if doing so would violate the affinity rule? (Choose two.)

    A. Virtual machines are migrated off an ESXi host that is being placed into maintenance mode.

    B. An ESXi host is removed from the cluster.

    C. The cluster is imbalanced, and DRS migrates one or more virtual machines.

    D. The administrator performs some manual migrations within the cluster.

Chapter

7

Backing Up and Recovering a vSphere Deployment

2V0-21.19 EXAM OBJECTIVES COVERED IN THIS CHAPTER:

✓ **Section 4 – Installing, Configuring, and Setting Up a VMware vSphere Solution**

- Objective 4.6 – Deploy and configure VMware vCenter Server Appliance (VCSA)

✓ **Section 5 – Performance-tuning and Optimizing a VMware vSphere Solution**

- Objective 5.1 – Determine effective snapshot use cases

✓ **Section 7 – Administrative and Operational Tasks in a VMware vSphere Solution**

- Objective 7.7 – Perform different types of migrations

- Objective 7.9 – Create and manage VMs using different methods

This chapter covers backing up the vCenter Server Appliance (VCSA) and virtual machines as well as replicating virtual machines. Backups are important for a lower-cost method of recovering (partially or completely) failed components as well as tracking changes of components over a period of time. Replication is important in order to provide rapidly available duplicates of components, either locally or remotely.

Replication is normally costlier than backups as replication tasks cause additional WAN network traffic when run to remote sites, and replication tasks are often run at a higher rate. While you might back up your virtual machines nightly, replications are often set to run every hour. With VMware's backup and replication solutions, only the data that changed since the last process ran is affected, making both processes very efficient.

While backup tasks are often run on most virtual machines in the environment, you might only replicate the most critical virtual machines.

VCSA Backup and Restore

With vSphere 6.5, the vCenter Server Appliance has the ability to make a file-based backup. While the backup is currently triggered manually from the appliance GUI and cannot be scheduled, the resulting backup is much smaller than a copy of the whole appliance would be. The primary downside to the file-based backup is that in order to restore the backup, you need to use the deploy utility to create a new appliance that used the backup files as the data source.

To start a backup of the VCSA, you need to log into the management interface of the appliance, which is https://<VCSA FQDN or IP>:5480. The login credentials are *root* plus the password created when the appliance was deployed.

Once logged in, you will see the Backup button on the summary page (Figure 7.1).

Clicking the Backup button will launch the Backup Appliance wizard. The first screen (Figure 7.2) configures the destination for the backup. The choices are HTTP, HTTPS, SCP, FTP, and FTPS. If you select HTTP or FTP, you will be warned that those protocols are not secure.

Note that the Location field requires the server FQDN or IP plus a directory (or folder) at a bare minimum. You can also supply a path. The directory doesn't need to exist, but if it does exist, it must not have an existing backup in it. The directory name will be used to set the virtual machine name during the restore process, so best practice would be to use the name of the appliance as the directory name.

FIGURE 7.1   Back up the VCSA from the Summary screen.

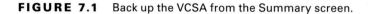

FIGURE 7.2   Configure the backup destination.

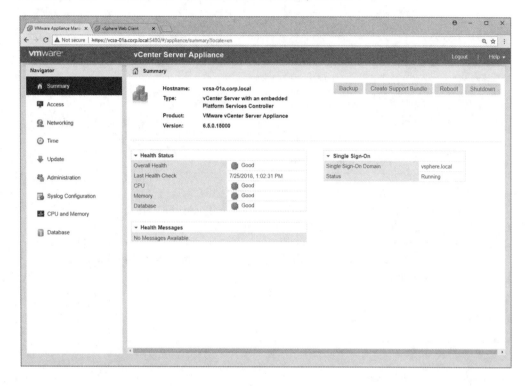

FIGURE 7.3   List of encrypted VCSA backup files

backup-metadata.json	7/30/2018 1:18 PM	JSON File	5 KB
config_files.tar.gz.enc	7/30/2018 1:18 PM	ENC File	1,773,631 KB
database_full_backup.tar.gz.enc	7/30/2018 1:13 PM	ENC File	21,762 KB
full_wal_backup_meta.tar.gz.enc	7/30/2018 1:13 PM	ENC File	1 KB
imagebuilder.gz.enc	7/30/2018 1:12 PM	ENC File	1 KB
lotus_backup.tar.gz.enc	7/30/2018 1:12 PM	ENC File	1,056 KB
rbd.gz.enc	7/30/2018 1:16 PM	ENC File	53 KB
statsmonitor_db_backup.gz.enc	7/30/2018 1:12 PM	ENC File	21,008 KB
vum.gz.enc	7/30/2018 1:16 PM	ENC File	1,015,303 KB
wal_backup_1.tar.gz.enc	7/30/2018 1:13 PM	ENC File	28 KB
wal_dir_struct.tar.gz.enc	7/30/2018 1:13 PM	ENC File	1 KB

You have the option of encrypting the files, which will add the .enc extension and a layer of encryption to each of the backup files (Figure 7.3).

The size of the backup will vary depending on the size of the inventory and the amount of historical data on the vCenter server; however, as shown in Figure 7.4, exporting the historical data is optional.

FIGURE 7.4   Select parts to back up.

Backing up the appliance is much more straightforward than restoring it. To restore, you run the graphical deploy utility (the CLI deploy utility does not offer restore) and choose the Restore option (Figure 7.5).

FIGURE 7.5   Starting a VCSA restore

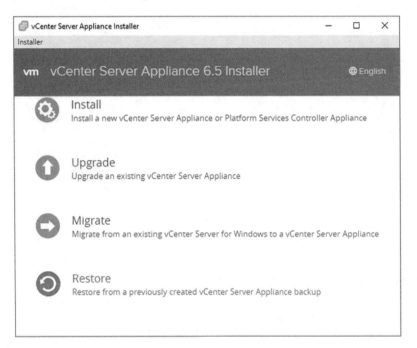

The Restore process will prompt you for the location of the backup files (Figure 7.6).

If you added a password during the backup, you will be prompted to enter the password during Stage 2 (Figure 7.7). The Windows system running *VCSA-Deploy* will download the backup-metadata.json file from the backup directory and check the supplied password against the PasswordValidator entry to verify that your entered password is correct before prompting to complete the restore.

The restore process is very similar to the VCSA upgrade and migrate processes, where a new appliance is deployed and then the configuration and data are imported. While this process takes longer to recover a VCSA appliance compared to restoring a copy of the VCSA virtual machine, the data backed up is considerably smaller and the backup process should be faster.

FIGURE 7.6   Enter the backup location.

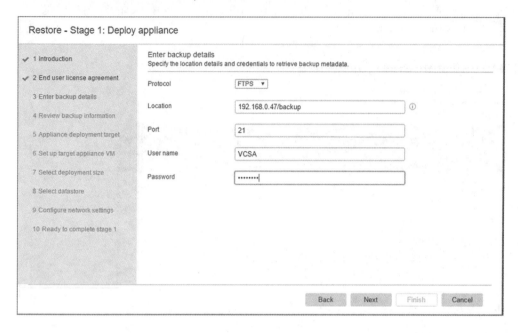

FIGURE 7.7   Specify the password if one was set during backup.

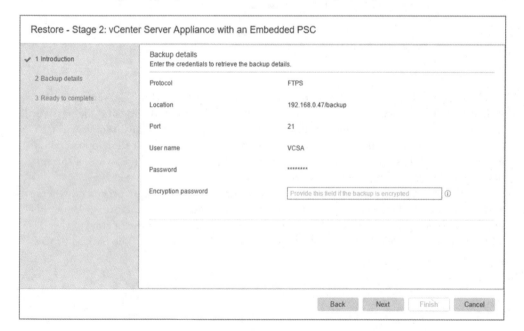

EXERCISE 7.1

Back up a VCSA appliance.

Required: VCSA server, FTPS server.

1. Connect to the management interface of your vCenter appliance at `https://<IP or FQDN>:5480` and log in as root with the password you set during deployment.

2. Click the Backup button.

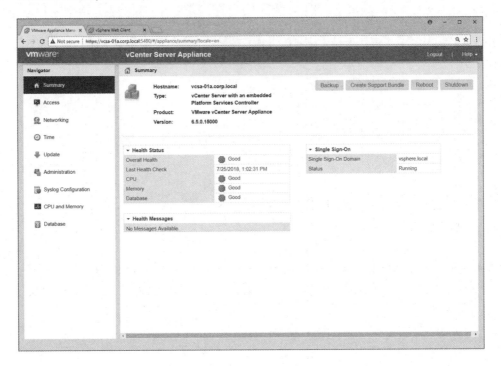

3. Select the FTPS protocol and enter the location and credentials for the file server. Add a password and check the Encrypt Backup Data box if you want the backup encrypted.

4. Ensure that Stats, Events, Alarms, and Tasks is selected and click Next.

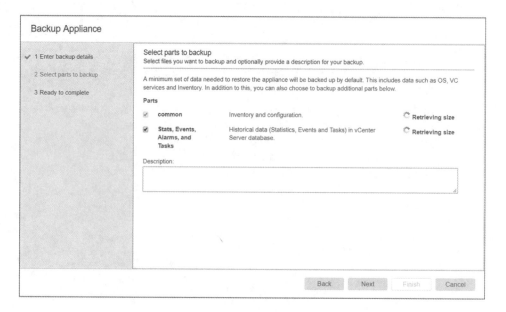

5. Click Finish to start backing up the VCSA appliance and copy the files to the storage server.

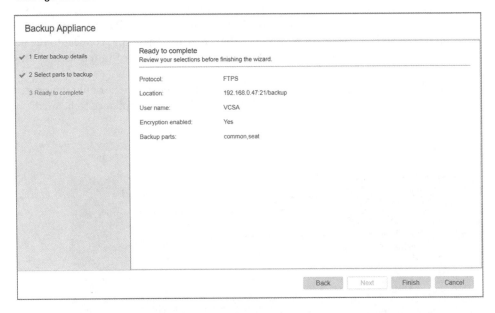

Backing Up Virtual Machines by Using VDP

VMware includes a license for vSphere Data Protection (VDP) with all versions of vSphere except the lowest-price vSphere Essentials license. Based on (or "Powered By" according to the plug-in) EMC's Avamar product, VDP provides virtual-disk-level backups of virtual machines, either powered on or powered off. Additional features include data deduplication, backup replication, user-controlled file-level restore, and guest-level backups of Microsoft services including Exchange, SQL, and SharePoint.

There are a few key "maximums" to know for VDP that will affect how they are deployed. The greatest number of virtual machines that can be protected by one VDP appliance is 400, and the greatest number of VDP appliances that can be supported per vCenter is 20. This means you can only protect up to 8,000 virtual machines on a single vCenter server. Of course, an environment that large should probably be using a third-party backup solution because each VDP appliance runs independently. With multiple appliances in use, you would have to manually keep track of which VMs are being backed up on which appliance and you would have at least one backup job and destination per appliance.

Installing VDP

To install vSphere Data Protection, you need a vCenter server, an ESXi host, and at least 873 GB of storage space. When you deploy the OVA file for the VDP appliance, you will be prompted to add IP information for the appliance. After deploying, connect to the new appliance using `https://<appliance FQDN or IP>:8543/vdp-configure` with a username of *root* and password of *changeme*.

During installation, you can "create" new storage for VDP or use (or migrate) existing VDP storage. Creating new storage adds VMDK files to the appliance to be used (Figure 7.8).

FIGURE 7.8   Create storage for VDP

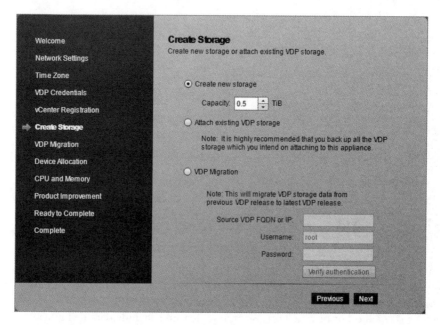

When creating storage for VDP your options are 0.5, 1, 2, 4, 6, or 8 tebibytes (TiB) as shown in Table 7.1. The appliance will deploy with a single 200 GB VMDK for the appliance plus additional VMDKs depending on your storage choice.

When adding storage to the appliance, you can choose to have all the storage VMDKs created in the same directory as the appliance, or you can distribute them among the available datastores (Figure 7.9).

If you initially select a storage amount less than 8 TiB, you can expand the storage later using the same `https://<appliance FQDN or IP>:8543/vdp-configure` link used for the initial setup. Select Expand Storage under the Storage tab (Figure 7.10) and then choose the new size and place the disks.

TABLE 7.1   VDP storage guide

Storage Choice (in TiB)	Number of VMDKs	Size of VMDKs (in GB)	RAM requirements (in GB)	vCPUs
0. 5	3	256	4	4
1	3	512	4	4
2	3	1024	4	4
4	6	1024	8	4
6	9	1024	10	4
8	12	1024	12	4

FIGURE 7.9   Specify datastore settings.

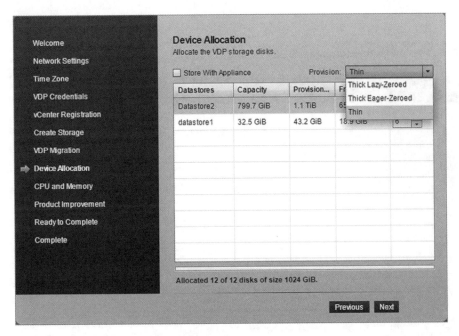

If the new storage size utilizes larger VMDKs (see Table 7.1), the existing VMDKs will be resized. When you initially add storage to the appliance, you can choose *thick lazy-zeroed*, *thick eager-zeroed*, or *thin* provisioned. This choice can be changed later using the Expand Storage wizard (Figure 7.11).

FIGURE 7.10   Launch the expand storage utility for VDP.

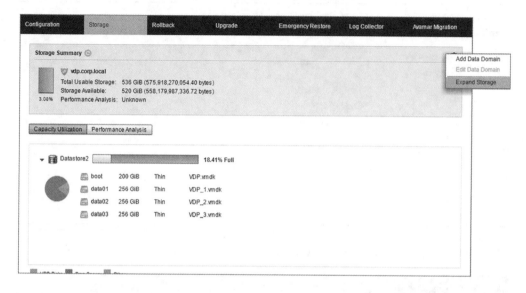

FIGURE 7.11   Resizing storage for VDP

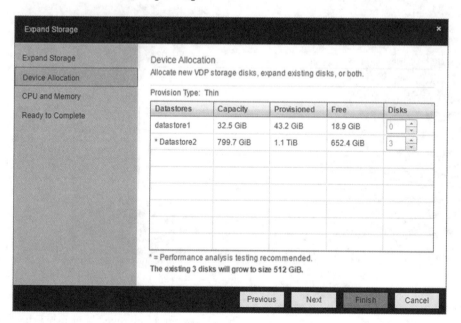

During the initial installation, you can choose the CPU and RAM settings for the appliance, which default to 4 CPUs and 4096 MB of RAM with the minimum storage setting. If you are choosing a higher amount of storage, the wizard may suggest more memory. If you later expand the storage, you may again be prompted to increase the memory for the appliance (Figure 7.12). While the CPU and Memory window for both the initial and Expand Storage wizards shows an entry for CPU, the value is set to 4 and can't be changed.

FIGURE 7.12 Changing the RAM setting for the VDP appliance

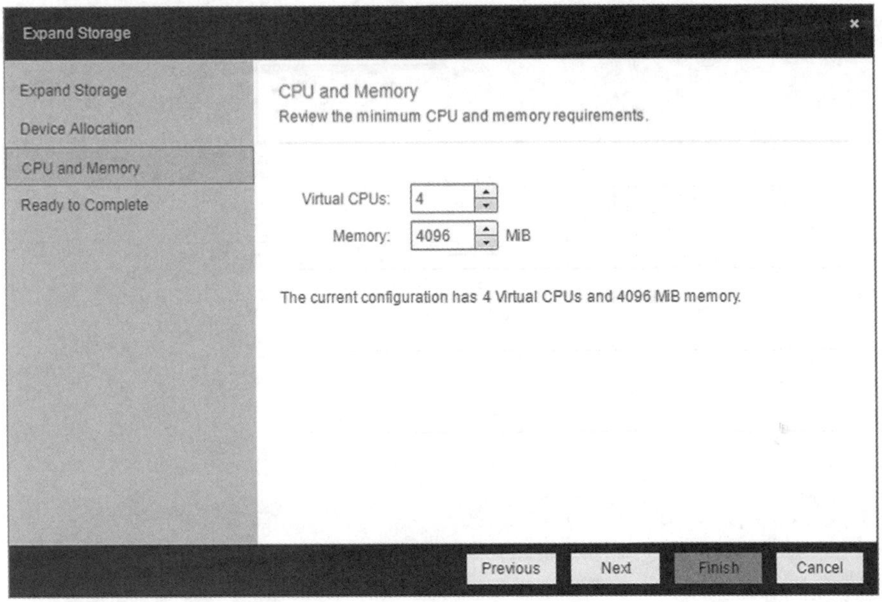

Creating Backup Jobs

Once the appliance has been initially configured, you can access the vSphere Data Protection plug-in using the vSphere client (Figure 7.13). If you do not see the plug-in on the client, you may need to log out and back in.

There are two types of backup job types: Applications and Guest Images. Applications jobs allow you to back up Exchange, SQL, and SharePoint servers (Figure 7.14) using a client installed in the guest. Note that the applications do not need to be running on virtual machines; as long as the VDP client can access the IP address of the VDP appliance, you can back up one of the supported applications. Guest Images jobs back up entire virtual machines or select VMDKs.

The application backup clients can be downloaded from the Downloads section of the Configuration tab (Figure 7.15).

Installation doesn't require much more than the VDP server's IP address, but each client

FIGURE 7.13 Accessing the VDP plug-in

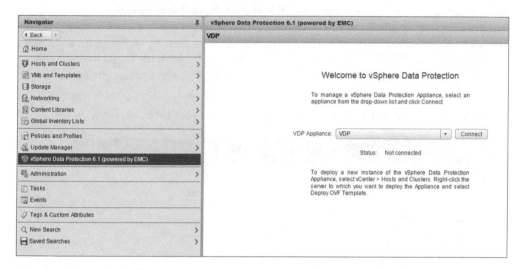

FIGURE 7.14 Application backup sources

will need to be configured after installation. Figure 7.16 shows the configuration tool for the Exchange client.

The tool will create the user specified with the permissions it needs. You will need to enter the information (username, password) into the backup job during creation. See Figure 7.17 for an example of creating an Exchange backup job.

When creating Guest Images backup jobs, you have the choice of backing up the virtual machine with all of its drives (Full Image) or selecting specific drives to back up with the Individual Disks option. Both methods will back up the virtual machine's .vmx configuration file, but Individual Disks is useful if you want different backup schedules for different drives or have incompatible drives on a virtual machine. Virtual machine disks set to Independent mode, RDMs, and VMDKs stored on VVols are not compatible with VDP backups. The backup job wizard will display an alert (Figure 7.18) if an incompatible disk is selected.

FIGURE 7.15   Application client downloads

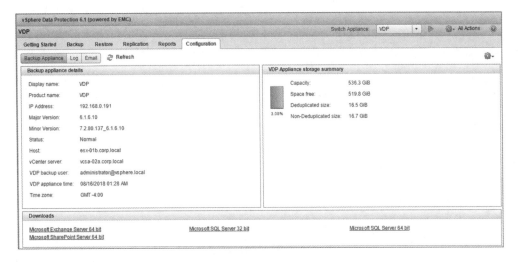

FIGURE 7.16   Exchange backup client configuration

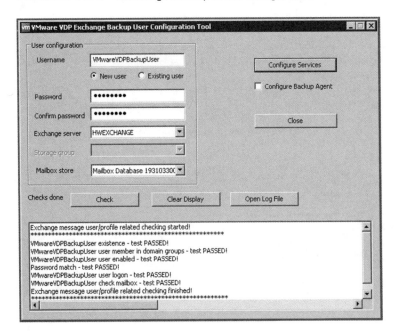

FIGURE 7.17   Exchange backup job creation

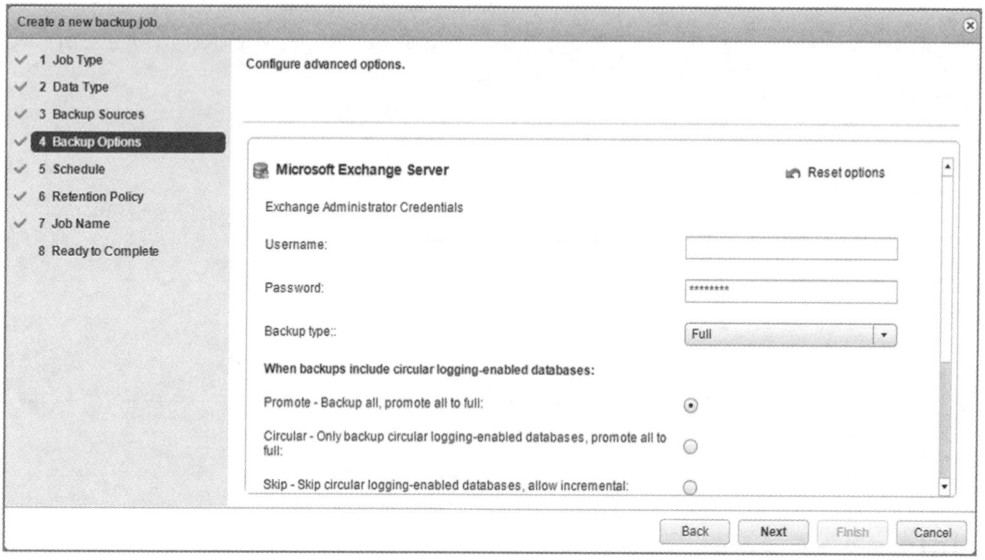

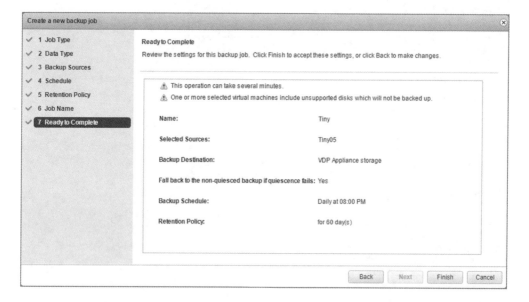

FIGURE 7.18   Incompatible disk alert

VDP has two options for backing up the VMDKs: HotAdd and network block transport (NBT). For HotAdd, the VDP appliance will take a snapshot of the VMDKs it is backing up (Figure 7.19) and then mount the VMDKs from the virtual machines as Independent-NonPersistent disks (Figure 7.20).

FIGURE 7.19   VDP snapshot on a VM to back up

```
PS C:\Users\Administrator> get-vm Win8Two |Get-Snapshot |ft -auto

Name                                                              Description                                                           PowerState
----                                                              -----------                                                           ----------
VDP-1534385231ea6f1340bc9ed4eb5fad50b2632a5d64b52ea3d3 Created by VDP workorder Backup VMs-1534385225837 on GMT-Thu Aug 16 02:07:10 2018 PoweredOff

PS C:\Users\Administrator> _
```

FIGURE 7.20   VDP mounting the VMDKs to back up

```
PS C:\Users\Administrator> get-vm vdp |Get-HardDisk |ft -auto
CapacityGB Persistence                                        Filename
---------- -----------                                        --------
200.000    Persistent                         [Datastore2] VDP/VDP.vmdk
256.000    IndependentPersistent              [Datastore2] VDP/VDP_1.vmdk
256.000    IndependentPersistent              [Datastore2] VDP/VDP_2.vmdk
256.000    IndependentPersistent              [Datastore2] VDP/VDP_3.vmdk
40.000     IndependentNonPersistent           [Datastore2] Win8One/Win8One.vmdk
40.000     IndependentNonPersistent [iSCSI-Datastore] Win8Two/Win8Two.vmdk

PS C:\Users\Administrator> _
```

If the virtual machine is powered on, the snapshot process of the HotAdd will include a quiesce attempt. When a snapshot is flagged for quiesce, the guest disk buffers will be flushed so that there are no outstanding writes. This prevents guest disk corruption. If the quiesce request is not successful, a crash-consistent snapshot will be taken, but noted in the backup log.

HotAdd is the default mechanism for backing up VMDKs; however, it requires the datastore the VMDK is on to be presented to the host the VDP appliance is on, and vSphere Flash Read Cache (vFlash) cannot be enabled for the virtual machine. If these requirements are not met, VDP will use NBT to back up the virtual disks and will leverage the ESXi server hosting the virtual machine to back up the VM over the network to the VDP appliance.

VDP utilizes Change Block Tracking (CBT) to improve backup and restore times. With CBT, the ESXi hosts can identify what disk sectors have changed since the last backup. Also, per VMware KB article 1020128, "On VMFS partitions, CBT can also identify all the disk sectors that are in use." This technology allows backup jobs to know which data to back up without scanning the data or to restore a backup by only replacing the blocks that changed. CBT is enabled on virtual machines by default.

After a backup job is run, you can create a Backup Verification job to ensure that the backup worked successfully.

Restoring from Backup

There are several options for restoring from backup. For Guest Images, you can overwrite the existing VMDK with the backup or overwrite the entire VM with the backup. You can also spin up a copy of the VM with the VMDKs attached. Using the VDP Restore client, you can also restore individual files from the Guest Images backups. Application restores can be full or partial, depending on the backup options. Unlike a backup job, a restore job can include Guest Images and Application restores.

If the virtual machine was not successfully quiesced before a Guest Images backup runs against it, the backups will be differentiated in the backup list with a red icon (Figure 7.21).

FIGURE 7.21   Backup jobs where the VM was not quiesced have a red icon.

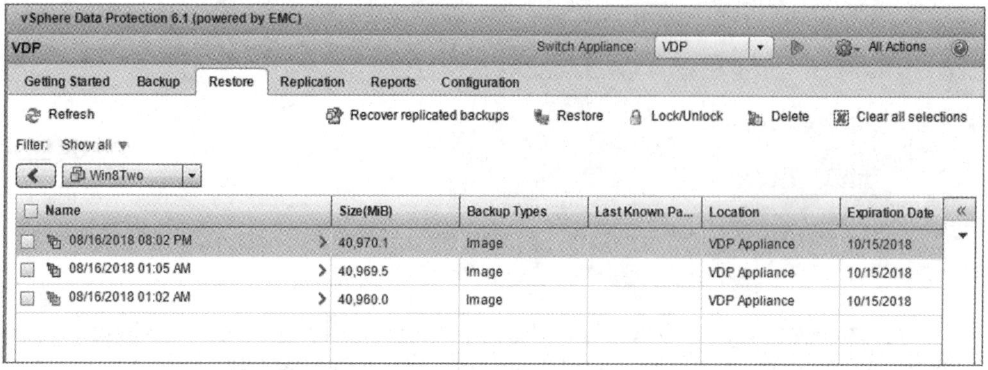

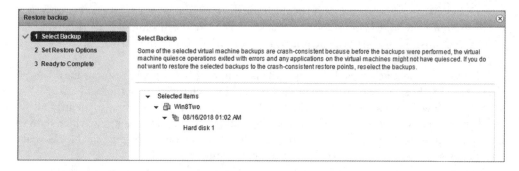

If you create a restore that includes backup jobs that were not quiesced, a warning will be displayed alerting you to the crash-consistent backup (Figure 7.22).

FIGURE 7.22   Warning that a crash-consistent backup has occurred

To restore individual files from a backup, access the VDP File Level Restore (FLR) client using `https://<IP or FQDN or VDP appliance>:8543/flr`. There are two methods of login, Local Credentials and Advanced Login.

Local Credentials gives an administrator on the VM that was backed up the ability to restore files locally. Only files backed up on the machine the FLR is running from can be restored using Local Credentials. If you attempt to use Local Credentials from a guest that has not been backed up by the VDP appliance, you will get an error message: "Cannot locate vm in vCenter" (Figure 7.23).

For username and password, enter the credentials for the local PC you are running the FLR client from to get a list of available backups (Figure 7.24). Only backups for the current VM are available when using Local Credentials.

FIGURE 7.23   FLR error when using Local Credentials from a guest that has not been backed up

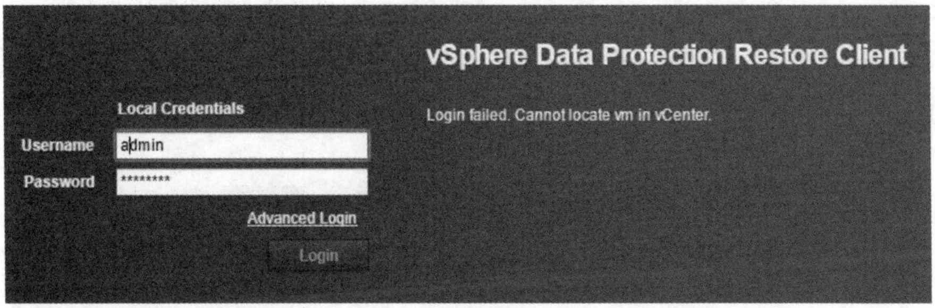

FIGURE 7.24   Local credential FLR backup jobs

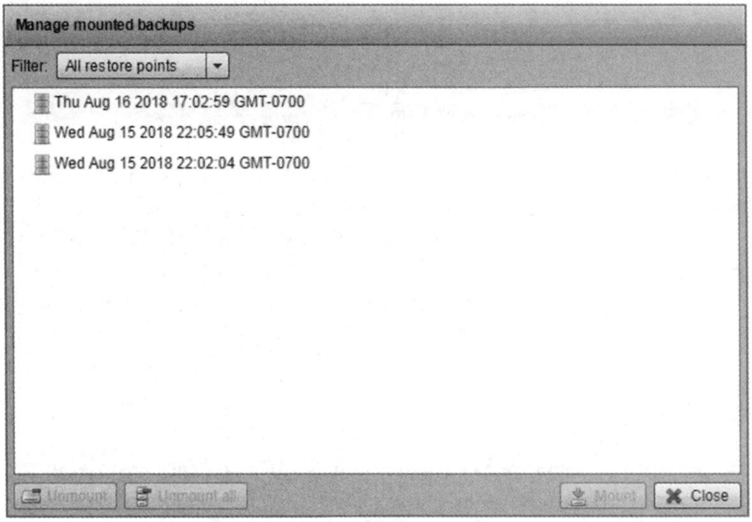

Selecting a backup job and clicking Mount will display the file structures of the VMDKs. You can restore files to their original locations by selecting the root disk or choose a new folder to restore to; however, the folder must already exist. You can monitor the restore from the Monitor Restores tab (Figure 7.25).

If you would like to restore files to a VM other than the original, or if the UUID of the virtual machine has changed from a restore of the VM or by moving it, you can use the Advanced Login. The Advanced Login screen takes the same local credentials but also requires the vCenter credentials used to register the VDP appliance with vCenter.

While any system administrator with the URL for the VDP appliance can restore backups for systems they administer, only a user with the proper vCenter credentials can restore files from the backup jobs of other systems.

FIGURE 7.25   Monitor restores

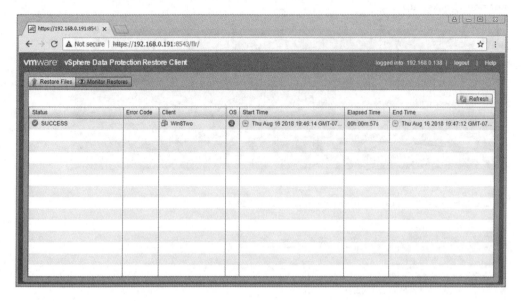

A few notes on restoring using the FLR client: You cannot restore ACLs, symbolic links, or more than 5,000 files or folders in one restore job. Browsing directories is also limited to no more than 5,000 files/folders. Also, you cannot use FLR if there is a NAT in front of the VM or if there is a firewall between the VDP and the VM. There are also several limitations to which VMDKs FLR can pull files from; GPT disks, Windows dynamic disks and VMDKs with multiple partitions are not supported.

Deploying Proxy Servers

VDP can also be provisioned with external proxy servers. The VDP appliance installs with an internal proxy server capable of 8 simultaneous backups. However, you can deploy up to 8 external proxy servers, although there is a limit of 24 concurrent backups per VDP appliance when external proxies are used. The internal proxy server will be disabled if an external proxy server is added (Figure 7.26).

Proxies can be deployed to increase the simultaneous number of backups running, to spread the backup and restore footprint across multiple appliances and hosts, or to provide a single VDP appliance with the ability to back up datastores that are not accessible on all hosts. Proxies are also required for backing up and restoring LVM and ext4 file systems.

Monitoring Backup Jobs

While vSphere Data Protection is very useful—and included with most licenses of vSphere—it doesn't have a way to monitor the backup jobs in real time from the GUI.

The command line of the appliance does, however, have a command to monitor the jobs in real time, but while this is very useful, it will not be on the VCP6.5-DCV certification exam.

To run the command, connect to the VDP appliance using PuTTY or another SSH client. You can log in with credentials *admin* and the password you set for the appliance. From the command line, run `mccli activity show --active`.

The mccli utility will display all running jobs in real time, including restore jobs.

FIGURE 7.26   VDP configured with an external proxy

Note: The VDP Appliance can be configured with up to 8 external proxies.

EXERCISE 7.2

Back up an Exchange server using VDP.

Required: Exchange server, VDP appliance deployed.

1. Log into vCenter and connect to the VDP appliance from the vSphere Data Protection menu.

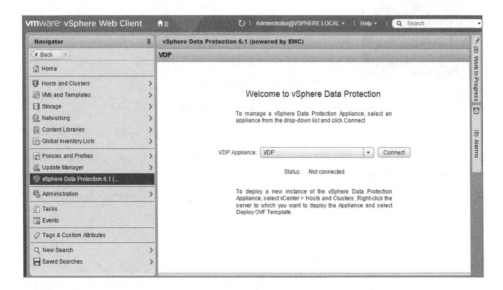

EXERCISE 7.2 *(continued)*

2. From the Configuration tab, download the Microsoft Exchange Server agent.

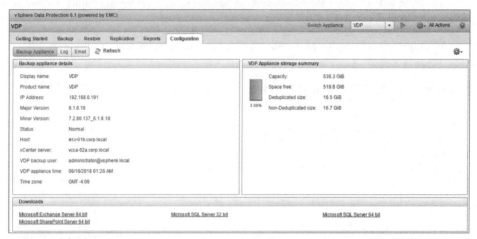

3. Install the agent on the Exchange server, entering the VDP appliance IP address or FQDN when prompted.

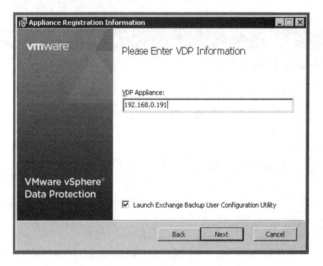

4. Launch the VMware VDP Backup User Configuration Tool from the Start menu.

5. Enter a password for the VMwareVDPBackupUser account and select your Exchange server and the mailbox store.

6. Click Configure Services to create the user and assign the appropriate permissions.

7. Click Check to verify that the user was created properly.

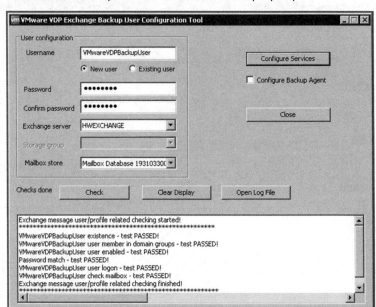

8. Using the vSphere Data Protection menu in the web client, start a new backup job.

9. Choose the job type Applications and click Next.

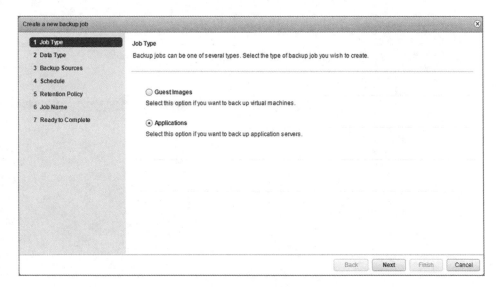

EXERCISE 7.2 *(continued)*

10. Choose the data type Full Server and click Next.

11. Choose your Exchange server and click Next.

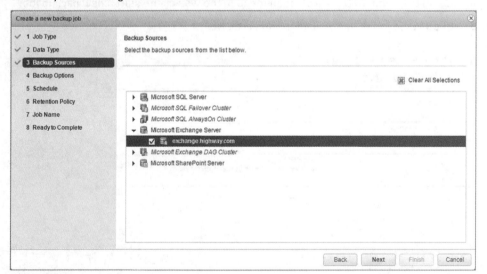

12. Enter the password you set for the VMwareVDPBackupUser account in step 4, choose the options appropriate for your environment, and click Next.

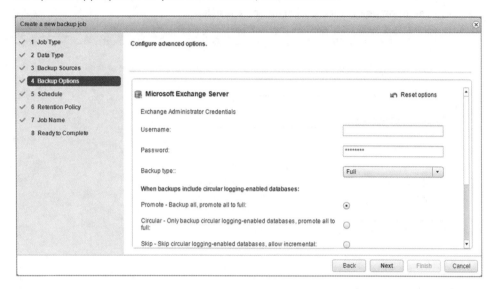

13. Set a backup schedule and click Next.

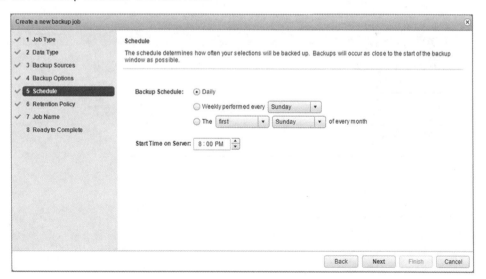

14. Set a retention policy for the backup and click Next.

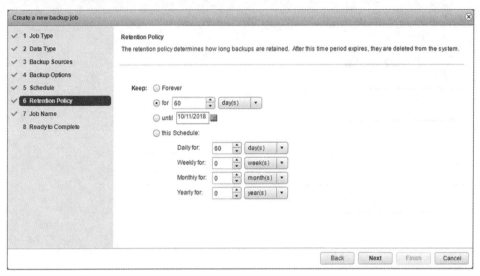

15. Set a name for the backup job and click Next.

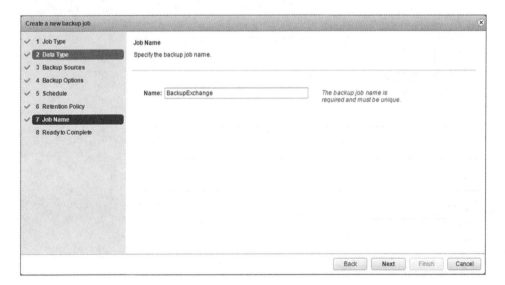

16. Click Finish.

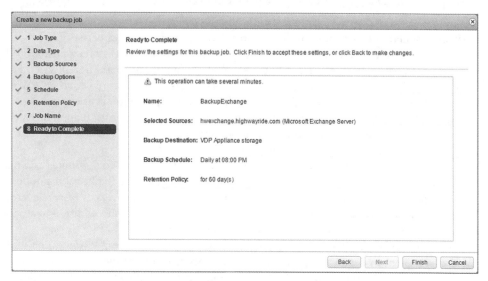

17. Select the new backup job and choose Backup All Sources.

18. Open the Reports tab and verify that the backup job completed.

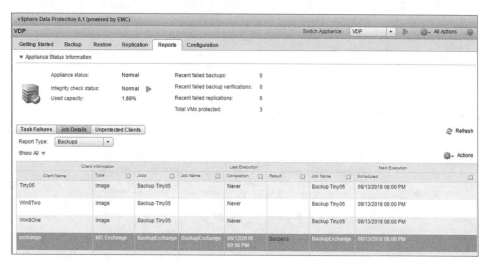

Replicating Virtual Machines

VMware vSphere offers a solution that can replicate virtual machines between hosts. With vSphere Replication, you can create copies of virtual machines in a different cluster on the same vCenter, to a different vCenter in the same SSO domain, or to a different vCenter and SSO domain. The destination can also be cloud platforms like VMware Cloud on AWS. All licenses of vSphere except Essentials include a license for vSphere Replication.

vSphere Replication uses an appliance (at least one vSphere Replication appliance per vCenter) to manage and monitor the replication between the hosts. There is a plug-in to add the management options to the web client.

Offering features such as recovery point objectives (RPOs) down to 5 minutes and multiple point in time recovery for protected virtual machines, vSphere Replication can be a very effective tool to migrate workloads or prepare for disaster recovery. VMware's Site Recovery Manager (SRM) product can leverage vSphere Replication in addition to storage replication to create a complete disaster recovery environment.

To deploy vSphere Replication, you need to download the ISO from VMware.com and use the web client to deploy the proper files. The /bin directory of the ISO image contains the files to deploy several versions of vRealize appliances, including the SRM and Cloud Service versions. The Cloud Service version can be leveraged by vCloud Director, vCloud Air, or other cloud services.

Deploying a Replication Appliance

For a basic implementation of vSphere Replication, you only need to deploy the vSphere Replication OVF with the files selected (Figure 7.27).

FIGURE 7.27   Files to deploy with the OVF for the vSphere Replication appliance

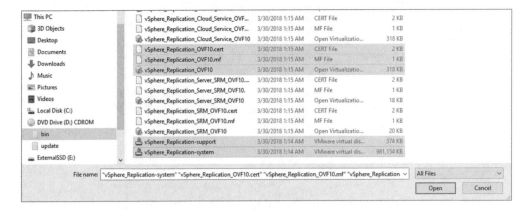

The other OVF file set - vSphere_Replication_Addon is needed to deploy "add-on" appliances that can help with scaling vSphere Replication.

During the deployment you will be prompted for the compute resource, how many CPUs the appliance is deployed with (4 is the default but can be changed to 2), storage, and network. You are also required to enter at least one NTP server and a new password for the root account of the appliance during the OVF deployment.

Once the appliance is deployed, you can connect to its management console at https://<IP or FQDN or vSphere Replication>:5480 and log on as root with the password you set during deployment. From the configuration screen, verify that the information is accurate and enter the password for the SSO administrator (Figure 7.28). Click the Save and Restart Service button to register the appliance with vCenter.

FIGURE 7.28   vSphere Replication appliance configuration

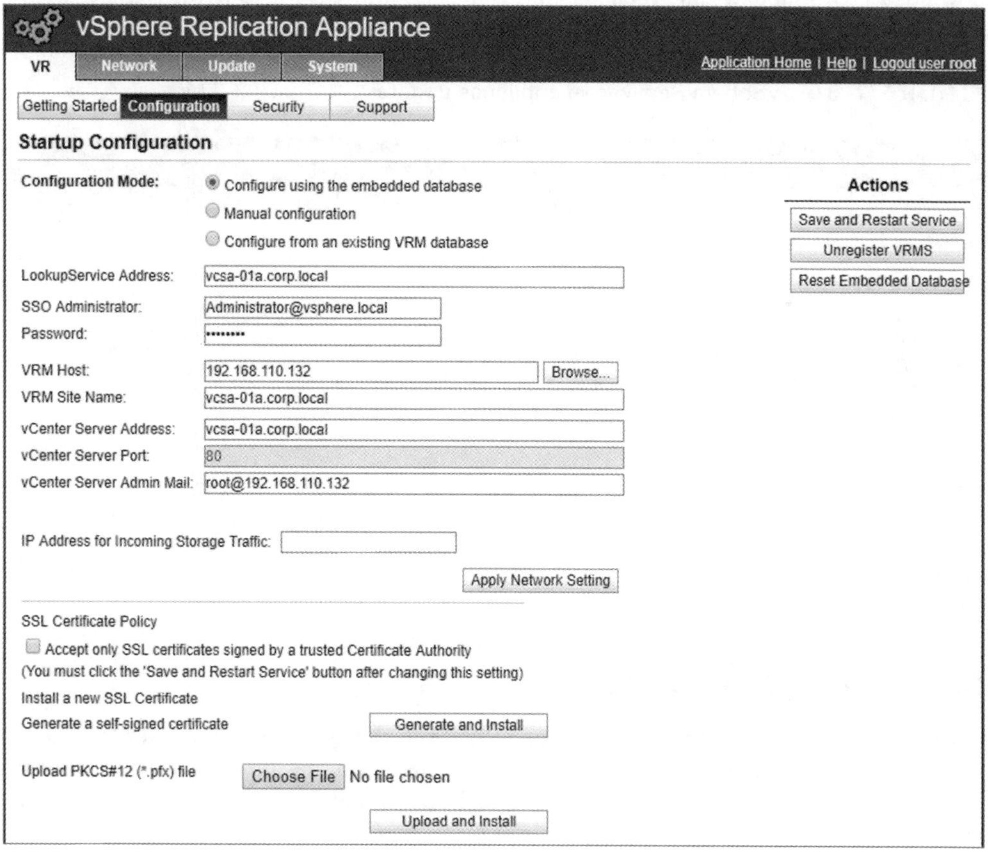

The appliance deploys with a self-signed certificate, but you can add a certificate generated from VMware Certificate Authority (VMCA) or the certificate authority used by your infrastructure. Once the appliance is registered with vCenter and the services are restarted, the Service Status at the bottom of the configuration page will change to "VRM service is running" (Figure 7.29).

FIGURE 7.29   vSphere Replication appliance configured and running

The appliance allows the administrator the ability to manually check the VMware download site for updates and then install them. This feature is found in the configuration site for the appliance on the Update tab (Figure 7.30).

FIGURE 7.30   vSphere Replication appliance updates

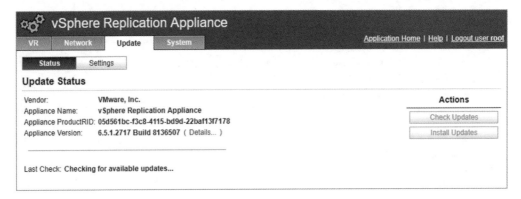

You can also schedule automated updates from the default repository, a CD, or a custom repository (Figure 7.31).

Configuring Replication

You can use vSphere Replication to replicate virtual machines between hosts in the same vCenter with no additional configuration. To replicate virtual machines to hosts connected to a separate vCenter, you will need a second replication appliance deployed and connected to the other vCenter, and the vSphere Replication servers need to be linked together.

When linking vSphere Replication servers, there are two site options: local and remote (Figure 7.32). Local sites are vCenter servers that share the same SSO domain, and remote sites are vSphere Replication servers that are connected to a vCenter server and have a different SSO domain.

FIGURE 7.31   Automatic vSphere Replication appliance updates

vSphere Replication Appliance

| VR | Network | **Update** | System | | Application Home | Help | Logout user **root** |

Status   **Settings**

Update Settings

Automatic Updates

- ⦿ No automatic updates
- ○ Automatic check for updates
- ○ Automatic check and install update

Schedule a frequency for the updates

[Every Day ▼] at [3:00 AM ▼]

Actions

[Save Settings]
[Cancel Changes]

Update Repository

- ⦿ Use Default Repository

  RepositoryURL   https://vapp-updates.vmware.com/vai-catalog/valm/vmw/05d561bc-f3c8-4115-bd9d-22baf13f7178/6.5.1.2717.latest

- ○ Use CDROM Updates

- ○ Use Specified Repository

  Repository URL   [   ]

  Username (Optional)   [   ]

  Password (Optional)   [   ]

FIGURE 7.32   Connecting to target sites

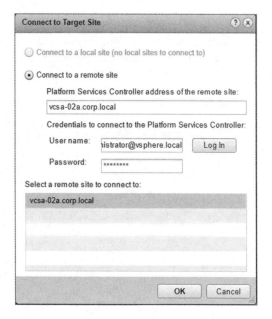

Connect to Target Site   ? ⊗

- ○ Connect to a local site (no local sites to connect to)
- ⦿ Connect to a remote site

  Platform Services Controller address of the remote site:

  [vcsa-02a.corp.local]

  Credentials to connect to the Platform Services Controller:

  User name: [nistrator@vsphere.local]   [Log In]

  Password: [********]

Select a remote site to connect to:

vcsa-02a.corp.local

[OK]   [Cancel]

To replicate a virtual machine, right-click the VM and select Configure Replication from the All vSphere Replication Actions menu (Figure 7.33). Virtual machines cannot have Fault Tolerance enabled to configure them to be replicated and must be powered on before replication will start.

FIGURE 7.33   Replicating a virtual machine

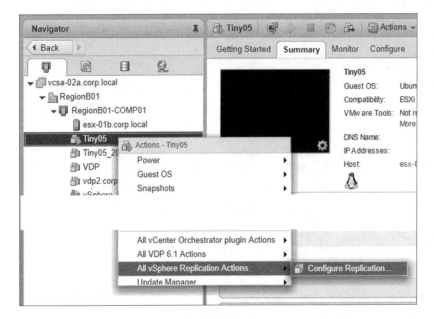

You can also select multiple VMs and create replication tasks for each of the selected VMs at one time. The tasks will share the same settings, although the storage location can be set for each VM during the Configure Replication wizard (Figure 7.34).

FIGURE 7.34   Replicating multiple virtual machines

Also on the Configure Replication window, you are prompted to enable Guest OS quiescing and/or Network Compression. We would suggest enabling Guest OS quiescing for all OSs that support it, to prevent issues with the replicated image. However, you may find that certain virtual machines do not respond well to quiescing attempts and may need that disabled.

The Network Compression setting compresses the data to replicate before it is sent to the target vSphere Replication appliance. According to a VMware blog on the topic (`blogs.vmware.com/vsphere/2015/03/vr-60-compression.html`), you can expect compression ratios of 1.6:1 to 1.8:1. While this results in a higher CPU load on the hosts running the source and target vSphere Replication appliances, the selected virtual machines will sync faster and there will be lower network utilization. While compression is a trade-off between network and CPU utilization, most environments have CPU resources to share, and we would suggest using network compression.

If there are ESXi 5.5 hosts in the environment, the Network Compression setting only works as advertised when the source and destination datastores are accessible by version 6.x ESXi hosts. If the virtual machine is running on a vSphere 5.5 host, then no compression will take place. If the destination datastore is only available by vSphere 5.5 hosts, the vSphere Replication appliance at the target site will decompress the data and send it to the ESXi 5.5 host.

FIGURE 7.35   Replication options

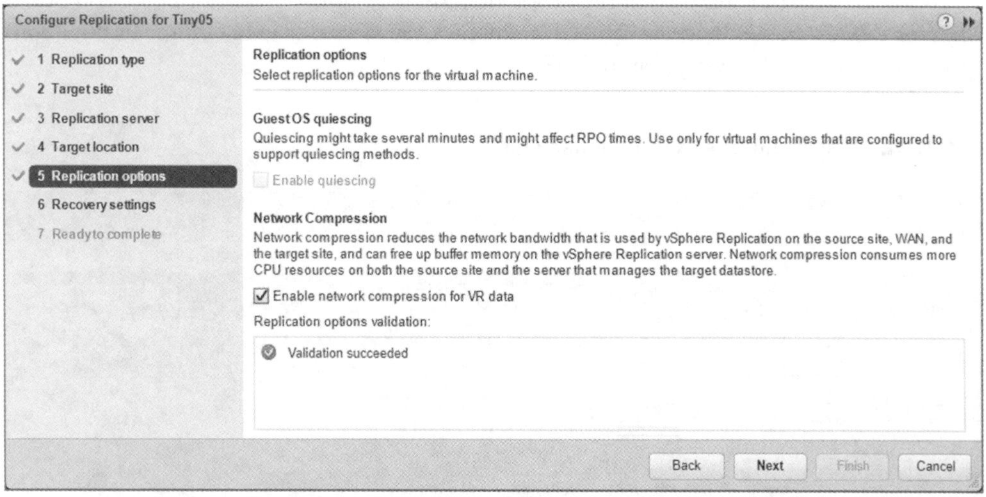

This can also affect vMotion and by extension DRS. Virtual machines that are being replicated with compression enabled cannot be moved to ESXi 5.5 hosts because the new host does not support compression.

Recovering Replicated VMs

The recovery settings of the virtual machine replication task include an adjustable RPO as well as optional point in time instances. The RPO setting is a balance between the most time you can lose and the system resources (CPU and networking primarily) it takes to replicate the changes. An RPO of 5 minutes means that in theory the most you can lose would be the last 5 minutes of changes. Every 5 minutes, the machine is replicated, so the most the destination could be behind is 5 minutes. However, this may be impractical for many servers as it could take 5 minutes to quiesce the guest or the CPU, and network impact of constantly replicating data may exceed the usefulness of the limited loss.

The multiple points in time feature allows multiple options for recovering the replicated VMs (Figure 7.36).

FIGURE 7.36   Multiple points of recovery

Replication Details	Point in Time		
Point in time recovery: Enabled (Keep 3 instances per day for the last 5 days)			
Instance Sync Point	Duration		Size
8/20/2018 11:27 PM	41 seconds		402.73 MB
8/20/2018 8:19 PM	59 seconds		631.12 MB

To recover a virtual machine at the target site, use the vSphere Replication Section of the Monitor tab for the destination vCenter. Right-click the virtual machine in Incoming Replications and choose Recovery (Figure 7.37).

FIGURE 7.37   Recover a virtual machine.

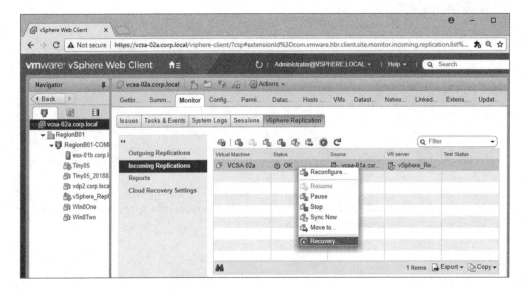

The Recovery wizard will prompt you to either use the latest sync or initiate a sync as the first step of the recovery. If the virtual machine is still available, then Synchronize Recent Changes is the preferred choice.

After recovery, the virtual machine will be powered off and the network connections will be disconnected. If the replication was configured with multiple points in time, those points will be available as snapshots on the recovered virtual machine (Figure 7.39).

FIGURE 7.38   Select whether to use the most recent changes.

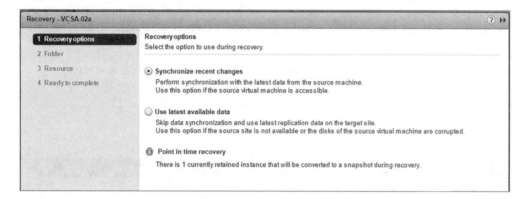

FIGURE 7.39   Multiple points in time snapshots

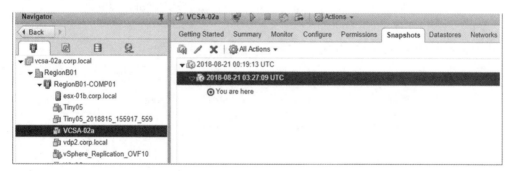

To fail the virtual machine back to the original configuration without Site Recovery Manager, you will need to create a vSphere Replication task for the recovered virtual machine with a destination of the original source.

Selecting When to Replicate Virtual Machines

vSphere Replication is a great tool even without Site Recovery Manager. However, you will probably want to take a varied approach to replications in the real world. Test and Dev machines might simply need a backup—or no backup at all depending on how the developers work. You might instead want to back up the VM templates and ensure that the code repository and deployment infrastructure is backed up.

For applications such as Active Directory (AD), Exchange, and SQL you will want to use either vendor tools (in the case of AD, deploy a live AD server to the remote environment) or replication/clustering methods, or look for third-party tools to replicate the data. A database-based application is not usually a good candidate for vSphere Replication due to change tracking by the application and interaction with other systems.

If you have SAN or NFS storage, you might also look at what those vendors offer in the way of replication tools.

EXERCISE 7.3

Recover a replicated virtual machine.

Required: vSphere Replication installed, VM replicated.

1.   Use the web client and view Incoming Replications from the vSphere Replication menu of the Monitor tab for the target vCenter.

2.   Right-click the virtual machine to recover and choose Recovery.

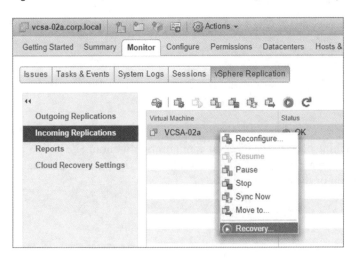

3. Select Use Latest Available Data and click Next.

4. Select a folder for the recovered virtual machine and click Next.

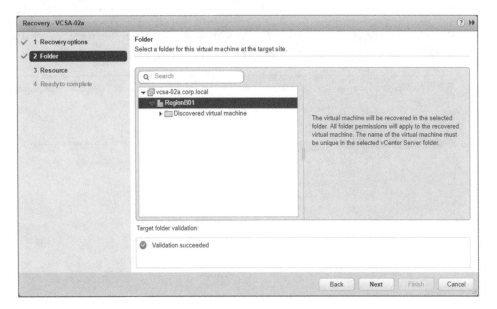

EXERCISE 7.3 *(continued)*

5. Select a host, cluster, or resource pool for the recovered virtual machine and click Next.

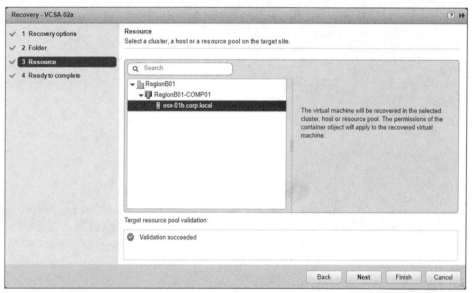

6. Verify your settings. Check "Power On the Virtual Machine after Recovery" to ensure that the VM has been recovered properly.

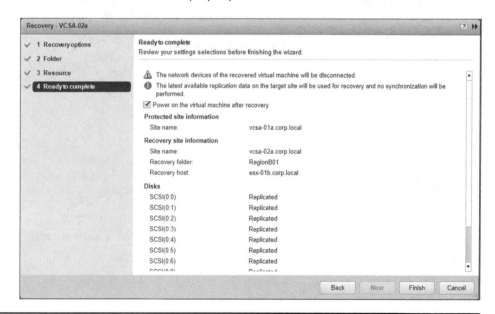

Summary

This chapter has covered backing up the VCSA appliance and backing up and replicating virtual machines. Backing up the configuration of VCSA is important to ensure quick recovery in the event of a problem, and the files can be reasonably small (depending on the size of your events and performance database).

The vSphere Data Protection Appliance will back up your virtual machines to storage locally to the appliance using deduplication to reduce the storage footprint of the backups. The backup jobs can be replicated to VDP appliances at other sites to ensure recoverability in the event of a site loss.

vSphere Replication will make duplicates of virtual machines that can be brought up fairly quickly for testing or in the event the original VM is unavailable. While backups are not intended to run very often, replications can be set down to every 5 minutes. vSphere Data Protection offers data deduplication to reduce the storage used; vSphere Replication offers compression to reduce the network bandwidth used.

A combination of vSphere Replication and vSphere Data Protection will ensure that your virtual machines are recoverable from issues on the local machines or in the local site while balancing storage and network impact.

Exam Essentials

Know how to back up the VCSA.   New to vSphere 6.5, you can back up a VCSA appliance into a set of files with options to only back up the configuration or include the historical data.

Understand how to deploy vSphere Data Protection.   VDP has limitations on the number of virtual machines it can back up simultaneously and how many VMs it can back up in total. While 1 VDP appliance can back up 8 virtual machines at once, you can deploy up to 8 proxy servers to back up a total of 24 virtual machines at a time. However, each VDP appliance is limited to a total of 8,000 virtual machines, so larger environments will need a different solution.

Know how to replicate virtual machines.   vSphere Replication manages virtual machine replication between clusters or vCenter servers. You should be able to describe deploying Replication, setting up a VM to replicate, and then recover that virtual machine at the target.

Know how Data Protection and Replication compare.   Know that both are included with all vSphere licenses except Essentials. Both have appliances that need to be deployed and both have primary or manager appliances that can only be installed once per vCenter. Data Protection offers data deduplication and Replication has network compression. Data Protection jobs can run daily; Replication jobs can run from every 5 minutes up to once per day.

Review Questions

The answers to the chapter review questions can be found in Appendix.

1. What features are offered by vSphere Data Protection? (Choose two.)

   A. Compression

   B. Deduplication

   C. Encryption

   D. Replication

2. What feature is offered by vSphere Replication?

   A. Compression

   B. Deduplication

   C. Encryption

   D. Guest agent

3. What is the minimum number of VDP proxy servers needed to back up 16 virtual machines simultaneously?

   A. 1

   B. 2

   C. 4

   D. 8

4. What product should be used to ensure that your Exchange server can be recovered in the event of a storage failure?

   A. vSphere Data Protection

   B. vSphere Replication

   C. vSphere High Availability

   D. vSphere storage clusters

5. What should be used to ensure that your MySQL database can be recovered in the event of a storage failure?

   A. vSphere Data Protection

   B. vSphere Replication

   C. vSphere High Availability

   D. A third-party utility

6. What option can be enabled to allow a virtual machine administrator to choose from multiple restore times after a virtual machine has been recovered?

   A. Snapshots

   B. Data deduplication

    C. Point in time instances

    D. Recovery point objective

7. What option reduces the amount of changes that can be lost for a virtual machine in the event of a recovery?

    A. Snapshots

    B. Data deduplication

    C. Point in time instances

    D. Recovery point objective

8. What options can be used to ensure that copies of your virtual machines are available in a remote environment in the event of a site loss? (Choose two.)

    A. vSphere Data Protection

    B. vSphere Replication

    C. vSphere High Availability

    D. vSphere storage clusters

9. What option can be enabled to reduce the likelihood of guest corruption?

    A. Guest OS quiescing

    B. Data deduplication

    C. Point in time instances

    D. Recovery point objective

10. What option should be disabled if the recovery point objective cannot be met?

    A. Guest OS quiescing

    B. Data deduplication

    C. Point in time instances

    D. Network compression

11. Why is the icon next to the object named "08/16/2018 1:02 AM" shown in red here?

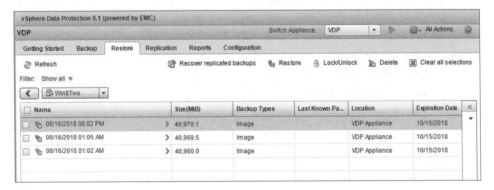

    A. It is the master for that sequence.

    B. It has not been replicated yet.

    C. It was not quiesced.

    D. It has been encrypted.

12. What would prevent a virtual machine from being replicated?

    A. Fault Tolerance enabled

    B. Unsupported guest OS

    C. VMDKs on virtual SAN

    D. VM power state is on

13. What steps would reduce the network traffic used by vSphere Replication?

    A. Increasing the RPO time

    B. Disabling point in time instances

    C. Decreasing the RPO time

    D. Enabling data deduplication

14. What steps would reduce the storage used by vSphere Data Protection?

    A. Increasing the RPO time

    B. Disabling point in time instances

    C. Decreasing the RPO time

    D. Enabling data deduplication

15. Unchecking which option would minimize the storage needed by VCSA backups?

    A. Stats, Events, Alarms, and Tasks

    B. Common

    C. Configuration, Events, and Tasks

    D. Configuration, Events, Tasks, and Performance Metrics

16. What is the best method for ensuring that a Windows vCenter server can be recovered in the event of a storage issue?

    A. vCenter backup wizard

    B. vSphere Data Protection

    C. vSphere High Availability

    D. vSphere datastore cluster

17. What step could be taken to resolve the issue shown here?

Recovery option validation:

◆ Source virtual machine is currently powered on.
Cannot recover the replicated virtual machine with the most recent changes as it might conflict with the source virtual machine.
Make sure that the source virtual machine is powered off or select the option to recover the virtual machine with the latest data that is available at the target site.

A. Select Use Latest Available Data.

B. Unselect Point in Time Recovery.

C. Power on the virtual machine.

D. Quiesce the virtual machine.

18. What steps are required to regain use of a virtual machine after it has been recovered using vSphere Replication? (Choose two.)

A. Power on the VM.

B. Quiesce the virtual machine.

C. Connect the network adapters.

D. Select the point in time.

Chapter

8

Troubleshooting a vSphere Deployment

2V0-21.19 EXAM OBJECTIVES COVERED IN THIS CHAPTER:

✓ **Section 4 – Installing, Configuring, and Setting Up a VMware vSphere Solution**

- Objective 4.1 – Understand basic log output from vSphere products

✓ **Section 5 – Performance-tuning and Optimizing a VMware vSphere Solution**

- Objective 5.2 – Monitor resources of VCSA in a vSphere environment

- Objective 5.3 – Identify impacts of VM configurations

✓ **Section 7 – Administrative and Operational Tasks in a VMware vSphere Solution**

- Objective 7.14 – Understand use cases for alarms

Troubleshooting is a key skill for anyone in today's technology-driven world. The ability to take a problem, look at it from different angles, break it into smaller pieces, or view the problem in a greater setting is crucial in many areas. From mechanical problems to political barriers, from network failures to development activities, the ability to solve problems quickly is a key component to productivity.

There are several stages to successful troubleshooting, including problem identification, hypothesis, and resolution testing. This chapter will focus on the information gathering and analysis for a vSphere environment, which are crucial to the identification of a problem. Knowing where to find logs and configuration information is a critical step, but understanding how the components function and what different settings do is just as important.

If you are actually troubleshooting a problem, don't forget the classic questions: "What was the last change made?" and "Have you tried rebooting it?"

Troubleshooting vCenter and ESXi

The following sections will cover some of the higher-level issues around the vCenter Server and ESXi hosts, such as services, overall monitoring, and health.

Some of the tools to use when troubleshooting vCenter include the web client (`https://<vCenter IP or FQDN>/vsphere-client`), the appliance UI (`https://<vCenter IP or FQDN>:5480`) for VCSA, and the Windows management tools for the installed version of vCenter. The VCSA has an additional tool, vimtop, which is available from the command line.

vCenter Connectivity and Services

If you cannot connect to the appliance or web client, or if your hosts cannot communicate with vSphere, check for network connectivity issues or a firewall between the components blocking the required ports. VMware has an extensive list of the ports needed in the vSphere documentation under "Incoming and Outgoing Firewall Ports for ESXi Hosts" and "Required Ports for vCenter Server and Platform Services Controller." A brief list of these ports is contained in Table 8.1.

TABLE 8.1   Common ports required for vSphere functionality

Port	Functionality
389 / 636	vCenter Single Sign-On LDAP / LDAPS
443	Web client
636	vCenter Server Enhanced Linked Mode
902	Web client and Data transfer between hosts
12345, 23451	vSAN clustering
53	DNS lookup
8100, 8200, 8300	Fault tolerance
8000	vMotion
80, 9000	vSphere Update Manager
3260	iSCSI
5480	VCSA appliance management

The vCenter server has several key services that are always required and optional services for functionality such as Auto Deploy. You can check the status of vCenter and its services from the System Configuration page for the node (see Figure 8.1).

FIGURE 8.1   The System Configuration section of the web client

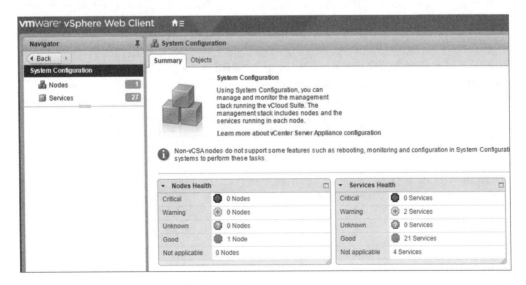

Or get a list of services and their status by using the Services menu as shown in Figure 8.2.

FIGURE 8.2   The Services menu of the web client

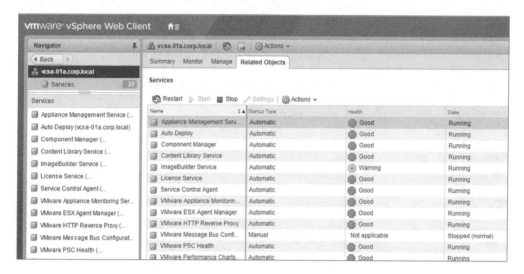

The full list of services includes the ability to start, stop, and restart services plus the ability to change the startup settings of each service. This is where you go to "enable" Auto Deploy and ImageBuilder by setting the services to always start. Note that if an upgrade of vCenter fails due to Tomcat (the VCSA web service) not stopping, the VMware Troubleshooting documentation suggests setting the VMware vCenter Management Webservices and VMware VirtualCenter Server services to manual and then rebooting the server.

One common source of issues for vCenter servers is the database holding the events and statistics. To avoid running the volume holding the database out of space, you can monitor it using the df -h command from the VCSA appliance or using the Windows Explorer or Disk Management tools if vCenter is installed on a Windows server.

To reduce the space used by the database, you can adjust the statistics levels kept as well as how long the levels are kept. The statistics settings are available in the Configure tab of the vCenter object (Figure 8.3). When you are changing the settings, the estimated maximum size of the database is displayed on the bottom right—but you need to set the host and VMs numbers for the best accuracy. When you're setting the levels, Level 1 saves the fewest number of statistics and thus takes up the least space, and Level 4 is for debugging and saves all statistics.

You can also adjust the time tasks and events will be retained in the database under the Database options of vCenter Server Settings; however, the Task Cleanup and Event Cleanup options must be selected before the time settings will be honored (Figure 8.4).

FIGURE 8.3 Viewing the statistics options for vCenter server settings

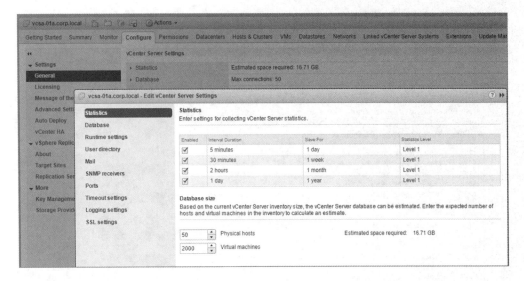

FIGURE 8.4 The event and task options for vCenter server settings

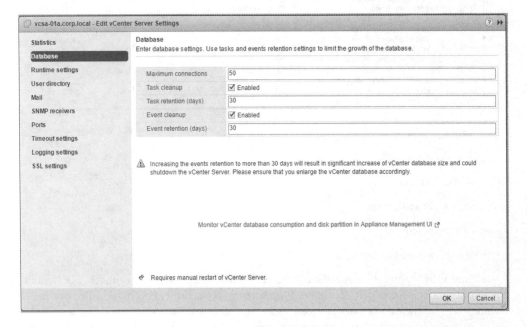

Additional statistics are available for the VCSA appliance in the form of a command-line tool called vimtop, which the VMware documentation refers to as a "plug-in." Very similar in look to the esxtop utility, vimtop will display the running tasks with their CPU and memory usage as shown in Figure 8.5.

FIGURE 8.5   Default view for the vimtop VCSA monitoring tool

```
VIMTop0.9 (Beta): uptime: 25 days 04:54:51, load average:  0.13,  0.16,  0.17
Tasks:     60 all,    1 run,   59 sleep,    0 block,    0 stop,    0 zombie
CPUs:    3.7%us   2.8%sy   0.0%ni 182.6%id   0.0%wa   0.0%hi   0.0%si   0.0%st  7008MHz
```

CPU	%USR	%SYS	%NI	%IDL	%IOW	%IRQ	%SIRQ	%STEAL	MHZ
0	3.75	3.75	0.00	89.91	0.00	0.00	0.00	0.00	3504.00
1	0.00	0.00	0.00	93.66	0.00	0.00	0.00	0.00	3504.00

```
Memory:  10230540KB total   8436492KB used     140020KB free    620556KB buffs
Swap:    27254776KB total   2315884KB used   24938892KB free   1033472KB cached
Vmalloc: 33554431MB total         0MB used   33554431MB free         0MB chunk
(Enter),(H)elp,(P)ause,(S)et period,(W)rite config,P(r)ocesses,Dis(k)s,Netw(o)rk,(Q)uit
```

PID	NAME THREADS		%CPU	MHZ	%MEM	MEM	VIRT
num	%	MHz %	MB MB				
30330	VIM Top	7	4.68	164	0.42	42.05	484.55
4781	VSAN Health Service	310	3.75	131	5.01	500.93	4077.39
4778	Image Builder Manager	1 06	1.87	65	0.17	17.06	817.26
2260	vSphere Client anager 6St	948	0.94	32	9.13	912.47	2902.71
2261	vSphere H5 Web Client	83	0.94	32	3.76	375.54	2397.82
2195	ESXi Agent Manager	76	0.94	32	1.49	149.09	1564.57
4872	Java Process	112	0.94	32	4.98	497.13	1981.07
2344	Appliance Management Serv	1	0.00	0	0.26	25.99	211.45
4225	vCenter Server	121	0.00	0	1.16	115.47	1323.33
5102	Autodeploy CGI	11	0.00	0	0.26	25.63	888.88
4782	Update Manager	75	0.00	0	2.37	236.38	1172.13
1288	VMware Virtual Machine To	2	0.00	0	0.04	4.02	149.52
1292	Authentication Framework	23	0.00	0	0.19	19.47	1338.19
2095	Reverse HTTP Proxy	27	0.00	0	0.16	16.02	1069.08
6815	Performance Charts	77	0.00	0	1.33	132.63	1819.55
2241	Service Control Agent	51	0.00	0	1.88	187.64	1533.63
2262	Component Manager	40	0.00	0	1.97	196.39	1645.31
2122	Licensing Manager	59	0.00	0	2.55	254.58	1636.49
19034	Autodeploy VC Monitor	2	0.00	0	0.51	50.75	252.99
4868	VMware Service Manager	33	0.00	0	1.55	154.90	1559.95
1469	VMware Domain Name Servic	18	0.00	0	0.08	7.98	602.59
3156	vAPI Endpoint	55	0.00	0	3.69	368.29	1683.40
5942	Update Manager Java subpr	26	0.00	0	0.61	60.68	4919.38
1375	Directory Service Control	32	0.00	0	0.31	30.97	21869.21
4852	vSphere Profile-Driven St	163	0.00	0	3.80	379.62	2003.35
3151	vCenter Services	387	0.00	0	4.08	407.95	2626.88
983	Platform Services Control	68	0.00	0	0.80	79.76	2059.77

Useful keystrokes for vimtop include the following:

p—pause the display

k—view disk stats

o—view network stats

c—change columns

w—write a configuration file

You can start vimtop with specific configuration files using the -c parameter. The default configuration file is located at /root/vimtop/vimtop.xml. Other command-line options include -n to set the number of iterations and -p or -d to set the update period in seconds.

If you are using encryption in your environment, you may be deploying KMS servers to manage the keys. If you encounter issues, be aware that round-trip latency between vSAN hosts and the KMS server cannot exceed 1 second. If you are using large SSL certificates (greater than 2,048 bits) or have network latency between the KMS and hosts, you could encounter problems.

You also need to ensure that vCenter can access the KMS server or cluster at all times to ensure that VMs can been unlocked when requested by hosts. If you encounter a key/ key ID mismatch on the KMS server, you can retrieve the key ID using the Managed Object Browser at `VirtualMachine.config.keyId.keyId`. Having the KMS administrator reactivate the key associated with that ID should resolve the issue.

vCenter Certificates

Connectivity to a vCenter server and between vSphere components (PSC, hosts, postgres database) depends on correct authentication of the certificates used to secure the communications. A default install of vSphere will generate certificates using the VMware Certificate Authority daemon running on vCenter, but for production use these should be replaced with certificates from your corporate authority or a commercial CA.

There are a few areas where you might run into issues after replacing your certificates.

General connectivity   Existing connections might remain open and continue to use the old certificate after replacement. You can shut the network interfaces or restart the vCenter Server service to ensure that all connections are reset.

Database connectivity   If vCenter can't connect to the database, use the vpxd -p {password} command to reset the password, which will re-encrypt it with the new certificate.

Host connectivity   If hosts cannot connect to the vCenter server after certificate updates, disconnect and reconnect them from vCenter. The official documentation suggests you do this from the ESXi hosts, but you can only disconnect—and that's not permanent, as rebooting the host should reconnect it.

HA enablement   You may encounter an error when enabling HA that "vSphere HA cannot be configured on this host because its SSL thumbprint has not been verified." Again, disconnecting and reconnecting the host from vCenter should resolve this issue.

vCenter Log Files

One of the first steps for troubleshooting a new problem is examining the log files. Common log files are described in the following paragraph, but note that you will need to check the specific host or machine having the issues for the correct log file. Troubleshooting using log files also depends on having the time accurate (and synchronized) on the machines in your environment. Troubleshooting connectivity or security issues between multiple machines is made much easier when you can match the log entries to the second and compare entries between the logs.

Installation logs for the installed version of Windows can be found at %PROGRAMDATA%\ VMware\vCenterServer\logs as well as the %temp% directory on the Windows server.

In the temp directory, look for vminst.log, pkgmgr.log, pkgmgr-comp-msi.log, and vim-vcs-msi.log. The VCSA installer has a log file at C:\Users\Administrator\AppData\Local\VMware\CIP\vcsaInstaller; however, if the installer encounters a problem, it should prompt you to create a zip file with the relevant logs for troubleshooting.

If you encounter problems with the web client, on the installed version you can check the same %PROGRAMDATA%\VMware\vCenterServer\logs directory, or for VCSA look in /var/log/vmware/vsphere-client/logs. The main log file for the vSphere web client is vsphere_client_virgo.log.

A comprehensive list of logs is available in the vSphere Troubleshooting guide, but I'll list some of the key ones here. For an installed version of Windows, the logs are found in the directories under %PROGRAMDATA%\VMware\vCenterServer\logs, and for VCSA they are in directories under /var/log/vmware/. I already mentioned installation and web client logs, but also be aware of these:

vpxd—main vCenter Server log

CM—VMware Component Manager

FirstBoot—first boot logs

EAM—ESX Agent Manager

InvSvc—Inventory Service

vPostgres—Postgres database service

Vmcad—VMware Certificate Authority

These are directories containing the relevant logs and will be all lowercase on the VCSA appliance. The vpxd log is the first one to check for general vCenter issue, including client and web services connectivity, internal tasks and events, and vpxa communications (the vCenter Server Agent running on managed hosts).

You can use the VCSA appliance management page (VAMI) to create a support bundle as shown in Figure 8.6 or execute vc-support.sh from the command line.

FIGURE 8.6   Generating a support bundle from the VCSA configuration page

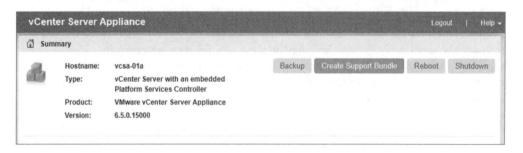

While the button in the VAMI will automatically download the support bundle to your browser, you will need to retrieve it via SCP from the VCSA appliance if you use the vc-support.sh script as shown in Figure 8.7.

FIGURE 8.7   Generating a support bundle from the VCSA command line

```
05:01:27: Adding /storage/log/vmware/vpxd/drmdump/domain-c7/0184776296-proposeNonResActions.dump.gz
05:01:27: Adding /etc/vmware/vsphere-ui/vc-packages/vsphere-client-serenity/com.vmware.vcHms-6.5.1.658128481/plugins/vr-ui-war-6.5
05:01:27: Adding /storage/log/vmware/vpxd/drmdump/domain-c7/8557456242-proposeNonResActions.dump.gz
05:02:28: Done.
Please attach this file when submitting an incident report.
To file a support incident, go to http://www.vmware.com/support/sr/sr_login.jsp
To see the files collected, check '/storage/log/vc-vcsa-01a-2019-05-01--04.56-60498.tgz'
root@vcsa-01a [ / ]#
```

You can also view and download the vCenter logs using the vSphere client as shown in Figure 8.8. While you can only view the vpxd logs using the client, you can download all of them. This method can also download ESXi log files.

FIGURE 8.8   View or download vCenter log files.

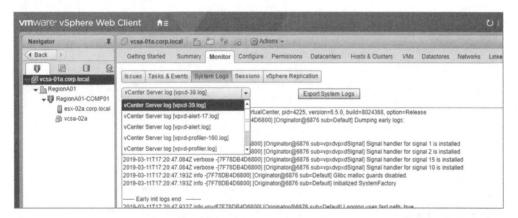

EXERCISE 8.1

Export ESXi and vCenter log files.

1. From the web client, select your vCenter server and open the System Logs view from the Monitor tab:

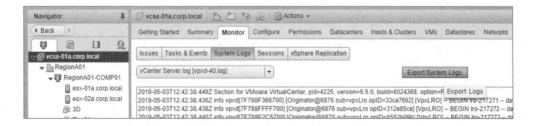

2. Click Export System Logs.

3. Select your ESXi hosts and select Include vCenter Server And vSphere Web Client Logs.

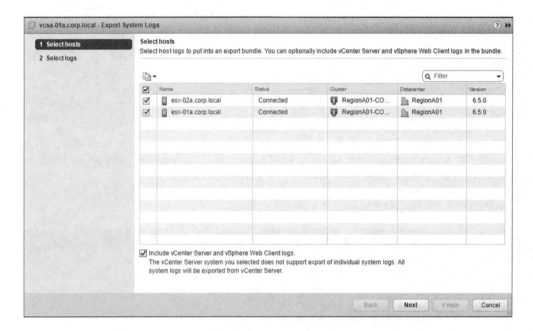

4. Select Password For Encrypted Core Dumps and enter a password.

5. Click Finish.

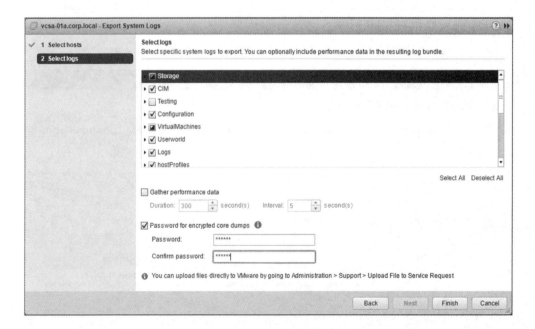

EXERCISE 8.1 *(continued)*

6. Select a directory and accept the default name for the log file.

7. Wait for the log files to download.

8. Extract the `.tar` file from one of the ESXi `.tgz` files.

9. Extract the log files from the `.tar` file and locate the `vmkernel.log` file in the `var/run/log` directory.

Real World Scenario

VMware Skyline

VMware has a little-known tool called Skyline that is included with every production support contract. Skyline is a proactive support product that collects, aggregates, and analyzes VMware product logs and telemetry information.

Skyline deploys as an appliance and connects to vCenter servers and NSX Manager to pull configurations, performance data, changes, and events, which are then sent to VMware for analysis.

Using data collected from customers around the world, Skyline can anticipate and predict issues in your environment.

If a problem is encountered, Skyline can be used to forward relevant logs to VMware— and associate them with your support ticket during uploading.

If you have a valid support contract, you should be looking into adding Skyline to your environment if only for the ease of sending logs to VMware if needed.

ESXi Troubleshooting

When you connect ESXi hosts to a vCenter server, a local user (vpxuser) is created and an agent service (vpxa) is configured and started, as shown in Figure 8.9. The vCenter host will leverage the vpxa service and vpxuser credentials when managing the host.

FIGURE 8.9 Generating a support bundle from the VCSA command line

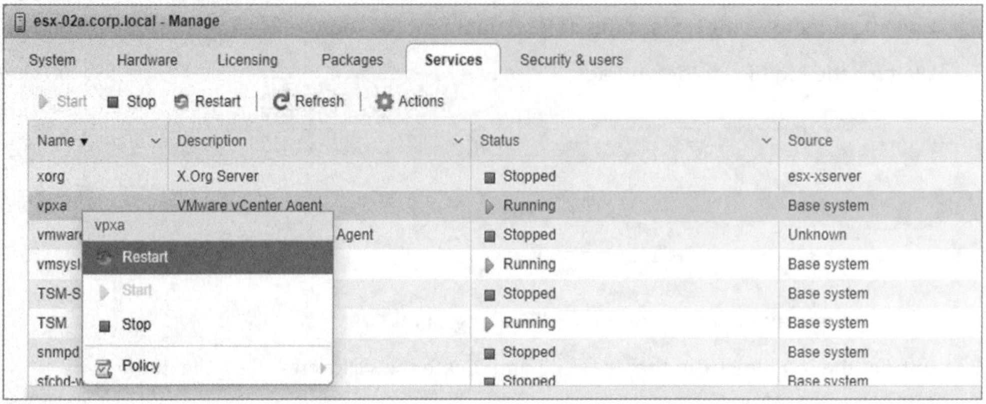

There are several issues you could experience regarding hosts. For the most basic of troubleshooting (after making sure everything is powered on and running), make sure you can ping the FQDN and IP address from the vCenter server to the host and from the host to the vCenter server. If you can't resolve the FQDNs, make sure the correct DNS server IP is in use and check the DNS servers. If there is no IP connectivity, you will need to look at the network hardware and work with the network team to test connectivity and things such as proper VLAN tagging.

If you encounter a "not responding" issue (see Figure 8.10) and the host is up and you have IP connectivity, there are a few steps to take to resolve it. First, as shown back in Figure 8.9, you can restart the vpxa service. You can also work with your network team to ensure that there is not a firewall between the hosts and vCenter blocking port 902; however, this would need to be a recent change as it would have prevented adding the host to vCenter in the first place.

FIGURE 8.10 Host not responding in vCenter due to a network issue

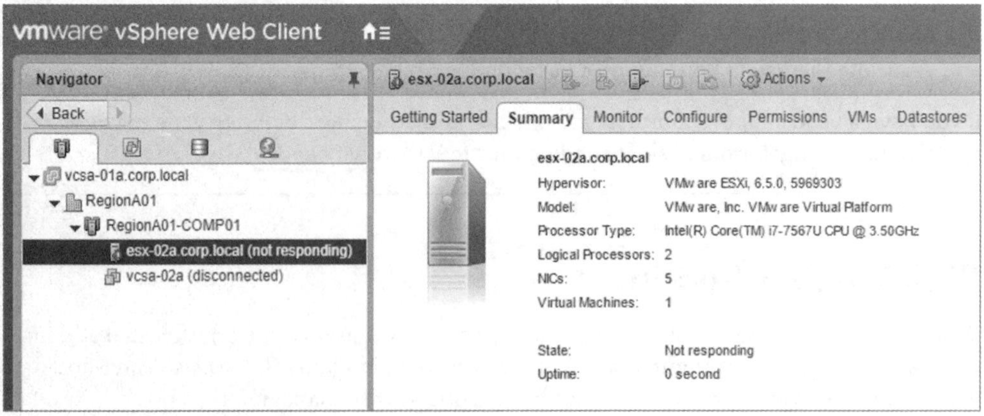

The final step for many issues (such as connectivity problems after replacing certificates) is often disconnecting and reconnecting the host from vCenter as shown in Figure 8.11.

FIGURE 8.11   Disconnecting/reconnecting a host in vCenter

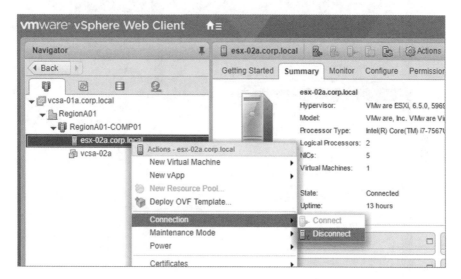

If High Availability is enabled on the host, there is an additional agent service (`vmware-fdm`) started on each host that manages elections and HA when vCenter is not available. If problems arise with HA, they are usually classified in one of these states:

Unreachable State   Host communication error or HA configuration is off. If the host is communicating with vCenter, reconfigure HA (Figure 8.12).

Uninitialized State   Host might have lost access to datastores; HA is misconfigured or stopped. If the host can see all datastores properly, reconfigure HA (Figure 8.12).

Initialization Error State   Host communication error, out of disk space, or host needs to reboot. If the host is communicating, free up disk space or reboot host as needed.

Uninitialization Error State   Usually host communication error. Resolve and reconfigure HA (Figure 8.12).

Host Failed State   Usually host communication error or lost access to datastores.

Network Partitioned State   Host communication error where the Master HA host can't access another host by network but can exchange heartbeats—often caused by physical network changes.

Network Isolated State   Host communication error where the host can't access the isolation addresses or any other hosts in the cluster. Usually a physical network problem.

FIGURE 8.12   Reconfiguring a host for vSphere High Availability

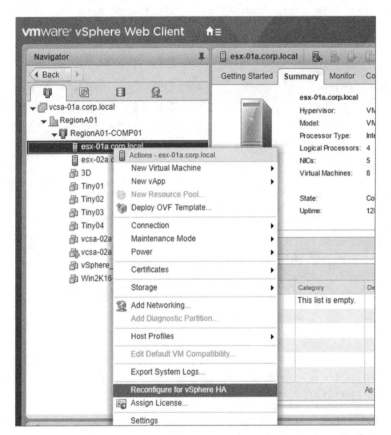

Coupled with High Availability is the Fault Tolerance option for virtual machines. VMware's FT technology requires low-latency network connectivity for proper operation. You should ensure that you have a 10 Gbps link between hosts and a dedicated VLAN and VMkernel adapter for Fault Tolerance, and you should work with the network team to ensure the lowest latency possible between the hosts.

Hair-pinning the traffic to a physical firewall or use of a bridge firewall or any other service that examines packets should be disabled for the Fault Tolerant network. The network does not need to be routed or extended beyond the hosts participating in Fault Tolerance. You should also ensure that all of your hosts' firmware and drivers are up-to-date and review any documentation from your vendor regarding VMware and Fault Tolerance best practices.

If you have several VMs with FT enabled, make sure you monitor the environment to ensure that one host isn't swamped with multiple FT-enabled machines. Since DRS won't migrate FT-enabled machines, you will need to balance them yourself—and periodically check, as power-cycling the virtual machines can change the location of the FT copy, as can activities like disabling FT for updates or other maintenance.

ESXi Monitoring

You can monitor your ESXi host using the host UI, from vCenter, or from the command line using `esxtop` (see Figure 8.13, Figure 8.14, and Figure 8.15).

FIGURE 8.13   Host client

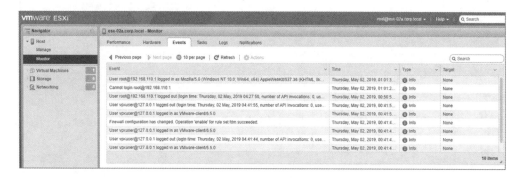

FIGURE 8.14   Monitoring a host using the vSphere web client

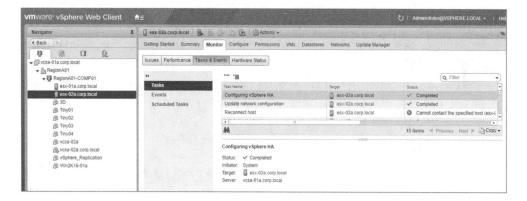

The host UI is great for standalone hosts, or to check on hosts that are having issues connecting to vCenter. The vSphere web client is the preferred method as it has more information than the host client—and has all of the configuration settings for the host. The command-line tool `esxtop` is great for granular examination and is the most detailed in the areas it covers, but is often too detailed to start troubleshooting with since it doesn't display things like recent tasks or events.

All three of these tools can report on performance, but the vSphere client is best for historical information, trends, readability, and export capabilities (image or CSV). The `esxtop` tool is best for fine detail and scheduling data captures.

FIGURE 8.15   Monitoring a host using `esxtop`

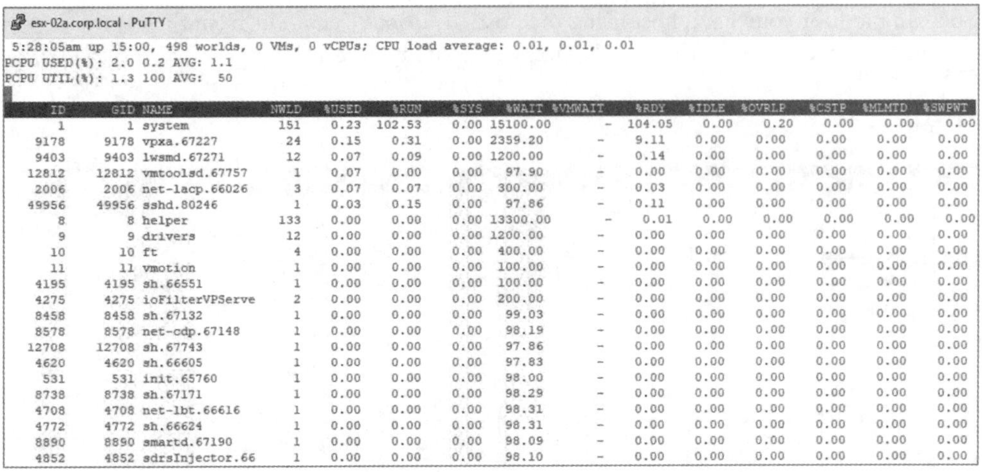

```
 esx-02a.corp.local - PuTTY

5:28:05am up 15:00, 498 worlds, 0 VMs, 0 vCPUs; CPU load average: 0.01, 0.01, 0.01
PCPU USED(%): 2.0 0.2 AVG: 1.1
PCPU UTIL(%): 1.3 100 AVG:   50
```

ID	GID NAME	NWLD	%USED	%RUN	%SYS	%WAIT	%VMWAIT	%RDY	%IDLE	%OVRLP	%CSTP	%MLMTD	%SWPWT
1	1 system	151	0.23	102.53	0.00	15100.00	–	104.05	0.00	0.20	0.00	0.00	0.00
9178	9178 vpxa.67227	24	0.15	0.31	0.00	2359.20	–	9.11	0.00	0.00	0.00	0.00	0.00
9403	9403 lwsmd.67271	12	0.07	0.09	0.00	1200.00	–	0.14	0.00	0.00	0.00	0.00	0.00
12812	12812 vmtoolsd.67757	1	0.07	0.00	0.00	97.90	–	0.00	0.00	0.00	0.00	0.00	0.00
2006	2006 net-lacp.66026	3	0.07	0.07	0.00	300.00	–	0.03	0.00	0.00	0.00	0.00	0.00
49956	49956 sshd.80246	1	0.03	0.15	0.00	97.86	–	0.11	0.00	0.00	0.00	0.00	0.00
8	8 helper	133	0.00	0.00	0.00	13300.00	–	0.01	0.00	0.00	0.00	0.00	0.00
9	9 drivers	12	0.00	0.00	0.00	1200.00	–	0.00	0.00	0.00	0.00	0.00	0.00
10	10 ft	4	0.00	0.00	0.00	400.00	–	0.00	0.00	0.00	0.00	0.00	0.00
11	11 vmotion	1	0.00	0.00	0.00	100.00	–	0.00	0.00	0.00	0.00	0.00	0.00
4195	4195 sh.66551	1	0.00	0.00	0.00	100.00	–	0.00	0.00	0.00	0.00	0.00	0.00
4275	4275 ioFilterVPServe	2	0.00	0.00	0.00	200.00	–	0.00	0.00	0.00	0.00	0.00	0.00
8458	8458 sh.67132	1	0.00	0.00	0.00	99.03	–	0.00	0.00	0.00	0.00	0.00	0.00
8578	8578 net-cdp.67148	1	0.00	0.00	0.00	98.19	–	0.00	0.00	0.00	0.00	0.00	0.00
12708	12708 sh.67743	1	0.00	0.00	0.00	97.86	–	0.00	0.00	0.00	0.00	0.00	0.00
4620	4620 sh.66605	1	0.00	0.00	0.00	97.83	–	0.00	0.00	0.00	0.00	0.00	0.00
531	531 init.65760	1	0.00	0.00	0.00	98.00	–	0.00	0.00	0.00	0.00	0.00	0.00
8738	8738 sh.67171	1	0.00	0.00	0.00	98.29	–	0.00	0.00	0.00	0.00	0.00	0.00
4708	4708 net-lbt.66616	1	0.00	0.00	0.00	98.31	–	0.00	0.00	0.00	0.00	0.00	0.00
4772	4772 sh.66624	1	0.00	0.00	0.00	98.31	–	0.00	0.00	0.00	0.00	0.00	0.00
8890	8890 smartd.67190	1	0.00	0.00	0.00	98.09	–	0.00	0.00	0.00	0.00	0.00	0.00
4852	4852 sdrsInjector.66	1	0.00	0.00	0.00	98.10	–	0.00	0.00	0.00	0.00	0.00	0.00

The VCP exam should not have significant questions on the `esxtop` tool, but here are some things you should know:

There are two versions, `esxtop` for your local host and `resxtop` to capture data from remote hosts. While `esxtop` is installed with any host deployed, `resxtop` is available with the vSphere CLI package or the vSphere Management Assistant (vMA) virtual machine.

You can use `esxtop` in interactive or batch mode. Simply running `esxtop` starts it in interactive mode where you can use keyboard keys to change the display panel:

h—help

f—add or remove displayed fields

W—write a configuration file to save your settings (~/.esxtop60rc)

k—kill a world (i.e., stop a virtual machine)

c—show CPU stats

m—show memory stats

n—show network stats

u—show disk device stats

x—show vSAN stats

In batch mode, you call `esxtop` using the default configuration or a customized config file with parameters to set how many sets of data to capture and how long to wait between captures. Note that you need to start `esxtop` and use an *uppercase* W to save a configuration file before using `esxtop` in batch mode.

a—all statistics (overrides the config file if it was saved with specific columns)

b—required to start `esxtop` in batch mode

d—the delay in seconds between captures; minimum of 2 seconds, default 5 seconds

n—number of iterations or datasets to capture

To start `esxtop` in batch mode, the minimum command line is `esxtop > filename .csv`, capture for the default 5 second intervals, and redirect the output to a CSV file in the directory you are in. Realistically you will want to specify `-n x` to set a specific number of intervals to capture or the utility will simply continue to run until it is manually stopped or the disk is out of space. For `resxtop`, you will also need `-server` and `-username` (you will be prompted for the password).

EXERCISE 8.2

View esxtop stats.

1. Connect to an ESXi host using SSH.

2. Start `esxtop`.

```
esx-01a.corp.local - PuTTY

[root@esx-01a:~] esxtop
```

3. Press **u** to switch to disk device view.

4.   Press f to show the column chooser.

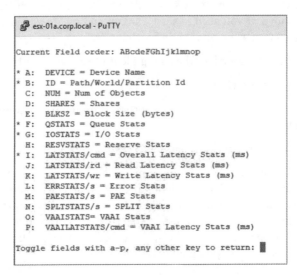

5.   Press **F** and **G** to remove the QSTATS and IOSTATS information.

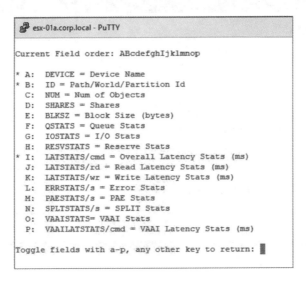

6. Press Enter to return to the stats screen and view the DAVG, KAVG, GAVG, and QAVG stats for your devices.

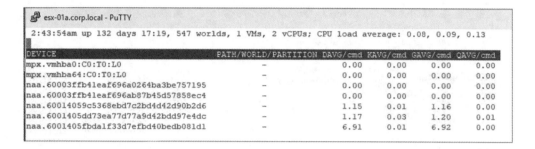

View vimtop stats.

1. Connect to a VCSA appliance using SSH. Disabling "auto wrap" in your SSH client may result in a better view for vimtop.

2. Start the shell.

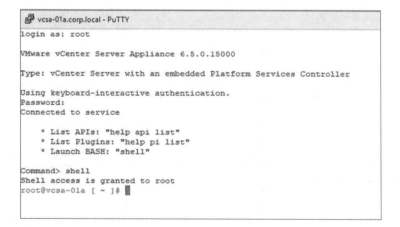

3. Enter **vimtop** to start the utility.

```
vcsa-01a.corp.local - PuTTY
VIMTop0.9 (Beta): uptime: 31 days 22:23:02, load average:  0.24,   0.46,   0.41
Tasks:     62 all,    1 run,    61 sleep,    0 block,    0 stop,    0 zombie
CPUs:    3.8%us   3.8%sy   0.0%ni 186.6%id   0.0%wa   0.0%hi   0.0%si   0.0%st  7008MHz
 CPU     %USR      %SYS      %NI      %IDL     %IOW      %IRQ     %SIRQ    %STEAL       MHZ
  1      2.81      3.75     0.00     90.96     0.00      0.00      0.00      0.00    3504.00
  0      0.94      0.00     0.00     95.65     0.00      0.00      0.94      0.00    3504.00
Memory:   10230540KB total    6630108KB used    1886400KB free    468012KB buffs
Swap:     27254776KB total    3031772KB used   24223004KB free   1246020KB cached
Vmalloc:  33554431MB total          0MB used   33554431MB free         0MB chunk
(Enter),(H)elp,(P)ause,(S)et period,(W)rite config,P(r)ocesses,Dis(k)s,Netw(o)rk,(Q)uit
 PID     NAME THREADS      %CPU     MHZ    %MEM MEM VIRT
         num        %       MHz  %  MB  ME
 5114    VIM Top 1th Service 310    1.8   7    4.69      164    0.42     42.11     485.15
 4852    vSphere Profile-Driven St  183   0.94  5.0332    3.91   391.11    2009.16
 2261    vSphere H5 Web Client       83   0.94   32      2.60   259.33    2397.82
 4781    VSAN Health Service        310   0.94   32      5.03   502.73    4079.89
 4778    Image Builder Manager        6   0.94   32      0.17    16.66     817.26
 2344    Appliance Management Serv    1   0.94   32      0.26    26.02     211.45
 2260    vSphere Client Client  St  970   0.00    0      9.85   984.48    2887.30
 2429    vPostgres Writer             1   0.00  0  INV   0.18    18.07     463.32
 2430    vPostgres Wal Writer         1   0.00  0  INV   0.14    14.05     463.21
 3608    vPostgres VCDB               1   0.00  0  INV   0.12    12.34     465.27
 3612    vPostgres VCDB               1   0.00  0  INV   0.14    13.62     464.39
 4439    vPostgres VCDB               1   0.00  0  INV   0.16    16.27     467.27
 6902    vPostgres VCDB               1   0.00  0  INV   0.09     8.68     464.18
 6934    vPostgres VCDB               1   0.00  0  INV   0.09     8.69     464.18
 6937    vPostgres VCDB               1   0.00  0  INV   0.09     8.69     464.18
 6951    vPostgres VCDB               1   0.00  0  INV   0.22    22.38     492.38
 6954    vPostgres VCDB               1   0.00  0  INV   0.14    13.86     466.54
 8252    vPostgres VCDB   Collector   1   0.00  0  INV   0.59    58.60     475.57
36825    vPostgres VCDB               1   0.00  0  INV   0.40    39.92     471.68
36903    vPostgres VCDB pointer       1   0.00  0  INV   0.22    21.94     464.92
36904    vPostgres VCDB               1   0.00  0  INV   0.19    19.44     464.93
61569    vPostgres VCDB               1   0.00  0   0.58    57.76   473.82649.20
62408    vPostgres VCDB               1   0.00  0   0.5   1.47    56.86     473.99
 2432    vPostgres Stats Collector    1   0.00  0   0.04  3.554  703.55    1670.46
 2424    vPostgres Logger             1   0.00  0   0.02  2.402    6 2.46    67.34
 2428    vPostgres Checkpointer       1   0.00      0   0.97    96.71     463.47
 2412    vPostgres                    1   0.00      0   0.12    11.59     463.04
 3151    vCenter Services           404   0.00      0   3.80   379.20    2649.20
 4225    vCenter Server             125   0.00      0   1.47   146.79    1366.09
 3156    vAPI Endpoint               55   0.00      0   3.01   300.46    1683.40
 1288    VMware Virtual Machine To     2   0.00     0   0.04     3.98     149.52
 4868    VMware Service Manager       33   0.00      0   1.12   111.78    1559.95
 1469    VMware Domain Name Servic    18   0.00      0   0.08     7.98     602.59
 5942    Update Manager Java subpr    26   0.00      0   0.52    51.75    4919.38
 4782    Update Manager               75   0.00      0   1.39   138.87    1172.13
 2210    Service Lifecycle Manager     9   0.00     0   0.06     6.20     629.98
```

4. Press **p** to pause the display. Use the arrow keys to scroll and view the processes.

5. Press **p** to resume.

EXERCISE 8.3 *(continued)*

6. Press **o** to view the network statistics.

```
vcsa-01a.corp.local - PuTTY

VIMTop0.9 (Beta): uptime: 31 days 22:28:26,  load average:  0.37,  0.42,  0.40
Tasks:      62 all,      1 run,     61 sleep,     0 block,     0 stop,     0 zombie
CPUs:     3.8%us    3.8%sy    0.0%ni  183.4%id    0.0%wa    0.0%hi    0.0%si    0.0%st   7008MHz
CPU      %USR      %SYS      %NI      %IDL      %IOW      %IRQ      %SIRQ     %STEAL        MHZ
0         3.82      2.87     0.00     90.74      0.00      0.00      0.00      0.00    3504.00
1         0.96      0.96     0.00     92.65      0.00      0.00      0.96      0.00    3504.00
Memory:   10230540KB total    6632684KB used    1882200KB free    468508KB buffs
Swap:     27254776KB total    3031508KB used   24223268KB free   1247148KB cached
Vmalloc:  33554431MB total          0MB used   33554431MB free         0MB chunk
(Enter),(H)elp,(P)ause,(S)et period,(W)rite config,P(r)ocesses,Dis(k)s,Netw(o)rk,(Q)uit
INTF RATE      RXRATE      TXRATE  RXXRATE  RXMCAST  DROPPED       ERRS   CLLSNS
        n     KBps KBps  KBps KBps     num      num         num      num
eth0 0.00 0.00 0.00 nagement0Serv       1     0.00          0 0 0
eth1 0.00 0.00 0.00 nagement Serv       1     0.00          0 0 0
lo 0.00 0.00 0.001Management0Serv 1   102     0.00          0 0 0
```

Troubleshooting Storage and Networking

With a vSphere environment, troubleshooting network and storage issues usually involves working with the physical hardware supplying the services. Even troubleshooting vSAN often involves the network team. Specific hardware troubleshooting steps should come from your vendors—and checking with them for documentation including design guides and white papers is always a good idea.

In the following sections, we will look at different storage and networking issues you might encounter and show you how to locate information that should help troubleshoot any issues with the hardware vendors.

Storage Issues

There are several storage technologies available to vSphere, including SAN (Fibre Channel and iSCSI), vSAN, and virtual volumes (VVols). All of these except for Fibre Channel leverage the TCP/IP networking stack and physical networking components, so make sure you are considering those areas when troubleshooting.

Common Storage Area Network Issues

Storage area networks (SANs) using Fibre Channel or iSCSI share many similar processes. I'll point out if steps are only for one technology or the other.

If you cannot see the LUNs you are expecting on a host, start by narrowing the problem down. Can you see any LUNs? If you can see some LUNs, do they have anything in common? You might need to work with the storage team to identify any similarities, such as all available LUNs are on one SAN or one storage processor (SP).

If you cannot see any LUNs at all on a host, you should be looking for a connectivity problem, either physical (bad, disconnected cable), digital (bad, wrong drivers) or logical (improper zoning for Fibre Channel devices, mapping, or security for iSCSI). Check the other hosts—do any of them see the LUNs? If so, what is different?

The zoning or mapping issues need to be addressed and worked on from the storage side. You can help by providing the IP address for the VMkernel port in use by iSCSI and the iSCSI name, as shown in Figure 8.16.

FIGURE 8.16   Locate the iSCSI name and VMkernel port.

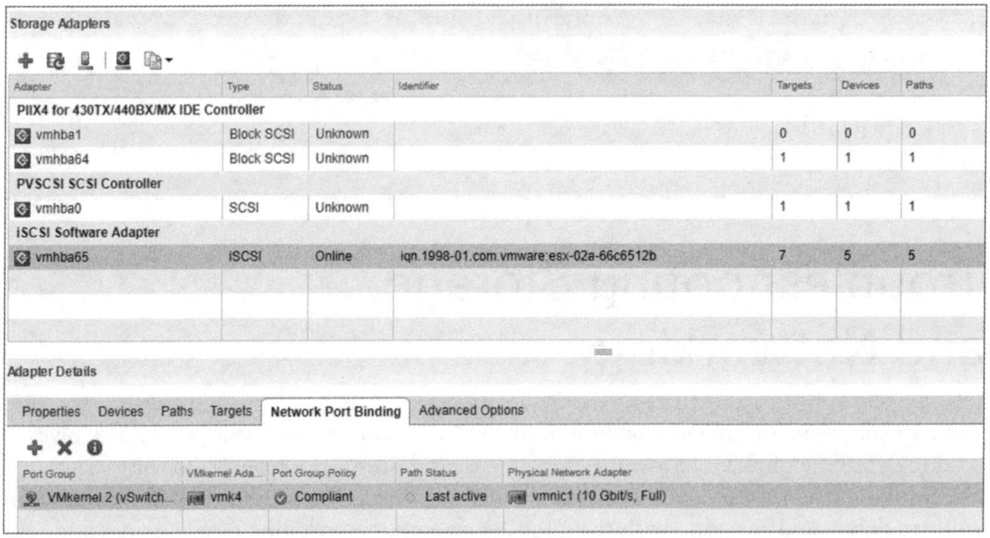

For Fibre Channel, provide the storage administrator with the worldwide node and worldwide port IDs used by the host so they can easily identify it from their end.

If you are using iSCSI with CHAP authentication, make sure no changes have been made to the password or CHAP requirements.

You can also check the MASK_PATH plug-in, as shown in Figure 8.17 using the `esxcli storage core claimrule list` command on the host to ensure that no LUNs have been masked at the host, preventing them from being used.

FIGURE 8.17   Listing claimrules to check for MASK_PATH usage

```
[root@esx-02a:~] esxcli storage core claimrule list
Rule Class   Rule   Class     Type        Plugin      Matches
----------   -----  -------   ---------   ---------   -------------------------------------
MP             50   runtime   transport   NMP         transport=usb
MP             51   runtime   transport   NMP         transport=sata
MP             52   runtime   transport   NMP         transport=ide
MP             53   runtime   transport   NMP         transport=block
MP             54   runtime   transport   NMP         transport=unknown
MP            101   runtime   vendor      MASK_PATH   vendor=DELL model=Universal Xport
MP            101   file      vendor      MASK_PATH   vendor=DELL model=Universal Xport
MP          65535   runtime   vendor      NMP         vendor=* model=*
[root@esx-02a:~]
```

Note that the MASK_PATHs shown in Figure 8.17 are created by default and likely exist in your environment.

Checking for VMFS Issues

If you experience problems with a VMFS datastore, including outages, files not being available, or error messages related to corruption, you can check the consistency of the datastore using the VOMA command-line tool. Note that if VOMA reports errors, you should contact support for assistance resolving them.

Before using VOMA, power off any VMs on the datastore.

VOMA requires the device name and partition for the datastore, so step one is identifying the device name using either the web client or the esxcli command as shown in Figure 8.18.

FIGURE 8.18   Identify the device name and partition for a datastore.

```
[root@esx-02a:~] esxcli storage vmfs extent list
Volume Name      VMFS UUID                            Extent Number  Device Name                            Partition
---------------  -----------------------------------  -------------  -------------------------------------  ---------
esx-02a-LOCAL    5ade5710-8216d59c-ecd8-000c29a418f1              0  mpx.vmhba0:C0:T0:L0                            3
RegionA01-iSCSI02  5b234fbe-49c4d954-a62a-000c296bdd1d             0  naa.60003ffb41eaf696a0264ba3be757195           1
RegionA01-iSCSI01  5b29944c-97913f44-cdb3-000c29422b9b             0  naa.60003ffb41eaf696a87b45d57858ec4            1
iSCSI-Datastore   5b737f0a-20597b2a-caa2-000c29a1cff7             0  naa.6001405fbda1f33d7efbd40bedb081d1           1
iSCSI-Datastore2  5bc7a75c-6ba5fe74-c91f-000c29422b9b             0  naa.60014059c5368ebd7c2bd4d42d90b2d6           1
iSCSI-Datastore3  5bc7a85f-c77f99d4-6845-000c29422b9b             0  naa.6001405dd73ea77d77a9d42bdd97e4dc           1
[root@esx-02a:~]
```

Once you have that, you can run VOMA using the parameters -m vmfs -f check and -d with the device and partition, as shown in Figure 8.19.

FIGURE 8.19   Identify the device name and partition for a datastore.

```
[root@esx-02a:~]  voma -m vmfs -f check -d /vmfs/devices/disks/naa.60003ffb41eaf696a0264ba3be757195:1
Checking if device is actively used by other hosts
Scanning for VMFS-3/VMFS-5 host activity (512 bytes/HB, 2048 HBs).
Running VMFS Checker version 2.1 in check mode
Initializing LVM metadata, Basic Checks will be done
Phase 1: Checking VMFS header and resource files
   Detected VMFS file system (labeled:'RegionA01-iSCSI02') with UUID:5b234fbe-49c4d954-a62a-000c296bdd1d, Version 5:81
Phase 2: Checking VMFS heartbeat region
Phase 3: Checking all file descriptors.
Phase 4: Checking pathname and connectivity.
Phase 5: Checking resource reference counts.

Total Errors Found:       0
[root@esx-02a:~]
```

The -m parameter can be used to check VMFS (version 3, 5, and 6), or you can include the lvm parameter to have it check the logical volume backing the VMFS datastore.

After any changes, be sure to rescan your HBAs (see Chapter 4, "Storage in vSphere," for more information).

Storage Performance

Storage performance issues can come from several areas—including the physical network if Fibre Channel is not in use. Common problem areas are SCSI reservations, path thrashing, and LUN queue depth.

SCSI Reservations

ESXi hosts can use SCSI reservations for file or metadata locks in VMFS. As SCSI reservations lock the LUN, an overabundance of them can cause performance issues. Changing the VMFS datastore, creating VMs or templates, powering on or migrating VMs, or using thin-provisioned disks (including snapshots) can all cause a host to issue a SCSI reservation.

One way to identify SCSI reservation issues is to examine the /var/log/vmkernel.log file on your host and look for "RESERVATION CONFLICT" messages.

To combat this, you can reduce the use of snapshots and the number of VMs per datastore. You can also work with your processes to limit how many datastore-impacting operations run at one time. You should also ensure that your firmware, BIOS, and drivers are up-to-date.

Path Thrashing

Path thrashing occurs when a LUN is being serviced by multiple storage processors and the storage processors are "fighting" over the LUN. Usually this occurs on active-passive LUNs when either the SAN or the hosts are misconfigured. Ensure that all hosts are configured to access the SAN and LUN in the same way and that all LUNs are set to use the Most Recently Used (MRU) path selection policy.

LUN Queue Depth

The LUN queue depth issue arises when a ESXi host queues storage requests due to the limits of the LUN queue depth setting. Note that while the SCSI drivers should have a configurable LUN queue depth setting, you should only make changes in conjunction with the vendor's support team.

You can adjust the queue depth using the esxcli command (note that this must be run on each host affected) as follows:

```
esxcli system module parameters set -p parameter=value -m module
```

For this command, module is the name of the SCSI driver.

Another way to examine SAN performance issues is to use the esxtop command. Once it's started, use the u command to switch to device view, shown in Figure 8.20. Note that here I have used the f command to remove many of the default columns to improve readability.

FIGURE 8.20   Identify the device name and partition for a datastore.

```
4:32:14am up 1 day 14:04, 495 worlds, 0 VMs, 0 vCPUs; CPU load average: 0.01, 0.01, 0.01

DEVICE                                  DAVG/cmd KAVG/cmd GAVG/cmd QAVG/cmd
mpx.vmhba0:C0:T0:L0                        0.00     0.00     0.00     0.00
mpx.vmhba64:C0:T0:L0                       0.00     0.00     0.00     0.00
naa.60003ffb41eaf696a0264ba3be757195       0.00     0.00     0.00     0.00
naa.60003ffb41eaf696ab87b45d57858ec4       0.00     0.00     0.00     0.00
naa.60014059c5368ebd7c2bd4d42d90b2d6       0.82     0.00     0.82     0.00
naa.6001405dd73ea77d77a9d42bdd97e4dc       0.72     0.02     0.74     0.01
naa.6001405fbda1f33d7efbd40bedb081d1       0.00     0.00     0.00     0.00
```

Here you can see the values for DAVG (device), KAVG (kernel), GAVG (guest), and QAVG (queue), which are the average (AVG) response times at different points in the SCSI request cycle.

- DAVG is the time for a command to leave the host and return from the array. This should be the longest value listed. This value can be tracked over time or compared to similar hosts. Generally speaking, this value should be less than 10 ms for top performance, but this could vary depending on your storage, current usage, and system design.

- KAVG is the time it takes the VMkernel to process a request, and QAVG is the time a request spends in the HBA driver. These should always be very short (<1 ms).

- GAVG is the sum of the other three times and is the time the request is waiting for storage requests to process.

Storage DRS and I/O Control

Storage DRS and Storage I/O control are useful tools, but there are some caveats and areas to examine if problems arise when using them.

For Storage DRS, be aware it can't be enabled for templates, ISO files, virtual machine swap files, independent disks, or virtual machines that have operations such as Storage vMotion currently affecting them. Storage DRS also cannot be used with Fault-Tolerant enabled virtual machines.

If you are trying to perform maintenance on a datastore but the datastore doesn't complete entering maintenance mode, ensure that any disks remaining on the datastore have Storage DRS enabled and are configured such that they can be moved.

If you cannot enable Storage DRS on a datastore, make sure the datastore isn't shared between datacenters and that all connected hosts are compatible and do not have Storage I/O control running.

For Storage I/O control issues, make sure all hosts connected to the datastore are compatible, support Storage I/O control, and have the appropriate license. If you see an "Unmanaged workload is detected on the datastore" message, you should check with the storage admin as Storage I/O is detecting activity on the datastore it cannot account for.

For more information on Storage DRS and Storage I/O control, see Chapter 4.

Network Issues

The network is a key component for a vSphere infrastructure since without it you can't manage a host or access network-driven storage (NFS, vSAN, iSCSI) and virtual machines can't communicate. Network issues usually revolve around vSphere configuration, hardware configuration, and hardware problems.

While hardware problems are outside the scope of this book, you can identify disconnected physical network interface cards (pNIC) using the web client, as shown in Figure 8.21. Also in Figure 8.21, you can see the observed network range(s) per adapter.

FIGURE 8.21   Examining physical network adapters in the web client

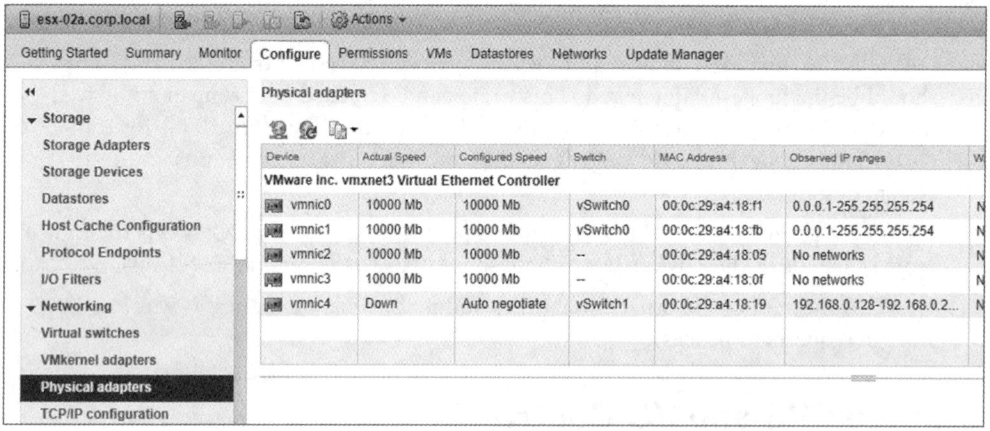

The observed traffic field is useful to determine what VLANs are configured for each pNIC, although it requires listening for broadcast packets. Networks with no or little traffic, or specialized traffic such as storage networks, might not have broadcast packets and might not appear in the list.

Another useful tool for troubleshooting network issues is enabling CDP or LLDP on distributed switches. This will report information from the physical switches (if configured), including port ID and switch name, and is key to ensuring that your configuration matches the physical configuration. See Chapter 3, "Networking in vSphere," for more information.

Finally, standard and distributed switches can be configured for network failure detection or beacon probing, as shown in Figure 8.22.

Network failure detection (the default setting) will stop vSphere from using a network adapter that is not connected to a network, while beacon probing will send packets down each path to determine if an adapter can reach the proper network. This prevents traffic from being sent down a network adapter that is plugged into the wrong port on a switch. Note that beacon probing requires at least three NICs to function properly. With only two NICs, if either had a problem, neither would be used since the host would not know which of the NICs had a problem.

FIGURE 8.22   Network failure detection

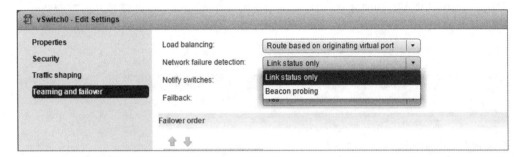

Verifying that your network connection is correct is a key step in troubleshooting issues. This is compounded if you are using standard switches since the configuration needs to be set on each host.

One useful tool for this is the network view in the web client, where you can quickly see the port groups on standard switches along with the number of hosts using each port group (listed under the Networks tab in the GUI) as shown in Figure 8.23.

FIGURE 8.23   Listing the standard switch port groups

Name	Type	Network Protocol Profile	VMs	Hosts
vCenter HA	Standard network		1	2
Management	Standard network		7	2
Bridged	Standard network		4	2
VM Network	Standard network		0	1
VM Networkk	Standard network		0	1

You can also select each network and view the virtual machines (or templates) connected to it (Figure 8.24).

To confirm the proper configuration, you need to access the settings of each network—and for standard switches you need to do this on each host. While it is possible to have different configurations on each host (VLANs used, failover), it is far easier to manage an environment where everything is configured the same way. If your environment requires differences (such as different VLAN tags for the same network on different hosts), make sure you have that documented. There is no place in the vSphere settings to make notes on configuration differences.

FIGURE 8.24   Listing the virtual machines on a network

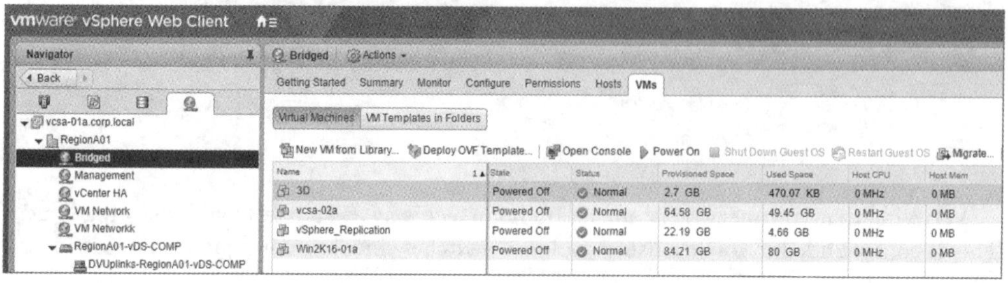

VLANs are a common area of concern, since an improper tag will prevent the traffic from being placed on the correct network—but your "connectivity" indicators such as green lights on the physical ports will look fine. A quick troubleshooting step is to place virtual machines on the same network/port group on the same host. If VMs can talk on the same host but can't talk when on different hosts, then you have a physical network issue, which could certainly be a VLAN tag mismatch.

Along with VLANs, the more specialized PVLANs can cause problems when not configured properly. Two VMs on the same network that are on an isolated PVLAN won't be able to talk, nor can they talk if they are on different community PVLANs. With PVLANs you also have another layer to configure on the physical switches, setting the PVLAN type properly for each network.

Again, moving VMs that should be able to talk together onto the same host will quickly isolate whether the issue is a physical network one.

Finally, network latency or performance issues can be caused by misconfigurations such as these:

- Manually setting the incorrect speed on a pNIC
- Configuring traffic shaping
- Configuring traffic filtering
- Manually setting failover order
- Disabling failback
- MTU mismatch on port groups, virtual or physical switches

You should also verify that your system BIOS, network card firmware, and drivers are up-to-date.

If no traffic is passing at all, make sure you check the VM's network connectivity and port blocking at the VM and port group levels.

Troubleshooting Upgrades

When updating your vSphere environment, the key first step is to do the upgrades in order, from the "top" down. VMware KB article 2147289 has all the VMware products in a table, in order, but in general terms you want to go as follows:

1. Automation
2. Operations
3. Network
4. PSC
5. vCenter
6. ESXi
7. vSAN and VDS (if needed)

Upgrading your host before your vCenter server is a common mistake. Also, make sure you have backed up anything you are upgrading, just in case.

After ensuring that you are backed up and upgrading in the correct order, there are some areas in which you might run into trouble. For instance, vCenter occasionally has issues stopping the Tomcat web service during an upgrade. If you see an error message about Tomcat, try stopping the service manually or rebooting the host.

As mentioned earlier, in the section " vCenter Connectivity and Services" regarding replacing SSL certificates, if your hosts can't connect to vCenter after an upgrade, try disconnect/connect.

For other upgrade issues you can check the log files at `C:\ProgramData\VMware\vCenterServer\logs` and in the `%TEMP%` directory—specifically the `vc-install.txt`, `vminst.log`, `pkgmgr.log`, `pkgmgr-comp-msi.log`, and `vim-vcs-msi.log` files.

If you are using Update Manager to apply updates, there is a log file (`vmware-vum-server-log4cpp.log`) that will include errors returned by the precheck script that runs before updates are performed.

Troubleshooting Virtual Machines

Virtual machines running on ESXi hosts need some occasional care and feeding, with both proactive and reactive processes. One good tool for both proactive and reactive monitoring of virtual machines is the performance view from the host (Figure 8.25).

Note that performance charts are available from the cluster, host resource pool, and individual virtual machine level. The host view is the most practical as it shows the virtual machines whose performance is directly impacting each other, but all of the views have their uses. Note that the CPU and memory used is from the point of view of the host and won't necessarily match from the guest point of view.

FIGURE 8.25 Listing the virtual machines on a network

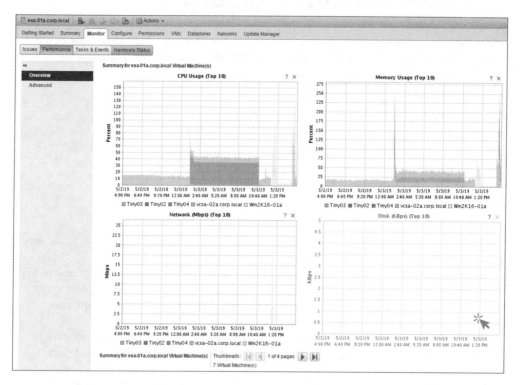

Contention managing tools such as shares, limits, reservations, and memory swapping can make the guest results considerably different.

One of the more useful counters is the CPU Ready value, available in the Advanced CPU charts (Figure 8.26).

Figure 8.27 shows the same host using the esxtop tool. Note the %RDY, which is the CPU ready as a percentage for each virtual machine.

This ms value from Figure 8.26 shows the time guest CPUs were waiting to run. This is often expressed as a percentage, which is the percent of time spent waiting over the sample period. A consistently high CPU Ready time (over 5%) implies the host is being overloaded and virtual machines should be moved off it.

You can use the performance charts (and esxtop) to view the memory usage also for the cluster, host resource pool, and individual virtual machine level. Remember that ballooning is taking memory back from virtual machines; this is an indication that you have overallocated RAM but isn't necessarily a problem. See Figure 8.28 for an example of a host using ballooning.

Swap, on the other hand, is always a problem as that indicates overallocated RAM. Virtual machines are actively contending for physical memory and the host is writing some guest RAM pages to a storage file. This usually results in significant performance penalties to the VM that is experiencing the swapped memory.

FIGURE 8.26 Showing CPU Ready on a host

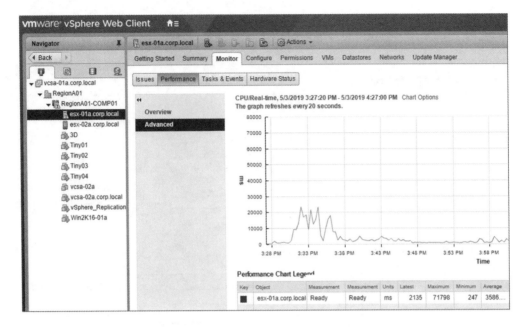

FIGURE 8.27 Showing CPU Ready using esxtop

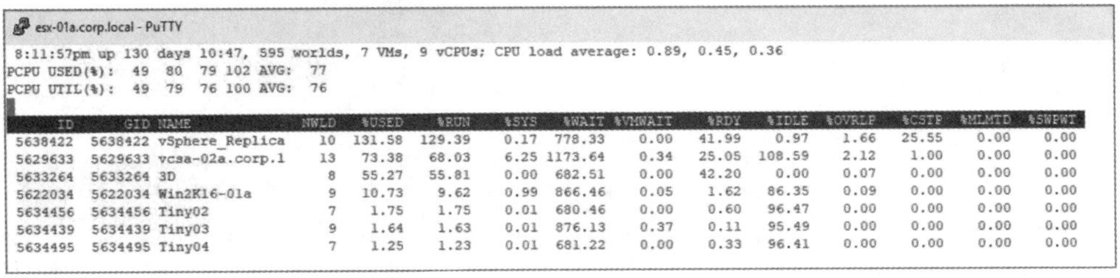

The performance charts are available as Overview with set values selected and Advanced charts where you can pick the values to display, as shown in Figure 8.29. Advanced charts can also be saved as image files or CSV files.

FIGURE 8.28   A host experiencing ballooning due to guest RAM overcommitment

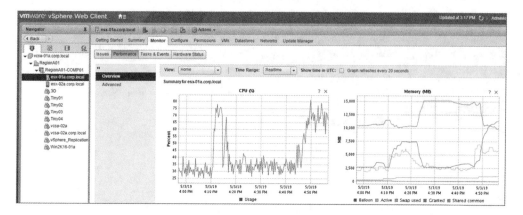

FIGURE 8.29   Advanced chart options

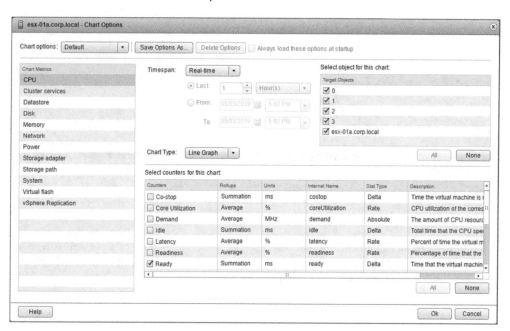

Troubleshooting HA and DRS

Issues encountered when using the High Availability and Dynamic Resource Scheduling features of vSphere can take a variety of forms. For starters, make sure you have the correct license version to enable the features. While vCenter Standard includes HA, you need Enterprise Plus to enable DRS and proactive HA. And only HA is included with the Essentials Plus level, but not even HA is included with Essentials.

Once the licensing is in place, you need to meet the prerequisites to enable HA or DRS (see Chapter 10, "Ensuring High Availability for vSphere Clusters and the VCSA," for more information). Once they are enabled, some of the situations you might run into include running out of resources, heartbeat datastore availability, and unprotected virtual machines.

One of the first places to go for issue troubleshooting is the Issues view of the Monitor tab, as shown in Figure 8.30 (note that most objects in vSphere have this view available).

FIGURE 8.30   Viewing current HA issues

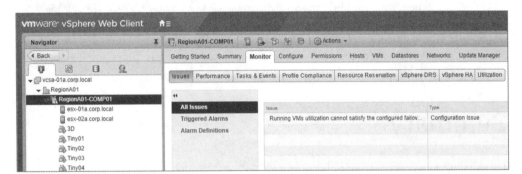

In this case, HA is reporting that it cannot satisfy the failover requirements. This would normally be the case if admission control was disabled, but it could happen if hosts are unavailable in the cluster, from being in a non-running state or in maintenance mode or from an HA agent problem or a connectivity problem.

Similarly, you could be prevented from powering on virtual machines in a cluster due to admissions control being set and either being set too high (large slots for small virtual machines or excessive resource percentage) or hosts not being available. If all the proper hosts are available, you can check the slot size using the summary section of the vSphere HA view for the cluster (Figure 8.31).

If you are not using a fixed slot size, powering on VMs with large reservations or enlarging the reservations on existing machines can set this high enough to block new VMs from powering on due to a reduced number of slots. For more information, see Chapter 10.

FIGURE 8.31   Viewing Admission control slot size

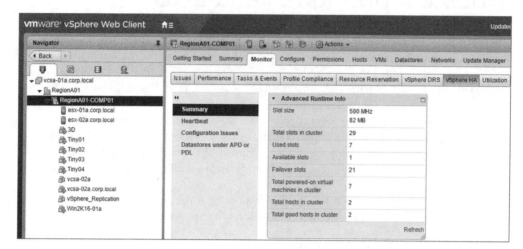

Heartbeat datastores could become an issue for your HA cluster if there are storage changes in your environment and you had manually selected datastores, or if there are no available shared datastores. Note that vSphere doesn't always use the datastores you manually select if you select more than two, if the ones you select are not shared, or if a datastore becomes unavailable.

Summary

This chapter has covered troubleshooting a vSphere environment. Key to troubleshooting is understanding how the product works and how your environment is configured. Past that, there are a few ways to pull log files and several tools that can be used to examine the current state of the environment.

Since understanding the functionality and settings of different components is crucial to troubleshooting, the other chapters in this book are important for referencing. Knowing that virtual machine reservations affect slot size, which affects admission control, which affects high availability and can prevent you from powering on new virtual machines, can be critical to troubleshooting a VM that won't power on.

Some of the best tools for troubleshooting are the same ones used for monitoring the day-to-day operations, such as the Performance tab. Using those tools periodically will keep you aware of the baseline performance of your environment and could give you a heads-up on potential problems. Other tools such as `esxtop` are usually only used during troubleshooting due to the depth of information they produce.

Finally, troubleshooting often involves vendors and other teams such as the networking and storage teams. Be sure you involve those other teams in your troubleshooting process and be prepared to discuss how vSphere interacts with those systems.

Exam Essentials

Know common network ports used by vSphere.   Especially 902 (ESXi connectivity), 8000 (vMotion), and 5480 (appliance management), but be familiar with the others listed also.

Be familiar with the most common vCenter services.   Know vpxd, Auto Deploy, Image-Builder, and Tomcat, where to start/stop them, and why.

Understand the different vCenter database settings.   Especially the ones controlling the size of the database (performance counters) and where to change the settings.

Know the difference between vimtop, esxtop, and resxtop.   The vimtop utility is available on the VCSA appliance and works with vCenter. esxtop is on each ESXi host and shows local stats, and resxtop is on the vMA management appliance or the vSphere CLI download and looks up performance stats on remote ESXi hosts.

Know how SSL certificates are replaced and the more common troubleshooting tasks around them.   Knowing the proper steps to replace them is key, but reconnecting hosts is a common resolution for certificate issues.

Know the most common log files and how to access them.   Especially vpxd and vmkernel. Make sure you have viewed files in the GUI and exported from vCenter and ESXi hosts.

Know the ESXi agents vpxa and vmware-fdm.   The vpxa agent communicates with vCenter and vmware-fdm managed HA (if HA is configured).

Know the basics of storage and network troubleshooting.   Much of storage revolves around networking, so be able to pinpoint a network issue vs. storage and then drill down on the network. Be familiar with CDP and LLDP and identifying network and storage configuration issues.

Know CPU Ready and how to pull performance reports.   Understand the uses of the performance charts vs. esxtop and what a high CPU ready state looks like.

Review Questions

The answers to the chapter review questions can be found in Appendix.

1. What tools can be used to create CSV files of virtual machine performance data? (Choose two.)

    A. `esxtop`

    B. vimtop

    C. Performance view of a cluster

    D. Performance view of a virtual distributed switch

2. What log file is considered the main vCenter log file?

    A. Vmcad

    B. EAM

    C. vpxd

    D. vimtop

3. Where can you download ESXi host logs? (Choose two.)

    A. VCSA command line

    B. vSphere Update Manager

    C. vSphere web client

    D. ESXi web client

4. Where are the install logs for the VCSA appliance located?

    A. `/var/logs` on the VCSA appliance

    B. `/var logs` on Update Manager

    C. `AppData\local` directory for the installing user

    D. `VMware\vCenterServer\logs`

5. When upgrading from vCenter 6.0 to vCenter 6.5, what should be your first step?

    A. Ensure that Update Manager is on the latest version.

    B. Upgrade all the ESXi hosts

    C. Back up vCenter.

    D. Obtain a new license from VMware.

6. What is the correct upgrade order to ensure a smooth upgrade?

    A. vRA, PSC, vCenter, ESXi, vDS

    B. PSC, vCenter, vRA, ESXi, vDS

    C. vRA, vDA, PSC, vCenter, ESXi

    D. ESXi, PSC, vCenter, vRA, vDS

7. Which performance counter is approximately the storage response time a guest OS will experience?

    A. DAVG

    B. KAVG

    C. QAVG

    D. GAVG

8. Which performance counter is the storage response time of the SAN?

    A. DAVG

    B. KAVG

    C. QAVG

    D. GAVG

9. What vSphere objects can the performance charts report on? (Choose two.)

    A. Virtual machines

    B. Virtual distributed switches

    C. ESXi hosts

    D. VVols

10. Which performance counter is approximately the time the host takes to process a storage request?

    A. DAVG

    B. KAVG

    C. QAVG

    D. GAVG

11. What command will capture 100 sets of data in 5-second intervals?

    A. `esxtop -b -n 5 -d 100 > capture.csv`

    B. `esxtop -b -n 100 -d 500 > capture.csv`

    C. `esxtop -b -d 5 > capture.csv`

    D. `esxtop -b -n 100 > capture.csv`

12. See the accompanying image. What three options are most likely to resolve the issue reported? (Choose three.)

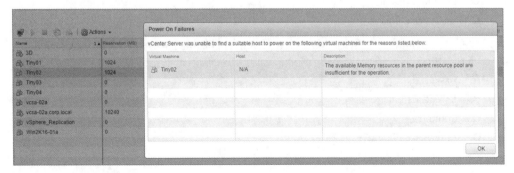

    A. Remove the reservation on vcsa-02a.corp.local.

    B. Remove the reservation on Tiny03.

    C. Disable admission control.

    D. Remove the reservation on Tiny02.

    E. Disable Dynamic Resource Scheduling.

13. Which two technologies can report on physical switch settings? (Choose two.)

    A. CDP

    B. PVLAN

    C. VDS

    D. LLDP

14. Which counter can indicate CPU contention?

    A. Ready

    B. Active

    C. Swap

    D. Balloon

15. Which counter can indicate significant guest impact due to memory contention?

    A. Ready

    B. Active

    C. Swap

    D. Balloon

16. Which counter indicates memory is being reclaimed?

    A. Ready

    B. Active

    C. Swap

    D. Balloon

17. What is the minimum licensing level required to enable High Availability?

    A. Essentials

    B. Essentials Plus

    C. Standard

    D. Enterprise Plus

18. What is the minimum licensing level required to enable the Distributed Resource Scheduler feature?

    A. Essentials

    B. Essentials Plus

    C. Standard

    D. Enterprise Plus

19. Which storage technologies are not affected by Ethernet network outages? (Choose two.)

   A. VSAN

   B. Fibre Channel

   C. SCSI

   D. NFS

20. Where can `resxtop` be run from by default?

   A. VCSA appliance

   B. vMA appliance

   C. PowerCLI

   D. ESXi hosts

Chapter

9

Deploying and Customizing ESXi Hosts

2V0-21.19 EXAM OBJECTIVES COVERED IN THIS CHAPTER:

✓ **Section 1 – VMware vSphere Architectures and Technologies**

- Objective 1.1 – Identify the pre-requisites and components for vSphere implementation

✓ **Section 4 – Installing, Configuring, and Setting Up a VMware vSphere Solution**

- Objective 4.4 – Set up ESXi hosts

✓ **Section 7 – Administrative and Operational Tasks in a VMware vSphere Solution**

- Objective 7.8 – Manage resources of a vSphere environment
- Objective 7.16 - Configure and manage host profiles

This chapter addresses deploying ESXi hosts using the Auto Deploy mechanism as well as utilizing Host Profiles to manage host configuration settings. The ability to simplify the deployment and configuration of hosts reduces the time to provision new hosts and apply changes. With a mechanism to compare host configurations, configuration drift can be managed, and the host settings can remain consistent between hosts, clusters, and datacenters.

A rapid and automatic method of standing up hosts with little or no manual intervention can improve the flexibility of an environment and eliminate the requirement to be physically at a server to deploy it—no more USB drive or inserted CDs. Hosts can also quickly be updated or reverted to previous versions as quickly as they can be rebooted.

Configuring Auto Deploy

With Auto Deploy configured, new hosts can be configured automatically as they boot, reducing the time to deploy and eliminating manual steps. Custom boot images and updates can be applied by simply rebooting the hosts, and troubleshooting some host problems can be skipped when rebooting the host rebuilds it from a known good image.

However, there are several steps required to properly configure Auto Deploy, and third-party resources (specifically a DHCP server and TFTP server) are required. We'll walk through the steps over the following pages.

Auto Deploy Steps

1. The new host server powers on and its PXE-enabled network card makes a DHCP request.

2. DHCP server responds with IP configuration and two options: a file server IP address and PXE boot loader filename.

3. The host server's PXE card sets the IP configuration received and queries the file server for the PXE boot loader file.

4. The file server sends the PXE boot loader file to the host server.

5. The PXE card uses the PXE boot loader file to start booting the host and queries the Auto Deploy server for an image file (a PXE boot file).

6. The Auto Deploy server uses the properties of the host to determine which image is appropriate and sends the host image file to the host server along with host profile settings.

7. The PXE process on the host server chainloads the ESXi boot process using the supplied image file and configuration settings.

The components needed for Auto Deploy include a host with a PXE-capable network card, a DHCP server, a TFTP server, and a vCenter server. Optionally, you can install PowerCLI if you would like to manage Auto Deploy rules and images using cmdlets. The ability to manage all settings from the GUI is new to vSphere 6.5, but if you used PowerCLI scripts in the past. they will still work with 6.5.

Enabling PXE Boot

The first step is to configure your host to boot from the network card. You may need to refer to your host server or network card documentation to enable PXE booting; however, many systems with PXE-enabled network cards will attempt to boot using PXE, either initially or if no other boot source is found. To speed up boot times, you may want to ensure that the PXE card is the first boot option in the host BIOS (Figure 9.1).

FIGURE 9.1   BIOS boot order

If your network requires VLAN tagging on the ESXi host management subnet, you will need to ensure that your host's network card supports tagging and is configured to supply the proper VLAN ID. If you can configure your network to use the native (or default) VLAN for the management network, you can avoid manually configuring each host.

Configuring DHCP

Once your host is set to boot from the network, a DHCP server is needed to supply the proper IP settings (address, subnet mask, default gateway) and the PXE boot parameters. If your DHCP server is not on the same network as your ESXi management NIC, you will need a DHCP helper server configured to forward the request to the DHCP server.

The DHCP server needs to be configured to supply the IP address of the TFTP server along with the filename of the PXE boot loader. While many DHCP servers use option 066 Boot Server Host Name and option 067 Bootfile Name to supply the values during a boot request, you may need to check your DHCP server's documentation on setting these values. VMware offers a Knowledge Base article (KB 2005071) that covers Windows, Infoblox, and Cisco DHCP server configuration.

A Windows 2008 R2 server uses options 66 and 67 (Figure 9.2). These should be configured as options for the management network (as opposed to DHCP server options) to prevent PXE boots from other networks from being directed to the Auto Deploy server. The boot file name will be undionly.kpxe.vmw-hardwired for normal Auto Deploy–linked boot but the TFTP server or boot server value will change for your environment.

FIGURE 9.2   Windows DHCP server with Auto Deploy options

Option Name	Vendor	Value	Class
003 Router	Standard	192.168.0.1	None
066 Boot Server Host Name	Standard	192.168.0.4	None
067 Bootfile Name	Standard	undionly.kpxe.vmw-hardwired	None
006 DNS Servers	Standard	192.168.0.47	None
015 DNS Domain Name	Standard	corp.local	None

There are scenarios where the boot file name can change, including in order for one TFTP server to support multiple Auto Deploy servers. You can find a blog post detailing one such scenario at

blogs.vmware.com/vsphere/2013/06/configuring-pxe-to-support-multiple-auto-deploy-servers.html.

Configuring TFTP

A TFTP server accessible from the management network is needed to supply the boot loader file during the iPXE boot process. We are using SolarWinds's free TFTP server for our lab, but you may want something more robust. Once the TFTP service is installed and running, make sure to create firewall rules on the TFTP server permitting access. You can use a TFTP client (there is one built into Windows) to test access to the TFTP server to verify connectivity.

After you configure Auto Deploy on your vCenter server, you will need to download the TFTP files and place them into the TFTP root directory (Figure 9.3).

FIGURE 9.3   TFTP root directory with Auto Deploy boot files

Name	Date modified	Type	Size
C:\TFTP-Root			
snponly64.efi	9/6/2018 10:37 PM	EFI File	261 KB
snponly64.efi.officialkey	9/6/2018 10:37 PM	OFFICIALKEY File	266 KB
snponly64.efi.testkey	9/6/2018 10:37 PM	TESTKEY File	263 KB
snponly64.efi.vmw-hardwired	9/6/2018 10:37 PM	VMW-HARDWIRE...	261 KB
snponly64.efi.vmw-hardwired.officialkey	9/6/2018 10:37 PM	OFFICIALKEY File	266 KB
snponly64.efi.vmw-hardwired.testkey	9/6/2018 10:37 PM	TESTKEY File	263 KB
tramp	9/6/2018 10:37 PM	File	1 KB
undionly.0	9/6/2018 10:37 PM	0 File	122 KB
undionly.kpxe	9/6/2018 10:37 PM	KPXE File	122 KB
undionly.kpxe.debug	9/6/2018 10:37 PM	DEBUG File	92 KB
undionly.kpxe.debugmore	9/6/2018 10:37 PM	DEBUGMORE File	96 KB
undionly.kpxe.nomcast	9/6/2018 10:37 PM	NOMCAST File	122 KB
undionly.kpxe.vmw-hardwired	9/6/2018 10:37 PM	VMW-HARDWIRE...	122 KB
undionly.kpxe.vmw-hardwired-nomcast	9/6/2018 10:37 PM	VMW-HARDWIRE...	122 KB

These files include the `undionly.kpxe.vmw-hardwired` boot loader and the `tramp` file, which includes the information needed for the iPXE boot process to find the Auto Deploy service. If your vCenter server IP address changes, you can edit the `tramp` file to direct hosts to the new IP.

Enabling Auto Deploy

One of the new changes with vSphere 6.5 is that Auto Deploy is bundled with vSphere and cannot be separated. After you install the Windows-based vCenter or deploy the VCSA, you can enable Auto Deploy by starting the services and configuring them to start with vCenter.

1. Go to the System Configuration section of the Administration menu in the web client (Figure 9.4).

2. Select your vCenter server, and under the Services section, open the Related Objects tab.

3. Start Auto Deploy and the ImageBuilder Service, and set them to start with vCenter by editing the startup type (Figure 9.5).

4. Once the two services are started, the Auto Deploy option will be available in the Operations and Policies menu (Figure 9.6). Log out and back into the web client if the icon is not available.

FIGURE 9.4 System Configuration

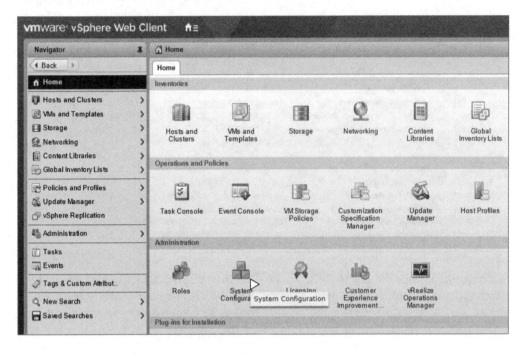

FIGURE 9.5 Edit the startup type.

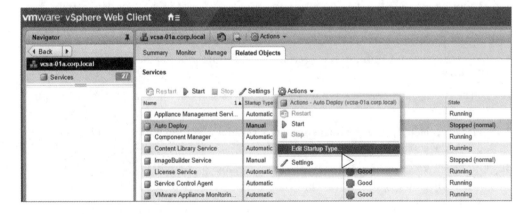

FIGURE 9.6 Auto Deploy in the Operations and Policies section

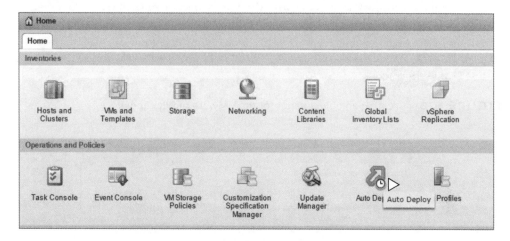

5. There are three tasks to accomplish after Auto Deploy is started:

   a. Add a software depot to pull images from.

   b. Create Auto Deploy rules to associate images with hosts.

   c. Copy the TFTP files to the TFTP server.

6. Use the Configure menu of the vCenter object to locate the TFTP boot file zip link (Figure 9.7). Extract the files from the zip archive to the TFTP root directory.

FIGURE 9.7 Download the TFTP boot files from vCenter.

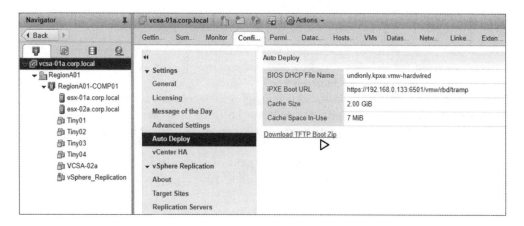

7. The Auto Deploy server needs a repository of images to associate with hosts. You can use a public repository such as the official VMware one, or you can create your own repository to hold custom images and software packages.

    To use the VMware public repository, create an Online depot referencing `hostupdate.vmware.com/software/VUM/PRODUCTION/main/vmw-depot-index .xml` (Figure 9.8).

FIGURE 9.8   Creating an online depot for the VMware public repository

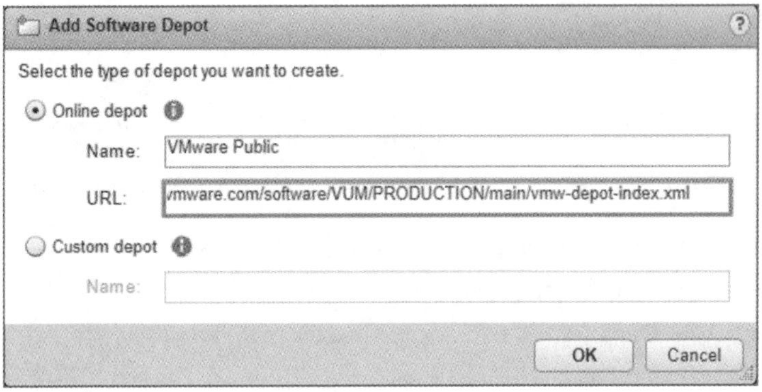

Once you have a depot available with images, you can create Auto Deploy rules to assign images to hosts, which we'll cover next.

Adding Deploy Rules

You can use the New Deploy Rule wizard from the Deploy Rules tab to create a new rule to associate images with hosts. Rules are required to automatically assign images; however, you can link a host to an image manually.

A host will continue to use an associated image until it encounters a new rule that assigns a different image. If you delete a rule, any host that used that rule for deployment will still use the assigned image until a new rule is created or the host is removed from inventory.

When you create a new rule, you must specify that it applies to all hosts or add a pattern for the host to meet. To see the properties supplied by your hosts, look at the error screen when one boots when there is no rule.

```
Machine attributes:
. asset=No Asset Tag
. domain=corp.local
. hostname=
```

. .ipv4=192.168.0.143
. mac=00:0c:29:e1:3e:cf
. model=VMware Virtual Platform
. oemstring=[MS_VM_CERT/SHA1/27d66596a61c48dd]
. oemstring=Welcome to the Virtual Machine
. serial=VMware-56 4d 22 ff 6d 41 82 19-9a 0f
. uuid=ff224d56-416d-1982-9a0f
. vendor-VMware, Inc.

Once the hosts are selected, you need to select the image to use, an (optional) host profile to assign, and the location in the datacenter the hosts should be assigned to.

After creating the rule, make sure you activate it using the Activate/Deactivate Rules wizard (Figure 9.9).

FIGURE 9.9   Activate the deploy rule.

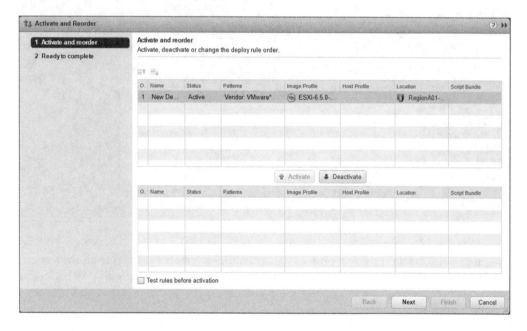

The Discovered Hosts tab (as shown in Figure 9.10) will display hosts that have contacted the Auto Deploy server and not been assigned an image. You can select a host from the list and use the Add to Inventory wizard to manually assign an image, host profile, and location.

Adding a Custom Image and Profile

Your server vendor may offer custom images for your server hardware that could include specific drivers, vendor-supplied VIBs, or patches specific to the server. They often are smaller than VMware-supplied images as they do not need to include drivers for other vendors or hardware.

You can import the ZIP file containing the image as a separate repository (Figure 9.10 and Figure 9.11).

FIGURE 9.10   Importing a custom image ZIP file

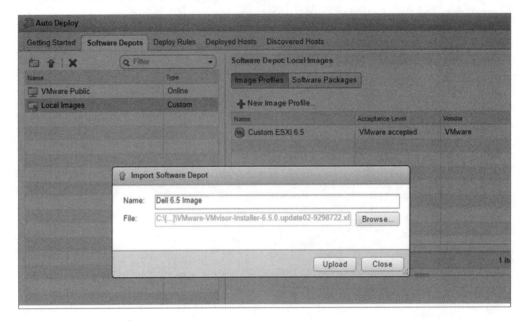

You can also create your own profiles to use, pulling software packages from the any of the depots, including the public VMware depot and uploaded vendor-specific ZIP packages. See Figure 9.12 for a sample image profile created using packages from public and vendor-specific depots.

Stateless Caching and Stateful Installs

There are two other methods of using Auto Deploy beyond reading an image from the Auto Deploy server at boot: Stateless Caching and Stateful Install. Either of these options requires changes to the boot order of the host and a host profile with the proper settings.

FIGURE 9.11   Listing available image profiles

FIGURE 9.12   Custom image profile

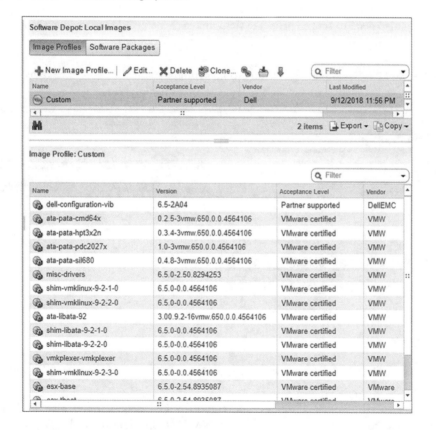

Stateless Caching enables the host to cache the software image obtained from Auto Deploy on a local or remote disk or a USB drive. This has the primary advantage of allowing the host to boot even if the Auto Deploy server is not available during startup.

Note that if the vCenter server is available but the Auto Deploy service is not available when a Stateless Cache host boots, it will not join the vCenter server automatically, but the hosts can be manually joined. If the vCenter server is unavailable, you will need to use the host client to manage the hosts.

Stateful Install will install the Auto Deploy–sourced image to a local, remote, or USB drive on the host. The host will not contact Auto Deploy again after the install.

Make sure you set the boot order of the host properly:

- Stateless Cache: Attempt to boot from network, then boot from disk.
- Stateful Install: Attempt to boot from disk, then boot from network.

For Stateless Cache, it will always attempt to contact the Auto Deploy server and if that fails will boot from the cached image. For Stateful Install, once the image is installed it will boot from there and not contact Auto Deploy.

You will also need to set the proper system image cache profile settings on the Host Profile assigned to the hosts. See Figure 9.13 for the possible options.

FIGURE 9.13 System image cache profile settings

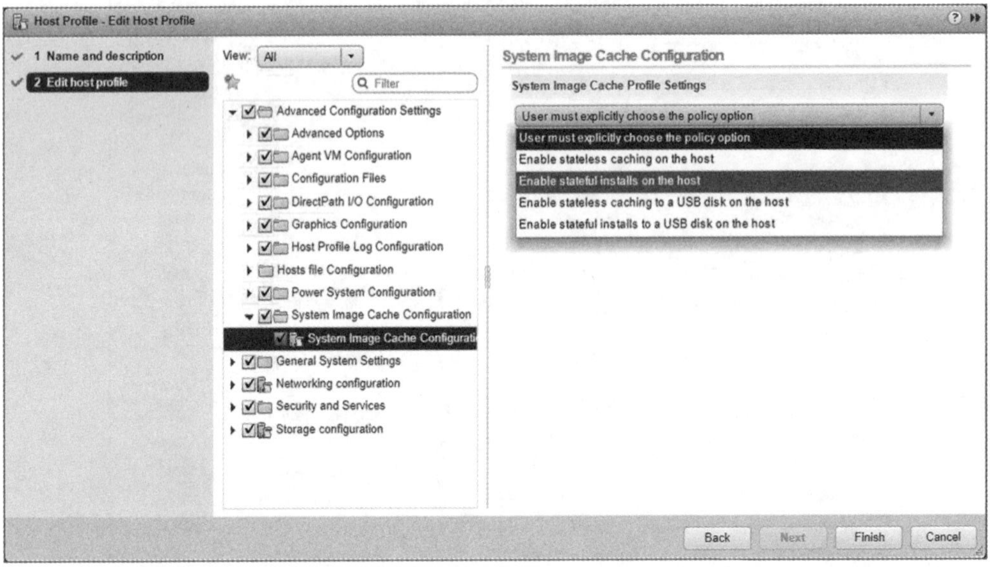

If you choose either of the options that do not use a USB disk, you will also need to specify the disk to use and choose to overwrite VMFS and/or ignore local SSD drives (Figure 9.14).

FIGURE 9.14   Configuring stateful installs

System Image Cache Configuration

System Image Cache Profile Settings

Enable stateful installs on the host	▼

*Arguments for first disk:	localesx,local
*Check to overwrite any VMFS volumes on the selected disk	☐ Enabled
*Check to ignore any SSD devices connected to the host	☐ Enabled

🌐 **Real World Scenario**

Troubleshooting Auto Deploy

Understanding the Auto Deploy sequence is key to troubleshooting the configuration.

1. Make sure the host received an IP address from DHCP.

   If you know your MAC address, you can also check your DHCP server for a valid lease for that address.

2. Make sure your host has requested the boot loader from the TFTP server by checking the log files of the server for the IP address or DNS name of the host.

   The process starts with the `undionly.kpxe.vmw-hardwired` file and ends with the `tramp` file.

3. Make sure the PXE process queries the Auto Deploy server by checking the boot screen of the host for an error message about not finding a rule set.

4. Make sure the Auto Deploy server has a rule that applies to the host and manually assign an image if no rule matches.

5. If a rule has been removed but a host still uses an image assigned by the removed rule, remove the host from inventory to reset the image assignment, or create a new rule that matches the host.

EXERCISE 9.1

Enable and configure Auto Deploy

Required: DHCP server configured to supply IP settings to the host management network, TFTP server available from the host management network, and a vCenter server.

1. Connect to the DHCP server and configure option 66 with the IP address of the TFTP server and option 67 with the filename `undionly.kpxe.vmw-hardwired`.

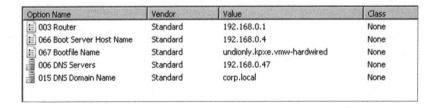

2.   Log into the web client and open System Configuration from the Home menu.

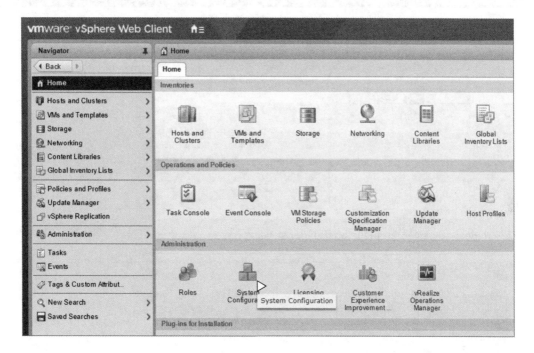

3.   Select the vCenter server from the Nodes section and open the Related Objects tab.

4.   Right-click Auto Deploy and choose Edit Startup Type.

5.   Choose Automatic for the startup type and click OK.

6. With Auto Deploy selected, click Start.

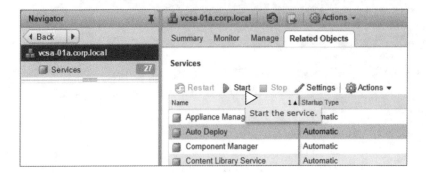

7. Repeat steps 4–6 for the ImageBuilder service.

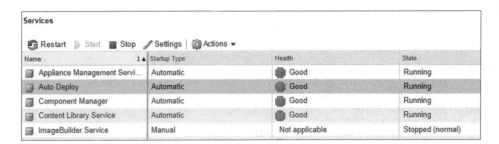

8. Open the Hosts and Clusters view from the vCenter menu.

9. Select Auto Deploy from the Configure tab for the vCenter object.

10. Click the Download TFTP Boot Zip link to download the bootloader archive.

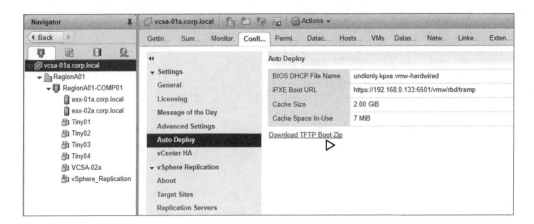

11. Extract the bootloader archive to the root directory of the TFTP server.

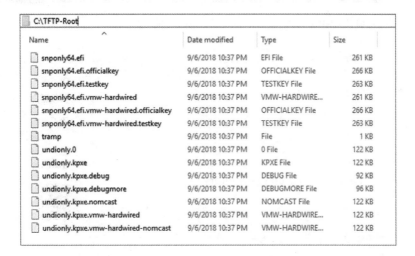

Name	Date modified	Type	Size
snponly64.efi	9/6/2018 10:37 PM	EFI File	261 KB
snponly64.efi.officialkey	9/6/2018 10:37 PM	OFFICIALKEY File	266 KB
snponly64.efi.testkey	9/6/2018 10:37 PM	TESTKEY File	263 KB
snponly64.efi.vmw-hardwired	9/6/2018 10:37 PM	VMW-HARDWIRE...	261 KB
snponly64.efi.vmw-hardwired.officialkey	9/6/2018 10:37 PM	OFFICIALKEY File	266 KB
snponly64.efi.vmw-hardwired.testkey	9/6/2018 10:37 PM	TESTKEY File	263 KB
tramp	9/6/2018 10:37 PM	File	1 KB
undionly.0	9/6/2018 10:37 PM	0 File	122 KB
undionly.kpxe	9/6/2018 10:37 PM	KPXE File	122 KB
undionly.kpxe.debug	9/6/2018 10:37 PM	DEBUG File	92 KB
undionly.kpxe.debugmore	9/6/2018 10:37 PM	DEBUGMORE File	96 KB
undionly.kpxe.nomcast	9/6/2018 10:37 PM	NOMCAST File	122 KB
undionly.kpxe.vmw-hardwired	9/6/2018 10:37 PM	VMW-HARDWIRE...	122 KB
undionly.kpxe.vmw-hardwired-nomcast	9/6/2018 10:37 PM	VMW-HARDWIRE...	122 KB

12. Boot the host and verify that it stops at the Machine Attributes error screen.

13. Open Auto Deploy from the Home menu.

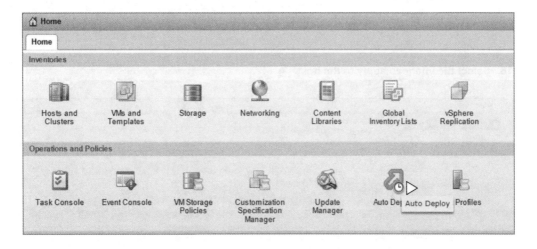

14. Find the host in the Discovered Hosts tab in Auto Deploy.

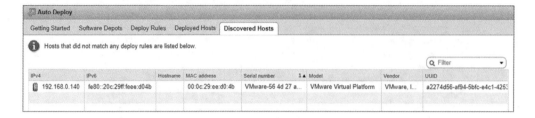

15. Select the host and choose Add to Inventory.

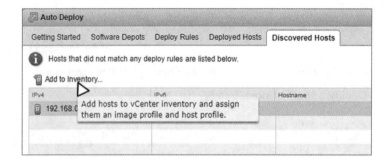

16. Select the image to apply to the host.

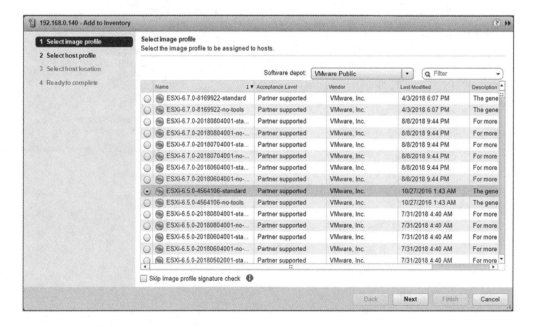

17. Select the host profile to apply to the host.

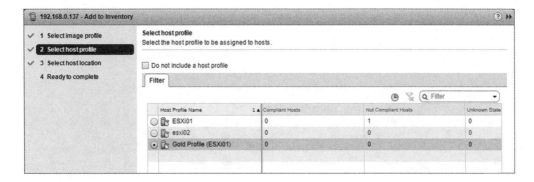

18. Select the inventory location for the host.

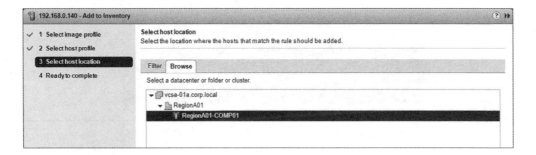

19. Verify the settings and finish adding the host to inventory.

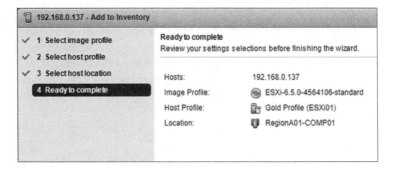

20. Verify that the host has booted and loaded the proper ESXi image and host profile.

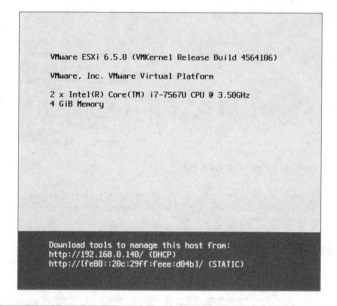

Employing Host Profiles

VMware vSphere Host Profiles offers a solution to manage and compare host settings. While host profiles are a key component of Auto Deploy, they have significant usage even if Auto Deploy is not used in the environment. Host profiles can be used to ensure that all of your hosts are configured identically across datacenters, to ensure that any new change is applied uniformly, to speed deployment of hosts, or to troubleshoot why hosts do not behave the same.

The standard host profiles workflow is as follows:

1. Build a "gold" host with all the appropriate settings.

2. Extract a host profile from the gold host.

3. Apply the profile to a new host.

4. Check for any differences between the new host and the profile.

5. Apply the changes from the profile to the new host.

However, not all steps have to be followed. Instead of applying the profile to hosts, you can export it to keep as a backup or use with a separate vCenter installation. You can also choose to only compare settings and not remediate.

Host profiles are managed using the Host Profiles menu option from the Operations and Policies section of the Home menu (Figure 9.15). You can also start Host Profiles management from Policies and Profiles, accessed from the Home drop-down menu.

FIGURE 9.15   Managing host profiles

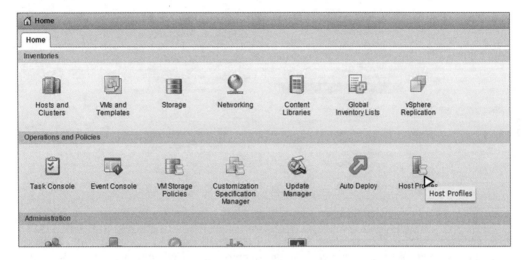

Creating and Using Host Profiles

To create a new host profile, you use the Extract Profile wizard (Figure 9.16).

FIGURE 9.16   Extracting a host profile

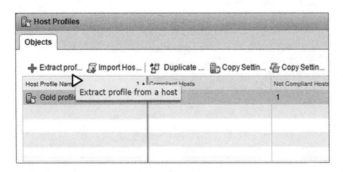

Once the profile is extracted you can review the settings captured and edit them by clicking the profile name (Figure 9.17).

FIGURE 9.17   Viewing host profile settings

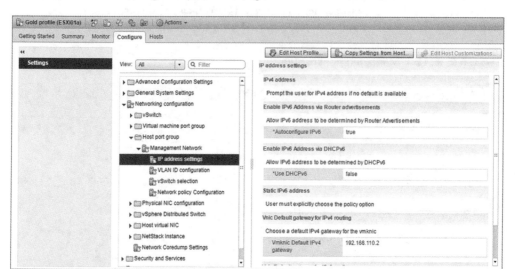

In addition to changing captured settings, you can also disable sections of the host profile (see Figure 9.18) so they will not be used for compliance checks or remediation. This can be useful when storage or networking parameters vary or you only want to remediate some settings.

FIGURE 9.18   Disabling host profile settings

Once the profile contains the settings desired you can attach it to individual hosts or all hosts in a cluster by using the Attach/Detach wizard in Host Profiles or the Host Profiles actions menu available from a cluster or host object (Figure 9.19). Be advised that you can only attach one profile to a host at a time.

When a profile is applied to a host, it may require customization—fields that typically have unique values for each host, such as IP address, MAC address, IQN name, and so on. When the profile is attached, the values will be read from the attached host and you will be prompted to validate those values (Figure 9.20).

FIGURE 9.19   Host Profiles menu on a cluster object

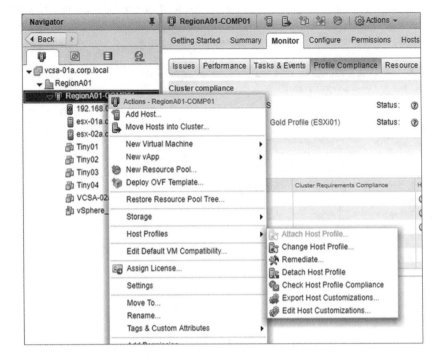

FIGURE 9.20   Customize hosts.

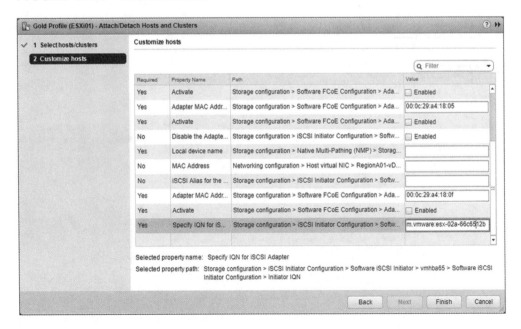

After a profile has been attached to a host, you can check host compliance and view the results from within the profile (Figure 9.21) from the host or from the cluster (Figure 9.22).

FIGURE 9.21 Checking host compliance from the profile

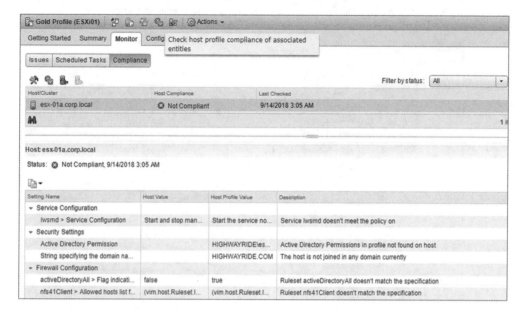

FIGURE 9.22 Checking host compliance from the cluster view

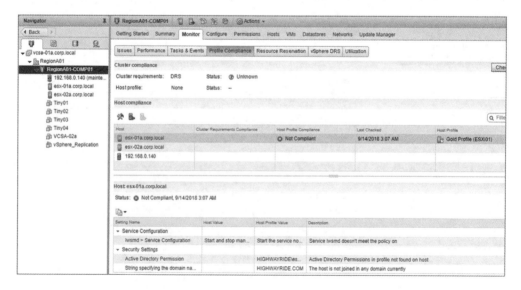

Whether or not you have checked the host's compliance with the profile, you can remediate the host to correct any differences (Figure 9.23).

FIGURE 9.23   Remediate a host from the cluster view.

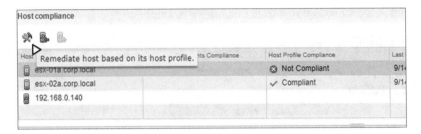

If you no longer wish to associate a host profile with a particular host or all the hosts in a cluster, you can detach the profile using the Action menu on the host or cluster object (Figure 9.24) or from within the host profile.

FIGURE 9.24   Detaching a host profile

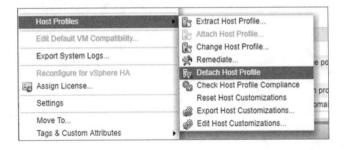

Note that if you want to switch profiles, there is a Change Profile wizard also available from the Action menu on the host or cluster object or from within the host profile.

Importing and Exporting Host Profiles

You can keep host settings in separate datacenters in sync by importing and exporting host profiles between them. By keeping a set master to compare against, you can ensure consistency between environments.

While you might be able to use one profile between all of your hosts with no changes, you will likely need to strip out a number of settings to avoid considerable overhead. Properties such as syslog and NTP servers, not to mention network and storage, would have to be either removed or adjusted for each environment.

However, you could use one "universal master" profile with settings that are consistent across the environments, such as security profiles, and use the Copy Settings to Host Profiles wizard to copy the settings from the master profile to the local "gold" profile (Figure 9.25).

FIGURE 9.25   Copy settings from one profile to another.

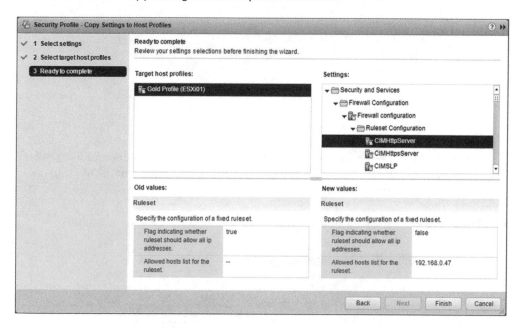

You can then export the profile with the security settings to use across all datacenters (Figure 9.26) and import it into the other vCenter environments (Figure 9.27). Host profiles use XML with a .vpf filename extension.

You will note that administrator passwords are not exported with the profile (Figure 9.28). They will need to be set when the policy is imported and applied.

Advanced Profile Modifications

One of the more advanced uses for host profiles is to change storage paths and network switch configuration.

For example, you can change the path section plug-in for a particular storage device using the PSP configuration branch of the storage configuration (Figure 9.29).

Edit the PSP Name field to the desired plug-in and then apply the profile.

You can also quickly update switch changes, including security policies and traffic shaping (Figure 9.30).

FIGURE 9.26 Exporting a host profile

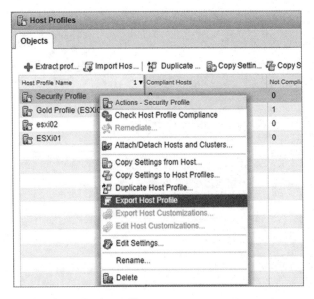

FIGURE 9.27 Importing a host profile

FIGURE 9.28 Passwords are not exported with the host profile.

FIGURE 9.29 Changing a storage device's PSP using a host profile

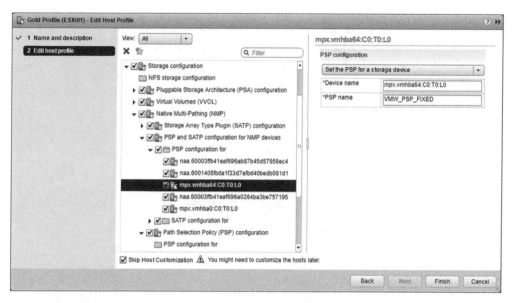

FIGURE 9.30 Changing security settings on a network switch using a host profile

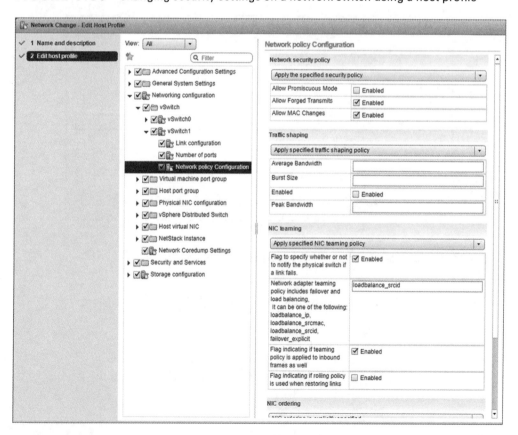

Using Answer Files

When applying host profiles across many hosts, it may be easier to supply the required customization settings using customization files instead of entering the values in the GUI. The file was referred to as an *answer file* in previous version of vSphere.

You can generate a customization file from a profile that has been attached to a host (Figure 9.31).

FIGURE 9.31 Changing security settings on a network switch using a host profile

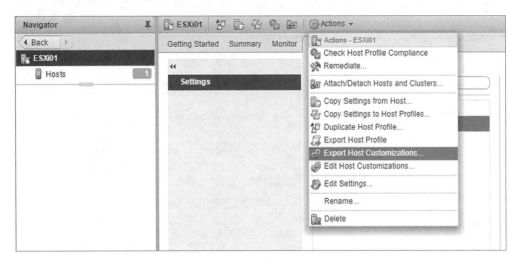

The customization file is a CSV (.csv) text file (Figure 9.32) that can be copied and edited for other hosts.

FIGURE 9.32 Sample customization file

You can use the Edit Host Customizations tool from inside the profile (Figure 9.33) to make changes to host customizations and upload customization files for specific hosts.

FIGURE 9.33 Launch the Edit Host Customizations wizard.

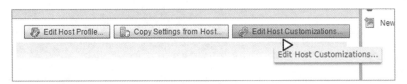

EXERCISE 9.2

Extract and edit a host profile, attach the profile to a cluster, and check for compliance

Required: vCenter Server, existing cluster with hosts.

1. Log into vCenter and open Host Profiles from the home menu.

2. Start the Extract Profile wizard.

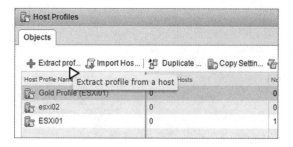

3. Select the host from which you want to extract the settings to create a profile.

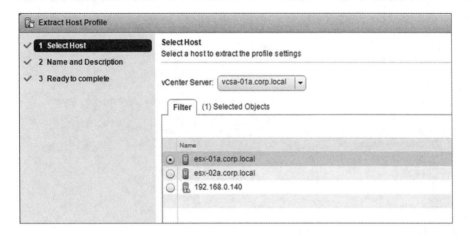

4. Add a name for the new host profile.

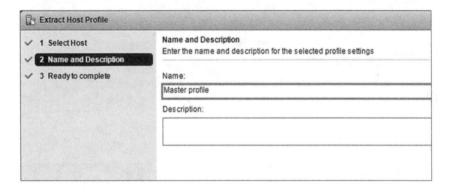

5. Complete the host profile creation.

6. Click the new host profile name to open the object.

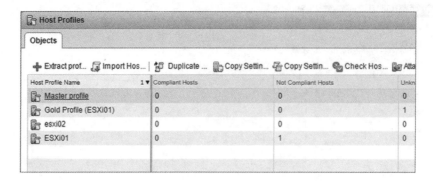

7. Click Edit Host Profile from the Configure tab.

8. Add a description if desired.

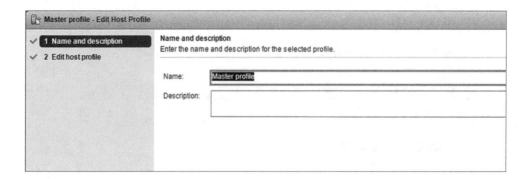

9. Make any changes to the profile needed and finish editing. In the example, the networking and storage configurations have been disabled.

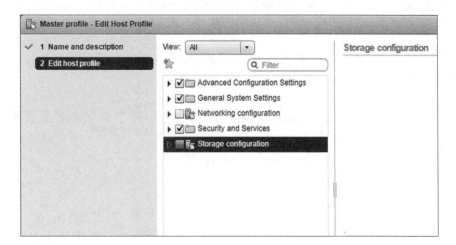

10. Start the Attach/Detach wizard.

EXERCISE 9.2 *(continued)*

11. Select the cluster to attach the profile to and use the Attach > button to move it to the right column.

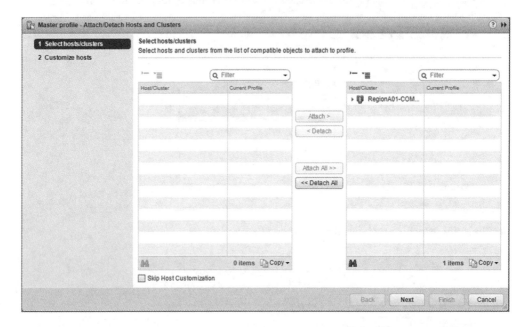

12. Change the customization settings if needed. You will be prompted if any changes are required.

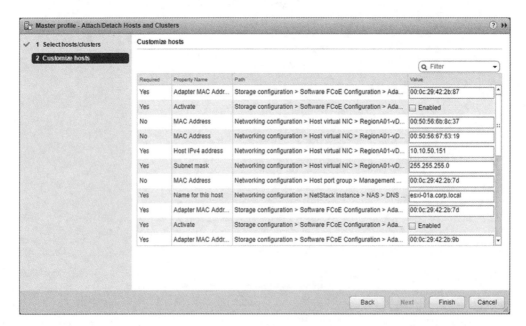

13. Open the Hosts and Clusters view from the home menu.

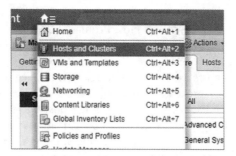

14. Open the Monitor tab for the cluster you attached the profile to and start the compliance check from the Profile Compliance menu.

15. View the results of the compliance check.

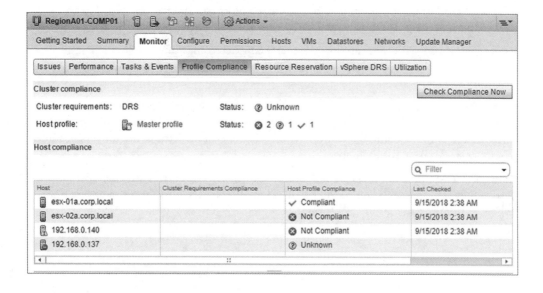

Summary

This chapter has covered Auto Deploy and Host Profiles. These two features provide methods for automatically deploying ESXi hosts and comparing and applying host settings between different hosts.

With Auto Deploy, ESXi hosts can be deployed without physical intervention. Those hosts can be stateless, cached stateless, or installed. With a stateless deployment, an ESXi image is pulled from the Auto Deploy server each time a host boots. With a stateless cached configuration, the image will be stored where the host can access it after the initial boot in case Auto Deploy isn't available during subsequent boots. Using the install settings, Auto Deploy is contacted only during the initial boot and ESXi is installed to the host.

With each of those Auto Deploy configurations, you can provide all of the settings required by the host using Host Profiles. These profiles can also be used to compare and remediate settings between hosts or exported to be used to ensure consistent settings in other vCenter installations.

Exam Essentials

Understand the Auto Deploy sequence.   The host queries DHCP for IP settings, a TFTP server, and a boot loader file. Then the server pulls the boot loader file and `tramp` file from the TFTP server. The PXE process on the host starts to boot with the bootloader and uses the `tramp` file settings to query the Auto Deploy server. The Auto Deploy server matches the host to an image and a profile and supplies those to the host.

Know the specifics of the Auto Deploy boot.   The DHCP options are 66 (boot server) and 67 (boot file). The default bootfile name is `undionly.kpxe.vmw-hardwired`. The third-party servers needed are DHCP and TFTP.

Know that a host will wait if no image is matched when using Auto Deploy.   These hosts can be found in the Discovered Hosts tab and can be matched to an image using the Add to Inventory wizard.

Understand how host profiles work.   Only one host profile can be attached to a host. You have to extract a profile from a host or import a profile to get started. You can copy settings between profiles using the Copy Settings wizard. Not all settings are universal; some require customization for each host.

Know how customization and customization files work.   When you attach a host, you must supply the customization settings that are unique to each host. You can export and import customization files in CSV format.

Review Questions

1. How many host profiles can be attached to a host?

    A. One on either the host or the cluster

    B. Two: One on the host and one on the cluster

    C. Three: One on the host, one on the cluster, and one on the datacenter

    D. Four: One on the host, one on the cluster, one on the datacenter, one on vCenter

2. You have settings in two host profiles that you would like applied to all hosts. What is the simplest method to do this?

    A. Create customization files for each server with the settings.

    B. Extract a new profile and edit the settings.

    C. Use the Copy Settings to Host Profiles wizard.

    D. Use the Copy Settings from Host wizard.

3. Where can profile compliance for all hosts in a cluster be checked?

    A. The datacenter object under Host Profiles

    B. The cluster object under Host Profiles

    C. The datacenter object under Profile Compliance

    D. The cluster object under Profile Compliance

4. Where can profile compliance for a specific host in a cluster be checked?

    A. The host object under Host Profiles

    B. The cluster object under Host Profiles

    C. The host object under Profile Compliance

    D. The cluster object under Profile Compliance

5. Why would you export a host's customization settings? (Choose two.)

    A. To enable Stateless Cache mode

    B. To back up before re-creating the host

    C. To use as a template for other hosts

    D. To use the host profile with a different vCenter

6. What steps are always required to compare settings between hosts? (Choose three.)

    A. Extract

    B. Remediate

    C. Attach

    D. Export

    E. Check

7. What file format do exported host customizations use?

    A. CSV

    B. VPF

    C. ZIP

    D. ISO

8. What file type does an exported host profile use?

    A. CSV

    B. VPF

    C. ZIP

    D. ISO

9. What file type does an imported software depot use?

    A. CSV

    B. VPF

    C. ZIP

    D. ISO

10. What is a custom depot?

    A. A URL-accessible image repository

    B. An uploaded software bundle

    C. A place to add image profiles

    D. A collection of deploy rules

11. A host console display is shown in the accompanying image. Where can this host be found in the web client?

```
* and add it to the rule set with Add-DeployRule or Set-DeployRuleSet.
* The rule should have a pattern that matches one or more of the
* attributes listed below.
*
* Machine attributes:
* . asset=No Asset Tag
* . domain=Highwayride.com
* . hostname=
* . ipv4=192.168.0.143
* . ipv6=fe80::20c:29ff:fee1:3ecf
* . mac=00:0c:29:e1:3e:cf
* . model=VMware Virtual Platform
* . oemstring=[MS_VM_CERT/SHA1/27d66596a61c48dd3dc7216fd715126e33f59ae7]
* . oemstring=Welcome to the Virtual Machine
* . serial=VMware-56 4d 22 ff 6d 41 82 19-9a 0f 69 71 f9 e1 3e cf
* . uuid=ff224d56-416d-1982-9a0f-6971f9e13ecf
* . vendor=VMware, Inc.
*
* To see the error details visit:
* https://192.168.0.133:6502/vmw/rbd/err/1000
*
* Sleeping for 5 minutes and then rebooting...
*********************************************************************
```

A. It cannot be found using the web client.

B. Discovered Hosts.

C. Deployed Hosts.

D. The cluster it was assigned.

12. Where should you look to resolve the error in the screenshot? (Choose two.)

```
Network boot from VMware VMXNET3
Copyright (C) 2003-2014  VMware, Inc.
Copyright (C) 1997-2000  Intel Corporation

CLIENT MAC ADDR: 00 0C 29 EE D0 4B  GUID: 564D27A2-94AF-FC5B-E4C1-425330EED04B
PXE-E51: No DHCP or proxyDHCP offers were received.

PXE-M0F: Exiting Intel PXE ROM.
Operating System not found
_
```

A. Network configuration

B. DHCP server

C. TFTP server

D. Auto Deploy server

E. Deploy rules

13. Where should you look to resolve the error in the following screen shot? (Choose two.)

```
Network boot from VMware VMXNET3
Copyright (C) 2003-2014  VMware, Inc.
Copyright (C) 1997-2000  Intel Corporation

CLIENT MAC ADDR: 00 0C 29 EE D0 4B  GUID: 564D27A2-94AF-FC5B-E4C1-425330EED04B
CLIENT IP: 192.168.0.140  MASK: 255.255.255.0  DHCP IP: 192.168.0.47
GATEWAY IP: 192.168.0.1
PXE-E32: TFTP open timeout
TFTP.
```

A. Network configuration

B. DHCP server

C. TFTP server

D. Auto Deploy server

E. Deploy rules

14. Where should you look to resolve the error in the following screen shot? (Choose two.)

```
VMware iPXE Build: 4446055 (undionly.kpxe.vmw-hardwired)
iPXE 1.0.0-vmw (4750) -- Open Source Network Boot Firmware -- http://ipxe.org
Features: DNS HTTP HTTPS iSCSI TFTP AoE ELF MBOOT PXE bzImage COMBOOT Menu PXEXT


net0: 00:0c:29:ee:d0:4b using undionly on UNDI-PCI0b:00.0 (open)
  [Link:up, TX:0 TXE:0 RX:0 RXE:0]
Configuring (net0 00:0c:29:ee:d0:4b).............. ok
net0: 192.168.0.140/255.255.255.0 gw 192.168.0.1
net0: fe80::20c:29ff:feee:d04b/64
Next server: 192.168.0.4
Filename: tramp
tftp://192.168.0.4/tramp... ok
tramp : 109 bytes [script]
https://192.168.1.133:6501/vmw/rbd/tramp.............. Connection timed out (ht
tp://ipxe.org/4c0a6035)
Could not boot image: Connection timed out (http://ipxe.org/4c0a6035)
Network error encountered while PXE booting.
Scanning the local disk for cached image.
If no image is found, the system will reboot in 20 seconds......
<3>BANK5: not a VMware boot bank
<3>BANK6: not a VMware boot bank
<3>No hypervisor found.
<3>Rebooting...
_
```

A. Network configuration

B. DHCP server

C. TFTP server

D. Auto Deploy server

E. Deploy rules

15. Where should you look to resolve the error in the following screen shot? (Choose two.)

```
* and add it to the rule set with Add-DeployRule or Set-DeployRuleSet.
* The rule should have a pattern that matches one or more of the
* attributes listed below.
*
* Machine attributes:
* . asset=No Asset Tag
* . domain=Highwayride.com
* . hostname=
* . ipv4=192.168.0.143
* . ipv6=fe80::20c:29ff:fee1:3ecf
* . mac=00:0c:29:e1:3e:cf
* . model=VMware Virtual Platform
* . oemstring=[MS_VM_CERT/SHA1/27d66596a61c48dd3dc7216fd715126e33f59ae7]
* . oemstring=Welcome to the Virtual Machine
* . serial=VMware-56 4d 22 ff 6d 41 82 19-9a 0f 69 71 f9 e1 3e cf
* . uuid=ff224d56-416d-1982-9a0f-6971f9e13ecf
* . vendor=VMware, Inc.
*
* To see the error details visit:
* https://192.168.0.133:6502/vmw/rbd/err/1000
*
* Sleeping for 5 minutes and then rebooting...
********************************************************************
```

A. Network configuration

B. DHCP server

C. TFTP server

D. Auto Deploy server

E. Deploy rules

16. What rules options are available to match a rule to multiple hosts? (Choose three.)

  A. All hosts

  B. Asset tag

  C. Serial number

  D. Network

  E. VLAN

17. A rule was created to provide an image for all hosts. (See the following screen shot.) However, no hosts are completing the boot process after powering on. What can resolve this issue?

  A. Set a host profile.

  B. Assign a compatible image.

  C. Activate the rule.

  D. Set a host location.

18. What will happen to a host in inventory if all deploy rules are deleted and the host is restarted?

  A. The host will boot properly.

  B. The host will boot but need to be added to vCenter manually.

  C. The host will not complete the boot process.

  D. You cannot delete all deploy rules.

19. What Auto Deploy method will always boot to ESXi regardless of access to the Auto Deploy server? (Choose two.)

  A. Stateless Caching

  B. Stateful Install

  C. Stateless Deploy

  D. Stateful Caching

20. What steps will prevent an existing host from receiving an image during bootup? (Choose two.)

  A. Remote the host from inventory.

  B. Create a new rule that only includes the host's vendor value.

  C. Create a new rule that doesn't include any of the host's values.

  D. Delete any existing rules that applied to the host.

Chapter

10

Ensuring High Availability for vSphere Clusters and the VCSA

2V0-21.19 EXAM OBJECTIVES COVERED IN THIS CHAPTER:

✓ **Section 1 – VMware vSphere Architectures and Technologies**

- Objective 1.2 – Identify vCenter high availability (HA) requirements

- Objective 1.6 – Describe and differentiate among vSphere, HA, DRS, and SDRS functionality

- Objective 1.9 – Describe the purpose of cluster and the features it provides

✓ **Section 2 – VMware Products and Solutions**

- Objective 2.2 – Describe HA solutions for vSphere

✓ **Section 4 – Installing, Configuring, and Setting Up a VMware vSphere Solution**

- Objective 4.2 – Create and configure vSphere objects

✓ **Section 7 – Administrative and Operational Tasks in a VMware vSphere Solution**

- Objective 7.13 – Identify and interpret affinity/anti-affinity rules

Ensuring that your resources are available when needed is a key requirement in a datacenter. In any environment, it takes a comprehensive plan to ensure availability, with participation from each of the teams with responsibilities in the datacenter. The infrastructure team needs to make sure there are no single points of failure; the development team needs to build resilient and self-healing applications; and the operations team needs to track, trend, and anticipate potential issues before they can cause outages.

The vSphere team members are responsible for ensuring that the system is designed for resiliency, updates are applied regularly, and the system is configured to take advantage of the availability features built into vSphere. This chapter will address two of those availability features, the High Availability (HA) option for vSphere clusters and the vCenter High Availability solution for the VCSA.

Configuring vSphere Cluster High Availability

When you create clusters in vSphere, there are two primary options to enable: Distributed Resource Scheduler (DRS) and High Availability (HA). The primary purpose of DRS is to balance workloads among hosts in a cluster, which is discussed in Chapter 6, "Allocating Resources in a vSphere Data Center." High Availability allows virtual machines to be restarted in the event of problems with the host or in the virtual machine.

All vSphere licenses Essentials Plus and above include High Availability. The primary benefits of High Availability are recovery from the following scenarios:

- A host failure—by restarting virtual machines on other hosts

- A virtual machine failure—by restarting the VM

- A storage loss on a host—by restarting virtual machines on other hosts

- A network loss on a host—by restarting virtual machines on other hosts

You can also configure Proactive HA, which gives you both manual and automatic options for evacuating virtual machines from hosts whose health has degenerated.

The only requirements to enable HA are licensing (Essentials Plus or higher) and a cluster object. No hosts or virtual machines are required to configure HA, although you will not be able to test your settings without them!

High Availability for a cluster can be enabled using the Edit Cluster Settings wizard (Figure 10.1), which is accessed from the vSphere DRS or vSphere Availability options under the Configure tab of the cluster.

FIGURE 10.1   Enable High Availability on a cluster.

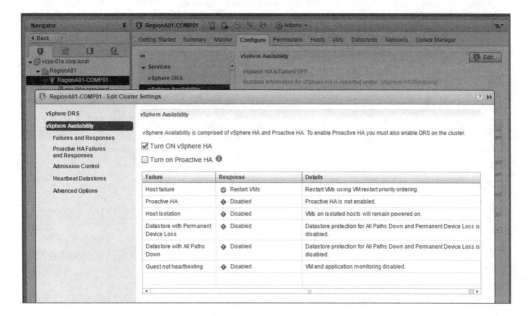

HA Failures and Responses

Figure 10.1 shows the availability failures and responses available from High Availability, and the single green check shows that by default it will only protect against a host failure. To recover from other scenarios, additional configuration is required.

Proactive HA allows vCenter to move virtual machines off a host that has reported health degradation via a third-party provider. Many major server vendors, including Dell, Lenovo, and Cisco, have providers available for their hardware and might have requirements such as licensing or homogeneous hosts in a cluster.

As shown in Figure 10.2, there are a few options available for Proactive HA.

When Proactive HA is enabled, it will default to the Manual automation level with Quarantine mode. Manual mode will only provide suggestions; you need to manually move virtual machines off flagged hosts. Automated mode will leverage vMotion to automatically move virtual machines off troubled hosts.

FIGURE 10.2 Configure Proactive HA.

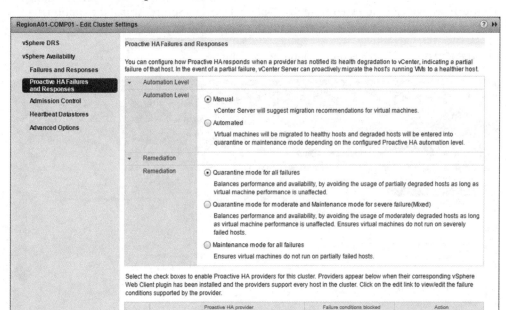

The remediation options allow you to adjust when virtual machines are migrated:

- Quarantine Mode for All Failures allows virtual machines to migrate as long as performance is unaffected.

- Maintenance Mode for All Failures moves all virtual machines off any host with a failure.

- Mixed (the middle option) sets quarantine mode for hosts with moderate issues and maintenance mode for hosts with severe failures. You can adjust what types of failures (such as redundant PSU or fan) are treated as moderate or severe.

The types of failures detected are dependent on the Proactive HA provider. Contact your hardware vendor for availability, licensing, and installation.

Host Isolation

Host isolation is when a host stops receiving HA heartbeats and cannot access the isolation address. Hosts in an HA cluster communicate continuously over any network with management traffic enabled. If a host does not receive any communications in 12 seconds, it attempts to ping any configured isolation address (by default, the gateway IP address of the management network). If no response is received from the isolation address, the host will check the HA folder in the heartbeat datastore. If the host determines that it is isolated, the host will initiate the host isolation response (Figure 10.3).

FIGURE 10.3   Configure host isolation response.

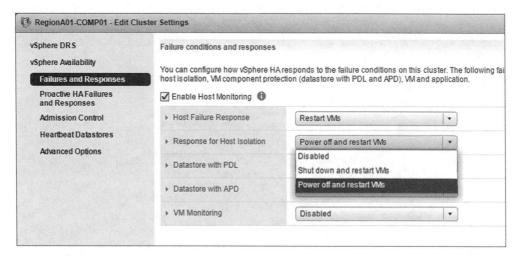

The default response is Disabled, which means a host will not react to being isolated. The other options can either power off the VMs or initiate a guest shutdown. If the uptime of the guests is a priority and they can handle being powered off, the Power Off and Restart VMs option will get the virtual machines back up faster as there is no wait time for the guest to gracefully power down.

The isolation response is governed by the Fault Domain Manager (FDM) agent, which runs on each host in the cluster. The FDM agents elect a master host to act as a primary point of contact with vCenter and the subordinate hosts, which are all of the other hosts in the cluster.

The master host listens for a *heartbeat message* from each subordinate host, which are sent every second. If a subordinate stops sending heartbeat messages, the master host will check the heartbeat datastore(s) for entries from the failed host. If the master determines that the subordinate is isolated from the management network and is not updating the heartbeat datastore, the master will initiate restarting the subordinate's virtual machines on other hosts in the cluster. If the master determines that the subordinate is isolated from the management network but is still updating the heartbeat datastore, the master host will watch for the virtual machines on that host to be powered off before attempting to restart them on other hosts in the cluster.

Heartbeat Datastores

The heartbeat datastores are selected automatically by default, but as seen in Figure 10.4, you have the option of specifying datastores to use. You can also specify datastores to use while allowing HA to choose additional datastores if needed. While it is best to use datastores available to all of the hosts, you at least need to ensure that all datastores are accessible by at least one host—the master designation will go to the host with the most datastores connected by default. High Availability will display a warning message if there are fewer than two datastores available or manually selected.

FIGURE 10.4 Configure heartbeat datastores.

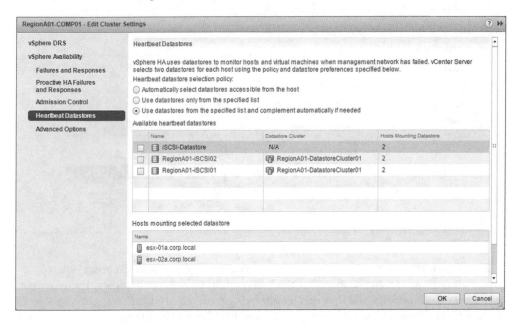

If you are on a converged network where your management, virtual machine, and storage traffic use the same NICs and switches, you might assume that any management traffic loss will result in VM network or storage loss and shut down the running virtual machines. On the other hand, if your management network is completely separate, then you may want to leave the virtual machines running by disabling host isolation response.

Advanced Options

There are a few common advanced settings for host isolation that are accessible under the Advanced Options section of the Edit Cluster Settings wizard (Figure 10.5):

- **das.ignoreRedundantNetWarning**: This setting prevents a warning from being displayed if there is not a second HA network or NIC. This can be set to true for test/dev environments with limited networks.

- **das.usedefaultisolationaddress:** This setting prevents the FDM from using the default gateway of the management network to test for host isolation.

- **das.isolationaddress[0–9]:** These settings (up to 10) set specific addresses to use for isolation response in addition to the default gateway if it is not disabled.

- **das.isolationshutdowntimeout:** This setting adjusts the amount of time the host waits for a virtual machine to shut down before it issues a power off command. This setting is only used if a response of "Shut down and restart" is used.

FIGURE 10.5   Configure advanced settings for host isolation.

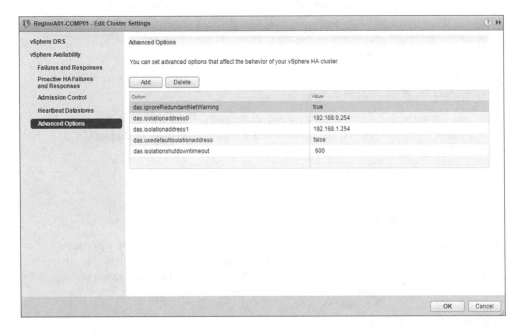

 **Real World Scenario**

Up and Down: Know Your Network Before Setting Isolation

I was called out to help a company that was experiencing virtual machines randomly powering off overnight. While putting this story right in the middle of the network isolation section gives a big clue as to why, it took several hours of troubleshooting to pin it down at the time.

The client had a three-node cluster and one of the hosts (not always the same one) would have a few (but not all) virtual machines powered off at night, right around the time of the systemwide backup. Some nights there would be no virtual machines powered off, but more often than not, a few would be powered off.

One way to verify that the FDM agent is shutting down your VMs is to check the FDM log file /var/log/fdm.log on the host the virtual machines were running on for lines such as these:

```
[LocalIsolationPolicy::TerminateVms] Terminating 1 vms
[LocalIsolationPolicy::DoVmTerminate] Terminating <path>/Tiny01.vmx
```

```
[InventoryManagerImpl::MarkVmPowerOff] Adding <path>/Tiny01.vmx to powering off set
[LocalIsolationPolicy::HandleNetworkIsolation] Done with isolation handling
```

It turned out the network team had initiated reboots of some of the network equipment, including the switches the hosts plugged into (which prevented the subordinates from talking to the master) and the firewall that acted as the default gateway. The devices didn't always take the same amount of time to reboot; they usually took just enough to time to start the isolation response, but the network would be available before the isolation response was completed.

To compound matters, they had disabled the datastore heartbeat during recent storage maintenance.

In the end, we reconfigured the datastore heartbeat and worked with the networking team to stagger the network switch reboots and identify IPs of devices that would respond to pings and always be available.

Configuring VMCP

High Availability can also protect against a host losing access to datastores in use by a virtual machine. *Virtual Machine Component Protection (VMCP)* refers to the capability for HA to respond to a Permanent Device Loss (PDL) or All Paths Down (APD) event. Figure 10.6 shows the response options for both scenarios.

FIGURE 10.6 Configure VMCP options.

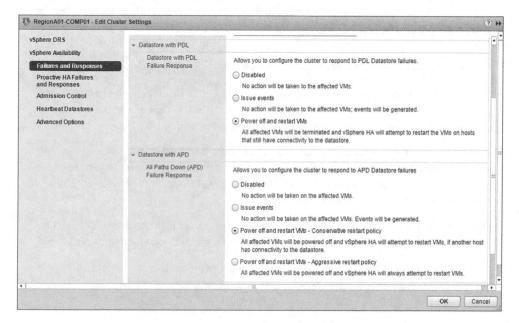

Whether a storage loss is considered PDL or APD depends on the response from the storage device.

- A PDL event occurs when the storage device responds to an I/O request with a SCSI sense code indicating the storage device is no longer available. This indicates to the host that the storage will not be coming back and requires virtual machines to be powered off before they can be recovered.

- An APD event occurs when there is either no response or any response other than "that device is no longer available."

 VMware's Knowledge Base article 2004684 lists the SCSI sense codes that will trigger a PDL state.

Permanent Device Loss Event

As PDL is the storage provider stating that the requested device is gone, the only options are to either issue an event message or power off affected virtual machines so they can be restarted on a host that still can access the storage device. If you have virtual machines with storage on multiple sources (OS on one datastore, data on another, logs on a third), you might not want to power off the virtual machines if one of the devices becomes unavailable. As shown in Figure 10.7, you can set per–virtual machine overrides for any of the monitored conditions including PDL.

All Paths Down Event

The possible response to an All Paths Down event are more varied because it is not clear why the storage is unavailable and when it might return. As with PDL, possible choices for APD events are to issue events and power off virtual machines. However, you have two options for powering off virtual machines, either conservative or aggressive. Conservative will power off VMs only if hosts are available with connections to the datastore. Choosing aggressive will start powering off the affected virtual machines without first seeing if other hosts can access the datastore.

While conservative should be the choice for most environments, there could be scenarios such as a stretched cluster where aggressive could be a valid choice. An environment where the storage could be isolated with some hosts in the cluster could be a candidate for aggressive as a remote host would not be able to check those hosts to know they have storage connectivity.

Monitoring Virtual Machines

The final failure vSphere High Availability addresses is virtual machine failures, monitoring both operating system and running applications (Figure 10.8). Virtual machine monitoring requires VMware Tools to be installed and running on the virtual machine. The VMware

FIGURE 10.7 Override VMCP settings for a virtual machine.

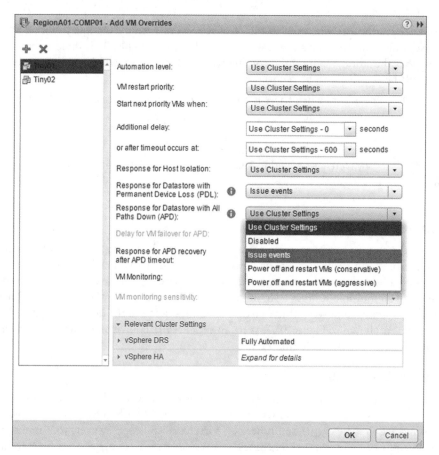

Tools application will send a "heartbeat" signal to the host periodically. If the host does not receive a heartbeat in a certain amount of time and no I/O activity is observed within 120 seconds, the guest OS will be restarted. You can change the amount of time the host will wait for I/O activity or disable the I/O check using the *das.iostatsinterval* advanced option.

Applications that support vSphere application monitoring can also send heartbeats to the host. If the application heartbeat is not received within the time period, the guest will be restarted.

Heartbeat monitoring defaults to High sensitivity. If the guest has been sending heartbeats for 120 seconds and there are no heartbeats received for 30 seconds, the recovery will proceed. A virtual machine will be reset no more than three times and not more than once in a 1-hour period. You can use the slider shown in Figure 10.8 to select Low, Medium, or High sensitivity (see the grayed-out Custom section to see what settings correspond to which preset) or choose Custom and set specific time limits.

As with VMCP settings, you can override the cluster settings on a per-VM basis (Figure 10.9).

FIGURE 10.8 Configure virtual machine monitoring.

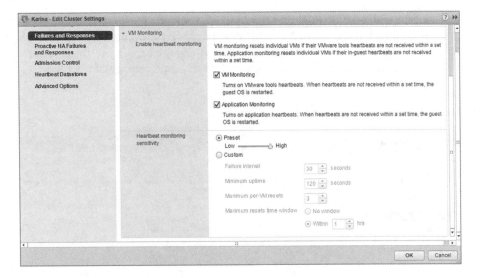

FIGURE 10.9 Configure monitoring for a specific virtual machine.

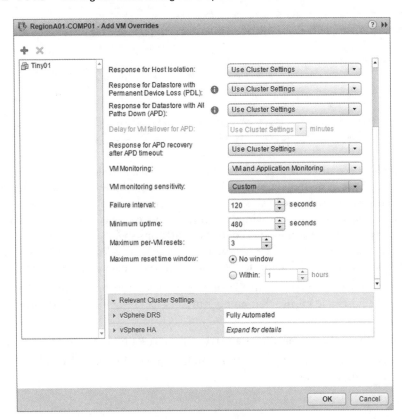

Admission Control

One key concept with High Availability is *admission control*: admitting virtual machines into the cluster in such a way that capacity is guaranteed in the event of a failure. As shown in Figure 10.10, the default configuration is to reserve enough capacity to tolerate one host failure and to calculate the capacity needed by using a percentage of the resources in the cluster.

FIGURE 10.10   Configuring admission control

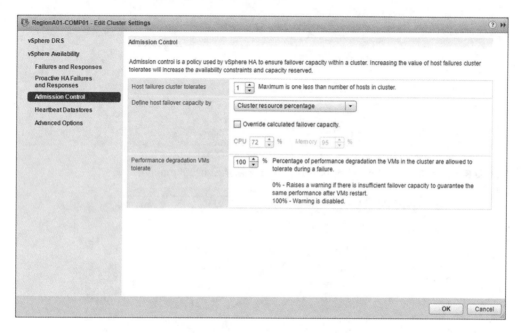

With admission control enabled, you need to have at least two hosts available in the cluster (powered on and not in maintenance mode) or no virtual machines will be allowed to power on because in the event that one host is unavailable, there will be no resources left.

Admission control works by providing vCenter with a capacity check before virtual machines power on. If the admissions control calculations specify that there will be sufficient resources available in the event of a failure, the virtual machine is allowed to power up. The options available for defining host failover capacity are as follows:

- Slot Policy: Uses a virtual machine "slot size" to determine how many slots are available on the hosts and ensure that number of slots will be available in the event of a failure.

- Cluster Resource Percentage: Uses a percentage of resources to hold in reserve.

- Dedicated Failover Hosts: Specifies hosts to hold in reserve. No VM will run on these hosts unless another host fails.

Slot Policy

Slot Policy (listed as Host Failures to Tolerate in vSphere prior to 6.5) uses the concept of a *slot*, which is a measurement of a virtual machine using memory and CPU reservation. The basic idea is to determine the "size" of the largest running virtual machine (by memory and CPU), determine how many virtual machines of this size can run on your hosts, and determine how much space needs to be kept free to account for the number of failed hosts you want the cluster to tolerate. See Figure 10.11.

FIGURE 10.11   Configuring Slot Policy

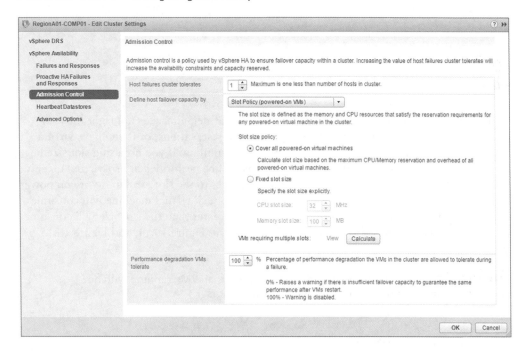

The default slot size is calculated by looking at all of the running virtual machines in the cluster for the largest memory reservation (plus overhead) and the largest CPU reservation. The largest values do not need to come from the same virtual machine. If VM A has a 1 GB memory reservation and a 500 MHz CPU reservation while VM B has CPU reservations of 768 MB and 1 GHz, the default slot size will be 1 GB memory and 1 GHz CPU.

The virtual machines currently running in the cluster are counted for the number of slots currently in use. The slot size is then compared to each host to determine how many slots each host can hold. If the hosts have different memory/CPU configurations, the largest hosts are used for the slots to reserve.

To view the slot size for your cluster along with the total slots, available slots, and failover slots, look at the Advanced Runtime Info in the vSphere HA summary under the Monitor tab of the cluster (Figure 10.12).

FIGURE 10.12   Viewing the slot information

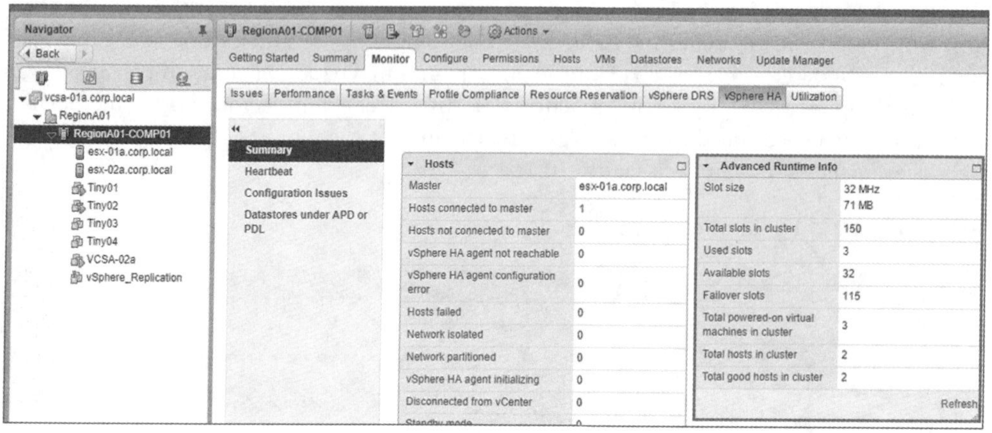

You can also manually set the slot size if you feel the default size is not right for your environment, if you have virtual machines of varying reservations, or if you have virtual machines with large reservations that are not always running. If you are using slot size but are not using a *fixed* slot size, the slot calculations will be performed at any virtual machine power state change. This can result in dramatic changes to the slot availability if you power on and off a virtual machine with a large reservation. Each virtual machine will consume one slot at least. Virtual machines with reservations greater than the slot size will consume enough slots to cover their reservation. See Figure 10.13, Figure 10.14, and Figure 10.15 for examples.

FIGURE 10.13   A small environment with three small VMs running with no reservations and automatic slot sizes. Note 664 total slots.

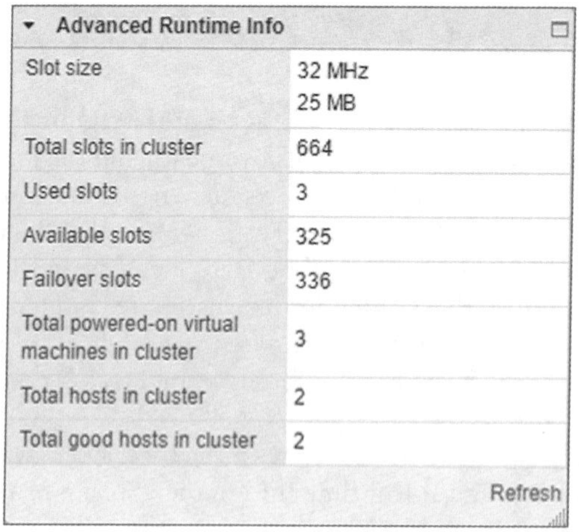

Advanced Runtime Info	
Slot size	32 MHz / 25 MB
Total slots in cluster	664
Used slots	3
Available slots	325
Failover slots	336
Total powered-on virtual machines in cluster	3
Total hosts in cluster	2
Total good hosts in cluster	2

FIGURE 10.14   A virtual machine with a 3000 MHz CPU reservation is powered on. Total slots in cluster changes to 6.

Advanced Runtime Info	
Slot size	3000 MHz 25 MB
Total slots in cluster	6
Used slots	4
Available slots	0
Failover slots	2
Total powered-on virtual machines in cluster	4
Total hosts in cluster	2
Total good hosts in cluster	2
	Refresh

FIGURE 10.15   Slot size is manually set to 1000 MHz. Total slots in cluster are now 20. There are 6 used slots as the large VM is consuming 3 slots.

Advanced Runtime Info	
Slot size	1000 MHz 25 MB
Total slots in cluster	20
Used slots	6
Available slots	4
Failover slots	10
Total powered-on virtual machines in cluster	4
Total hosts in cluster	2
Total good hosts in cluster	2
	Refresh

EXERCISE 10.1

Configure a cluster for Slot Policy.

Requires a vCenter server with a datacenter created.

1. Create a new cluster in the datacenter named SlotPolicy and enable HA.

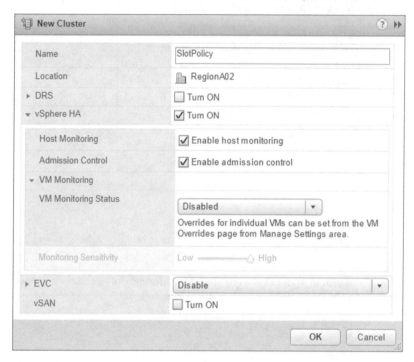

2. Open the HA settings of the new cluster.

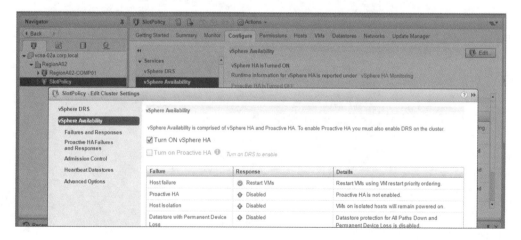

3. Set Admission Control to Slot Policy.

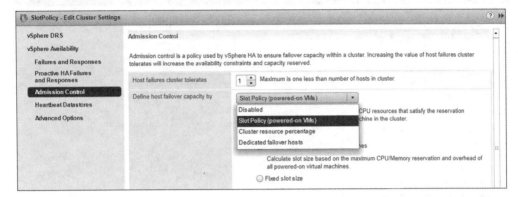

4. Configure a fixed slot size of 250 MHz and 256 MB. Set a warning if performance is expected to drop more than 20% during a failure.

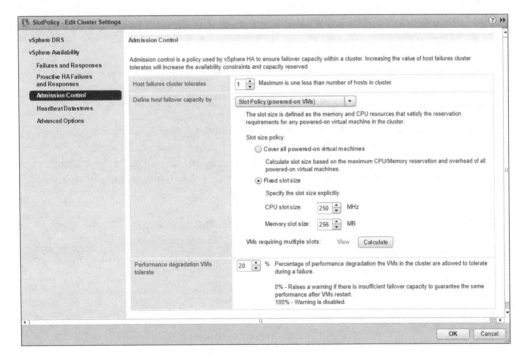

EXERCISE 10.1 *(continued)*

5. Open the Advanced Options and set the *das.isolation* to default and create two new isolation addresses:

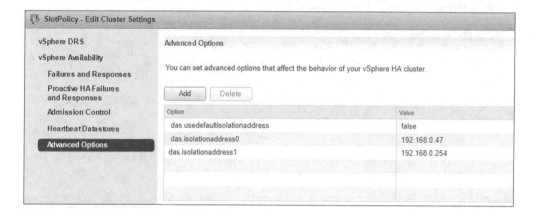

6. Click OK to save the settings.

Cluster Resource Percentage

The next choice for admission control is Cluster Resource Percentage, where a specific percentage of cluster resources (CPU and memory) are held in reserve. By default, the percentage will be the total resources available divided by the resources of the n largest hosts, where n is the number of host failures to tolerate. You can also manually set the percentage of CPU and memory reserved (Figure 10.16).

FIGURE 10.16 Manually setting Cluster Resource Percentage

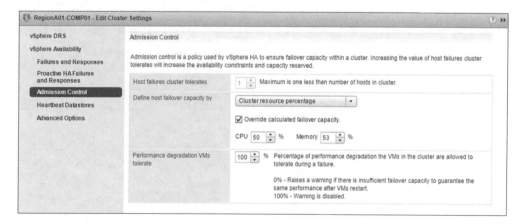

When you view the Advanced Runtime Info in the vSphere HA summary under the Monitor tab of the cluster (Figure 10.17), you will not see any information about running virtual machines as you would with the Slot Policy.

FIGURE 10.17   Viewing Cluster Resource Percentage

▼ Advanced Runtime Info	□
Cluster total memory	24.25 GB
Failover capacity (Memory)	51% (12.37 GB)
Cluster total CPU	28.03 GHz
Failover capacity (CPU)	50% (14.02 GHz)
Failover resource auto-computation	On

However, you can use the Resource Reservation tab to view Cluster Total Capacity for CPU and Memory as well as Total Reservation Capacity for each resource (Figure 10.18).

FIGURE 10.18   Viewing total cluster CPU capacity and VM CPU reservations

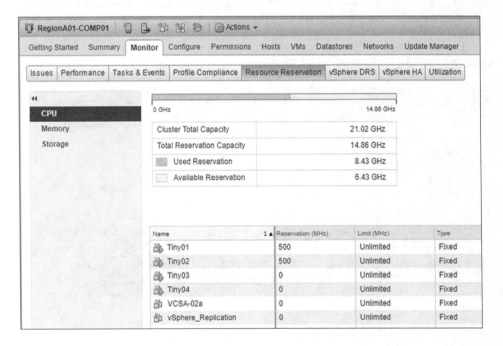

Dedicated Failover Hosts

Using a dedicated failover host is the simplest configuration as it sets up a "hot standby" list. This ensures that a comparable amount of resources is available in the event of a failure, assuming your failover hosts have the same capacity as the largest hosts in the cluster. Virtual machines cannot power up on the specified hosts, and attempting to vMotion a virtual machine to a listed host will result in the message shown in Figure 10.19.

FIGURE 10.19 Message received when migrating a virtual machine to a failover host

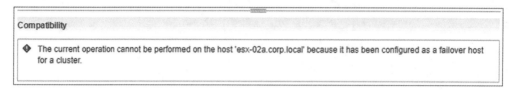

The downside to dedicated hosts is that you cannot use those hosts for any workloads and you have less flexibility in workload placement. Using dedicated hosts also does not adjust to changing workloads or demands over time. You also need to ensure that the selected failover host has sufficient resources if not all of the hosts have the same specifications. In a cluster where not all hosts have the same CPU type or count or amount of RAM, choosing a smaller host will result in a warning (Figure 10.20).

FIGURE 10.20 Choosing a smaller host can result in a warning.

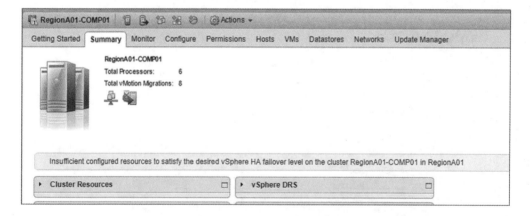

EXERCISE 10.2

Configure a cluster for dedicated hosts.

Requires a vCenter server and two hosts, each with VMs. Assumes hosts are in an existing cluster.

1. Open the vSphere Availability settings of the cluster.

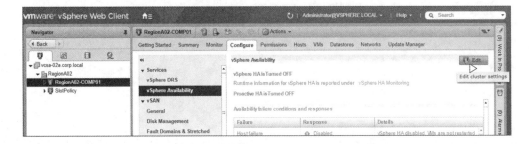

2. Enable HA.

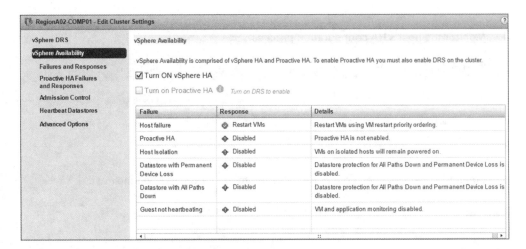

3. Under Admission Control, set the host failover capacity to Dedicated Failover Hosts, select a host for the list, and click OK.

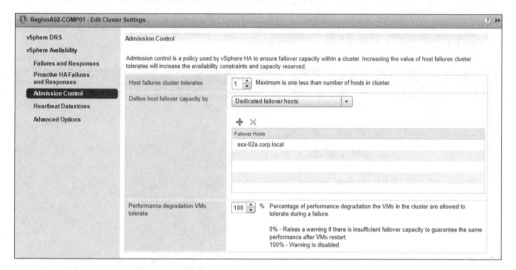

4. Monitor the host's HA configuration process.

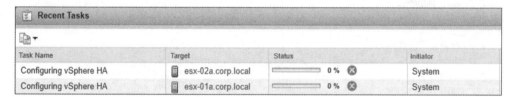

5. When the host has been configured, attempt to power on a VM on the host.

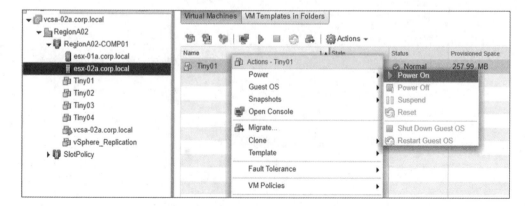

6. Verify that the virtual machine cannot power on.

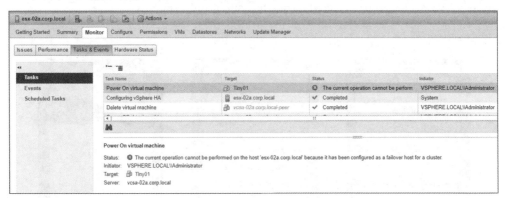

Resource Fragmentation

Resource fragmentation refers to a problem of virtual machines not being able to boot because while the capacity to hold the virtual machine exists, it may not exist on one host. Resource fragmentation cannot occur with dedicated failover hosts or Slot Policy if a fixed slot size is not used. However, with Cluster resource percentage, you can run into resource fragmentation.

In Figure 10.21 we see three hosts with 5000 MHz each in a cluster. If Cluster Resource percentage is enabled it will reserve 33% CPU and 33% of memory. In this example, in a failover scenario, while 33% of the total cluster resources are still available, VMK cannot be powered on to a surviving host as neither host has sufficient resources.

If we used a custom slot size of 500 MHz with our example in Figure 10.21, we could have the same problem. A slot size of 500 MHz allows each host to have 10 slots, with 10 slots total being held in reserve. In the event of a failure, those slots would not necessarily be on the same host—and in this case VMK, which requires 6 slots, would not be able to power on.

Performance

For Cluster resource percentage and Slot Policy, calculations are made to determine the current load and possible load and the amount of resources needed to reserve in case of a failure. Both of these policies use virtual machine reservations plus VM overhead memory to determine capacity. If you do not have any CPU or memory reservations set for your virtual machines, only the memory overhead of the running machines is used. This will result in a very low figure for running capacity and a very high figure for total capacity, which will result in oversubscribing the environment in the event of a failure.

To help with this, vSphere 6.5 introduced a new setting that is only available when DRS is also enabled: Performance Degradation VMs Tolerate is specified as a percentage (Figure 10.22).

This setting will raise a warning if the virtual machines' performance is expected to degrade more than a set percentage during a failure. If the current CPU or memory utilization is greater than the percentage of reserved capacity specified, a warning will be set.

FIGURE 10.21 Resource fragmentation example showing that virtual machine "VMK" cannot be powered on due to insufficient resources

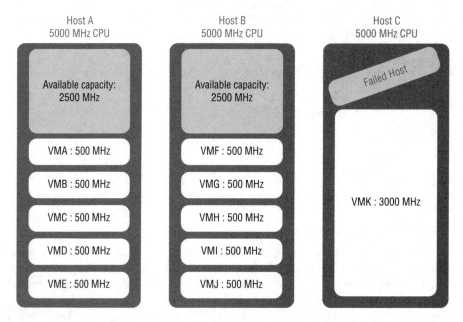

FIGURE 10.22 The Performance Degradation VMs Tolerate setting

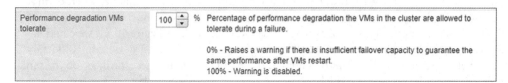

The VMware documentation gives the formula as follows:

performance reduction = current utilization × percentage set

If *current utilization - performance reduction > available capacity*, a warning will be issued (Figure 10.23).

FIGURE 10.23 Performance degradation warning

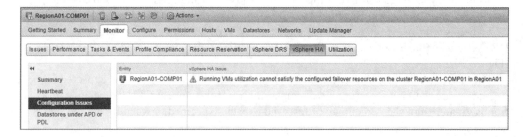

From the white paper "VMware vCloud Architecture Toolkit for Service Providers" (download3.vmware.com/vcat/vmw-vcloud-architecture-toolkit-spv1-webworks/index.html):

- Host Failures Cluster Tolerates admission control policy: When virtual machines have similar CPU/memory reservations and similar memory overheads.

- Percentage of Cluster Resources Reserved admission control policy: When virtual machines have highly variable CPU and memory reservations.

- Specify a Failover Host admission control policy: To accommodate organizational policies that dictate the use of a passive failover host, most typically seen with the use of virtualized business critical applications.

For best results, your hosts should all be about the same size with regard to CPU and RAM capacity. You should also either disable Distributed Power Management (DPM) or configure it to have enough hosts running to allow the reserve capacity to survive a host failure. If DPM has consolidated VMs and powered down all other hosts, HA will not have the capacity to recover a failed host.

You also need to keep an eye on any Distributed Resource Scheduler (DRS) rules created. DRS rules that are VM-to-Host "must" rules or rules to separate virtual machines will be enforced by HA during failures unless HA Advanced Options are set.

- **das.respectvmvmantiaffinityrules:** Can be set to false to ignore VM anti-affinity rules during a failure

- **das.respectvmhostsoftaffinityrules:** Can be set to false to restart a VM on any available host regardless of VM-to-host rules

Please refer to Figure 10.5 for configuring Advanced Options such as advanced isolation or DRS rule options.

NOTE   VMware recommends disabling HA before enabling or upgrading vSAN. Once the vSAN operation is complete, re-enable HA.

vCenter Server Appliance High Availability

With vSphere, the vCenter server provides centralized management, monitoring, and security. Keeping your vCenter server available will ensure that DRS is always working, new VMs can be deployed, and you know where all of your virtual machines are in your environment. With vSphere 6.5, there is a new feature available for the vCenter Server Appliance called vCenter High Availability, which provides a managed active/passive cluster of VCSAs to ensure that VCSA is not a single point of failure.

VCSA HA can be enabled using the web client in the vCenter HA section of the Configure tab of the vCenter server (Figure 10.24).

FIGURE 10.24   vCenter HA in the web client GUI

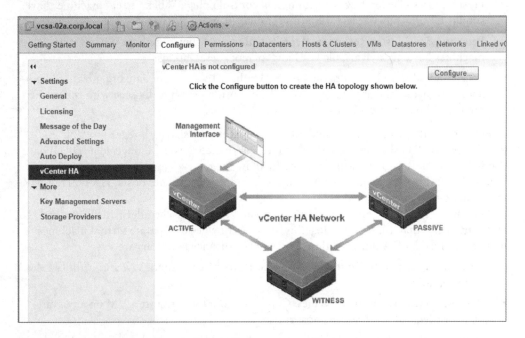

As shown in Figure 10.24, a vCenter HA configuration consists of active and passive vCenter hosts plus a witness virtual machine. The passive and witness appliances are clones of the original VCSA. Once vCenter HA is configured, two of the nodes must be available at all times. If the active node becomes unavailable, the passive node will take over. If the passive or witness node goes down, the active node will continue to run. However, if any two nodes go down, the remaining node will stop responding to requests.

There are two methods of setting up vCenter HA: Basic and Advanced (Figure 10.25). You should create a new port group to use for the vCenter HA network.

If you use the Basic option, the VCSA must reside in the environment it manages or reside on a cluster managed by a 6.5 vCenter server in the same Single Sign-on domain. The cluster the VCSA is running on should have DRS enabled and at least three hosts for best practices. The Basic option will add a NIC to the VCSA before cloning the VCSA twice.

During the Basic wizard, you will be able to set the IP addresses for the vCenter HA network and add IP addresses for the management NIC of the passive appliance. You can also approve where the two new appliances will be created. The wizard will attempt to place them, but if the default options have problems, you will be prompted (Figure 10.26).

FIGURE 10.25　vCenter HA configuration options

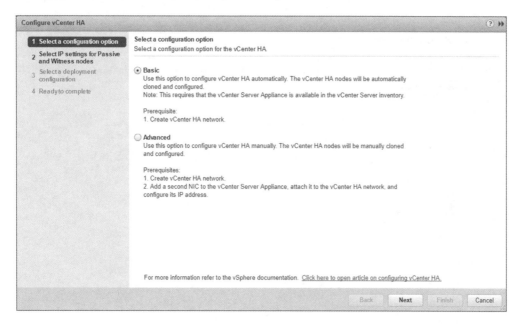

FIGURE 10.26　Basic option compatibility errors (left) and the issues expanded (right)

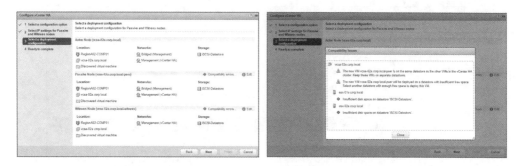

Correct the issues and set the configuration as needed before continuing (Figure 10.27).

If you use the Advanced option to configure vCenter HA, you must add a second NIC to the vCenter server appliance before starting the Advanced Option wizard. During the wizard, you will be prompted to enter the IP addresses for the passive and witness virtual machines. The last step of the Advanced option is Clone VMs. While on this window, use the Clone to Virtual Machine wizard (Figure 10.28) to make two copies of the VCSA. During that wizard, use the Customize the Operating System option and create a Guest Customization Spec to change the hostname and IP address of NIC0 to the one specified in the Advanced Option wizard. For a detailed walkthrough, visit the following URL:

featurewalkthrough.vmware.com/t/vsphere-6-5/enabling-vcenter-ha-advanced/26

FIGURE 10.27 Completing the Basic option process

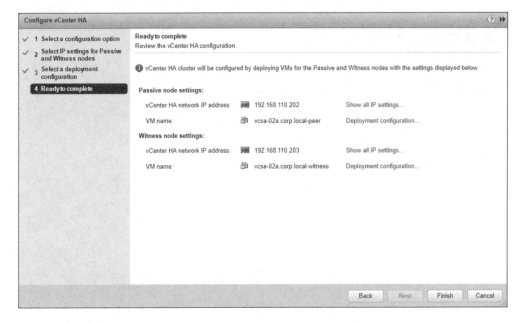

FIGURE 10.28 Use the Clone to Virtual Machine wizard to copy the VCSA.

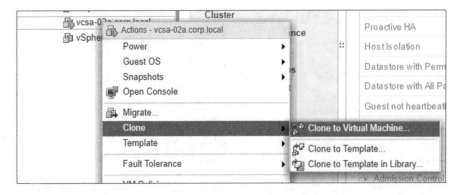

The Basic option will default to using `<VCSA name>-peer` for the passive appliance and `<VCSA name>-witness` for the witness appliance.

With either configuration, the witness appliance will only be connected to the HA network. You also need to ensure that SSH is enabled on the VCSA before cloning is performed or you will receive the errors shown in Figure 10.29 and/or Figure 10.30.

FIGURE 10.29 Tasks message regarding enabling SSH before the VCSA is cloned

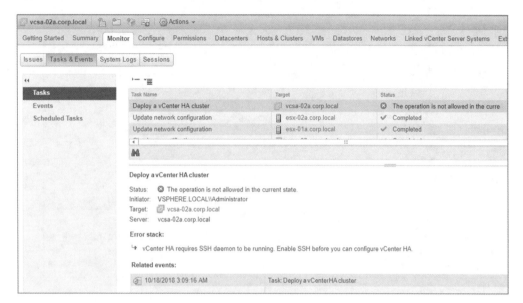

FIGURE 10.30 Error message in the Configure vCenter HA window if SSH is not enabled

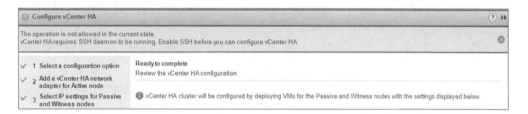

After vCenter HA is configured, you can monitor its status using the Monitor tab (Figure 10.31) or monitor the status and review the configuration using the Configure tab (Figure 10.32).

If a problem is detected, the Monitor tab will suggest some remedies. In this case (see Figure 10.33), the network connections for the passive node have been disconnected.

If the active node fails, the failover process (Figure 10.34) will start and the passive node will assume the hostname and management IP address of the active node (Figure 10.35).

When the failed node returns, it will become the passive node. There is no automatic failback. However, there is an Initiate Failover button on the Configure tab to trigger a failback. Also, on the Configure tab after vCenter HA is enabled is an Edit button that allows you to enter maintenance mode in case of infrastructure changes that could affect connectivity, since if the active node loses connectivity to the passive and witness nodes, it will stop responding to requests. You can also disable or remove vCenter HA using the Edit button (Figure 10.36).

FIGURE 10.31   Monitor tab for vCenter HA

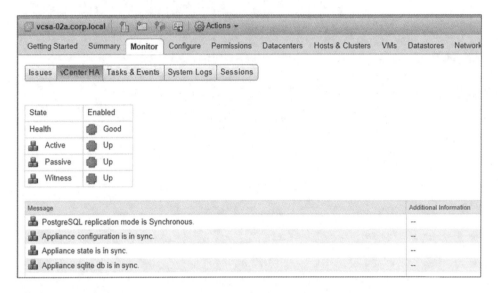

FIGURE 10.32   The Configure tab after vCenter HA is enabled

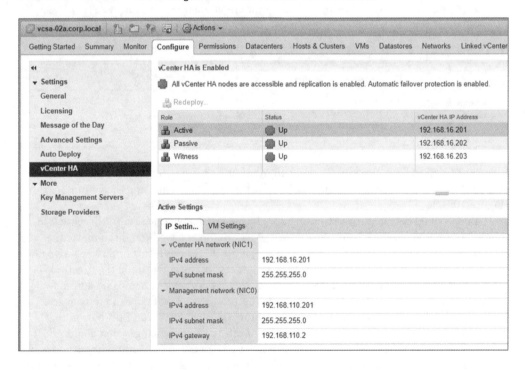

FIGURE 10.33   The Monitor tab after the passive node has been disconnected

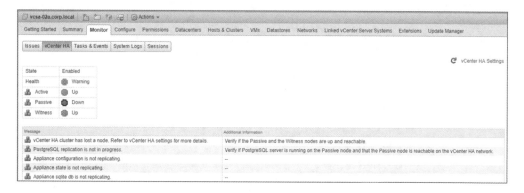

FIGURE 10.34   Failover notification from the web client

FIGURE 10.35   The passive node has claimed the .201 IP address of the active node.

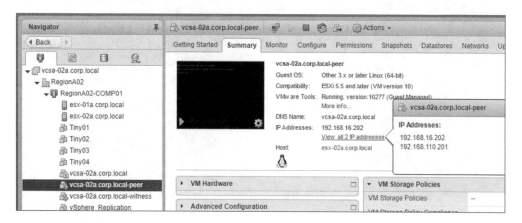

FIGURE 10.36 Four options are provided to edit the configurations after vCenter HA has been enabled.

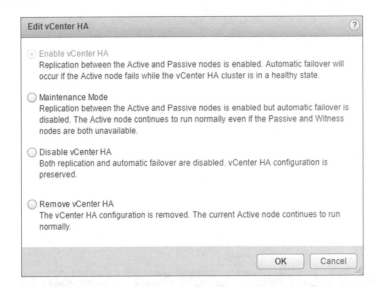

EXERCISE 10.3

Enable vCenter HA and test failover.

Requires a VCSA residing in the cluster it manages.

1. Ensure that the VCSA has SSH enabled.

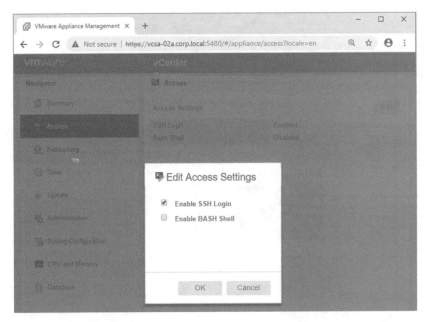

2. Create a new port group named HA Network either on a vDS or on a vSS on each of your hosts and allocate an IP domain for it. This will be a closed network and will not need routing.

3. Open the Config tab for your VCSA and click the Configure button on the Settings ➢ vCenter HA page.

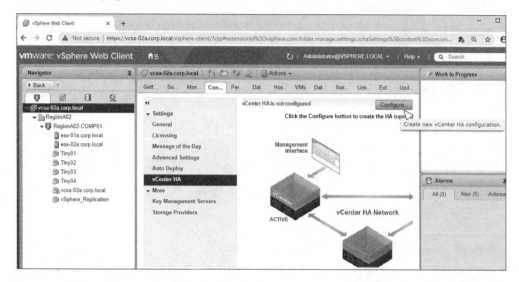

4. Leave Basic selected and click Next.

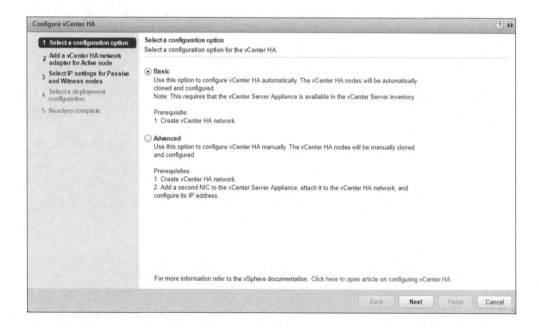

EXERCISE 10.3 *(continued)*

5. Enter the vCenter HA network IP address for the active node and select the port group (network) to use.

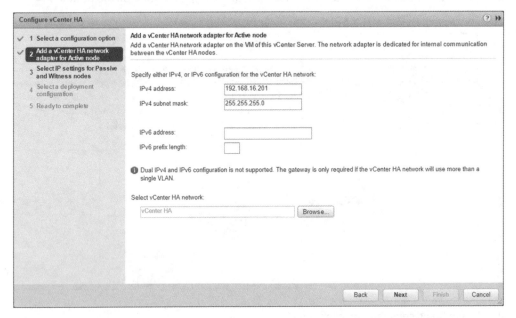

6. Enter the vCenter HA network IP addresses for the passive and witness nodes.

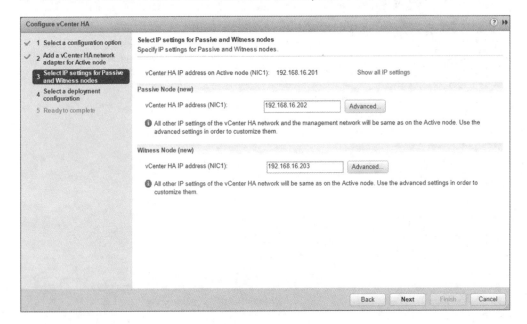

7. Verify that the selected configuration is appropriate for your environment and check any compatibility errors or warnings.

8. Double-check your settings and then click Finish to start the clone process.

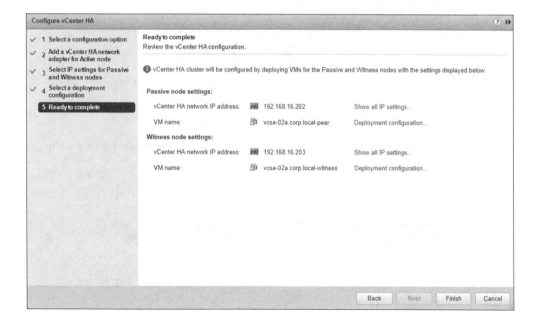

9. Monitor the deployment via vCenter and watch the Monitor tab for vCenter HA to complete the process and start replicating.

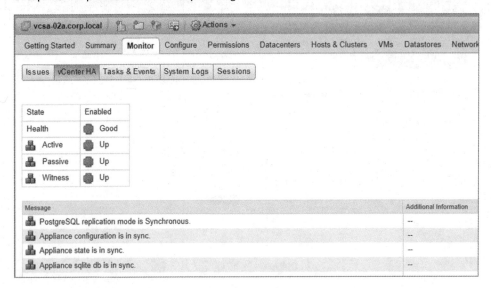

10. When vCenter HA shows that its health is Good, suspend the active VCSA.

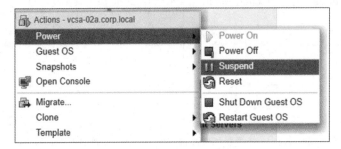

11. You can monitor the failover by pinging the public IP of the vCenter server or waiting for the web client to resume.

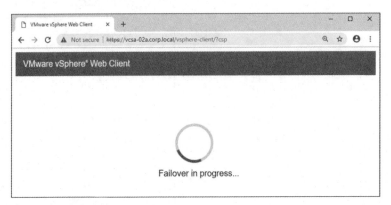

12. Verify that the passive appliance has taken over and the vCenter HA is in a degraded state.

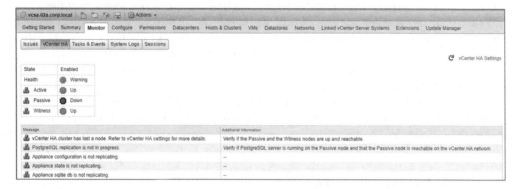

13. Unsuspend the original active node and verify that vCenter HA has a Good status.

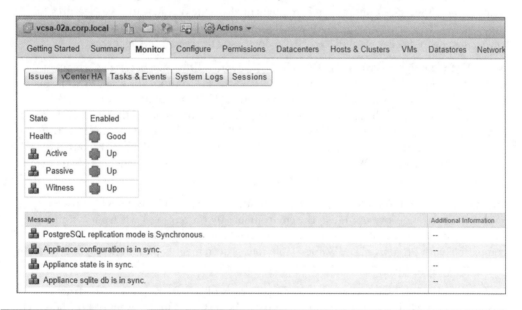

Summary

In a production vSphere environment, ensuring that the virtual machines are available is a priority. Part of keeping virtual machines available is recovering them from a failed host and reviving virtual machines that experienced a failure. Using vSphere High Availability, you can configure automated recovery from those scenarios.

The primary purpose of vSphere HA is to restart VMs from a failed host onto a running host, and this feature is turned on if all you do is enable High Availability. However, HA has the ability to also monitor virtual machines (using VMware Tools) and restart the VM if the OS or an application being monitored stops. HA can also recover from storage issues on a host, where virtual machines can be restarted on other hosts not experiencing an issue.

New to vSphere 6.5, High Availability can also be proactive, leveraging vendor monitoring tools to evacuate virtual machines from hosts that experience problems such as failed power supply or overheating.

Also new to vSphere 6.5 is the ability to create an active/passive cluster from a VCSA. With vCenter HA, you can increase the availability of your vCenter server to improve management uptime.

Exam Essentials

Understand vSphere HA and how it is implemented.   One of VMware's key features for many years, HA's primary goal is to restart VMs from failed hosts. Know that this is a per-cluster setting and the VMs will experience downtime during an HA recovery.

Know VM Component Protection (VMCP).   Know the difference between Permanent Device Loss (PDL) and All Paths Down (APD) and the HA options for each. PDL means the array has reports (via SCSI code) that the storage device is no longer available. APD means the storage can't be reached by your host. The key difference is that with PDL, the array is reporting that the storage is gone while APD means the host has no idea why it can't reach the storage. PDL assumes your VMs need to be powered off and restated on a host that can reach them. With APD, you have a conservative option where HA won't stop VMs before it determines that other hosts can restart them.

Describe Proactive HA and know its requirements.   Proactive HA is a new feature in vSphere and can improve uptime in the environment by preventing VMs from running on suspect hosts. However, it requires your server vendor to provide a monitoring solution compatible with Proactive HA. While an obvious requirement is that all hosts must be from the same vendor, your vendor may have other requirements.

Understand HA admission control.   Admission control is there to prevent you from starting more VMs in your environment than can be restarted in the event of host failure(s). Admission control has three methods for calculating how much capacity to reserve for the event of a failure: Slot Policy, Cluster Resource Percentage, and Dedicated failover hosts.

Know Slot Policy vs. Cluster Resource Percentage.   Two of the admission control policies use calculations and VM reservations to determine how much CPU and memory capacity to hold in reserve. Slot Policy uses the maximum RAM reservation and the maximum CPU reservation to set a "slot" size. Each running VM takes up one slot, and enough extra slots are reserved to account for a host to fail. Cluster Resource Percentage keeps free the amount of resources that equal the CPU and memory capacity of one host.

Understand vCenter HA architecture.   With vCenter HA, there are three virtual machines set up in an active-passive-witness trio. The passive and witness appliances are clones of the active appliance and can be created by the Enable wizard using Basic mode or by the administrator manually if the Advanced option is used.

Be able to describe the requirements for vCenter HA.   You can only enable vCenter HA on a vSphere 6.5 VCSA with SSH enabled. If the appliance is not managing itself or is not managed by a vCenter server in the same SSO domain, you must use the Advanced option. You need a separate network for the HA traffic. The Advanced option requires the admin to add a second NIC on the HA network prior to cloning and use the Guest Customization option to change the host name and IPs before the Advanced option wizard is completed.

Review Questions

The answers to the chapter review questions can be found in the Appendix.

1. What is the minimum licensing level required for vSphere High Availability?
   - **A.** Essentials
   - **B.** Essentials Plus
   - **C.** Standard
   - **D.** Platinum

2. What recovery is provided if no High Availability configuration is performed beyond enabling HA on a cluster?
   - **A.** Host failure
   - **B.** Storage failure
   - **C.** vCenter failure
   - **D.** Virtual machine failure

3. Which options should be used if the default gateway of the management network does not respond to ICMP? (Choose two.)
   - **A.** *das.failuredetectiontime*
   - **B.** *das.isolationaddress0*
   - **C.** *das.usedefaultisolationaddress*
   - **D.** *das.isolationshutdowntimeout*

4. Which admission control policy should be used when regulations require passive failover capacity?
   - **A.** Slot Policy
   - **B.** Cluster resource percentage
   - **C.** Host Failures Cluster Tolerates
   - **D.** Dedicated failover hosts

5. Which admission control policy should be used when virtual machines have very different reservation settings for CPU and memory?
   - **A.** Slot Policy
   - **B.** Cluster resource percentage
   - **C.** Host Failures Cluster Tolerates
   - **D.** Dedicated failover hosts

6. Which admission control policy should be used when virtual machines have very similar resource reservations?
   - **A.** Slot Policy
   - **B.** Cluster resource percentage

C. Host Failures Cluster Tolerates

D. Dedicated failover hosts

7. Which admission control policy, when configured by vSphere, could result in resource fragmentation?

A. Slot Policy (fixed slot size)

B. Cluster resource percentage

C. Host Failures Cluster Tolerates

D. Dedicated failover hosts

8. What could prevent virtual machines from restarting during a failure in an environment using a Slot size policy that covers all powered-on virtual machines?

A. A new virtual machine with a very large reservation

B. Fragmented resources

C. DRS affinity rules

D. Performance degradation set to 0%

9. Which option will set a warning if the environment is anticipated to have insufficient performance during a failure?

A. Cluster resource percentage set to 0%

B. Cluster resource percentage set to 100%

C. Performance degradation set to 0%

D. Performance degradation set to 100%

10. An environment has the following virtual machines in a cluster configured with the default Slot Policy admission control.

•   Twenty virtual machines with a 500 MHz CPU reservation

•   Twenty virtual machines with a 750 MHz CPU reservation

•   Five virtual machines with a 3000 MHz CPU reservation

An administrator cannot power on a new virtual machine. What are two options that could allow the administrator to power on the VM? (Choose two.)

A. Remove the CPU reservation on the new VM.

B. Reduce the 500 MHz reservations to 250 MHz.

C. Reduce the 750 MHz reservations to 500 MHz.

D. Reduce the 3000 MHz reservations to 750 MHz.

11. An environment has the following virtual machines in a cluster configured with the default Slot Policy admission control.

•   Twenty virtual machines with a 500 MHz CPU reservation and 1024 MB memory reservation

•   Twenty virtual machines with a 750 MHz CPU reservation and no memory reservation, 250 MB overhead

- Five virtual machines with a 3000 MHz CPU reservation and no memory reservation, 512 MB overhead

What is the slot size currently in use?

A. 500 MHz and 1 GB

B. 3000 MHz and 1 GB

C. 3000 MHz and 512 MB

D. 3000 MHz and 1786 MB

12. What options are available if a monitored VM appliance stops sending heartbeats?

A. Restart the VM on a new host.

B. Power off the VM after confirming that another host has connectivity.

C. Restart the guest OS.

D. Restart the application.

13. What could account for a virtual machine configured for VM monitoring not being restarted after a failure? (Choose two.)

A. No VMware Tools.

B. VM failed too quickly.

C. HA cannot find a host that can access the datastore.

D. Admission control is disabled.

14. Which HA technologies require vendor support for implementation? (Choose two.)

A. Proactive HA

B. VMCP

C. Heartbeat datastores

D. Application monitoring

15. What components are required for vCenter High Availability? (Choose two.)

A. VCSA

B. Load balancer

C. Windows server

D. Dedicated network

16. Which HA failure scenarios will not allow usage of vCenter?

A. Witness appliance failure

B. Active appliance failure

C. Passive or witness appliance failure

D. Passive and witness appliance failure

17. What steps are required to be taken manually for the vCenter HA Basic option? (Choose two.)

   A. Add a second NIC.

   B. Enable SSH.

   C. Clone the VCSA.

   D. Create a new network.

18. What manual steps are required for the Advanced option for vCenter HA? (Choose two.)

   A. Clone the VCSA.

   B. Customize the guest.

   C. Configure PostgreSQL replication.

   D. Enable VMCP.

19. Which step should be taken prior to initiating infrastructure changes in an environment configured for vCenter HA?

   A. Set the host to maintenance mode.

   B. Suspend the witness and passive nodes.

   C. Initiate a failover before working on the active host.

   D. Set vCenter HA to maintenance mode.

20. What is the default number of heartbeat datastores per host?

   A. One

   B. Two

   C. Three

   D. Same as the number of hosts in the cluster

21. How many more virtual machines without a reservation can be started in this environment? (See exhibit.)

Advanced Runtime Info	
Slot size	1000 MHz 68 MB
Total slots in cluster	20
Used slots	2
Available slots	8
Failover slots	10
Total powered-on virtual machines in cluster	2
Total hosts in cluster	2
Total good hosts in cluster	2

Refresh

   A. 20

   B. 2

C. 8

D. No limit

22. How many slots will a virtual machine with a 200 MB reservation take in this environment? (See exhibit.)

▾ Advanced Runtime Info	□
Slot size	1000 MHz 68 MB
Total slots in cluster	20
Used slots	2
Available slots	8
Failover slots	10
Total powered-on virtual machines in cluster	2
Total hosts in cluster	2
Total good hosts in cluster	2
	Refresh

A. One

B. Two

C. Three

D. Four

Chapter 11

Administering and Managing vSphere Virtual Machines

2V0-21.19 EXAM OBJECTIVES COVERED IN THIS CHAPTER:

✓ **Section 1 – VMware vSphere Architectures and Technologies**

- Objective 1.10 – Describe virtual machine (VM) file structure
- Objective 1.11 – Describe vMotion and Storage vMotion technology

✓ **Section 4 – Installing, Configuring, and Setting Up a VMware vSphere Solution**

- Objective 4.2 – Create and configure vSphere objects
- Objective. 4.3 – Set up a content library

✓ **Section 5 – Performance-tuning and Optimizing a VMware vSphere Solution**

- Objective 5.1 – Determine effective snapshot use cases
- Objective 5.3 – Identify impacts of VM configurations

✓ **Section 7 – Administrative and Operational Tasks in a VMware vSphere Solution**

- Objective 7.7 – Perform different types of migrations
- Objective 7.9 – Create and manage VMs using different methods
- Objective 7.10 – Create and manage templates

Running virtual machines is the main objective of a vSphere environment. While the VMware vSphere 6.7 Foundations Exam 2019 covers creating virtual machines, it doesn't address advanced information and options that are covered, along with Content Library and Converter tools, on the VMware Certified Professional exam.

This chapter will include a more in-depth discussion of the configuration files that make up virtual machines and exist behind the GUI and how changes to the virtual machine are reflected in those files. I will also address some advanced topics around virtual processor configuration, optional virtual hardware, and the effect USB devices can have in an environment.

The second part of this chapter will go into detail around content libraries, a vSphere-integrated method of sharing VM and vApp templates and other files across vSphere environments. A central repository of VMs encourages consistency and compliance in the environment and improves efficiencies when templates don't have to be manually created in or copied to environments.

Finally, I will address a method of creating virtual machines using the Converter tool. While primarily used for Physical-to-Virtual (P2V) migration, the tool could also be used to import virtual machines, and there are a variety of options around managing the migration process. Although the frequency of P2V conversions has been in sharp decline as virtualization has become a vital part of the modern datacenter, Converter is still a useful tool.

Virtual Machine Advanced Settings

Virtual machines primarily consist of a .vmx configuration file and a boot device, which is normally a pair of files: a .vmdk configuration file and a flat.vmdk data file. While the .vmdk files are the virtual hard drive presented to the virtual machine, the .vmx file holds all of the configuration information for the VM—such as CPU and memory and network configuration. The .vmx file is a plaintext file and can be manually edited if needed.

One of the key settings for a virtual machine is the operating system, which controls the default settings for the virtual machine (including default storage and network controllers), the minimum and maximum for various settings, and which virtual machine features are available for the virtual machine. If you cannot set a specific value for a virtual machine, check the operating system setting. Other limiting factors for VM values include host hardware and virtual machine hardware version. Examples of these limitations are shown in Figure 11.1, Figure 11.2, Figure 11.3, and Figure 11.4.

FIGURE 11.1   Setting the operating system to Windows 95 as shown in 11.a will limit you to one CPU and 2 GB RAM as shown in 11.b.

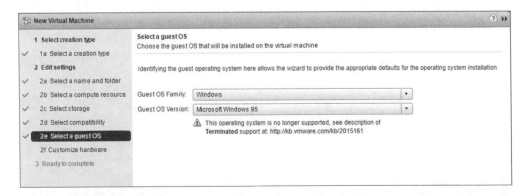

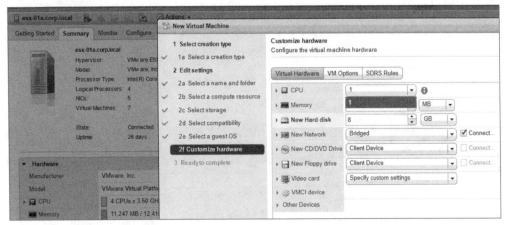

FIGURE 11.2   A VM cannot be created with more vCPUs than the host has logical processors.

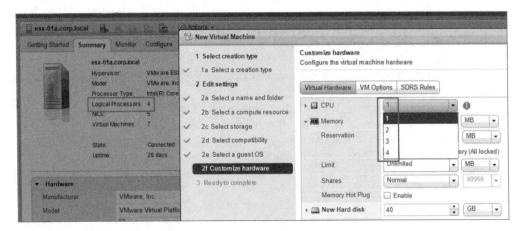

FIGURE 11.3   Hot Plug cannot be enabled if the operating system is Other 32-bit Linux.

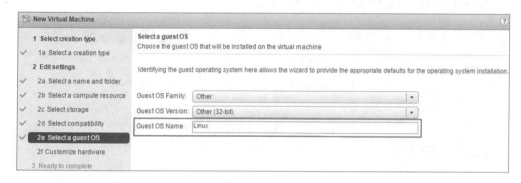

These are examples of limitations set by the OS selected, VM hardware version, and host configuration and do not represent a comprehensive list.

Virtual Machine Configuration File

When a virtual machine is edited in the GUI, the .vmx file for that VM is modified to match. A VM with hardware version 8, one vCPU, and 48 MB of RAM is shown in Figure 11.5.

The partial .vmx file for the VM is shown in Figure 11.6. I have removed most of the lines from the file to illustrate the basics—the hardware version of the VM, the memory configured, the hard drive (.vmdk) filename, the name of the VM, and the guest OS selected. The number of CPUs is not shown as the setting is not always present if there is just one vCPU.

FIGURE 11.4   If the virtual machine hardware version is 4, you cannot add a VMXNET3 network adapter.

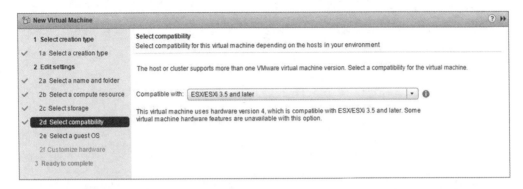

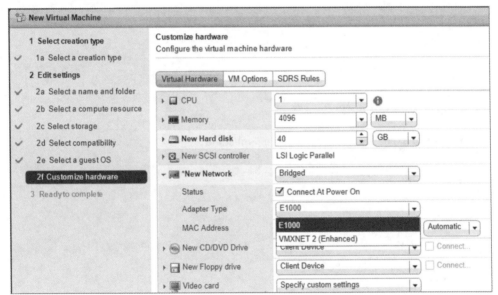

The hardware version for the virtual machine has been upgraded to 13 (the version compatible with vSphere 6.5 and above), the RAM increased to 64 MB, and a second vCPU added. The updated VM is shown in Figure 11.7.

The .vmx file now shows the changes. The virtualHW.version is now 13, memSize is 64, and the numvcpus setting has been added with a value of 2, as shown in Figure 11.8.

When adding multiple vCPUs to a virtual machine, you have the option of presenting multiple cores per processor to the guest. This can come in handy if your guest OS or application licensing has processor/core requirements. A virtual machine with four vCPUs is

FIGURE 11.5 Virtual machine as shown in the WebClient

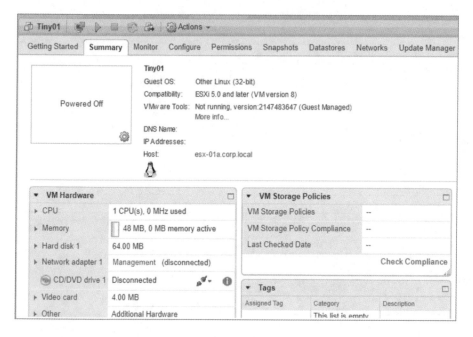

FIGURE 11.6 The .vmx file for the virtual machine

```
[root@esx-01a:/vmfs/volumes/5b234fbe-49c4d954-a62a-000c296bdd1d/Tiny01] cat Tiny01.vmx
.encoding = "UTF-8"
config.version = "8"
virtualHW.version = "8"
....
memSize = "48"
....
ide0:0.fileName = "Tiny01.vmdk"
ide0:0.present = "TRUE"
....
ethernet0.virtualDev = "e1000"
ethernet0.generatedAddress = "00:50:56:94:75:2d"
ethernet0.present = "TRUE"
displayName = "Tiny01"
guestOS = "linux"
uuid.bios = "42 14 91 30 fb ef 91 cb-70 c0 0c 9f 4d 40 8f 5f"
```

shown in Figure 11.9 along with the available cores per socket options. With four vCPUs set for the virtual machine, you have the options of presenting the guest with one CPU with four cores, two CPUs with two cores each, or four CPUs with one core each. You set this by choosing how many cores each CPU will have.

Changing the core count adds a new setting, cpuid.coresPerSocket, to the .vmx file, as shown in Figure 11.10.

FIGURE 11.7   Updated virtual machine as shown in the web client

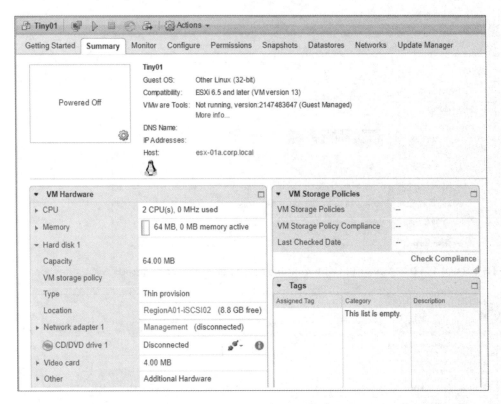

FIGURE 11.8   The vmx file for the updated virtual machine

```
[root@esx-01a:/vmfs/volumes/5b234fbe-49c4d954-a62a-000c296bdd1d/Tiny01] cat Tiny01.vmx
.encoding = "UTF-8"
config.version = "8"
virtualHW.version = "13"
...
memSize = "64"
...
ide0:0.fileName = "Tiny01.vmdk"
ide0:0.present = "TRUE"
...
ethernet0.virtualDev = "e1000"
ethernet0.generatedAddress = "00:50:56:94:75:2d"
ethernet0.present = "TRUE"
displayName = "Tiny01"
guestOS = "linux"
uuid.bios = "42 14 91 30 fb ef 91 cb-70 c0 0c 9f 4d 40 8f 5f"
numvcpus = "2"
```

When a hard drive is added to a virtual machine, the .vmx file of the VM is updated with the location of the .vmdk configuration file and the virtual controller presented to the VM for local storage access. Figure 11.11 shows the GUI view and a partial .vmx file for a virtual machine with the LSI Logic SAS controller and one hard drive.

FIGURE 11.9 Setting multiple cores per socket for a virtual machine

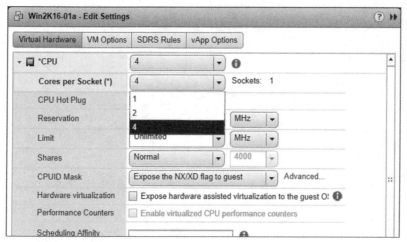

FIGURE 11.10 A .vmx file with multiple cores per socket configured

The .vmdk configuration file will include geometry information and the location of the binary *-flat*.vmdk file as shown in Figure 11.12.

If a snapshot is taken of the virtual machine, the VM's .vmx file is updated with the .vmdk location of the current snapshot location, Win2K16-01a-000001.vmdk (Figure 11.13).

A new .vmdk pair is created that consists of a .vmdk configuration file and a *-sparse*. vmdk file (see Figure 11.14). The *-sparse* file holds changes that the virtual machines writes to its hard drive after the snapshots are committed to the new *-flat*.vmdk. While a *-flat*. vmdk file can be thin or thick provisioned, the *-sparse* file is always thin provisioned.

FIGURE 11.11 GUI and .vmx file for a VM with a SCSI drive

```
.encoding = "UTF-8"
config.version = "8"
...
scsi0.virtualDev = "lsisas1068"
scsi0.present = "TRUE"
scsi0:0.deviceType = "scsi-hardDisk"
scsi0:0.fileName = "Win2K16-01a.vmdk"
```

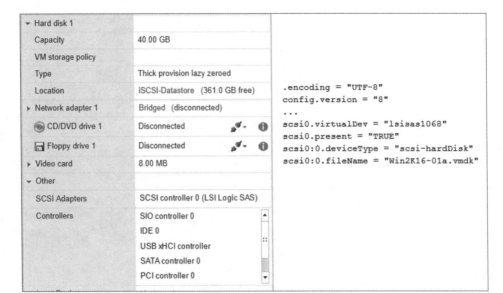

FIGURE 11.12 The configuration file for a virtual hard drive

```
[root@esx-01a:/vmfs/volumes/5b737f0a-20597b2a-caa2-000c29a1cff7/Win2K16-01a] cat Win2K16-01a.vmdk
# Disk DescriptorFile
version=1
encoding="UTF-8"
CID=fffffffe
parentCID=ffffffff
isNativeSnapshot="no"
createType="vmfs"

# Extent description
RW 83886080 VMFS "Win2K16-01a-flat.vmdk"

# The Disk Data Base
#DDB

ddb.adapterType = "lsilogic"
ddb.geometry.cylinders = "5221"
ddb.geometry.heads = "255"
ddb.geometry.sectors = "63"
ddb.longContentID = "ed5e8075419cb4b1355002c1fffffffe"
ddb.uuid = "60 00 C2 91 b3 2f ba 70-26 d2 16 5e 7b f6 99 ab"
ddb.virtualHWVersion = "13"
```

The snapshot .vmdk file includes a link to the "parent" .vmdk configuration file as shown in Figure 11.15.

When the snapshot is removed, the changes from the *-sparse* file are written to the *-flat* file, the *-sparse* and its .vmdk are removed, and the virtual machine's .vmx file is updated to point to the .vmdk for the *-flat* file.

FIGURE 11.13 Updated vmx after a snapshot

```
[root@esx-01a:/vmfs/volumes/5b737f0a-20597b2a-caa2-000c29a1cff7/Win2K16-01a] cat Win2K16-01a.vmx
.encoding = "UTF-8"
config.version = "8"
virtualHW.version = "13"
...
scsi0:0.deviceType = "scsi-hardDisk"
scsi0:0.fileName = "Win2K16-01a-000001.vmdk"
sched.scsi0:0.shares = "normal"
```

FIGURE 11.14 New .vmdk pair created for the snapshot

```
[root@esx-01a:/vmfs/volumes/5b737f0a-20597b2a-caa2-000c29a1cff7/Win2K16-01a] ls -l -h
total 41944128
-rw-------    1 root      root        165.0M Nov 20 17:26 Win2K16-01a-000001-sesparse.vmdk
-rw-------    1 root      root           340 Nov 20 17:26 Win2K16-01a-000001.vmdk
-rw-r--r--    1 root      root           242 Nov 12 18:48 Win2K16-01a-268148ba.hlog
-rw-------    1 root      root         10.1K Nov 20 17:26 Win2K16-01a-Snapshot1.vmsn
-rw-------    1 root      root         40.0G Nov 12 18:48 Win2K16-01a-flat.vmdk
-rw-------    1 root      root           473 Nov 12 18:48 Win2K16-01a.vmdk
-rw-r--r--    1 root      root           419 Nov 20 17:26 Win2K16-01a.vmsd
-rwxr-xr-x    1 root      root          2.0K Nov 20 17:26 Win2K16-01a.vmx
```

FIGURE 11.15 The snapshot .vmdk showing the parent .vmdk

```
[root@esx-01a:/vmfs/volumes/5b737f0a-20597b2a-caa2-000c29a1cff7/Win2K16-01a] cat Win2K16-01a-000001.vmdk
# Disk DescriptorFile
version=1
encoding="UTF-8"
CID=ffffffe
parentCID=ffffffe
isNativeSnapshot="no"
createType="seSparse"
parentFileNameHint="Win2K16-01a.vmdk"
# Extent description
RW 83886080 SESPARSE "Win2K16-01a-000001-sesparse.vmdk"

# The Disk Data Base
#DDB

ddb.grain = "8"
ddb.longContentID = "ed5e8075419cb4b1355002c1ffffffe"
[root@esx-01a:/vmfs/volumes/5b737f0a-20597b2a-caa2-000c29a1cff7/Win2K16-01a]
```

Advanced Virtual Machine Options

There are quite a few advanced options available from the virtual machine settings window that are available to resolve compatibility issues, provide guest operating systems with greater insight into host resources, and make it easier to manage large environments.

CPU Settings

There are a few advanced CPU settings, as shown in Figure 11.16, that affect the features available to guest vCPUs. These features are normally changed at the behest of application vendor support or VMware support to resolve or avoid issues.

FIGURE 11.16   Virtual machine CPU settings

CPUID Mask   This setting toggles the guest's ability to use AMD's NX or Intel's XD feature set.

CPUID Mask > Advanced   This will open the CPU Identification Mask window where you can create specific mask strings. Before Enhanced vMotion Compatibility (EVC) was available, this was used to ensure vMotion compatibility between hosts with different CPUs.

Hardware Virtualization   Exposes CPU virtualization to the guest. Usually used to nest hypervisors.

Scheduling Affinity   Allows you to specify which CPU core or hyperthread the guest vCPUs will use.

CPU/MMU Virtualization A host can provide CPU and Memory Management Unit (MMU) virtualization using software and/or hardware, which can be set here or left on automatic.

Video Card Options

In Figure 11.17 we see the video card options available for virtual machines. While the defaults are sufficient for most workloads, you may need to make changes for specialty VMs.

FIGURE 11.17 Video card options

Specify Custom Settings This setting defaults to Specify Custom Settings but you could set it to Auto-detect Settings. This has the effect of setting a cap on the video resources used by VMs. In automatic mode, the video memory can increase dramatically if the connected resource has multiple high-resolution screens.

3D Graphics Enable this setting to allow your virtual machine additional video resources for 3D.

3D Renderer This setting can be set to Automatic, Software, or Hardware. If you choose Hardware, your host must have a compatible GPU. If Hardware is set, your virtual machine can only vMotion to hosts with hardware GPU. On Automatic, virtual machines can vMotion between hosts with and without GPUs.

3D Memory This setting defaults to 256 MB once 3D Graphics is enabled, but it can be changed to fit your needs.

Note that these options are separate from the capabilities of units like the NVIDIA Grid vGPU, which shows up in virtual machines as a separate PCI device as shown in Figure 11.18.

FIGURE 11.18 An NVIDIA Grid vGPU configured for a virtual machine

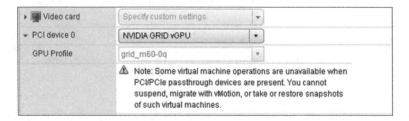

General and Remote Console Options

Moving to the VM Options tab, there are a few sections to look into, starting with General Options and VMware Remote Console Options, which are shown in Figure 11.19.

FIGURE 11.19 General Options and VMware Remote Console Options

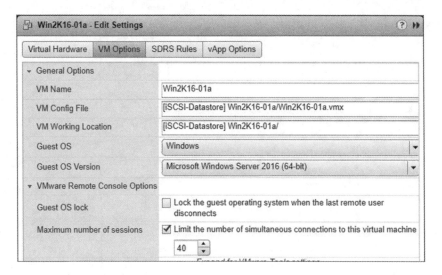

VM Working Location This sets the location of the temporary files such as .vswp plus the .vmem and .vmsn snapshot files. You can change this by adding the working-dir value to the .vmx file. Snapshot VMDKs are created in the same directory as the parent VMDK.

Guest OS and Guest OS Version These set the primary OS and version for the guest installed on the virtual machine. These settings only affect how vSphere treats the guest.

You can install any OS on the virtual machine. However, you will need to verify that the default VM hardware and settings are compatible with the guest you install.

Guest OS Lock   With a Windows guest, the guest desktop will be locked each time a user closes the VM console.

Maximum Number of Sessions   You can limit the number of vSphere consoles open to a virtual machine at one time.

VMware Tools

Additional options for virtual machines include the VMware Tools options (Figure 11.20) that set how the host will relate to the VMware Tools suite installed on the guest.

FIGURE 11.20   VMware Tools options

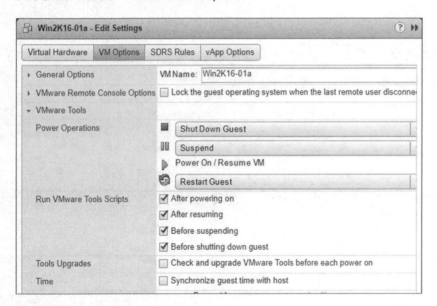

Run VMware Tools Scripts   VMware Tools includes scripts for each power change that can perform tasks such as release or renew an IP or respond to OS queries about shutting down.

Time   While virtual machines always get the time from the host at startup, you can set them to periodically get time updates from the host via VMware Tools. This is most useful for isolated or security VMs that have their network traffic restricted.

Boot Options

Figure 11.21 shows the available Boot Options settings for a VM that can change how a guest OS boots as well as ways to get into the VM BIOS settings.

FIGURE 11.21   Boot Options

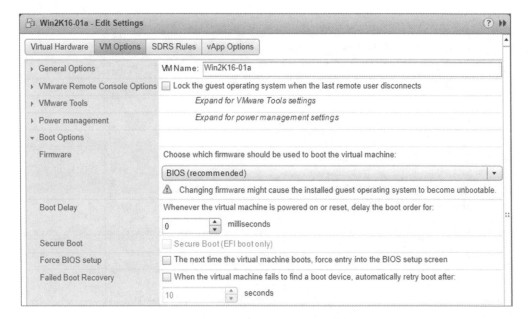

Firmware   The default is BIOS, but you can select the new Extensible Firmware Interface (EFI) boot mode if your operating system supports it.

Boot Delay   This sets a delay (in milliseconds) between power-on and booting the guest OS. This setting is useful if you want to change VM BIOS settings or select a boot device at startup.

Secure Boot   This setting enables UEFI secure boot, which requires the boot components of the VM to be signed. It also requires the EFI setting under Firmware.

Force BIOS Setup   Starts the virtual machine into the BIOS or EFI setup at the next power-on.

Failed Boot Recovery   Useful if your storage takes longer to bring up than your hosts, this setting will retry a boot attempt after a set delay if the storage is not available.

Advanced Options

The Advanced section of VM Options (Figure 11.22) includes ways to set where a VM's swap file is, indirect editing of the VMX file, and how DRS affects the VM.

Swap File Location   By default, all virtual machine files are in the same directory, selected when the VM was created. You can set the default location of the swap file for VMs at the cluster or host level or on a per-virtual-machine basis. You can also configure VMs to try to use the host settings and use the default directory if needed.

FIGURE 11.22   Advanced options

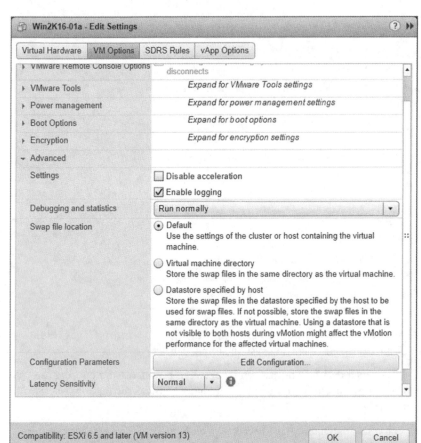

Edit Configuration   This will pull up a window where you can view and edit many of the settings in the VM's .vmx file. Not all settings are available, and if you add commands directly to the file, they will likely not show up here.

Latency Sensitivity   Setting a VM's latency sensitivity to High will create a soft affinity rule in DRS (if DRS is configured), which will reduce the likelihood that the VM will be moved. VMware suggests that a VM with Latency set to High should have the maximum CPU reservation set and will not power on unless all memory is reserved.

DirectPath I/O

You can give a virtual machine greater control and access to hardware on your host using DirectPath I/O, a VMware technology designed to give VMs direct access to hardware devices. If your host is equipped with a DirectPath I/O compatible network card or other PCI card, you can configure the host to allow DirectPath I/O access from virtual machines. From the virtual machine, you can then add the card directly to the VM. In most cases, this will prevent vMotion from working for that virtual machine; however, the Cisco USC platform allows vMotion if you have the Cisco UCS Virtual Machine Fabric Extender (VM-FEX) distributed switch.

SR-IOV

VMware vSphere supports Single Root I/O Virtualization (SR-IOV) for compatible Peripheral Component Interconnect Express (PCIe) devices. This allows virtual machines to bypass the VMkernel to reduce latency and CPU load. As with DirectPath I/O, you need to configure the host to allow SR-IOV before adding the appropriate SR-IOV component (a passthrough adapter) to the virtual machine.

While SR-IOV and DirectPath I/O are similar, SR-IOV allows sharing of the hardware with multiple virtual machines.

USB Considerations

You can present USB devices to virtual machines using either a client redirection (see Figure 11.23) or a virtual connection to the USB devices on the host as shown in Figure 11.24.

FIGURE 11.23 Connecting a USB device from a client

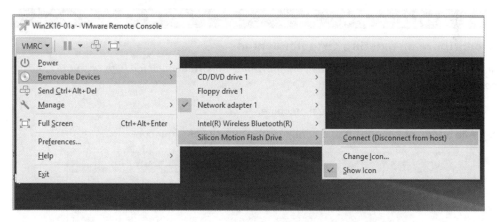

Virtual machines connected to USB resources on a host can still be vMotioned to a different host, assuming the USB device was enabled for vMotion when it was added to the host. See Figure 11.25 for the configuration message for a host-connected USB device enabled for vMotion.

You should disable VMware Distributed Power Management (DPM) for any host with a shared USB device to prevent DPM from powering off that host.

FIGURE 11.24 Connecting a host's USB device to a client

FIGURE 11.25 USB enabled for vMotion

EXERCISE 11.1

Reconfigure an existing virtual machine

Requires a vCenter server, ESXI host, and powered-off virtual machine with one vCPU and no snapshots.

1. Open the settings for the virtual machine.

2. Add a total of four vCPUs and configure the guest to see four cores.

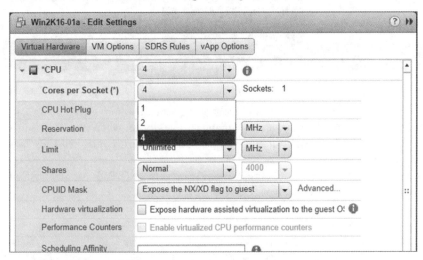

3. Open an SSH session to the host and examine the `.vmx` file for the virtual machine. Verify the `numvcpus` and `cupid.coresPerSocket` settings.

```
[root@esx-01a:/vmfs/volumes/5b737f0a-20597b2a-caa2-000c29a1cff7/Win2K16-01a] cat Win2K16-01a.vmx
.encoding = "UTF-8"
config.version = "8"
virtualHW.version = "13"
nvram = "Win2K16-01a.nvram"
...
numvcpus = "4"
cpuid.coresPerSocket = "4"
```

4. Verify that the `.vmx` file points to a `<vm name>.vmdk` file and make a note of the filename.

```
.encoding = "UTF-8"
config.version = "8"
...
scsi0.virtualDev = "lsisas1068"
scsi0.present = "TRUE"
scsi0:0.deviceType = "scsi-hardDisk"
scsi0:0.fileName = "Win2K16-01a.vmdk"
```

5. Take a snapshot of the virtual machine. Verify that the `.vmx` has a new entry for the VMDK file:

```
.encoding = "UTF-8"
config.version = "8"
...
scsi0.virtualDev = "lsisas1068"
scsi0.present = "TRUE"
scsi0:0.deviceType = "scsi-hardDisk"
scsi0:0.fileName = "Win2K16-01a-000001.vmdk"
```

Content Library

Content libraries are very useful central repositories for vSphere-related objects such as virtual machine templates and ISO files. Once one content library is created, other vCenter servers can subscribe to it, which allows them to access the files shared by that library. As shown in Figure 11.26, Content library management is accessed from the Home menu in the web client.

Once you have supplied a name for the library, you need to decide if this vCenter server will manage the files itself (a local library) or if it will subscribe to a library managed by a separate vCenter server. See Figure 11.27.

A local library has the option of being published for other vCenter servers to access it—and if it will be published, you can choose to optimize the catalog, which compresses the files immediately, allowing streams to be faster over HTTP and lower CPU utilization when

FIGURE 11.26 Managing content libraries

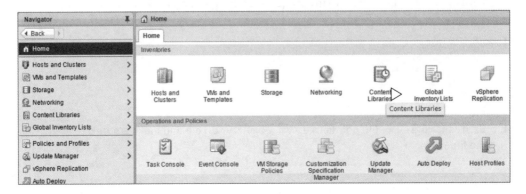

FIGURE 11.27 Choose local or subscribed for a new library.

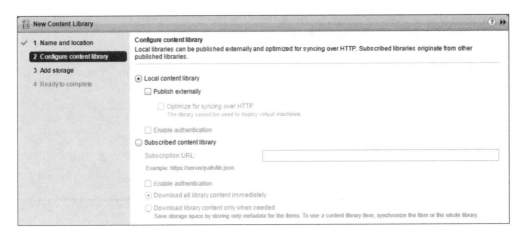

streaming. This is intended for environments where Enhanced Linked Mode (where multiple vCenter servers are connected into one domain) is not used. As shown by the alert in Figure 11.28, optimized catalogs cannot be used to deploy virtual machines by the hosting vCenter server. You can also not "unoptimize" a catalog. It would need to be deleted and re-created.

FIGURE 11.28 Warning message when optimizing a local library

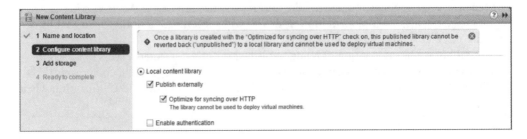

When a catalog is published, you have the option of setting a password as shown in Figure 11.29. The password will need to be set for a subscribing vCenter server.

FIGURE 11.29   Enabling authentication for a published library

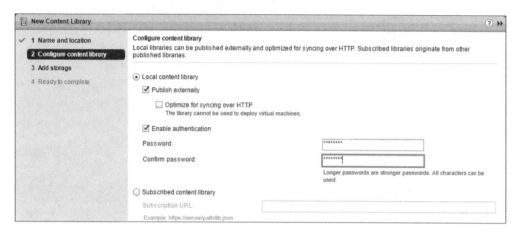

When configuring local storage (see Figure 11.30), note that SMB only works with Windows-installed vCenter servers. While a VCSA server will allow you to choose SMB, it will never connect to the share and will use local storage on the appliance for the library.

FIGURE 11.30   Configuring local storage

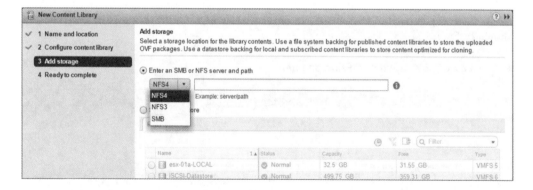

As shown in Figure 11.31, a subscribed library can download all content or only keep metadata for objects and download content as needed. This setting defaults to downloading all, but it can be set when the library is created or at any time later.

Keeping only the metadata results in greatly reduced network traffic and local storage, but attempting to use the objects will result in an error such as the one shown in Figure 11.32 when a VM is attempting to deploy using a library template that has not been synchronized.

FIGURE 11.31   Library options

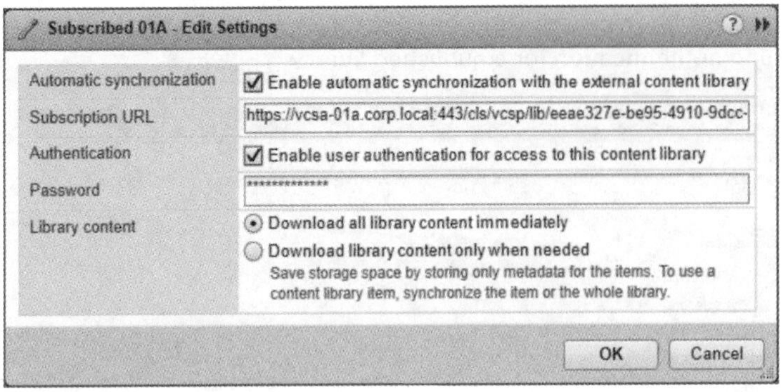

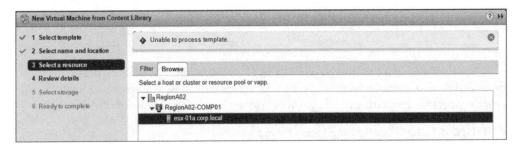

FIGURE 11.32   Deploying a template that is not synchronized

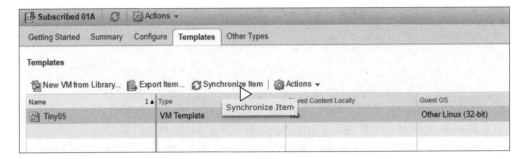

To resolve, you need to find the object in the library and select Synchronize Item as shown in Figure 11.33.

FIGURE 11.33   Synchronizing one item

Another option also shown in Figure 11.31 is the ability to turn off automatic synchronizations. This will prevent the subscribed library from receiving changes and can be useful to reduce the network traffic if many synchronized files are being added or updated.

When files need to be deployed from a catalog to an ESXi host, there are two modes: direct copy and streaming.

Direct copy mode—File copy from one host to another, used if the hosts are connected to the same vCenter server and the destination host doesn't have direct access to the datastore holding the files. This is also used for subscribed libraries where the vCenter servers are using Enhanced Linked Mode.

Streaming mode—HTTP file transfer used when Enhanced Linked Mode is not config-ured or when the library is hosted on an NFS or SMB share. This involves compressing and decompressing the files on the fly to improve transfer speeds.

While the Content Library's Transfer Service will initiate and monitor each of these file transfers, the data flow only directly involves the vCenter server when the library is hosted on an NFS or SMB share.

As shown in Figure 11.34, there are a series of privileges associated with the Content Library function in vCenter, and vCenter has a sample role created to make use of them.

FIGURE 11.34   User role and permissions

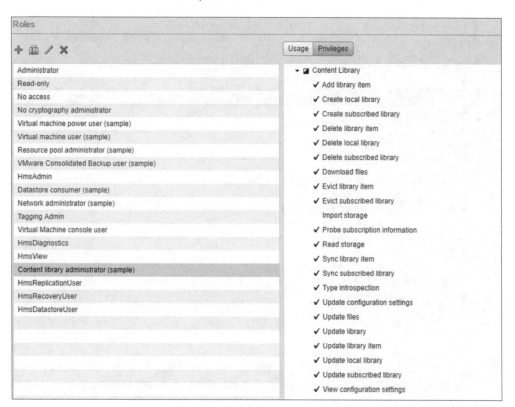

While this sample role would be useful to allow a user to manage the content library, it must be set at the vCenter level in the inventory, and the user will receive access to all of the libraries configured on that vCenter server.

EXERCISE 11.2

Create a subscribed content catalog

Requires two vCenter servers with one host each.

1. On one vCenter server, launch the Create a New Content Library Wizard.

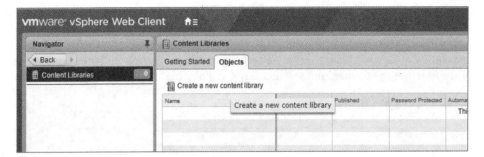

2. Give the new content library a name:

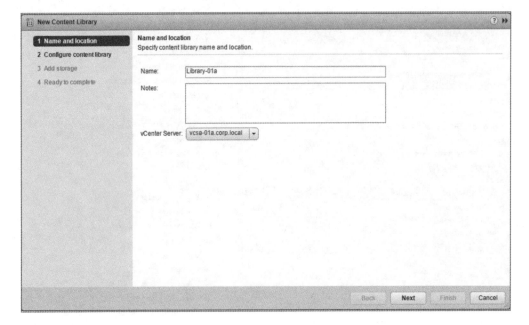

3. Select Local Content Library with Publish Externally and Enable Authentication. Enter and confirm a password.

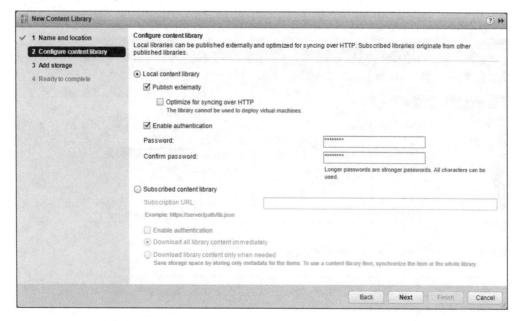

4. Select a datastore and finish the wizard.

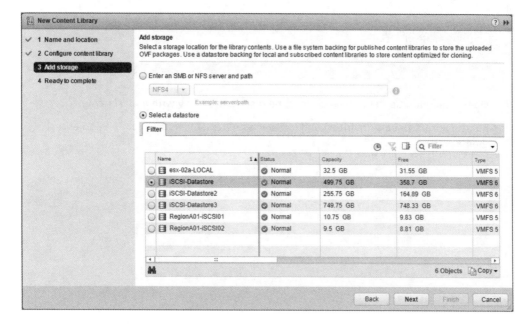

EXERCISE 11.2 *(continued)*

5. Open the settings for the new library.

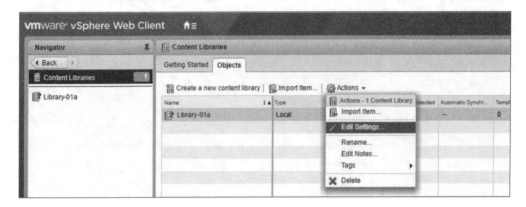

6. Copy the link for the published library.

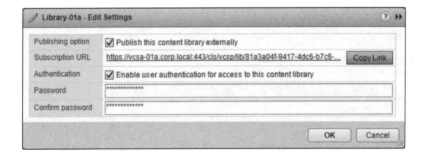

7. On the second vCenter server, create a new content library with a local name.

8. Set the library to be subscribed and paste the link. Enable authentication and enter the password.

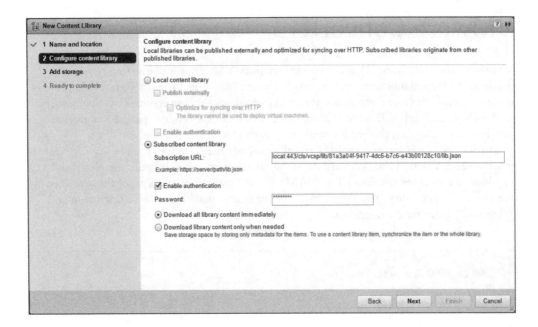

9. Select a datastore and complete the wizard.

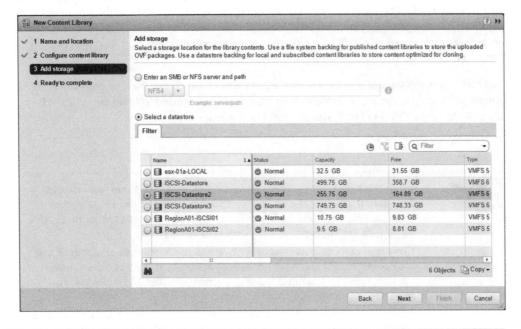

VMware Converter

VMware Converter Standalone is a free utility from VMware for converting physical machines to virtual machines and from other virtual machine formats. Careful planning is required as not all virtual machines are good candidates for conversion. Database servers such as SQL and Active Directory often work better using a vendor-specified migration process. Note also that the vendor might not support a P2V migration.

During the migration you should carefully evaluate the resources used by the physical machine and how that should translate to the virtual world. Just because the physical machine has 16 cores and 256 GB of RAM does not mean it requires all of those resources for proper functionality. You should monitor the source machine prior to migration and "rightsize" it during the migration.

Real World Scenario

The Importance of Rightsizing

While helping a company move to virtualization, I found a physical server that was managing the physical security of the building. Specifically, it managed the door locks and security cards. The server had two dual-core processors and 24 GB of RAM and was continuously pegged at 100 percent CPU. With a little research, I noticed that only two cores were ever in use, but it still did not seem to be a good candidate for P2V with the CPU usage.

After talking to the vendor and experimenting anyway, it turned out that the application simply used all CPU cycles available to it. In the end, the converted VM had two vCPUs, 6 GB of RAM, and a CPU limit of 2 GHz and ran fine for years.

While the exam will focus on converting physical machines, you should be aware that Converter will convert running Windows or Linux virtual machines on any VMware hypervisor, Hyper-V, Red Hat KVM, or RHEL XEN, as long as the VM is not using a paravirtualized kernel.

Converter can use powered-off VMware virtual machines as a source, but the converted VM will have hardware version 11. If the VM is on a newer version, it will be downgraded and any post–version 11 features will be removed.

VMware Converter can also migrate powered-off Hyper-V virtual machines; see the documentation for the specific list of host/VM combinations supported.

VMware Converter can migrate powered-on Windows or Linux servers (including those running as AWS EC2 instances) and can also migrate powered-off VMware or Hyper-V virtual machines; see the documentation for the specific list of host/VM combinations supported for virtual machine conversions.

During installation, you are prompted to select a setup type—either Local or Client-Server (See Figure 11.35)

FIGURE 11.35   Choose Local or Client-Server

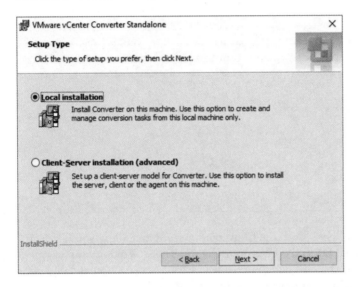

Converter has three installable components: server, agent, and client. The server does the actual work, the agent is installed on Windows machines to perform tasks such as quiescing, and the client is the GUI interface to the server. Choosing a local install places all of these components on the machine on which you are running the installer. Choosing Client-Server allows you to place the server and client components on one server and the agent on a different server. The Client-Server install is required to convert powered-on Linux machines as the Converter server will only install on Windows.

Once Converter has been installed, the client will allow you to launch the Converter Standalone client, as shown in Figure 11.36.

Whereas the Convert Machine button will take a running server and create a virtual machine copy of it, the Configure Machine button will take an existing VMware virtual machine and make changes to it. Existing vSphere or Workstation virtual machines can have VMware tools installed or Windows customization edited. You can also use the tool to get a virtual machine to boot properly with the Reconfigure Destination Virtual Machine option. This option will try some known repair methods for common issues to get the virtual machine to boot.

FIGURE 11.36   Choose Convert or Configure

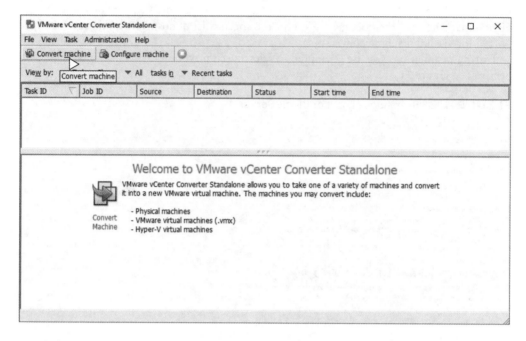

Clicking the Convert button will launch the Conversion wizard and allow you to select the source. If you select Powered On and a Linux remote source or a Windows server you have not installed the agent on, you will be prompted whether or not to automatically uninstall the agent after the conversion is complete, as shown in Figure 11.37.

FIGURE 11.37   Choose to uninstall the agent automatically

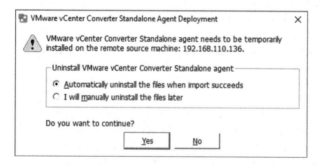

After the source has been chosen and connected (if remote), you are prompted to set the destination. For a VMware infrastructure virtual machine, you will need to enter either vCenter or ESXi credentials and set the inventory and storage options for the virtual machine. If you are not choosing vSphere as a destination, you need to select the hosting product and set the destination directory.

Once the destination has been set, you can edit the options for the virtual machine. These options include storage, devices, networks, services, and advanced options.

For storage options, you can choose to resize the existing disks as shown in Figure 11.38. There are three copy types for the Data Copy Type option:

Select volumes to copy—This is the only option for powered-on servers and will let you select and resize volumes and change the cluster size.

Copy all disks and maintain layout—This is the default for powered-off servers and copies the disks with no changes.

Linked Clone—Only available for vSphere source and destination, this creates a linked clone of the source virtual machine instead of a full copy of the virtual machine.

FIGURE 11.38   Editing the storage options

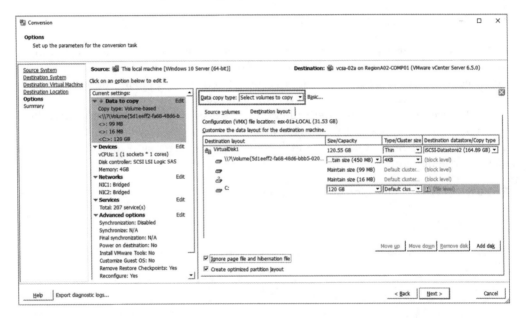

In Figure 11.38, the C: partition of the destination has been increased to 120 GB and the cluster size has been changed to the default size for the datastore (cluster). However, as this is different from the cluster size of the source, the copy mechanism has been changed to file instead of block. While block copy is faster, you cannot change the cluster size using block copy. Notice that the .vmx file location is listed (the datastore esx-01a-LOCAL in this instance) and there is a Destination Datastore drop-down (iSCSI-Datastore2 is selected here). You can use the drop-down list to change where the VMDKs will be placed during the conversion.

The Devices section will let you rightsize the memory and CPU of the destination VM, including choosing cores per CPU. As shown in Figure 11.39, you can also change the default storage controller; however, this is not recommended as other controllers might not have drivers installed in the OS.

FIGURE 11.39   Changing the CPU and storage controller

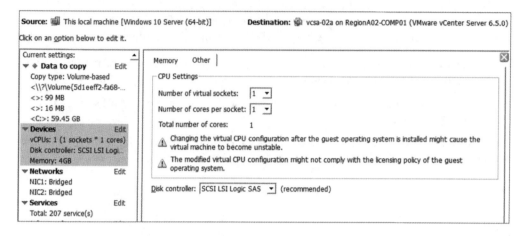

You can also change the number of network adapters, what networks they connect to, and whether they will be connected at the end of the conversion. If you are not planning on powering off the source virtual machine after the conversion, you should consider disabling the NICs on the destination so the IP address will not conflict.

The Services section (Figure 11.40) allows you to stop services before the migration and set service startup options on the destination. Some options for this would be disabling database services before a migration and disabling services for physical components such as an uninterruptible power supply.

FIGURE 11.40   Changing the services options

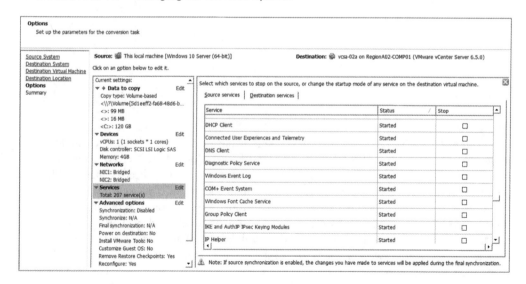

The last section for virtual machine settings is for the advanced options. Here you can enable synchronization—where after the initial copy, Converter will copy any changes since the copy started. Note that there are a few things that will prevent syncing, including resizing NTFS volumes or changing the cluster size.

Once you have the settings configured for how the destination machine will be configured, you can set throttling, as shown in Figure 11.41.

FIGURE 11.41   Throttling the conversion process

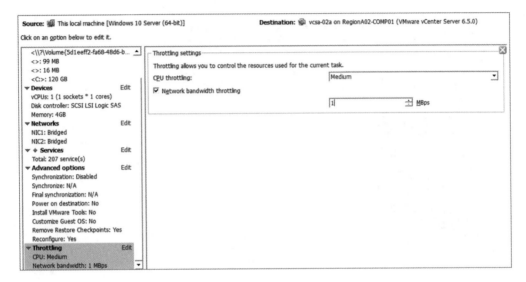

CPU throttling will affect the priority of the running conversion process and only affects powered-on Windows machines. The network throttling affects the bandwidth used to the destination ESXi host for VMware Infrastructure jobs.

EXERCISE 11.3

Convert a physical server to a vSphere virtual machine

Requires a physical Windows server and a vCenter server with a host. Assumes you have downloaded the Converter application to the Windows server.

1. Install the Converter application on the Windows server.

2. Choose Local Installation when prompted.

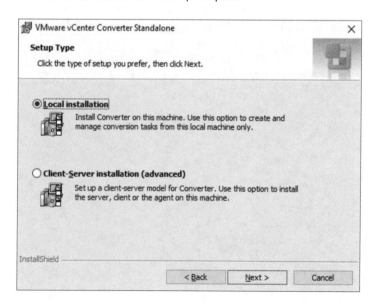

3. Launch the client after installation is complete.

4. Select Convert Machine.

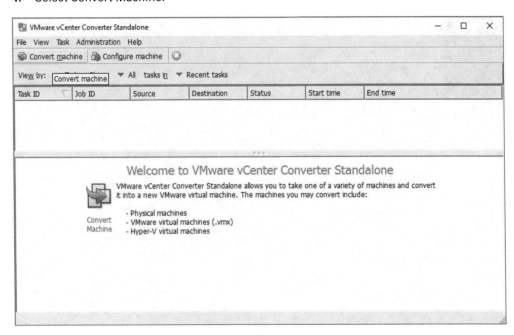

5. Choose Powered On and This Local Machine.

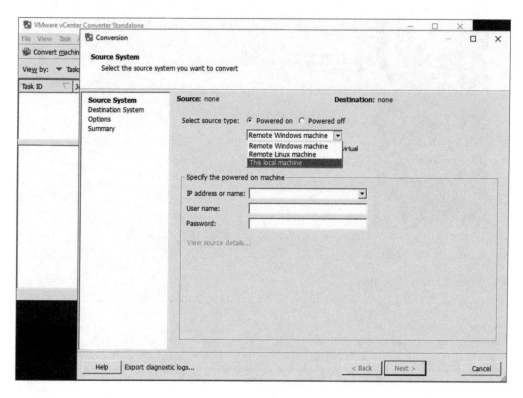

6. Choose VMware Infrastructure Virtual Machine and enter the credentials for the vCenter server.

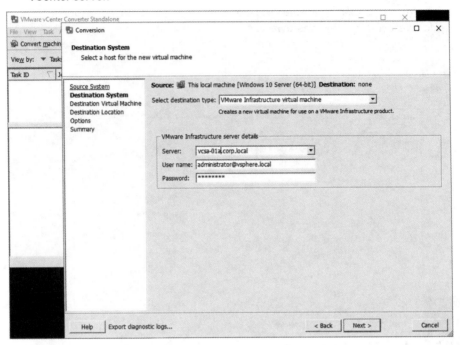

7. Select the virtual machine name and choose an inventory location for the converted virtual machine.

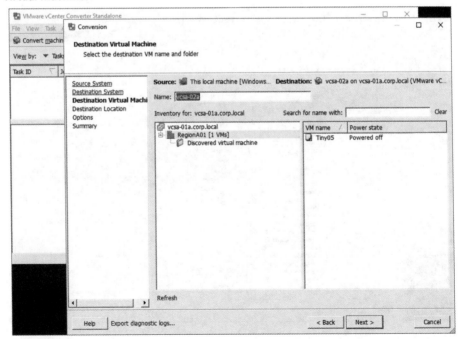

8. Choose the resource location for the virtual machine along with the datastore and version for the virtual machine hardware.

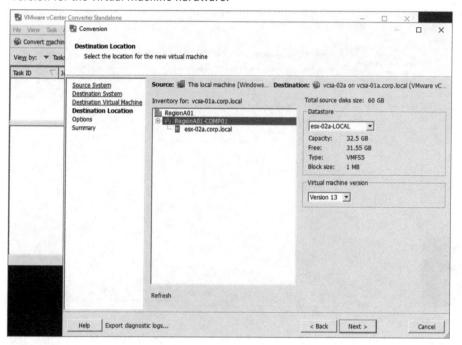

9. Verify that the storage information is correct and make any changes needed.

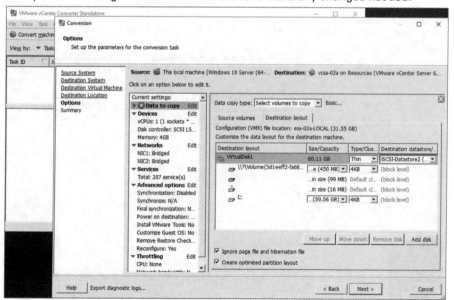

10. Make any other changes needed for the VM such as reduced CPU or memory. Set the appropriate network configuration also.

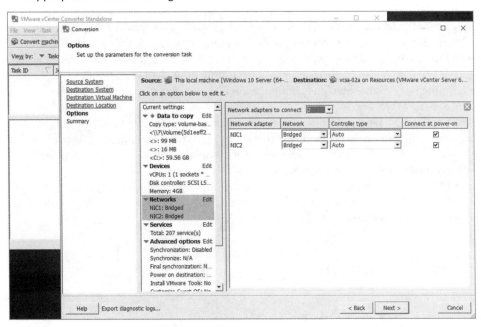

11. Verify that the choices are correct and click Finish to start converting the system.

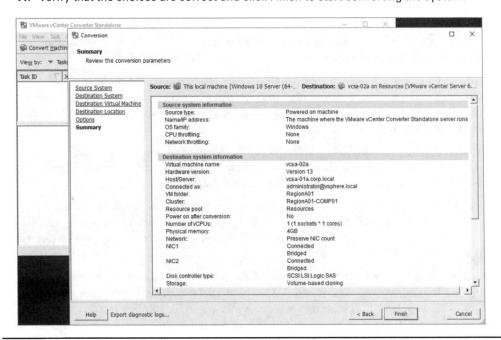

Summary

Running virtual machines is the main focus of any vSphere environment. Ensuring that virtual machines are created with the right options improves the reliability and efficiency of the environment and makes Day 2 operations easier. Knowing what options set defaults and add limitations is also important for understanding how virtual machines work, and understanding how virtual machine configuration files are structured makes troubleshooting easier.

Using the Content Library also improves efficiencies and reliability in the environment by both reducing duplicate work and ensuring that your virtual machines all start from the same known-good point. Using the subscription method also allows environments that are not fully meshed to still share resources in a read-only fashion.

The VMware Converter tool has been around for many years and is still useful for physical-to-virtual conversion. New features have been added, allowing it to work with third-party platforms and perform updates to VMware VMs.

Exam Essentials

Understand how VMX and VMDK files work. A virtual machine exists in the inventory as an object but sits on a datastore as a collection of files. The VMX file contains all of the virtual machine settings shown in the GUI and can be manually edited for advanced settings.

Know which VMX values correspond to which GUI options. Have a basic understanding of the most commonly used values, especially memory, CPU, and VMDK.

Understand CPU settings for a virtual machine. The ability to set the number of cores per processor presented to a virtual machine can help with licensing or OS limitations. Hiding NX/DX or setting the MMU might be needed for specific guests. CPU affinity lets you choose which physical cores to run on.

Know DirectPath I/O vs. SR-IOV. While both allow improved access to physical hardware for virtual machines, DirectPath I/O allows one VM to access the hardware device and SR-IOV can allow multiple VMs to access the hardware.

Understand the content library. Creating a library of files (templates or any file) on a vCenter server for access from the local hosts or publishing to remote vCenters results in a central repository of shared information. The library can be shared to vCenters that are not connected using Enhanced Linked Mode—and you can set a password on the share to secure it.

Know how VMware Converter Standalone works. Converter will convert powered-on physical machines or virtual machines to VMware virtual machines. There are limitations to know—like powered Linux machines need a Windows server running the server process. Know options such as the disk modes and file/block mode and understand throttling.

Review Questions

1. What are the minimum files needed to power on a virtual machine? (Choose three.)

   A. vm.vmx

   B. vm.vmsn

   C. vm-sparse.vmdk

   D. vm-flat.vmdk

   E. vm.vmdk

2. What core options are available if you are creating a VM with four CPUs on a host with eight logical processors?

   A. 1,2,3,4

   B. 1,2,4,8

   C. 1,2,4

   D. 1,4,8

3. What could restrict the number of CPUs an administrator can set on a VM?

   A. Host configuration

   B. Windows 2016 selected as the operating system

   C. CPUID Mask set to Hide

   D. CPU/MMU set to Automatic

4. What value might an administrator need to add to a .vmx file to change the number of CPUs a virtual machine has?

   A. cupid.coresPerSocket

   B. config.version

   C. parentCID

   D. numvcpus

5. Which files contain the data written to a virtual machine? (Choose two.)

   A. vm.vmdk

   B. vm-sparse.vmdk

   C. vm-flat.vmdk

   D. vm.vmsn

6. A virtual machine was created with one thin hard drive and one thick provisioned hard drive. If a snapshot is taken of the VM, how many thin provisioned disks will be referenced in the .vmx file?

   A. None

   B. One

    C. Two

    D. Depends on the storage policy

7. An administrator would like to modify an existing VM (see the following screen shot) to present one socket with eight cores to the guest OS. Which setting needs to be changed first?

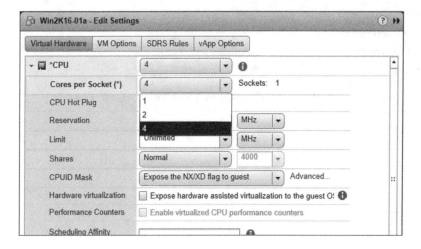

    A. Guest OS to a 64-bit OS

    B. CPU to 8

    C. Cores per Socket to 8

    D. Hardware version to 13

8. What is required before 3D Renderer can be set to Software for a new virtual machine??

    A. Guest OS to a 64-bit OS

    B. A supported GPU installed in the host

    C. 3D Graphics enabled

    D. Hardware version to 13

9. A developer has requested 4k display support for a virtual machine. What setting will accomplish that?

    A. Video card set to Auto

    B. Total video memory set to 16 MB

    C. 3D Graphics enabled

    D. A supported GPU installed in the host

10. Refer to the following screen shot. In what directory are the snapshot VMDKs stored for the virtual machine in the exhibit?

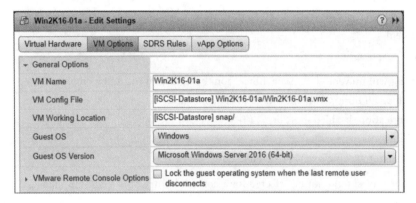

A. /Win2k16-01a

B. /snap

C. The directory specified by the host

D. The directory specified by the storage policy

11. What setting could best help an administrator choose an ISO image for a onetime boot?

A. Boot Delay

B. Force BIOS Setup

C. Secure Boot

D. Firmware

12. What setting could best help an administrator require manual intervention after a guest restart?

A. Boot Delay

B. Force BIOS Setup

C. Secure Boot

D. Firmware

13. What settings could best help an administrator prevent a rootkit virus from starting a VM? (Choose two.)

A. Boot Delay

B. Force BIOS Setup

C. Secure Boot

D. Firmware

14. What setting creates a DRS rule for the virtual machine?

    A. Latency Sensitivity

    B. Secure Boot

    C. SDRS rules

    D. Enable vApp options

15. What setting will prevent virtual machines from being deployed from a catalog?

    A. Download all library content immediately enabled

    B. Authentication disabled

    C. Publishing option enabled

    D. Optimize for syncing over HTTP enabled

16. What storage type should not be selected for a content library on a VCSA appliance?

    A. VMFS datastore

    B. SMB share

    C. NFS v3 share

    D. NFS v4 share

17. What could resolve the error shown in the following screen shot? (Choose two.)

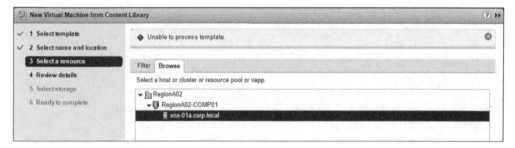

    A. Enable automatic synchronization

    B. Manually synchronize the item

    C. Add the template to the library again

    D. Change the library content setting to Immediately

18. What steps can resolve the error shown in the following screen shot? (Choose two.)

   A. Remove and re-add the USB device from the VM.

   B. Remove and re-add the USB device from the host.

   C. Configure the host to allow vMotion on the USB device.

   D. Configure the guest to allow vMotion on the USB device.

19. What could resolve the error shown in the following screen shot?

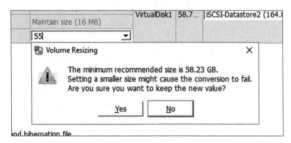

   A. Choose a larger datastore.

   B. Choose block for the copy type.

   C. Set a larger size for the partition.

   D. Set the VMDK to thin provisioned.

20. What could resolve the issue shown in the following screen shot?

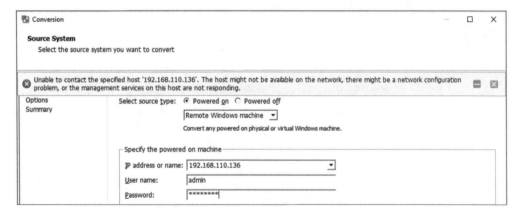

   A. Turn off the firewall on the source machine.

   B. Ensure that the ESXi host is reachable on the network.

   C. Ensure that the agent has been installed on the source machine.

   D. Ensure that the source files are in a compatible format.

Appendix

Answers to Review Questions

Chapter 1: What's New in vSphere 6.7

1. A. The management of VCSA services has been moved into the VAMI UI.

2. C. The Virtual Flash configuration has not yet moved to the HTML5 client.

3. B. The vSphere Management SDK includes the storage SDK, the vSAN.

4. C. All of these deployments support Enhanced Linked Mode, but VMware is recommending embedded PSCs for all deployments.

5. D. The Topology and Upgrade tool is an online utility used to ask questions and present a suggested solution.

6. C. The *vcsa-util* tool will converge or decommission external PSCs.

7. C. The *cmsso-util* can repoint vCenter servers, allowing you to merge or split vSphere SSO domains.

8. D. The loadESXCheckCompat script on the ESXI host will report on why Quick Boot isn't enabling.

9. A. Quick Boot only restarts the kernel, which can be far quicker than initializing the hardware during a full reboot.

10. C. Legacy virtual machines can be provisioned with drives created in Persistent Memory to improve their storage access time.

11. A. Using iSCSI across RDMA requires the iSER software adapter to be enabled on each host.

12. B. The Adaptive Resync feature will balance the I/O requirements of vSAN, primarily to ensure that VM I/O is prioritized over resync I/O during times of contention.

13. A. vSAN support for TRIM/UNMAP will drive storage efficiency by flagging for reuse blocks that guests have released.

14. A. WSFC is supported by using iSCSI targets accessed by the guest OS.

15. B. The latest storage technology, 4k, provides for higher efficient space utilization by reducing the number of gaps without the performance penalty of 512e.

16. A. TPM 2.0 security hardware is built into most modern servers and can be leveraged to ensure boot integrity for the ESXI host and guests running on the host.

17. D. The new VM hardware revision that ships with vSphere 6.7 is version 14. It is required for the 6.7-specific VM hardware such as NVDIMM.

18. B. OVA files are now converted to OVF during upload.

19. B, C. Virtual machines can be cloned to a Content Library as VM templates or converted to OVFs.

20. A. Setting the EVC option for a virtual machine improves portability by allowing it to migrate, resume, or have powered-on snapshots be started on more hosts.

Chapter 2: Configuring and Administering Security in a vSphere Datacenter

1. A. Privileges are very granular and can include actions like copying and pasting within a virtual machine or allowing the use of the datastore browser. To properly complete most actions, like the creation of a virtual machine, several privileges are required. When grouping privileges together, it makes sense to determine what actions are required by a user or group of users in their job role, then create a role that has all of those privileges.

2. A, B. When vSphere is initially deployed, several system roles are created by default to ensure that certain access levels are available at launch. These include the Administrator role and the No Access role, for example. Beyond these roles, organizations need to create customized roles to match their business needs. To simplify this process, VMware includes a number of sample roles covering typical infrastructure activities like creating virtual machines and administering datastores. These can be cloned and edited to create the exact roles required by the organization.

3. A. When a user belongs to multiple groups, they inherit the privileges of both groups. While this makes sense if you think about how they may need to take actions related to the role of each group, it is contrary to most security configurations.

4. A, C. Exception Users are users that can access the host even after it has been placed into Lockdown Mode. Regular auditing should be performed to ensure that the users in this group are valid and should have this degree of access. Another way to access an ESXi host is through SSH. SSH is disabled by default, but regular auditing should be performed to ensure that this remains disabled, or if it must be enabled, that the list of users who can access the host is closely monitored. Guest Operations and Datastore Access are both valid settings that should be properly secured, but these settings are specific to vCenter Server and not the host.

5. D. By default, log files on an ESXi host are stored in a scratch partition that is created during installation. Because the partition is configured as a ramdisk, data stored in the partition is not persistent. To ensure that log files are persistent, you can either change the log directory to a persistent location or change the scratch partition to a persistent location. However, since vm-support data is also stored in the scratch partition, moving this to a persistent location could result in the partition becoming full over time.

6.   C. By default, versions 1.0, 1.1, and 1.2 are all active. From a security hardening standpoint, VMware recommends disabling older versions. However, some third-party applications require TLS 1.1, so in some cases you may have to keep versions 1.1 and 1.2 and just disable 1.0. This can be done using the TLC Reconfiguration Utility. Version 1.3 was released in August 2018 but has not been widely incorporated and is not supported in vSphere 6.

7.   B. When Lockdown Mode is enabled using the **Strict** option, it is no longer possible to access the host using SSH or from the console unless the user is on the **Exception Users** list, in which case they can access the host from the console, via SSH, or from vCenter Server. Using this option does not force the use of the **Exception Users** list, it simply requires users to access the host via vCenter Server.

8.   C. All four of the components listed here are part of vCenter Single Sign-On. STS generates the tokens, the Administration Service allows configuration, vmdir provides an LDAP directory, and the Identity Management Service handles identity sources. Effective with vSphere 6.0, vmdir stores Single Sign-On and certification data. This component is also the piece that replicates this data to other Platform Services Controllers in a highly available deployment.

9.   A, C. The embedded Platform Services Controller should only be used for small, stand-alone deployments. This type of deployment will not allow additional PSC instances or vCenter Server instances to be joined to the vCenter Single Sign-On domain. For larger deployments, external PSC instances are required, which would sit behind a load balancer, but it is not a component that would be joined to the domain, nor are ESXi hosts.

10. B. A minimum of two PSC instances are required to create a highly available deployment. This is because data is replicated between the instances and the solution is designed to auto-failover in the event that an instance becomes unreachable. Additional instances can be deployed as needed but are not required to make the solution highly available.

11. C. The No Access role prevents viewing or editing and can be used to mask off areas of the hierarchy from the users assigned to that role.

12. D. The No Cryptography Administrator role will prevent an administrator from encrypting a virtual machine.

13. A. The port for SSH is disabled by default. The other ports are open by default. Note that starting the SSH service will also open the port.

14. A, C. With normal lockdown enabled, only root and a local user added to *DCUI.Access* can log into the DCUI.

15. D. The Strict Lockdown Mode disables the DCUI, or ESXi host console for the ESXi server.

16. A, B. Two of the available identity providers are Active Directory and OpenLDAP. Other options are Active Directory as an LDAP server and LocalOS.

17. A. Secure Boot requires hardware version 13. You must also have a compatible operating system to use Secure Boot, but that is not required to enable it.

18. A, B. The older versions of TLS (1.0 and 1.1) should be disabled, allowing TLS 1.2 to be used.

Chapter 3: Networking in vSphere

1. B. The virtual machine currently has a guarantee of 250 Mbit/s but a performance cap or limit of 500 Mbit/s. Increasing the limit to 1000 Mbit/s for the VM is the only option that will improve the performance. Note that you will not be able to set the reservation to 1000 Mbit/s (option D) before you increase the limit.

2. B. Traffic shaping is performed per-port group, so using that will immediately affect just the VMs on that VLAN.

3. C, D. If the virtual machines worked on one host and don't work on another, the first place to check is the physical network connection, including making sure the host has a physical NIC assigned to that switch.

4. A, C. The main function of private VLAN is to isolate traffic on the same VLAN or network. You can also use traffic filtering with IP ranges to block traffic.

5. C, D. Increasing the reservation on the virtual machine would guarantee it higher network performance. However, it cannot have more reserved than the pool quote, so that must increase also.

6. C. Of all the shown options, only vSAN can be selected as a traffic type.

7. C. This service handles incoming traffic for the host; vSphere Replication handles outgoing.

8. A, B. LLDP will retrieve information from the physical switch about port connectivity and configuration. The `vmkping` command can be used to verify that the host's VMkernel ports can access the default gateway and other hosts on the network. Note that beacon probing requires at least three NICs.

9. B. Creating a VMkernel adapter for Provisioning traffic will allow you to separate traffic for cloning and cold migrations for further improvements. Also, none of the other options could improve performance for VMkernel traffic.

10. D. LAGs cannot currently be used with software iSCSI initiator multipathing.

11. A. You would need completely separate networks and gateways to accomplish this, which can only be done with custom TCP/IP stacks.

12. B. With only one network connecting to the host, and multiple default gateways on that network, the simplest option is to override the default gateway.

13. D. The number of uplinks is set directly on the switch, settings are adjusted on the uplink group, and physical NICs can be set or changed in the virtual switch on the host.

14. C. VGT mode is the only one that passes VLAN headers to the guest.

15. A. EST mode is required for an access port, when the physical switch is handling all VLAN operations.

16. B. Promiscuous mode will essentially turn a port group into a hub where all traffic on the host for that switch and VLAN is forwarded to all ports in the port group.

17. B. Failover settings are done at the port group level. Use Explicit Failover Order will allow you to pick which NIC is used and during which fail conditions.

18. C. If Explicit Failover is configured with some NICs in Unused, those NICs will never be utilized regardless of the state of the other NICs.

19. C. Reservations can be set at a maximum of 75 percent of the speed of the slowest connected pNIC. If no pNICs are connected, a reservation cannot be set.

20. A, C. If the VMs are using jumbo frames but not all switches are configured, you will see inconsistent results. If the physical switch has the wrong VLAN tags configured, some networks will not be available for the host.

Chapter 4: Storage in vSphere

1. C. VMFS6 is only supported for 6.5 hosts.

2. A. This is not only the simplest method, it is also the only method that will work.

3. B, C. Block storage requires ESXi to maintain the file structure. Both iSCSI and local disks are block storage.

4. A, B, D. HBAs allow boot from SAN. FBFT and FBPT are the technologies required for non-HBAs to support boot-from-FCoE.

5. D. An IQN on the host is required for iSCSI. The other choices are all optional.

6. C. CHAP is only for iSCSI and needs to be set per target to allow for multiple arrays.

7. C, D. Deduplication and compression require vSAN Disk Format 3 and an All-Flash array.

8. B. Currently NFS v4.1 is not supported for Storage DRS.

9. A, B. A disk group consists of one SSD and between one and seven capacity disks. C is not right because there is only one SSD. D is not right because if you make one disk group (1+3), you only have three disks left, which is not enough.

10. C. A disk group consists of one SSD and between one and seven capacity disks. C is the only option with more than 8 disks or more than two SSD plus HDD drives.

11. B. A, C, and D all leverage external storage arrays or servers. vSAN only uses local disks on the hosts.

12. B. While storage arrays and servers can be used to supply storage for physical servers, only vSAN can be used by vSphere to provide storage using the iSCSI target.

13. A, B. CHAP is available for iSCSI, Kerberos for NFS. Both storage technologies use TCP/IP.

14. A. NFS 4.1 has the option to ensure data integrity using Kerberos.

15. B. vSAN offers data-at-rest encryption. While storage servers and arrays might offer the capability, it is not configured in vSphere.

16. C. Storage profiles created for vSAN actually create the capabilities when they are applied to VMs. All of the other profiles reference capabilities previously created.

17. B, C. VVols are only supported by iSCSI and NFS servers and arrays.

18. A, D. VVols need providers and profiles but are not compatible with traditional LUNs or datastores.

19. D. NFS 4.1 offers multipathing, which will improve performance at all times. NFS datastores do not have cache drives, Storage DRS would require other NFS datastores with lower I/O demands, and SIOC shares only matter during times of contention.

20. B, D. Out of these options, only iSCSI and Fibre Channel are supported for booting a host.

Chapter 5: Upgrading a vSphere Deployment

1. B. During the upgrade, an embedded SQL Express database will be replaced with an embedded PostgreSQL database. Any other database migration must be performed before the upgrade.

2. B. UMDS can be installed on a Linux-based or Windows server and has no topology dependencies other than not being installed on a server with VUM.

3. C, D. All vCenter components are now installed with vCenter. VUM is installed with VCSA but can be installed separately to support Windows. UMDS can always be installed on a Windows or Linux-based server.

4. A, C. VUM is primarily used to update hosts but can also update VMs and VAs. VUM cannot update vCenter or distributed switches.

5. B, D. VUM is primarily used to update hosts but can also update virtual machine hardware and VMware Tools. VUM cannot update vCenter or distributed switches.

6. B, C. The CLI migration tool is `vcsa-deploy`, which can be run from a Windows machine, and `vmware-umds` is the download service for VUM, which can run on Windows or a Linux-based machine.

7. D. The `migration-assistant` utility must be started on the Windows vCenter server.

8. A. The export directory can be removed from the migration host as a cleanup step. The directory will not be removed by the migration utility.

9. D. The `vcsa-deploy` utility, like the GUI utility, can upgrade, install, or migrate a vCenter instance.

10. A. The embedded database used by vCenter 6.5 is PostgreSQL, and an embedded SQL Express database will migrate to that by default.

11. A, B, C. While the embedded database used by vCenter 6.5 is PostgreSQL, it can be installed with SQL or Oracle. There are also steps to take to prevent the SQL Express database from being migrated to PostgreSQL.

12. D. The proper upgrade plan is "top down" with the Platform Services Controller (or SSO for version 5.5) being upgraded before vCenter and hosts. VM Hardware should be upgraded last.

13. A, C. The presumption here is that the hosts were upgraded before vCenter. Reverting the hosts to their previous version or upgrading vCenter would resolve the issue.

14. A, B. After the migration, Auto Deploy will be running on the VCSA server. The old server should be decommissioned and the DHCP parameters should be changed so booting hosts can find the new Auto Deploy service.

15. A, C. During the migration, data is copied from most of the services to the new vCenter appliance; however, ESXi Dump Collector and Syslog Collector data is not included.

16. B. After a migration, hosts will need to be manually repointed to the new ESXi Dump Collector service on the VCSA appliance.

17. A, D. If you have multiple vCenter servers, you must have external Platform Services Controllers.

18. A. By default, VUM will update one host in a cluster at a time. You can change this to be a set number of hosts or allow VUM to decide the maximum number of hosts to update at one time.

19. C, D. VUM can attach baselines to several inventory objects, including VM folders and vCenter.

20. B, D. VUM can attach host and VM/VA baselines to several inventory objects, including datacenters and vCenter.

21. B. VUM can snapshot virtual machines before updating to allow for easy rollback of changes.

Chapter 6: Allocating Resources in a vSphere Datacenter

1. B. When DRS is disabled on a cluster, it removes all of the resource pools that are a part of the cluster. This information is not restored automatically when DRS is re-enabled. Creating a snapshot of the resource pool tree allows this information to be restored if DRS has to be disabled temporarily.

2. A. Shares are a way to determine what allocation of resources happens when a resource is under contention. In this scenario, because the Sales pool has a share value of High, it will receive twice the amount of resources as the Engineering pool, which has a share value of Normal.

3. C, D. When a resource pool is established and the Expandable Reservation option is unchecked, the virtual machines using the pool are only able to reserve the amount of resources available in the pool. If a virtual machine in a pool will not power on, it is typically because the Admission Control mechanism is preventing the action due to a lack of resources available to reserve. To resolve this, you can either reduce the reservation requirements of one or more virtual machines in the pool or turn on the Expandable Reservation mechanism. A third option, though not provided as an answer here, would be to provide additional resources to the pool.

4. B. Resource pools can be used in a few different ways. One way is to control priority access to resources using shares. In this method, it is not necessary to provide a fixed amount of resources to the pool. However, if there are virtual machines that need dedicated resources, the pool needs to reserve an amount of that resource to provide to the virtual machines in the pool.

5. C. If a resource pool runs out of a resource, virtual machines with reservation requirements will be unable to power on. This could be resolved by adding additional resources, or you can enable the Expandable Reservation parameter. This allows the child pool to request resources from its parent pool to satisfy a virtual machine's requirements.

6. A, C. A resource pool is used to provide memory and/or CPU resources to virtual machines. vSphere uses other mechanisms to manage storage and network resources.

7. A. The hierarchy of resource pools begins at the cluster, which is referred to as the root pool. From there, a top-level resource pool is referred to as a parent pool, and pools created within that pool are referred to as child pools. When two pools exist at the same level (as would two child pools created under the same parent pool), they are referred to as sibling pools.

8. B. When a virtual machine powers on, it is able to use as much of the resources configured for it as are available in the cluster. For example, if a virtual machine is configured with 1 vCPU and 4 GB of memory is powered up on a host with 2.4 GHz CPUs, the VM can use as much as 2.4 GHz of CPU resources. However, the VM may only require a much smaller amount, such as 500 MHz. A limit can be used to prevent overallocation of resources and manage user expectations. The overallocation of resources may result in performance gains that will diminish as additional VMs are added to the cluster.

9. A. When setting share values, you can enter a custom value or use the default settings of High, Normal, and Low. When these settings are used, they conform to a ratio of 4:2:1, where High is twice as much of a resource as Normal and four times as much as Low.

10. C. In this case, there is no contention. Shares are only applied when there is resource contention, so the configuration shown in the scenario is not applied and all pools get all the resources they require.

11. B, D. Even though this use case involves only a single VM, you must still create a VM group in order to create a VM-Host affinity rule. You cannot create a simple VM-VM affinity rule because this type of rule does not take specific hosts into account when migrating the VM.

12. C. VM-VM affinity rules cannot be used in conjunction with HA if HA is configured with the Dedicated failover hosts option and multiple failover hosts have been configured.

13. B. Because VM-Host affinity rules are cluster based, the virtual machines in the DRS VM group must all reside within the same cluster. When a VM in an existing group is removed from the cluster, it loses its DRS group affiliation, even if it is added back into the cluster. To resolve the issue, the VM must be manually added back into the group.

14. C. Predictive DRS requires an understanding of the way workloads utilize resources over time. The collection and analysis of workload metrics is one of the key features of vRealize Operations Manager and is required in order for Predictive DRS to know when to migrate workloads in advance to avoid resource contention.

15. D. Network-aware DRS does not migrate virtual machines due to a network resource issue. What it does do is take into consideration the network utilization of hosts in the cluster when migrating a virtual machine due to a compute resource that is in contention in order to ensure that the migration solves the compute resource issue without creating a network resource issue.

16. A, C. Generally speaking, anti-affinity rules exist to maximize availability, and achieving that goal should apply to all hosts in a DRS cluster. However, in some specific cases, such as licensing or nonuniform hardware concerns, the rule may need to be applied to a subset of hosts in the cluster, resulting in the need for a VM-Host rule.

17. A. Network-aware DRS monitors the utilization of the physical uplinks of ESXi hosts in the cluster. An ESXi host is considered saturated when the collective utilization of the uplinks reaches or exceeds 80 percent. This setting is the default and can be adjusted using an advanced option if needed.

18. A, B, D. DRS generates migration recommendations when a CPU or memory imbalance occurs. Storage DRS generates migration recommendations in the event of a storage imbalance; DRS does not. There are other conditions that would generate migration recommendations, including satisfying a resource pool and accommodating an affinity or anti-affinity rule. DRS will also generate migration recommendations when a host in the cluster has planned downtime and enters Maintenance mode but is unable to migrate VMs from a host that experiences an unplanned downtime event.

19. A. When two VM-VM affinity rules conflict, the older one takes precedence and the newer rule is disabled. DRS only tries to satisfy enabled rules, and disabled rules are ignored.

20. A, C. This DRS will never take an action that would violate a VM-Host rule if the rule is set using the Must Run On or Must Not Run On option. Options A and C could both result in a violation of the rule. Because both B and D are manual options and are not performed by DRS, they can be accomplished. When possible, VM-Host rules should use preferential options to allow DRS maximum flexibility.

Chapter 7: Backing Up and Recovering a vSphere Deployment

1. B, D. vSphere Data Protection offers deduplication of backups as a core feature. It can also replicate backup jobs to remote sites.

2. A. vSphere Replication can compress the data before sending it to the remote site. This increases CPU usage but lowers sync time and network usage.

3. B. While the VDP appliance and proxies can each back up 8 VMs at a time, adding a proxy appliance disables the internal proxy, so you need to deploy two proxy appliances to back up 16 virtual machines at the same time.

4. A. vSphere Data Protection offers guest agents to back up certain applications, including Microsoft Exchange. An application-aware backup should be used for any database or database-like guest.

5. D. An application-aware backup should be used for any database or database-like guest. While vSphere Replication offers guest agents for some applications, it does not protect MYSQL.

6. C. vSphere Replication offers point-in-time instances, which provides multiple snapshots with a recovered VM, allowing you to choose which point in time to recover that virtual machine to.

7. D. vSphere Replication offers recovery point objectives (RPOs), which is a measure of how often a virtual machine is replicated. The more often a VM is replicated, the less data is lost.

8. A, B. vSphere Replication and vSphere Data Protection both offer the ability to replicate to remote sites.

9. A. vSphere Replication offers Guest OS quiescing to ensure that no writes are outstanding before the VM is replicated. This helps to ensure that the guest will be in a good state when it is recovered.

10. A. While guest OS quiescing can improve the state of the guest when it is recovered, it could interfere with a very low RPO setting if the guest takes too long to quiesce.

11. C. A red icon on a VDP backup job indicates that it was not able to quiesce the guest prior to backing up the virtual machine.

12. A. vSphere Replication does not support virtual machines with Fault Tolerance enabled.

13. C. Decreasing the RPO time will decrease the frequency of capturing and replicating the virtual machine, which will significantly reduce network traffic.

14. D. Enabling data deduplication for vSphere Data Protection will significantly reduce the storage used for backups.

15. A. There is only one option for backing up VCSA, and that is whether to include stats, events, alarms, and tasks in the backup.

16. B. VDP is the only option shown that could back up a vCenter server on Windows.

17. A. If the VM is powered on, vSphere Replication will not allow Synchronize Recent Changes to be used. You can power off the VM or select Use Latest Available Data to recover the VM.

18. A, C. When vSphere Replication recovers a VM, it will be powered off with the network connections disconnected. While you can choose from point-in-time snapshots if they are available, that is not a required step.

Chapter 8: Troubleshooting a vSphere Deployment

1. **A, C.** Using `esxtop` in batch mode, the output can be redirected to create a CSV file. A CSV file is an option in the performance view of a cluster. A vDS doesn't have a performance view.

2. **C.** The vpxd log file is considered the main vCenter log file.

3. **C, D.** The ESXi web client and vSphere web client can be used to download host files.

4. **C.** VCSA is installed with a Windows utility and the install log is found in the `appdata\ local\VMware\CIP` directory for the user that runs the utility.

5. **C.** The first step of upgrade should always be backing up whatever you are upgrading. Note that option A will be performed with the update, option B cannot be performed before the upgrade, and option D isn't needed.

6. **A.** The correct order is "biggest to smallest" and especially PSC before vCenter and vCenter before ESXi. vDS and vSAN are upgraded last if needed.

7. **D.** The Guest Average is the sum of the Device, Kernel, and Queue response times and should be approximately what the guest sees for storage response time.

8. **A.** The Device average is the time it takes a request to be sent to and returned from the storage array.

9. **A, C.** The performance charts are to report on performance of hosts and virtual machines.

10. **B.** The kernel average is the time the host spends processing a storage request.

11. **D.** The `esxtop` command when run in batch mode (-b) will capture data for a number of times specified (-n) in intervals specified. While -d sets the time interval, the default interval is 5 seconds.

12. **A, C, D.** The error is reporting that admission control (a part of High Availability) is preventing Tiny02 from powering on. This is because Tiny02 has a reservation set, and the admission control calculations concluded that there is not enough capacity available to meet Tiny02's reservation. From the list, only 3D, Tiny01, and vcsa-02a.corp.local are powered on and thus can have active reservations. Disabling the reservation on Tiny02 or one of the active VMs or disabling admission control should resolve the issue.

13. **A, D.** Cisco Discovery Protocol and Link Layer Discovery Protocol will report on upstream physical switch information and capabilities.

14. **A.** CPU Ready reports on guest CPU instructions that are waiting to be scheduled.

15. **C.** The memory swap counter reports when guest memory is being written to disk, which has a significant performance impact on the guest.

16. D. The memory balloon counter indicates that memory is being reclaimed from guests.

17. B. The minimum vSphere license level needed for High Availability is Essentials Plus.

18. D. The minimum vSphere license level needed for DRS is Enterprise Plus.

19. B, C. Local SCSI disks and LUNs accessed over Fibre Channel are not affected by Ethernet network outages.

20. B. The optional vMA management appliance has `resxtop` built in. Otherwise, you need to download the vSphere CLI and install it on a workstation.

Chapter 9: Deploying and Customizing ESXi Hosts

1. A. You can only attach one profile to a host.

2. C. If you have settings in two different profiles, you can combine them using the Copy Settings to Host Profiles wizard. While option B would work, it would take more effort.

3. D. The Profile Compliance section of the Monitor tab for the cluster object is a good place to view compliance. You can also use the Monitor tab of the host profile.

4. D. While the Summary screen of a host will display a message if the host is not in compliance, there is no view available on the host object showing host profile compliance. You can also use the Monitor tab of the host profile.

5. B, C. Exporting the customizations to use as a template for other hosts is a common practice. You can also use it to quickly re-create a host that is being removed from inventory.

6. A, C, E. The basic steps to compare settings with host profiles are extract, attach, and check. You do not need to remediate if you are only checking the settings, and you won't export unless you have multiple datacenters.

7. A. Host customizations export as CSV files.

8. B. Host profiles export as VPF files.

9. C. If you download a custom ESXi installation image from a server vendor, make sure you get the ZIP version so you can import it into Auto Deploy.

10. C. A custom depot is required to have image profiles created on the Auto Deploy server.

11. B. The host displays that message when it finds the Auto Deploy server but no rule matches it.

12. A, B. The host is not receiving a DHCP address. Either the DHCP server is not running or the host cannot reach it.

13. A, C. The host is receiving a DHCP address but cannot reach the TFTP server. Either the TFTP server is not running or the host cannot reach it.

14. A, D. The host is receiving a DHCP address and is pulling the bootloader but cannot reach the Auto Deploy server. Either the Auto Deploy server is not running or the host cannot reach it with the supplied information—note the URL with IP address pulled from the `tramp` file.

15. D, E. The host is receiving a DHCP address and pulling the bootloader from TFTP and is querying the Auto Deploy server but not receiving an image. The most likely issue is that no deploy rule is created that applies to that host.

16. A, B, C. Rules can apply to all hosts or any host that matches a pattern or patterns. Pattern types include asset tag, serial number, and vendor name.

17. C. The rule is not activated, which is a requirement to provide the boot image.

18. A. After a host is assigned an image, it will continue to use that image until a new rule applies to it or the existing rule is changed to a different image.

19. A, B. Stateless Caching will copy the image to the host after the first deployment, allowing the host to boot with the image on subsequent starts if Auto Deploy is not available. Stateful Install installs ESXi, similar to using a CD to install.

20. A, D. After a host is assigned an image, it will continue to use that image unless the host is removed from inventory. Auto Deploy will match any rule that applies to a host and will send the indicated image.

Chapter 10: Ensuring High Availability for vSphere Clusters and the VCSA

1. B. All licenses other than Essentials include HA.

2. A. Enabling HA allows VMs to be restated on other hosts only if a host fails.

3. B, C. These advanced HA options will prevent HA from using the default gateway (setting *das.usedefaultisolationaddress* to false). A new IP address will be used instead.

4. D. Dedicated failover hosts configures specific hosts to have no VMs running unless there is a host failure.

5. B. Cluster resource percentage is recommended for environments where VMs have very different resource reservations.

6. A. Slot Policy is recommended for environments where VMs have very similar resource reservations because the slot size will be very close to the average VM size.

7. B. With cluster resource percentage, you could have a failure scenario where sufficient capacity is available but spread across several hosts, preventing a VM with a large reservation from starting.

8. C. By default, HA will obey DRS affinity and anti-affinity rules during a failure recovery.

9. C. The performance degradation VMs tolerate will trigger a warning message if performance is estimated to drop after a failure. A setting of 100% will disable the warning; a setting of 0% will trigger a warning for any estimated performance drop.

10. A, D. A new VM would not be able to power on if the available capacity of the cluster (total MHz minus slot sizes of running VMs minus reserved capacity) is less than the reservation of the new VM. Removing the reservation will allow the VM to power up. The other option is to reduce the slot size of the environment, which (if the Slot Policy is set to the default) can only be done by reducing the reservation of the largest VM.

11. B. The default slot size is the largest CPU reservation and the largest memory reservation.

12. C. VM application monitoring can only restart the guest OS.

13. A, B. VMware Tools is required for VM monitoring, and a VM (by default) must be up for 120 seconds before failing for VM monitoring to restart it.

14. A, D. Proactive HA requires a compatible monitoring solution from your server vendor. Application monitoring requires your application to send heartbeats to the running host.

15. A, D. vCenter HA only works with VCSA, and you need a dedicated network for the HA traffic.

16. D. If two appliances fail, the third will not respond to requests.

17. B, D. The Basic option handles cloning and configuring but requires SSH and a dedicated network for HA traffic.

18. A, B. The Advanced option requires the admin to clone the VCSA twice, using the Guest Customization options to change the hostname and IP addresses.

19. D. Setting HA to maintenance mode will enable the active node to continue to respond to requests even if it loses connectivity to the passive and witness nodes.

20. B. The default is two heartbeat datastores per host. There may be more than two in use in a cluster if not all hosts have access to the same datastores.

21. C. When Slot Policy is used, each virtual machine uses one slot unless it has a reservation greater than the slot size. The environment has 8 available slots of the 20 it has total.

22. C. When Slot Policy is used, each virtual machine uses one slot unless it has a reservation greater than the slot size. If the reservation is greater, it will consume enough slots to cover its reservation.

Chapter 11: Administering and Managing vSphere Virtual Machines

1. A, D, E. A virtual machine needs its configuration file (.vmx) plus the two vmdk files—the .vmdk config file and the -flat.vmdk binary file.

2. C. The default for a four-CPU VM would be one core per VM. You could also set two cores per CPU (the guest would see two sockets) or four cores with just one socket presented to the guest.

3. A. A virtual machine is restricted to the number of CPUs as its host has logical processors.

4. D. A VM with just one CPU might not have the numvcpus value. You would need to add the value to increase the CPUs.

5. B, C. The binary files for virtual machine are the -flat file and the -sparse file; the -sparse file contains snapshot changes.

6. C. Snapshots are always thin provisioned. The .vmx file will reference the two new snapshot files, which in turn will reference the original/parent disks.

7. B. The existing VM has only four vCPUs selected. Once it has been changed to 8, the cores per socket can be set to 8.

8. C. Once 3D Graphics is enabled, you can change the 3D Renderer setting.

9. A. The default setting of one 8 MB display will not support 4k; a setting of Auto will scale to support a larger display.

10. A. Snapshot VMDKs are always stored with their parent VMDKs.

11. A. Boot Delay is intended to wait on the initial BIOS screen for a set period of time and will allow an administrator to perform tasks such as launch the boot menu.

12. B. Force BIOS Setup will leave the VM in the BIOS menu until an administrator exits the menu or restarts the VM.

13. C, D. Secure EFI boot is intended to prevent scenarios such as rootkits from infecting your guest at boot. Changing the firmware to EFI and enabling Secure Boot are the virtual hardware requirements for this.

14. A. Enabling latency sensitivity will create a soft DRS rule to keep a VM on the current. This helps to ensure that the VM will not be vMotioned off.

15. D. No VMs can be deployed from an optimized catalog.

16. B. While SMB is an option for a VCSA appliance, a VCSA appliance can't actually use an SMB share.

17. B. This error occurs when the Download Library Content Only When Needed option is configured for a published catalog.

18. A, D. A USB device must be configured for vMotion when it is added to the VM.

19. C. The error is due to resizing the partition to a smaller-than-suggested size.

20. A. In this case, the default firewall is preventing connectivity from the Converter server. While this is not apparent from the error, option B cannot be the answer as the ESXi host has not been contacted, option C cannot be the answer as the agent will be installed after the source machine is contacted (if not found), and option D cannot be the answer as this is a Powered On conversion.

Index

T

W–Z

Comprehensive Online Learning Environment

Register to gain one year of FREE access to the online interactive learning environment and test bank to help you study for your VMware® Certified Professional-Data Center Virtualization on vSphere 6.7 Exam 2V0-21.19 —included with your purchase of this book!

The online test bank includes the following:

- **Assessment Test** to help you focus your study to specific objectives
- **Chapter Tests** to reinforce what you've learned
- **Practice Exams** to test your knowledge of the material
- **Digital Flashcards** to reinforce your learning and provide last-minute test prep before the exam
- **Searchable Glossary** to define the key terms you'll need to know for the exam

Register and Access the Online Test Bank

To register your book and get access to the online test bank, follow these steps:

1. Go to www.wiley.com/go/sybextestprep.
2. Select your book from the list.
3. Complete the required registration information, including answering the security verification to prove book ownership. You will be emailed a pin code.
4. Follow the directions in the email or go to www.wiley.com/go/sybextestprep.
5. Enter the pin code you received and click the "Activate PIN" button.
6. On the Create an Account or Login page, enter your username and password, and click Login. A "Thank you for activating your PIN!" message will appear. If you don't have an account already, create a new account.
7. Click the "Go to My Account" button to add your new book to the My Products page.

SYBEX®
A Wiley Brand